GERMAN GRAMMAR
A Contrastive Approach

Stephen Clausing
UNIVERSITY OF UTAH

HOLT, RINEHART AND WINSTON

New York   Chicago   San Francisco   Philadelphia
Montreal   Toronto   London   Sydney
Tokyo   Mexico City   Rio de Janeiro   Madrid

Publisher: Nedah Abbott
Acquisitions Editor: Vincent Duggan
Project Editor: Biodun Iginla
Production Manager: Lula Als
Design Supervisor: Renée Davis
Design: Ruth Riley
Cover Design: Stephen Clausing

Library of Congress Cataloging-in-Publication Data

Clausing, Stephen
  German grammar.

  Includes index.
  1. German language—Grammar—1951.
  2. German language—Text-books for foreign speakers—
English. I. Title.
PF3112.C59   1986   438.2′421   85-17546

ISBN 0-03-001897-8

CBS COLLEGE PUBLISHING

Holt, Rinehart and Winston
The Dryden Press
Saunders College Publishing

PREFACE

The Nature of the Book

This textbook is intended as an intermediate grammar review to be used as a supplemental text in a typical curriculum of reading, conversation, and some writing. The grammar traditionally taught in first-year texts is thoroughly reviewed, but the book also provides additional grammar essential at the intermediate level.

The emphasis of the text is on contrastive analysis of English and German, that is, the problems that arise in learning German as a result of English interference. This method helps the student avoid mistakes such as those shown below:

*Als ein Kind würde ich jeden Tag in den Zoo gehen.

The sentence is wrong for two reasons. First, **als ein Kind** is a direct translation of the English phrase *as a child;* correct German would be **als Kind.** The second mistake involves the incorrect use of **würde** in German to indicate habitual action in the past (the intended meaning) on the pattern of English *would.* The problem arises because the student has been taught the German subjunctive without any regard to the English forms which appear to be equivalent. As a result, the student has no way of knowing that the sentence is incorrect. Linguistic interference is an inevitable facet of second language acquisition, as an analysis of student errors will demonstrate. To neglect this aspect of the grammar is to send the student ill-prepared into more advanced courses. This textbook represents a logical application of the modern principles of contrastive linguistics to pedagogy—without the distraction of linguistic jargon.

The reader should not, however, construe from the previous remarks that the text is concerned solely with contrastive analysis: the teacher will find much that is familiar and traditional. In other words, fundamental aspects of German grammar are not neglected for the sake of the text's unique method, nor is the contrastive method applied artificially or unnecessarily to areas where it has no value.

Where necessary, the student is shown the actual mistakes that arise when English patterns are transferred directly into German. The use of incorrect German examples is an integral part of the contrastive approach because it shows in concrete form the practical manifestations of the theory. All of the errors shown in the book are adaptations of actual student errors. The student is made aware of potential mistakes, understands why they occur, and knows how they can be corrected. Each incorrect German sentence is clearly marked as being incorrect and is followed by the correct sentence. Many student errors have nothing to do with English interference, and these are also discussed in the book. In short, the book teaches the student to proofread his own material—an important skill that most textbooks do not address.

Some teachers may be apprehensive about showing the student incorrect German for fear that the student will learn the incorrect pattern. The author has found no evidence that this occurs. Furthermore, students are exposed to incorrect German in any class, for example, when they speak German, write essays, listen to other students, look at student answers on the blackboard, and so on. Rather than avoiding any mention of these errors, it makes better sense to develop the student's ability to recognize and correct them. Finally, it should be noted that the exercise dealing with German errors is put at the end of each chapter and is specially marked off from the other exercises; thus, the teacher who is still opposed to the idea of showing students incorrect German can essentially eliminate this feature of the book.

The material covered is "digestible": each chapter can be split up into numerous subunits. The student does not need to read the entire text portion of the chapter before beginning the exercises. The text is also "teacher-friendly"; for example, each section is clearly marked as to topic and each exercise is preceded by a short description of the topic and prerequisites for the exercise, that is, what is the content and goal of the exercise and which section(s) must the student read in order to do the exercise. The exercises themselves are structured into six main groups:

1. **Comprehension Check exercises:** These short exercises *with answers* occur at the end of sections. This exercise enables the student to test his immediate understanding of the fundamentals of the section.
2. **Section exercises:** These occur after the text portion of the chapter and are detailed exercises dealing with individual sections.
3. **Comprehensive exercises:** These follow the section exercises and summarize the material of the chapter.
4. *Gedankenproblem:* Many chapters also have a *Gedankenproblem* which asks the student to go beyond the material in the text and draw conclusions on his own regarding more advanced topics.
5. **"What's wrong with these?"** This exercise tests the student's proofreading ability.
6. **Review Exercises:** These are given after every three chapters and summarize the material of those chapters. As a further review, the German-English vocabulary is restricted to words from preceding chapters.

As with most review grammars, the topics discussed become more advanced as the student progresses through the text. Special care has been given to arrange the chapters so that topics introduced in one chapter will be naturally reviewed in the following chapters.

Many student errors involve problems in vocabulary, particularly as a result of lexical interference. Most textbooks, however, ignore these problems because they do not fall under the rubric of "grammar." This text devotes the final third of the book to lexical problems.

In order to help the student complete the exercises, the book has German and English end glossaries as well as chapter vocabulary lists. In order to make the initial vocabulary manageable without resorting to simplistic German, the chapter vocabulary lists in chapters 1–9 cover only the "core" vocabulary of the chapter, that is, the words that apply directly to the answer portion of the sentences in the exercises. The remaining words are given in the end glossary. After Chapter 9, the entire German vocabulary of the chapter is given in the vocabulary list. Vocabulary items, once introduced, are not repeated in subsequent vocabulary lists unless the word is used in a different meaning or usage. The chapter vocabulary lists are presented in column format so that the student can test his knowledge of the vocabulary by covering the English column or vice versa. The chapter vocabulary lists contain about 1600 words; the total German vocabulary of the book is approximately 1950 words. The English end glossary contains about 800 words. This vocabulary is essentially a subset of the German-English vocabulary and is therefore not listed separately by chapter.

Finally, the book contains detailed instructions on the use of a German-English and English-German dictionary—a skill which many teachers unwisely take for granted. With some exercises, the student must consult a dictionary in order to do the exercise. In short, the student is weaned from the artificiality of a glossary to the real-world problem of having to use a dictionary for reference.

How to Use This Book

The exercises in a given chapter progress from specific to comprehensive coverage and from passive to active knowledge. As a result, the exercises will work best if done in sequence and not all at once. This will enable the student to progress stepwise through the material with help along the way. By studying the prerequisites for the exercises, the teacher can quickly determine a syllabus for each chapter.

The book is designed to be as self-explanatory as possible, though the teacher may have to explain grammatical terms with which individual students are not familiar. Most of the work can be done by the student at home leaving valuable classroom time for other matters. The review exercises mark a natural break for a major test and help prepare the student for such a test.

Incorrect German sentences used as examples are identified as incorrect by an asterisk. The teacher should explain this convention to the class before beginning the book. The student must also be told what to do with the "What's wrong with these?" exercise. Specifically, the student should do the following:

   a. *identify* the mistake.
   b. *correct* the mistake.
   c. *explain* why the mistake occurs.

Inform the student also that some sentences may contain more than one mistake. Finally, the teacher should by all means include this type of exercise on tests.

The entire text can be completed in about two semesters at the second-year level. Since the material of one chapter builds on that of the previous chapters, the teacher should do the chapters in sequence without skipping any chapters. However, the teacher can save time by omitting some exercises within individual chapters. For example, the teacher can skip the section exercises and do only the comprehensive exercises, or vice versa. The review exercises can also be deleted without affecting the continuity of the material. Ideally, the student should learn the entire vocabulary in the chapter vocabulary lists, but if time is limited, the teacher can skip the vocabulary entirely by allowing students to use the glossary or a dictionary on tests. In this manner, the book can be condensed to a one-semester course. For a very quick survey of the material, the student should merely read the text portion and do the comprehension check exercises.

CONTENTS

Chapter

Verb Stem Forms and Endings: Present and Simple Past Tense

1

A. Reference Information: Present and Simple Past Tense

The verb conjugations of the present and simple past tense are listed below (the endings are in boldface). In this book, verbs that form the simple past tense by adding **-te,** such as **machen** *(to make),* **machte** *(made),* are referred to as *weak* verbs. Verbs that form the past tense by changing the verb stem, such as **kommen** *(to come),* **kam** *(came),* are *strong* verbs.

Weak Verbs EXAMPLES: **machen** *(to make, to do),* **arbeiten** *(to work)*

	PRESENT TENSE	SIMPLE PAST TENSE
singular		
ich	mach**e** (arbeit**e**)	mach**te** (arbeit**ete**)
du	mach**st** (arbeit**est**)	mach**test** (arbeit**etest**)
er, sie, es	mach**t** (arbeit**et**)	mach**te** (arbeit**ete**)
plural		
wir	mach**en** (arbeit**en**)	mach**ten** (arbeit**eten**)
ihr	mach**t** (arbeit**et**)	mach**tet** (arbeit**etet**)
sie, Sie	mach**en** (arbeit**en**)	mach**ten** (arbeit**eten**)

Strong Verbs EXAMPLES: **fahren** *(to go, to drive)*, **lesen** *(to read)*

	PRESENT TENSE	SIMPLE PAST TENSE
singular		
ich	fahre (lese)	fuhr (las)
du	fährst (liest)	fuhrst (lasest)
er, sie, es	fährt (liest)	fuhr (las)
plural		
wir	fahren (lesen)	fuhren (lasen)
ihr	fahrt (lest)	fuhrt (last)
sie, Sie	fahren (lesen)	fuhren (lasen)

A complete list of the past tense stem forms of strong verbs can be found on page 00 of this book.

B. Stem Vowel Changes in the Present Tense of Strong Verbs

In the present tense, *strong* verbs with certain vowels in the stem of the infinitive change these vowels in the second- and third-person singular (see the examples of **fahren** and **lesen** in the table in section A). Specifically:

a → ä (see **fahren** example in section a)

au → äu in two verbs: **laufen** *(to run)* and **saufen** *(to drink)* (used for animals drinking or humans drinking alcohol). The complete conjugation of **laufen** is listed here for reference:

ich	laufe	wir	laufen
du	läufst	ihr	lauft
er, sie, es	läuft	sie, Sie	laufen

o → ö in one verb: **stoßen** *(to strike):*

ich	stoße	wir	stoßen
du	stößt	ihr	stoßt
er, sie, es	stößt	sie, Sie	stoßen

There is only one other strong verb with **o** in the infinitive stem, **kommen** *(to come),* but it does not have a stem vowel change.

long e → ie (see **lesen** example in section a)

short e → i, e.g., **treffen** *(to meet)*

ich	treffe	wir	treffen
du	triffst	ihr	trefft
er, sie, es	trifft	sie, Sie	treffen

If you do not hear the difference between long **e** in **lesen** and short **e** in **treffen,** here are a few more examples:

long		*short*	
befehlen	*to command*	brechen	*to break*
geschehen	*to happen*	gelten	*to apply to*
sehen	*to see*	stechen	*to prick, sting*

Three verbs with long **e** nevertheless change the stem vowel to **i:**

geben	*to give*	ich gebe	du gibst	er gibt
nehmen	*to take*	ich nehme	du **nimm**st	er **nimm**t
treten	*to step*	ich trete	du **tritt**st	er **tritt**

Notice the doubling of the consonants in **nehmen** and **treten,** which accompany the vowel change.

Finally, four strong verbs with long **e** in the stem never show any stem vowel change: **gehen** *(to go),* **genesen** *(to get better),* **heben** *(to raise),* **stehen** *(to stand).*

COMPREHENSION CHECK: *Fill in the blank with the appropriate present-tense form of the strong verb shown in parentheses.*

    EXAMPLE: Meine Katze _____ gerne Milch. (saufen)
    ANSWER: säuft

1. Das Geburtstagskind _____ die Kerzen aus. (blasen)
2. Was _____ der Kellner? (empfehlen)
3. Du _____ mir selten. (helfen)
4. Franz _____ das Geld. (nehmen)

    ANSWERS: 1. bläst 2. empfiehlt 3. hilfst 4. nimmt

C. Verbs with Special Conjugations

To ease pronunciation, verb stems ending in **-d** or **-t** insert an **e** before a verb ending, unless the verb ending already contains an **e.** This can be seen in the example of

arbeiten shown in section A. The same principle holds true for certain verbs ending in **-m** or **-n**. The following table illustrates a verb stem ending in **-d, melden** *(to report)*, **-m, atmen** *(to breathe)*, and **-n, ordnen** *(to order, to arrange)*:

	PRESENT TENSE			SIMPLE PAST TENSE		
ich	melde	atme	ordne	meldete	atmete	ordnete
du	meldest	atmest	ordnest	meldetest	atmetest	ordnetest
er, sie, es	meldet	atmet	ordnet	meldete	atmete	ordnete
wir	melden	atmen	ordnen	meldeten	atmeten	ordneten
ihr	meldet	atmet	ordnet	meldetet	atmetet	ordnetet
sie, Sie	melden	atmen	ordnen	meldeten	atmeten	ordneten

The preceding examples all involved weak verbs; the same principle applies to strong verbs as well, as shown below for the verb **finden** *(to find)*:

	PRESENT TENSE	SIMPLE PAST TENSE
ich	finde	fand
du	findest	fandest
er, sie, es	findet	fand
wir	finden	fanden
ihr	findet	fandet
sie, Sie	finden	fanden

The verbs above ending in **-m** or **-n** would have been difficult to pronounce without the inserted **e**, but certain verbs ending in **-m** or **-n** can be easily pronounced without the **e**, for example: **wärmen** *(to warm)*, ich **wärme**, du **wärmst**, er **wärmt**, etc. Let the sound tell you when to insert the **e** for verb stems ending in **-m** or **-n**.

Three strong verbs are irregular in the second- and third-person singular of the present tense: **halten** *(to hold)*, **laden** *(to load)*, and **raten** *(to advise)*. Since these verbs are strong verbs, they also have stem-vowel changes:

ich	halte	lade	rate
du	**hältst**	**lädst**	**rätst**
er, sie, es	**hält**	**lädt**	**rät**
wir	halten	laden	raten
ihr	haltet	ladet	ratet
sie, Sie	halten	laden	raten

Some *weak* verbs have **-n** instead of the usual **-en** infinitive ending. In the conjugation of such verbs, the **-n** always substitutes for **-en;** for example: the verb **zweifeln** *(to doubt)*:

	PRESENT TENSE	SIMPLE PAST TENSE
ich	zweifle	zweifelte
du	zweifelst	zweifeltest
er, sie, es	zweifelt	zweifelte
wir	zweifeln	zweifelten
ihr	zweifelt	zweifeltet
sie, Sie	zweifeln	zweifelten

Note: Verbs ending in **-eln** drop the **e** in the first-person singular of the present tense as shown above. **Tun** (*to do*) is the only strong verb that has **-n** as the infinitive ending. Its conjugation in the present tense is given here:

ich	tue	wir	tun
du	tust	ihr	tut
er, sie, es	tut	sie, Sie	tun

Finally, if the verb stem ends in an **s**-sound (**-s, -ss, -ß, -z**), then the **du**-form adds only **-t** in the *present* tense of all verbs, weak or strong, and inserts **e** in the simple *past* tense of *strong* verbs (weak verbs simply add the usual **-test**). The verb **lesen** shown in section A is an example of this rule. The following table illustrates the application of the rule to a weak verb, **reisen** *(to travel),* and to a strong verb, **sitzen** *(to sit):*

	PRESENT TENSE		SIMPLE PAST TENSE	
ich	reise	sitze	reiste	saß
du	reist	sitzt	reistest	saßest
er, sie, es	reist	sitzt	reiste	saß
wir	reisen	sitzen	reisten	saßen
ihr	reist	sitzt	reistet	saßt
sie, Sie	reisen	sitzen	reisten	saßen

COMPREHENSION CHECK: *Fill in the blank with the appropriate form of the present and simple past tense of the verb given in parentheses. Both weak and strong verbs are used.*

1. _____ du sehr? (leiden)
2. Er _____ auf den Zug. (warten)
3. Du _____ dieses Ende des Seils. (halten)
4. Wer _____ die Tür? (öffnen)
5. Warum _____ du ihn so unfreundlich? (grüßen)

6. Er _____ Briefmarken. (sammeln)
7. Warum _____ du mich? (stoßen)

ANSWERS: 1. leidest, littest 2. wartet, wartete 3. hältst, hieltest 4. öffnet, öffnete 5. grüßt, grüßtest 6. sammelt, sammelte 7. stößt, stießest

D. The Imperative

The imperative (command) forms of a regular verb are as follows:

Geh weg!	*Go away.*	(**du**-form)
Geht weg!	*Go away.*	(**ihr**-form)
Gehen Sie weg!	*Go away.*	(**Sie**-form)
Gehen wir weg!	*Let's go away.*	(**wir**-form)

Imperative statements in German are usually followed by an exclamation mark regardless of the degree of intensity implied.

In the imperative, strong verbs with **e** in the stem undergo stem-vowel change in the **du**-form, but strong verbs with **a** or **au** do not, nor does the vowel in **stoßen**:

Iß dein Brot!	*Eat your bread.*	(from **essen**, short **e**)
Lies das Buch!	*Read the book.*	(from **lesen**, long **e**)
Laß das!	*Stop that!*	(from **lassen**, compare: **du läßt**)
Lauf nicht!	*Don't run!*	(from **laufen**, compare: **du läufst**)

In very formal German, an **e** is sometimes added to the **du**-form of the imperative:

Schlafe wohl!   *Sleep well!*

In more colloquial German, this same sentence would be simply:

Schlaf gut!

The **e** is, however, always added to the **du**-form of the imperative when the verb is one of those discussed in section C which insert **e** before a verb ending, e.g., **arbeiten, finden, atmen**, etc. With such verbs, the **e** is not formal. These verbs also insert **e** in the **ihr**-form of the imperative:

Finde das Geld sofort! *Find the money immediately!*
Findet das Geld sofort! (**ihr**-form)

Arbeite nicht so viel! *Don't work so much.*
Arbeitet nicht so viel! (**ihr**-form)

Atme tief! *Breathe deeply.*
Atmet tief! (**ihr**-form)

In addition, verbs ending in **-ig** also add **e** in the **du**-form of the imperative, but not in the **ihr**-form:

Beschuldige mich nicht! *Don't accuse me!*
Beschuldigt mich nicht! (**ihr**–form)

The imperative forms of **sein** *(to be)* are irregular:

Sei vorsichtig!	*Be careful!*	(**du**-form)
Seid vorsichtig!	*Be careful!*	(**ihr**-form)
Seien Sie vorsichtig!	*Be careful!*	(**Sie**-form)
Seien wir vorsichtig!	*Let's be careful!*	(**wir**-form)

COMPREHENSION CHECK: *Fill in the blank with the **du-, ihr-, Sie-** and **wir**-form of the imperative of the verb given in parentheses.*

1. _____ weiter! (spielen)
2. _____ leise! (sprechen)
3. _____ ihm zu kommen! (befehlen)
4. _____ die Kinder nicht! (schlagen)
5. _____ bitte ruhig! (sein)
6. _____ die Koffer! (öffnen)
7. _____ hier! (warten)
8. _____ die anderen Schüler nicht! (belästigen)

ANSWERS: 1. spiel, spielt, spielen Sie, spielen wir 2. sprich, sprecht, sprechen Sie, sprechen wir 3. befiehl, befehlt, befehlen Sie, befehlen wir 4. schlag, schlagt, schlagen Sie, schlagen wir 5. sei, seid, seien Sie, seien wir 6. öffne, öffnet, öffnen Sie, öffnen wir 7. warte, wartet, warten Sie, warten wir 8. belästige, belästigt, belästigen Sie, belästigen wir

E. Mixed Verbs

In the past tense, a small group of so-called *mixed* verbs have the endings of weak verbs, but change the stem like strong verbs. This group consists of the following:

INFINITIVE	SIMPLE PAST TENSE	MEANING
brennen	brannte	*to burn*
kennen	kannte	*to know*
nennen	nannte	*to name*
rennen	rannte	*to run*
senden	sandte (sendete)	*to send*
wenden	wandte (wendete)	*to turn*
bringen	brachte	*to bring*
denken	dachte	*to think*

The first four in this list are easiest to recognize because of the characteristic double **n** in the stem; in the past tense the **e** simply becomes an **a**. Senden and wenden also have regular past-tense forms as shown in parentheses above, but these are not common. The complete conjugation of both **kennen** and **denken** is given here:

	PRESENT TENSE		SIMPLE PAST TENSE	
infinitive:	*kennen*	*denken*	*kennen*	*denken*
ich	kenne	denke	kannte	dachte
du	kennst	denkst	kanntest	dachtest
er, sie, es	kennt	denkt	kannte	dachte
wir	kennen	denken	kannten	dachten
ihr	kennt	denkt	kanntet	dachtet
sie, Sie	kennen	denken	kannten	dachten

COMPREHENSION CHECK: *Fill in the blank with the appropriate past-tense form of the verb given.*

1. Das Holz _____ schnell. (brennen)
2. Wir _____ unsere Katze Ilse. (nennen)
3. Ein Freund _____ mir diese Gitarre aus Spanien mit. (bringen)
4. Die Studenten _____ alle an die Prüfung. (denken)
5. Michael _____ uns diese netten Blumen. (senden)

ANSWERS: 1. brannte 2. nannten 3. brachte 4. dachten 5. sandte

F. The Spelling *ss* Versus *ß*

A spelling problem that often occurs in verb conjugations is deciding when to write **ss** (called **doppel-s**) and when **ß** (called **eszett**). The rule is this:

> **ss** is used after short vowels, **ß** after long vowels and diphthongs, but **ss** → **ß** before consonants and at the end of a word regardless of the preceding vowel.

If you do not know the sound difference between a long vowel, a diphthong, and a short vowel, look up the infinitive of the verb in question. If it is written with **ß**, then the vowel is long or a diphthong; if it is written with **ss,** then the vowel is short. Here are a few practical examples:

müssen	*must*	(short vowel)
er muß	*he must*	(short vowel, but end of word)
vermissen	*to miss*	(short vowel)
er vermißt	*he misses*	(short vowel, but before consonant)
heißen	*to be called*	(diphthong, remains ß in all forms)

The same principle applies to nouns:

der Fuß	*foot*	(long vowel)
die Füße	*feet*	(long vowel)
der Fluß	*river*	(short vowel, but end of word)
die Flüsse	*rivers*	(short vowel)

Clearly, the same word may alternate between **ss** and **ß** depending on the exact form. As a further example of this, the full conjugation of vermissen (short vowel) and heißen (diphthong) in the present tense is given below:

infinitive:	*vermissen*	*heißen*
ich	vermisse	heiße
du	vermißt	heißt
er, sie, es	vermißt	heißt
wir	vermissen	heißen
ihr	vermißt	heißt
sie, Sie	vermissen	heißen

COMPREHENSION CHECK: *Fill in the blank with the present-tense form of the verb given in parentheses.*

1. a. Ich _____ gern Fisch. (essen)
    b. Er _____ gern Fisch.
2. a. Wie _____ Ihr Freund mit Vornamen? (heißen)
    b. Wie _____ Sie mit Vornamen?
3. Aber Mitzi! _____ den Mantel doch in der Garderobe. (lassen)

ANSWERS: 1.a. esse b. ißt 2.a. heißt b. heißen 3. laß

G. Modal Verbs and *Wissen*

For reference, the various forms of the *modal* verbs and of **wissen** are listed below:

PRESENT TENSE

infinitive:	*dürfen*	*können*	*mögen*	*müssen*	*sollen*	*wollen*	*wissen*
ich	darf	kann	mag	muß	soll	will	weiß
du	darfst	kannst	magst	mußt	sollst	willst	weißt
er, sie, es	darf	kann	mag	muß	soll	will	weiß
wir	dürfen	können	mögen	müssen	sollen	wollen	wissen
ihr	dürft	könnt	mögt	müßt	sollt	wollt	wißt
sie, Sie	dürfen	können	mögen	müssen	sollen	wollen	wissen

SIMPLE PAST TENSE

ich	durfte	konnte	mochte	mußte	sollte	wollte	wußte
du	durftest	konntest	mochtest	mußtest	solltest	wolltest	wußtest
er, sie, es	durfte	konnte	mochte	mußte	sollte	wollte	wußte
wir	durften	konnten	mochten	mußten	sollten	wollten	wußten
ihr	durftet	konntet	mochtet	mußtet	solltet	wolltet	wußtet
sie, Sie	durften	konnten	mochten	mußten	sollten	wollten	wußten

The meanings of the modals and **wissen** are illustrated in the following sentences:

Ich darf es tun. *I may (am allowed to) do it.*
Ich durfte es tun. *I was allowed to do it.*

Ich kann es tun. *I can (am able to) do it.*
Ich konnte es tun. *I was able to do it.*

Ich mag es tun. *I like to do it.*
Ich mochte es tun. *I liked to do it.*

Ich muß es tun. *I must (have to) do it.*
Ich mußte es tun. *I had to do it.*

Ich soll es tun. *I am supposed to (should) do it.*
Ich sollte es tun. *I was supposed to do it.*

Ich will es tun. *I want to do it.*
Ich wollte es tun. *I wanted to do it.*

Ich weiß, was ich tue. *I know what I am doing.*
Ich wußte, was ich tat. *I knew what I was doing.*

COMPREHENSION CHECK: *Fill in the blank with the present-tense form of the German verb corresponding to the English word in parentheses. Then give the simple past tense of the same verb.*

1. Er _____ die Autoschlüssel nicht finden. *(can)*
2. Ich _____ den Kuchen nicht. *(like)*
3. Er _____ keinen Alkohol trinken. *(is allowed)*
4. Wir _____ ein Doppelzimmer mit Bad bestellen. *(want)*
5. _____ du das bestimmt? *(know)*
6. Ihr _____ pünktlich um drei Uhr da sein. *(must)*

ANSWERS: 1. kann, konnte 2. mag, mochte 3. darf, durfte 4. wollen, wollten 5. weißt, wußtest 6. müßt, mußtet

H. Common Mistakes

Do not forget the stem vowel change in the second- and third-person singular of *strong* verbs in the present tense:

> *Du fallst.   *Er fallt.
> *You are falling.*   *He is falling.*
> correct: Du fällst.   Er fällt.

This mistake occurs most often in the imperative **du**-form:

> *Sprech lauter!
> *Speak more loudly.*
> correct: Sprich lauter!

Do not use a strong verb as a weak verb in the past tense:

> *Er **fallte**.
> *He fell.*
> correct: Er **fiel**.

The best way to avoid this mistake is to memorize the strong verbs and their past-tense forms.

Sometimes students use the correct past-tense form of a strong verb, but then add a weak ending:

> *Er fiel**te**.
> *He fell.*
> correct: Er **fiel**.

Another mistake that frequently occurs in the *past* tense of strong verbs is the addition of the *present*-tense ending:

> *Ich kame.   *Er kamt.
> *I came.*   *He came.*
> correct: Ich **kam**.   Er **kam**.

Do not forget the stem change in the past tense of mixed verbs:

*Der Läufer **ren**nte schnell.
The runner ran fast.
correct: Der Läufer **ran**nte schnell.

*Der Gepäckträger **bringte** die Koffer.
The porter brought the suitcases.
correct· Der Gepäckträger **brachte** die Koffer.

Do not put the usual present-tense endings as shown in section A on *modal* verbs or **wissen:**

*Er kann**t** nicht kommen.
He cannot come.
correct: Er **kann** nicht kommen.

Furthermore, do not use the infinitive (plural) stem of a modal verb in the singular in the present tense:

*Ich **wisse** es nicht.   Sie **müß** es tun.
I don't know.   *She has to do it.*
correct: Ich **weiß** es nicht.   Sie **muß** es tun.

Most modal verbs have an umlaut in the plural form of the present tense, but you must not extend this principle to all modals:

*Wir s**ö**llen kommen.
We are supposed to come.
correct: Wir s**o**llen kommen.

Finally, be careful about the **ss–ß** alternation, particularly with modals:

*Er muss kommen.   *Wir mü**ß**en kommen.
He must come.   *We must come.*
correct: Er mu**ß** kommen.   Wir mü**ss**en kommen.

German Core Vocabulary

Note: strong verbs are listed as follows: **fahren (fährt), fuhr,** i.e., *infinitive (third-person singular), simple past* form. The third-person singular is listed only when the verb has a stem-vowel change. This list includes all the verbs used in the answer portion of the exercises.

Study the imperative forms of **sein** on page 7, the mixed verb forms on page 7, the modals on page 10, and the following list:

ähneln	*to resemble*	beenden	*to end*
arbeiten	*to work*	befehlen (befiehlt),	*to command, order*
atmen	*to breathe*	befahl	
beantworten	*to answer*	beginnen, begann	*to begin*

belästigen	to bother	ölen	to oil
besuchen	to visit	passen	to fit
beweisen, bewies	to prove	raten (rät), riet	to advise
bieten, bot	to offer	rechnen mit	to expect
bitten um, bat	to ask for	reden	to talk
blasen (bläst), blies	to blow	regnen	to rain
bleiben, blieb	to remain	reinigen	to clean
brauchen	to need	reisen	to travel
brummen	to purr	retten	to save
empfehlen	to recommend	rufen, rief	to call
(empfiehlt),		sagen	to say, tell
empfahl		sammeln	to collect
erfassen	to comprehend	saufen (säuft), soff	to drink (of
erschrecken	to terrify		animals), to
erwidern	to return (greeting)		consume alcohol
essen (ißt), aß	to eat	schlafen (schläft),	to sleep
fahren (fährt), fuhr	to drive	schlief	
fallen (fällt), fiel	to fall	schlagen (schlägt),	to hit, beat
festigen	to bolt, secure	schlug	
finden, fand	to find	schließen, schloß	to close
fliegen, flog	to fly	schluchzen	to sob
fressen (frißt), fraß	to eat (of animals)	schmeißen, schmiß	to fling
	to devour (of	schmelzen	to melt
	humans)	(schmilzt),	
geben (gibt), gab	to give	schmolz	
gehen, ging	to go	schneiden, schnitt	to cut
genießen, genoß	to enjoy	schweigen,	to be silent
geschehen	to happen	schwieg	
(geschieht),		schwimmen,	to swim
geschah		schwamm	
grüßen	to greet	sehen (sieht), sah	to see
halten (hält), hielt	to hold	singen, sang	to sing
halten von	to think of, to be	sitzen, saß	to sit
	of an opinion	spenden	to donate
hassen	to hate	spielen	to play
heißen, hieß	to be called	sprechen (spricht),	to speak
helfen (hilf), half	to help	sprach	
kämmen	to comb	stehlen (stiehlt),	to steal
kommen, kam	to come	stahl	
küssen	to kiss	stellen	to put
laden (lädt), lud	to load	stoßen (stößt),	to knock, shove
lassen (läßt), ließ	to leave	stieß	
laufen (läuft), lief	to run	studieren	to study
leiden, litt	to suffer	tragen (trägt), trug	to carry
lernen	to learn	treten (tritt), trat	to step
lesen (liest), las	to read	verachten	to despise
lügen, log	to (tell a) lie	vergessen	to forget
machen	to do	(vergißt), vergaß	
nehmen (nimmt),	to take	vergeuden	to squander
nahm		verkaufen	to sell
öffnen	to open	vermeiden	to avoid

vermissen	*to miss*	werfen (wirft),	*to throw*
verteidigen	*to defend*	warf	
warnen	*to warn*	widmen	*to dedicate*
warten	*to wait*	wohnen	*to live*

EXERCISE 1 (prerequisite: section A, topic: present-tense verb conjugation)

Fill in the blank with the appropriate present-tense form of the verb in parentheses. Then exchange the subject of the sentence with each of the pronouns given in the second parentheses and make any necessary changes in the verb.

> EXAMPLE: Er _____ zum Abendessen. (kommen) (wir,du)
> ANSWERS: Er kommt zum Abendessen. Wir kommen zum Abendessen. Du kommst zum Abendessen.

1. Ich _____ einen neuen Kugelschreiber. (brauchen) (Sie, sie = *she*)
2. _____ du mich morgen? (besuchen) (sie = *she*, ihr)
3. Wir _____ Deutsch. (studieren) (sie = *they*, ich)
4. Hoffentlich _____ ihr gesund. (bleiben) (du, er)
5. Er _____ Englisch. (lernen) (ich, wir)
6. Warum _____ Sie in dieser kleinen Wohnung? (wohnen) (ihr, sie = *they*)
7. _____ du nach Frankfurt? (fliegen) (Sie, er)
8. Ich _____ gern Schach. (spielen) (mein Bruder, viele Leute)
9. Sie (= *she*) _____ das Auto. (verkaufen) (wir, ihr)
10. Herr Klopke _____ sehr gut. (singen) (ich, du)

EXERCISE 2 (prerequisite: section A, topic: simple past tense, weak verbs)

Fill in the blank with the appropriate past-tense form of the weak verb given in parentheses. Then exchange the subject with the pronouns as in exercise 1.

1. Gestern _____ er seine Verwandten in Kassel. (besuchen) (wir, ich)
2. Warum _____ du das? (machen) (er, sie = *they*)
3. Regina _____ meinen Gruß. (erwidern) (sie = *they*, er)
4. Ihr _____ mich furchtbar! (erschrecken) (sie = *they*, er)
5. Die Mutter _____ das Kind. (küssen) (ich, du)
6. Wir _____ mehr Geld. (brauchen) (Sie, er)
7. Ich _____ Medizin. (studieren) (sie = *she*, wir)
8. Luise _____ die Teller auf den Tisch. (stellen) (ich, er)
9. Der Mechaniker _____ die Fahrräder. (ölen) (ich, sie = *they*)
10. _____ du ihm die Wahrheit? (sagen) (Sie, ihr)

EXERCISE 3 (prerequisite: section A, topic: simple past tense, strong verbs)

Fill in the blank with the appropriate past-tense form of the strong verb given in parentheses. Then exchange the subject with the pronouns as in exercise 1.

1. Jürgen _____. (schweigen) (wir, ich)
2. Wann _____ Sie nach Hause? (fahren) (wir, du)
3. Ich _____ ihm eine Zigarette. (geben) (wir, sie = *she*)
4. Du _____ mit dieser Bemerkung zu weit! (gehen) (Sie, er)
5. Wir _____ zu lachen. (beginnen) (du, sie = *she*)
6. Zwei alte Zeitungen _____ auf dem Sofa. (liegen) (ich, er)
7. Ich _____ den Hund des Nachbarn. (rufen) (wir, ihr)
8. Der Politiker _____. (lügen) (beide Politiker, sie = *she*)
9. Ein Alligator _____ im Wasser. (schwimmen) (du, sie = *they*)
10. Jemand _____ihm. (helfen) (die Männer, wir)

EXERCISE 4 (prerequisite: section B, topic: stem-vowel change)

Fill in the blank with the proper present-tense verb form and then exchange subjects.

1. Bis wann _____ du jeden Tag? (schlafen) (Sie, er)
2. Ich _____ gern. (lesen) (er, sie = *they*)
3. Das Pferd _____ das Wasser. (saufen) (zwei Pferde)
4. Warum _____ du niemals Obst? (essen) (er, Sie)
5. Er _____ alles mit. (nehmen) (Sie, du)
6. Wo _____ du hin? (laufen) (sie = *they*, er)
7. Mein Chef _____ mir nicht genug Geld. (geben) (du, sie = *she*)
8. _____ du die Pakete mit? (nehmen) (er, wir)
9. Meine Klasse _____ nächsten Sommer nach Europa. (fahren) (ich, wir)
10. Er _____ ins Zimmer. (treten) (wir, du)
11. _____ du irgendwo meine Brille? (sehen) (ihr, Sie)
12. Wann _____ er mir eine Antwort auf meine Frage? (geben) (Sie, du)
13. Du _____ auf meinen Fuß! (treten) (jemand, Sie)
14. Meine Schwester _____ mir oft bei den Hausaufgaben. (helfen) (meine Eltern, er)
15. Er _____ uns zu kommen. (befehlen) (sie = *they*, du)
16. Warum _____ du die schmutzigen Kleider auf das Bett? (werfen) (er, Sie)
17. Ein Eichhörnchen _____ die Nüsse. (stehlen) (drei Eichhörnchen, du)
18. Der Schneemann _____ . (schmelzen) (Die beiden Schneemänner)
19. Der Mann neben mir im Zug _____ mich ständig. (stoßen) (ihr, du)
20. Warum _____ du diesen armen Mann? (schlagen) (er, ihr)

EXERCISE 5 (prerequisite: section C, topic: present tense of verbs with special conjugations)

Use the present-tense form of the verb given.

1. _____ du meine neue Frisur hübsch? (finden) (Sie, er)
2. Er _____ uns um Hilfe. (bitten) (du, sie = *they*)
3. _____ du gern? (reisen) (er, Sie)
4. Er _____ Französisch. (lernen) (wir, ich)
5. Der Patient _____ schwer. (atmen) (du, ich)
6. Du _____ immer neben dem Ausgang. (sitzen) (ihr, er)
7. Wir _____ mit einer Niederlage. (rechnen) (sie = *she,* du)
8. Er _____ offensichtlich nicht viel von mir. (halten) (du, Sie)
9. Ich _____ dieses Denkmal den Kriegsopfern. (widmen) (wir, er)
10. _____ du mir, dieses Auto zu kaufen? (raten) (Sie, er)
11. Ich _____ Sie! (warnen) (er, sie = *they*)
12. Es _____ schon wieder! (regnen)
13. Was _____ er uns dafür? (bieten) (du, Sie)
14. Du _____ den Wagen. (laden) (Sie, er)
15. Wie _____ du? (heißen) (sie = *she,* ihr)

EXERCISE 6 (prerequisite: section C, topic: past tense of verbs with special conjugations)

Give the past-tense form of the strong or weak verb given.

1. Wir _____ (arbeiten) (ich, er)
2. Ich _____ Blut. (spenden) (wir, sie = *she*)
3. Wir _____ die frische Bergluft. (atmen) (ich, sie = *they*)
4. Wie _____ du als ledige Frau? (heißen) (Sie, sie = *she*)
5. Leise _____ er die Tür. (öffnen) (ich, wir)
6. Ich _____ dem Kind die Haare. (kämmen) (er, du)
7. Wann _____ Sie den Brief? (beantworten) (du, er)
8. Ich _____ zwei Stunden. (warten) (wir, er)
9. _____ du dieses Buch? (lesen) (er, ihr)
10. Dieser Mann _____ das ganze Geld. (vergeuden) (Sie, ich)
11. Er _____ mich. (verachten) (du, sie = *they*)
12. Voriges Jahr _____ es oft. (regnen)
13. Vater _____ den Streit. (beenden) (sie = *they,* ich)
14. Warum _____ du seine Bemerkung lustig? (finden) (ihr, Sie)
15. Wann _____ er um Erlaubnis, das zu tun? (bitten) (du, Sie)

EXERCISE 7 (prerequisite: section D, topic: imperatives)

*Give the correct imperative form of the verb shown. Use the **du**-form when the person is addressed with the first name and the **Sie**-form when the family name is used.*

1. Andreas, _____ hierher! (kommen)
2. _____ dieses Buch, du wirst es interessant finden! (lesen)
3. _____ mir nicht böse, aber ich kann heute abend nicht mit dir ausgehen. (sein)
4. _____ das nicht, egal, wie hungrig Sie sind! (essen)
5. Frau Lohner, _____ bitte ein bißchen lauter! (sprechen)
6. Peter, _____ nicht vom Dach herunter! (fallen)
7. _____ beruhigt, Frau Jost! Wir werden Ihre Koffer finden. (sein)
8. _____ mich, wenn ihr Schwierigkeiten habt! (rufen)
9. Erika, _____ mir bitte das Buch! (geben)
10. _____ die Nebenstraßen, wenn du durch dieses Land fährst! (vermeiden)
11. _____ gut, liebes Kind! (schlafen)
12. _____ Blut und hilf deinen Mitmenschen! (spenden)
13. _____ wir nicht hastig! (sein)
14. Martin, _____ nicht mit meiner Hilfe! (rechnen)
15. _____ deutlicher, wenn du vorliest! (sprechen)
16. _____ brav, Kinder, wenn Oma zu Besuch kommt! (sein)
17. _____ schnell zur Apotheke und hol mir Kopfwehtabletten! (laufen)
18. _____ dein Vaterland! (verteidigen)
19. _____ wir nach Hause! (fahren)
20. Max und Gerhard! _____ mir bitte! (helfen)
21. _____ bitte die Schuhe, bevor ihr ins Haus kommt! (reinigen)
22. Frau Ebenbauer! _____ bitte Platz! (nehmen)
23. Kinder! _____ nicht so laut! (reden)
24. Herr Friedemann, _____ bitte herein! (kommen)
25. Fräulein Braun! _____ bitte! (warten)

EXERCISE 8 (prerequisite: section E, topic: mixed verbs)

Insert the correct present-tense form of the verb given. Then do the same for the simple past tense of the verb.

1. Das Lagerfeuer _____ zu hoch. (brennen)
2. _____ du jemand in dieser Stadt? (kennen)
3. Wir _____ jeden Tag in der Frühe. (rennen)
4. Zwei Arbeiter _____ der alten Frau die Lebensmittel. (bringen)
5. Ich _____ ihn immer Hansi. (nennen)
6. _____ Sie wirklich an das Wohl Ihrer Kinder? (denken)
7. Eine Kosmetikfirma _____ ihr einige Lippenstifte zum Ausprobieren. (senden)
8. Wir _____ ihn nicht besonders gut. (kennen)

9. Die Verkäuferin _____ sich an den Kunden. (wenden)
10. Woran _____ du? (denken)

EXERCISE 9 (prerequisite: section F, topic: **ss-ß** alternation)

Use the present-tense form of the verb given. Then exchange the subject as usual,
unless the sentence is an imperative.

1. _____ du ihn wirklich? (hassen) (Sie, ihr)
2. Dieser Anzug _____ mir gut. (passen) (diese Anzüge)
3. Hartmut, _____ die Tür! (schließen)
4. Er _____ die Ferien. (genießen) (wir, du)
5. _____dein Versprechen nicht! (vergessen)
6. Er _____ die Bücher auf den Tisch. (schmeißen) (du, wir)
7. Niemand _____ diese Theorie. (erfassen) (sie = *they*, ich)
8. Wir _____ zuerst Wasser auf das Feuer. (gießen) (er, du)
9. Du _____ wie ein Schwein! (fressen) (er, Sie)
10. Das Kind _____ seinen Teddybären. (küssen) (ich, sie = *she*)

EXERCISE 10 (prerequisite: section G, topic: modal verbs and **wissen,**
present tense)

*Fill in the blank with the present-tense form of the modal or **wissen**, as indicated by*
the English verb in parentheses. Then exchange subjects.

1. _____ Sie Kaffee? *(like)* (du, ihr)
2. Wir _____ , daß er der Verfasser des Werkes ist. *(know)* (ich, Sie)
3. _____ ihr heute abend ins Kino gehen? *(want)* (du, er)
4. Niemand _____ die Antwort geben. *(can)* (wir, ich)
5. _____ Sie das wirklich tun? *(may)* (du, ihr)
6. Ich _____ nächste Woche ein Referat halten. *(to be supposed to)* (wir, er)
7. Meinetwegen _____ du weggehen. *(can)* (ihr, sie = *she*)
8. _____ man hier rauchen? *(may)* (sie = *they*, ich)
9. Wieso _____ du zur Bibliothek gehen? *(must)* (Sie, er)
10. Ich _____ neue Schuhe kaufen. *(want)* (wir, sie = *she*)
11. Du _____ mich nicht anschreien. *(should)* (ihr, Sie)
12. Die Touristen _____ ein besseres Hotel finden. *(must)* (ich, er)
13. Ich _____ seine Art nicht. *(like)* (wir, sie = *she*)
14. _____ du nicht, wie er heißt? *(know)* (ihr, sie = *they*)
15. _____ ich Sie stören? *(may)* (wir, er)
16. Wir _____ sofort den Arzt holen. *(must)* (Sie, du)
17. Was _____ Sie bestellen? *(want)* (du, sie = *she*)
18. Jeder _____ , wo der Präsident wohnt. *(know)* (sie = *they*, ich)
19. _____ ihr heute abend kommen? *(can)* (du, er)
20. Er _____ Tante Wanda besuchen. *(should)* (wir, du)

EXERCISE 11   (prerequisite: section G, topic: modal verbs and **wissen,** simple past tense)

Fill in the blank with the simple past-tense form of the verb given in parentheses. Then exchange subjects.

1. Wir _____ das Klassenzimmer nicht verlassen. (dürfen) (ich, sie = *they*)
2. _____ Sie es nicht begreifen? (können) (er, ihr)
3. Die Vermieterin _____ keine Ausländer haben. (wollen) (sie = *they*, wir)
4. Wir _____ um elf Uhr am Flughafen sein. (sollen) (ich, ihr)
5. Er _____ mich nicht. (mögen) (Sie, du)
6. Ich _____ wirklich nicht, daß es ein Feiertag war. (wissen) (sie = *they*, der Student)
7. Warum _____ du gestern zum Schuldirektor gehen? (müssen) (Sie, er)
8. Wann _____ du, daß jemand die Juwelen gestohlen hatte? (wissen) (Sie, ihr)
9. Wir _____ die Hitze nicht mehr aushalten! (können) (ich, sie = *she*)
10. _____ du mit ihm sprechen? (dürfen) (er, Sie)

EXERCISE 12   (comprehensive, excluding section H)

Fill in the blank with the present-tense form of the verb given.

1. Niemand _____ gerne. (warten)
2. Wir _____ ihn sehr gut. (kennen)
3. Er _____ ein grünes Hemd. (tragen)
4. Kinder, _____ draußen! (spielen)
5. _____ es keine andere Möglichkeit? (geben)
6. Bitte, _____ so lieb, und machen Sie die Tür für mich auf! (sein)
7. Er _____ seine Freunde von der Schule. (vermissen)
8. Warum _____ du so? (schluchzen)
9. Er _____ sich seinem Studium. (widmen)
10. Wir _____ unser Haus. (verkaufen)
11. Mein Aufsatz _____ morgen fertig sein. (müssen)
12. Die Katze _____. (brummen)
13. Wer _____ einen Bleistift? (brauchen)
14. Du _____ mir niemals! (helfen)
15. Er _____ auf den Teppich. (treten)
16. Erich, _____ das Silberbesteck nicht! (stehlen)
17. Mein Deutschlehrer _____ mir, ein Jahr in Deutschland zu verbringen. (raten)
18. Was _____ , wenn man bei einer Prüfung schwindelt? (geschehen)
19. _____ bitte deinen Teller in die Küche! (tragen)
20. Heinz _____ die Arbeit. (machen)
21. _____ dein Leben, solange du kannst! (retten)
22. Es _____ oft im April. (regnen)
23. Du _____ nichts mit deiner Erklärung. (beweisen)

24. Klaus, _____ bitte das Brot! (schneiden)
25. _____ Sie lieber zu Hause bleiben? (wollen)
26. Dann _____ er mich einfach nieder! (stoßen)
27. _____ mit einer großen Rechnung, wenn du zum Zahnarzt gehst! (rechnen)
28. Franz, _____ nicht so blöd! (sein)
29. Wie _____ ich ihn anreden? (sollen)
30. Da _____ du falsch! (denken)
31. _____ die Gartentür, bevor der Sturm kommt! (festigen)
32. Er _____ das Buch. (halten)
33. Wo _____ wir übernachten? (wollen)
34. Er _____ uns eine Einladung zur Party. (senden)
35. Er _____ das komisch. (finden)
36. _____ deine Suppe, bevor sie kalt wird! (essen)
37. Er _____ den Wagen mit Sachen für die Reise. (laden)
38. Du _____ das alles viel zu ernst. (nehmen)
39. Brigitte _____ einfach alles. (wissen)
40. Die Wolke _____ einem Schaf. (ähneln)

EXERCISE 13 (comprehensive excluding section H)

Do the sentences in exercise 12 with the verb in simple past tense except where the verb is an imperative.

What's wrong with these?

1. Was empfehlst du?
2. Ich rufte sie, aber sie hörte mich nicht.
3. Wann sollt er kommen?
4. Du fahrst immer zu schnell!
5. Was mächst du da?
6. Fress nicht so viel!
7. Ich sange im Chor.
8. Weisst du immer noch, wie wir dich damals nennten?
9. Wöllen Sie hier etwas kaufen?
10. Er aßt das ganze Grillhendl.
11. Das Haus brennte in 15 Minuten nieder.
12. Erika laste das Buch bis spät in die Nacht.

Verbs: Present and Simple Past Tense: Separable and Inseparable Prefixes

2

A. Separable and Inseparable Prefixes

The German language has a large number of prefixes which can be attached to virtually any verb. For example, the prefix **weg-** can be added to the verb **laufen** *(to run)* to produce **weglaufen** *(to run away)*. Similarly, the prefix **er-** when added to the verb **kennen** *(to know)* produces **erkennen** *(to recognize)*.

Prefixes in German can be separable or inseparable. This distinction is explained in the rule below:

> *Separable prefixes detach from the verb and go to the end of the clause except when the verb is itself at the end of the clause. Inseparable prefixes are always attached to the verb.*

The examples below illustrate the rule using the separable prefix **mit-** and the inseparable prefix **er-**:

SEPARABLE PREFIX

Mein Bruder fährt **mit.**
My brother is coming along.
(present tense)

INSEPARABLE PREFIX

Ich **er**kenne ihn nicht mehr.
I don't recognize him anymore.

SEPARABLE PREFIX	INSEPARABLE PREFIX
Mein Bruder fuhr **mit.**	Ich **er**kannte ihn nicht mehr.
My brother came along.	*I didn't recognize him anymore.*
(simple past tense)	
Mein Bruder will **mit**fahren.	Ich kann ihn nicht mehr **er**kennen.
My brother wants to come along.	*I can't recognize him anymore.*
(verb at end of clause)	

In this book, the verb minus its prefix will be called the *base verb*. Verbs with prefixes are conjugated according to the following principle:

> *The conjugation of a verb with a prefix is the same as the conjugation of the base verb with the prefix added.*

For example, **erkennen** has the base verb **kennen.** The simple past of **kennen** is **kannte**; therefore, the simple past of **erkennen** is **erkannte.**

Separable prefixes are almost always words that exist in their own right, chiefly as adverbs or prepositions. In addition, the meaning they impart to the base verb is often similar to their meaning as separate words. For example, **zusammen** means *together* in the sentences that follow:

Heinrich war **zusammen** mit seiner Freundin da.
Heinrich was there together with his girlfriend.
(adverb)

Heinrich und seine Freundin kamen heute **zusammen.**
Heinrich and his girl friend met today.
(prefix of the verb **zusammenkommen**)

In contrast to separable prefixes, inseparable prefixes usually do not exist as individual words; they are simply sound combinations such as **er-.** Furthermore, they generally do not change the meaning of the verb in as consistent a fashion as in the case with separable prefixes, e.g., **kennen** *(to know),* **erkennen** *(to recognize).*

But separable prefixes can also cause unpredictable changes in meaning. For example, when the separable prefix **an-** is added to **fangen** *(to catch),* it produces **anfangen** *(to begin).* Ironically, inseparable prefixes sometimes do impart consistent meanings to the base verb, but these are left for you to discover in the **Gedankenproblem** at the end of this chapter.

The type of prefix a word has determines which syllable has the main stress:

> *A word with a separable prefix is stressed on the prefix, a word with an inseparable prefix is stressed on the base word.*

For example, the stress in **mítfahren** (separable prefix **mit-**) is on the prefix **mít-**, the stress in **erkénnen** (inseparable prefix **er-**) is on the first syllable of the base verb **kénnen.**

When dealing with separable prefixes, always remember that the prefix goes to the end of the *clause,* not necessarily the end of the *sentence.* This distinction is illustrated in the example below where the separable prefix is **zurück-:**

*Er kam nach einigen Stunden und war äußerst aufgeregt **zurück.**
He came back after several hours and was extremely upset.
correct: Er kam nach einigen Stunden **zurück** und war äußerst aufgeregt.

For reference, the most common *separable* prefixes are listed here:

PREFIX	MOST COMMON MEANING	EXAMPLE	TRANSLATION
ab-	*off*	abdrehen	*to turn off*
an-	*on*	anbinden	*to tie on*
auf-	*up*	aufspringen	*to jump up*
aus-	*out*	ausschließen	*to shut out*
bei-	many meanings	beilegen	*to add to*
ein-	*in*	einsteigen	*to get in*
empor-	*upward*	emporragen	*to project upward*
entgegen-	*against, toward*	entgegengehen	*to go toward, approach*
		entgegensetzen	*to set against, contrast*
fort-	*away, continue*	fortschwemmen	*to wash away*
		fortfahren	*drive away; to continue*
heim-	*home*	heimgehen	*to go home*
los-	*free, loose*	loslassen	*to let go, to set free*
mit-	*along*	mitkommen	*to come along*
nach-	*after*	nachlaufen	*to run after*
nieder-	*down*	niederwerfen	*to throw down*
statt-	no specific meaning	stattfinden	*to take place*
teil-	*part*	teilnehmen	*to take part*
vor-	*before, forward*	vordringen	*to press forward*
		vorlegen	*to set before*
weg-	*away*	wegrennen	*to run away*
zu-	*to, closed*	zuwinken	*to wink to*
		zumachen	*to close*
zurück-	*back*	zurückkommen	*to come back*
zusammen-	*together*	zusammenbinden	*to tie together*

The most common *inseparable* prefixes are listed below. For each prefix, an example is given to show the effect of the prefix on that particular verb:

PREFIX	BASE VERB	MEANING	WITH PREFIX	MEANING
be-	schließen	*to close*	beschließen	*to conclude, to decide*
emp-	finden	*to find*	empfinden	*to feel, to perceive*
ent-	sprechen	*to speak*	entsprechen	*to correspond to*
er-	geben	*to give*	ergeben	*to produce*
ge-	hören	*to hear*	gehören	*to belong to*
hinter-	bleiben	*to remain*	hinterbleiben	*to remain behind*
miß-	trauen	*to trust*	mißtrauen	*to mistrust*
ver-	sprechen	*to speak*	versprechen	*to promise*
zer-	stören	*to disturb*	zerstören	*to destroy*

Most lists of strong verbs, including the one in this book, list only base verbs, e.g., **fahren.** You must realize on your own that a word with a prefix, such as **mitfahren,** is also a strong verb. In other words, you should be able to recognize a prefix as such so that you can in turn recognize the base verb to which the prefix is attached.

Note: In the vocabulary lists in this book, a verb with a separable prefix will be shown with a period between the prefix and the base verb, e.g., **an.fangen.** A verb with an inseparable prefix will have no such period, e.g., **zerstören.** For your own benefit, check your German-English dictionary to see how it indicates the distinction between separable and inseparable prefixes (for example, look up **anfangen** and **zerstören**).

COMPREHENSION CHECK: *Part A: Fill in the blank(s) with the present tense of the verb given in parentheses. You may need to use only one of the two blanks.*

1. Eberhard _____ die Tür _____ . (aufmachen)
2. Das Eis _____ in der heißen Sonne _____ . (zerfließen)
3. Rewrite sentence #1 in the simple past tense.
4. Rewrite sentence #2 in the simple past tense.
5. Which syllable has the stress in **aufmachen?**
6. Which syllable has the stress in **zerfließen?**

Part B: Fill in the blank with the separable prefix most likely to translate the English word given in parentheses.

7. Der Dieb bricht _____ . (*in*)
8. Wirf den Ball _____ . (*back*)

ANSWERS: 1. macht... auf   2. zerfließt (*first blank*)   3. machte... auf   4. zerfloß (*first blank*)   5. aúf-   6. -flíe-   7. ein   8. zurück

B. Her-/Hin-

Two separable prefixes not listed in section A deserve special attention: **her-** *(to here)* and **hin-** *(to there):*

> Erika, geh **hin!**   Erika, komm **her!**
> *Erika, go there.*   *Erika, come here.*

Her- should not be confused with the German word **hier** *(here)*. The difference in meaning is this: **her-** means *to here,* whereas **hier** means *here* (no motion). The two are not interchangeable. Thus, the following sentence is wrong:

> *Herr Fink, kommen Sie bitte **hier!**
> *Mr. Fink, come here please.*
> correct: Herr Fink, kommen Sie bitte **her!** (**hierher** can also be used instead of **her** for greater emphasis).

A sentence in which **hier** is correct is this:

> Wo ist meine Krawatte? Sie ist **hier.**
> *Where is my tie? It's here.*

Her- and **hin-** are most commonly used in combination with a second separable prefix, e.g., **hinein-, heraus-, hinab-,** etc. The addition of **hin-** or **her-** tends to make the meaning of the second prefix more literal and, in particular, emphasizes the idea of motion. Furthermore, **her-** indicates that the motion is towards the speaker, **hin-** implies that the motion is away from the speaker:

> Er brachte eine Beschwerde **ein.**
> *He brought in a complaint.*
> (i.e., He complained.)

> Er brachte den Beschwerdebrief in das Büro **herein.**
> *He brought the complaint letter into the office.*
> (i.e., He physically walked into the office; he came toward the speaker, who must have been in the office.)

> Er ging mit dem Beschwerdebrief in das Büro **hinein.**
> *He went into the office with the complaint letter.*
> (i.e., He physically went into the office; he went away from the speaker, who must have been outside the office.)

Another example:

> Willst du den Mantel **auf**hängen?
> *Do you want to hang up your coat (somewhere)?*

> Willst du den Mantel **hinauf**hängen?
> *Do you want to hang up your coat (up there)?*

COMPREHENSION CHECK: *Choose the separable prefix that correctly completes the meaning of the sentence.*

1. Gehst du weg? Wo läufst du _____ ? (her, hin)
2. a. Bring mir den Zucker _____ ! (her, hier, hin)
   b. Der Zucker ist _____ . (her, hier, hin)
3. a. Maria, lauf _____! (heraus, hinaus)
   (Both Maria and the speaker are inside.)
   b. Maria, lauf _____ ! (heraus, hinaus)
   (Maria is inside, the speaker is outside.)
4. Explain the difference in meaning between **ausgehen** and **hinausgehen** in the examples below:
   a. Willst du heute abend mit mir ausgehen? Ich habe Karten für ein Konzert.
   b. Willst du jetzt hinausgehen? Nein, ich will drinnen bleiben.

ANSWERS: 1. hin 2.a. her 2.b. hier 3.a. hinaus 3.b. heraus 4.a. ausgehen = *to go out on a date* 4.b. hinausgehen = *to go out of (leave) some building*

C. Uncertain Prefixes

The prefixes shown below are called *uncertain prefixes* because they can be either separable or inseparable:

durch-, über-, um-, unter-, voll-, wieder-, wider-

Sometimes with such prefixes, a given verb will have both a separable and an inseparable form, each corresponding to a different meaning:

Die neue Fähre setzte uns **über.**
The new ferry took us across.

Ulrike **über**setzte ein Gedicht.
Ulrike translated a poem.

Most of the time, the prefix will be separable with one verb and inseparable with another:

Die Sonne ging im Westen **unter.**
The sun went down in the west.

Der Diktator **unter**jochte sein Volk.
The dictator subjugated his people.
(**unterjochen** means literally *to yoke under*)

Most verbs with uncertain prefixes tend to have literal meanings when the prefix is separable and figurative meanings when it is inseparable. This tendency can be seen in the examples above. When an uncertain prefix is separable, it has the stress, when the uncertain prefix is inseparable, then the base verb has the stress. Finally, an uncertain prefix may be combined with **her-** or **hin-**. In such cases, the combined prefix is always separable:

Reich mir das Salz **herüber!**
Pass the salt over here.

Here are a few more examples to illustrate the use of the remaining uncertain prefixes:

Durch-

Er dringt **durch.**
He forces his way through.

Ein Schrei **durch**dringt die Stille.
A scream pierces the silence.

Um-

Ein böses Gerücht geht jetzt **um.**
A nasty rumor is now circulating.

Man **um**geht solche Probleme niemals.
One never avoids such problems.

Voll-

Die Kinder füllten ihre Taschen mit Süßigkeiten **voll.**
The children filled their pockets with candies.

Endlich **voll**endeten wir die Arbeit.
Finally we completed the work.

(When **voll-** imparts the meaning *to make full,* it is separable; when it means *to make complete,* it is inseparable.)

Wieder-

Ich sah ihn nach vielen Jahren **wieder.**
I saw him again after many years.

Das Klasse **wieder**holte alles, was der Lehrer sagte.
The class repeated everything that the teacher said.
(**Wieder-** is almost always separable, **wiederholen** is the most common exception.)

Wider-

Der Redner **wider**legte alle Beschuldigungen.
The speaker refuted all accusations.

Das Wasser spiegelte ihr Gesicht **wider.**
The water reflected her face.
(**Wider-** is usually inseparable, **widerspiegeln** is the most common exception.)

In most cases, you cannot predict whether an uncertain prefix will be separable or inseparable with a given verb; the problem can only be resolved by consulting a German dictionary to determine the correct usage.

COMPREHENSION CHECK: *Translate these sentences into English.*

1. a. Das Wasser lief in der Badewanne über.
   b. Die Studenten überliefen den Lehrer mit ihren Beschwerden.
2. a. Ich flog von Chicago nach Frankfurt durch.
   b. Ich durchflog das Buch.
3. Which syllable has the stress in **überlaufen** when it has the meaning shown in question 1.a. above?
4. Which syllable has the stress in **überlaufen** when it has the meaning shown in question 1.b.?

ANSWERS: 1.a. The water ran over the bathtub. 1.b. The students bombarded the teacher with their complaints. 2.a. I flew straight through from Chicago to Frankfurt. 2.b. I skimmed through the book. 3. über- 4. lauf-

German Core Vocabulary

This list contains all the new verbs used in the exercises.

ab.führen	to lead away
ab.schneiden, schnitt	to cut off, to slice off
an.fangen (fängt), fing	to begin
an.kommen, kam	to arrive
an.machen	to turn on
auf.blasen (bläst), blies	to blow up (put air into)
auf.machen	to open
auf.stehen, stand	to get up
aus.gehen, ging	to go out (on a date)
aus.rufen, rief	to call out
aus.sehen (sieht), sah	to look (like)
aus.spritzen	to rinse out
begreifen, begriff	to understand
bei.stehen	to stand by (someone)
betreten (betritt), betrat	to enter
brechen (bricht), brach	to break
durch.fliegen, flog	to fly (straight) through
durchfliegen, durchflog	to skim
ein.atmen	to breathe in
ein.streuen	to slip in, insert
empfangen (empfängt), empfing	to receive
empor.arbeiten (reflexive)	to work oneself up
entgegen.wirken	to work against, to hinder
entwickeln	to develop
erfinden, erfand	to invent
fort.setzen	to continue
gefallen (gefällt), gefiel	to please
hängen	to hang (something)
heim.fahren (fährt), fuhr	to go home (by car or train)
hinab.führen	to lead down

hinab/herab.lassen (läßt), ließ	*to lower*	nieder.stellen	*to put down*
		reichen	*to pass, to hand over*
hinauf.blasen (bläst), blies	*to move upward by blowing*	statt.finden, fand	*to take place*
		überlaufen (überläuft), überlief	*to bombard*
hinaus.gehen, ging	*to go out*		
hinaus.spritzen	*to squirt out*		
hinterlassen (hinterläßt), hinterließ	*to leave behind*	über.laufen (läuft), lief	*to run over*
		umarmen	*to embrace*
hinweg.schauen	*to look away*	verbrennen, verbrannte	*to burn*
lassen (läßt), ließ	*to let*		
los.lassen (läßt), ließ	*to let go*	vor.legen, lag	*to submit*
		weg.jagen	*to chase away*
mißverstehen, mißverstand	*to misunderstand*	weg.schauen	*to look away*
		weiter.gehen, ging	*to go farther*
mit.kommen, kam	*to come along*	zerfließen, zerfloß	*to melt away*
mit.spielen	*to join in the game*	zerreißen, zerriß	*to tear*
nach.schlagen (schlägt), schlug	*to look (something) up*	zurück.halten (hält), hielt	*to hold back, to keep to oneself*
nieder.fahren (fährt), fuhr	*to run (someone) over*	zusammen.stellen	*to put together*
		zu.sperren	*to lock*

EXERCISE 1 (prerequisite: section A, topic: common meanings of separable prefixes)

Fill in the blank with the separable prefix most likely to translate the English word given in parentheses.

1. Kommst du _____ ? *(along)*
2. Helmut stellte die heiße Pfanne _____ . *(down)*
3. Ich fahre jetzt _____ . *(home)*
4. Geh ein bißchen _____ ! *(farther)*
5. Er machte das Licht _____ . *(on)*
6. Ich setzte die Teile des Fahrrads _____ . *(together)*
7. Jemand rief meinen Namen _____ . *(out)*
8. Ich halte meine Meinung niemals _____ ! *(back)*
9. Der Hund jagte die Kinder _____ . *(away)*
10. Atmen Sie tief _____ ! *(in)*

EXERCISE 2 (Prerequisite: section A, topic: usage of separable and inseparable prefixes)

Each sentence in this exercise has two blanks. Fill in the blank(s) using the present tense of the verb(s) given in parentheses. Then rewrite each sentence in the simple past tense except those that involve imperatives. In some sentences only one blank need be filled.

1. Das Haus _____ immer noch gut _____ . (aussehen)
2. Niemand _____ seine Erklärung _____ . (begreifen)
3. Ich _____ ein Stück Brot _____ . (wollen, abschneiden)
4. Die Gastgeberin _____ ihre Gäste _____ . (empfangen)
5. Das Fotogeschäft _____ meinen Film _____ . (entwickeln)
6. Doris _____ sich zur Chefin _____ . (emporarbeiten)
7. Ihr Freund _____ mir nicht _____ . (gefallen)
8. Bitte, _____ Sie mich nicht _____ ! (mißverstehen)
9. Wer _____ mir _____ ? (beistehen)
10. Der neue Lehrer _____ die Arbeit seines Vorgängers _____ . (fortsetzen)
11. Wir _____ alte Zeitungen _____ . (verbrennen)
12. Ich _____ ihn um jeden Preis _____ . (müssen, vermeiden)
13. Du _____ das ganze Papier _____ ! (zerreißen)
14. _____ mich _____ ! (loslassen)
15. Seine Hilfe _____ dem Projekt nur _____ . (entgegenwirken)
16. _____ du die Tür _____ ? (zusperren)
17. Susi _____ nicht _____ . (dürfen, mitspielen)
18. Mein reicher Onkel in Amerika _____ mir ein Vermögen _____ . (hinterlassen)
19. Wann _____ er heute _____ ? (aufstehen)
20. Ein besoffener Autofahrer _____ einen Verkehrspolizisten _____ . (niederfahren)
21. Er _____ dem Direktor den Plan _____ . (vorlegen)
22. _____ Sie das Wort im Wörterbuch _____ ! (nachschlagen)
23. Du _____ immer solche Geschichten _____ ! (erfinden)
24. Die Vorstellung _____ _____ . (anfangen)
25. Wann _____ die Vorstellung _____ ? (stattfinden)

EXERCISE 3   (Prerequisite: section B, topic: **her-** and **hin-**)

Each pair of sentences in the exercise has two possible separate prefixes given in parentheses. Choose the prefix that best fits the context of the sentence. Do not use the same prefix for both sentences.

1. a. Wirf mir den Pullover _____ !
   b. Wirf ihm den Pullover _____ ! (her, hin)
2. a. Häng den Hut auf den Haken _____ !
   b. Reich mir den Hut _____ ! (herauf, hinauf)
3. a. Wollen Sie zu uns _____ kommen?
   b. Wollen Sie zum Direktor _____ gehen? (herein, hinein)
4. a. Wir müssen alles hier drinnen _____ tragen.
   b. Peter, lauf schnell ins Haus and bring mir den Regenschirm _____ ! (heraus, hinaus)
5. a. Langsam ließ ich das Klavier zu den Arbeitern _____ .
   b. Die Arbeiter ließen das Klavier langsam zu mir _____ . (herab, hinab)

EXERCISE 4 (Prerequisite: section B, topic: **her-** or **hin-** + prefix versus prefix alone)

Translate these sentences into English.

1. a. Ich spritzte das schmutzige Auto mit Wasser aus.
   b. Das Wasser spritzte aus dem Schlauch hinaus.
2. a. Kannst du diesen Ballon für mich aufblasen?
   b. Kannst du diesen Ballon zum Dach hinaufblasen?
3. a. Die Polizei führte den Verbrecher ab.
   b. Die Polizei führte den Verbrecher die Treppe hinab.
4. a. Er streute französische Ausdrücke in seine Rede ein.
   b. Er streute Heu in die Kiste hinein.
5. a. Sie mußte einfach wegschauen.
   b. Sie schaute über seinen Kopf hinweg.

EXERCISE 5 (Prerequisite: section C, topic: uncertain prefixes)

Fill in the blanks as necessary with the verb given in parentheses using the present tense unless otherwise indicated. The verbs in question are not necessarily listed in the vocabulary list; you may have to use a German-English dictionary to determine if the prefix is separable or inseparable.

1. a. Kinder, _____ eure Gummistiefel _____ ! (wiederholen)
   b. Kinder, _____ alles _____ ,was ich sage! (wiederholen)
2. a. Wir _____ das Auto mit Leuten _____ . (vollstopfen) *(simple past tense)*
   b. Wir _____ die Tat _____ . (vollbringen) *(simple past tense)*
3. a. Ich _____ dich _____ ! (durchschauen)
   b. _____ Sie hier _____ ! (durchschauen)
4. a. Die Armee _____ die Truppen in Privathäusern _____ . (unterbringen)
   b. Warum _____ Sie mich ständig _____ ? (unterbrechen)
5. a. Die Tatsachen _____ der Theorie _____ . (widersprechen)
   b. Der Glas _____ das Licht _____ . (widerspiegeln)
6. a. Der Fluß _____ die Stadt _____ . (überfluten) *(simple past tense)*
   b. Er _____ schließlich zum Katholizismus. (übertreten) *(simple past tense)*
7. a. Er _____ das Bild mit einem Blumenkranz. (umlegen) *(simple past tense)*
   b. Er _____ sich einen Mantel _____ . (umlegen) *(simple past tense)*
8. In the sentences above, mark the syllable of the infinitive that carries the stress.

EXERCISE 6 (Comprehensive)

This exercise has four sections with five sentences in each section and five possible prefixes listed at the top of each section. Use the five prefixes to complete the sentences of each section. You can use each prefix only once. In order to avoid giving the answers away, the verbs are not listed in the chapter vocabulary list. You will have to use a German dictionary for reference.

fort-, um-, ab-, be-, er-

1. Wann fährt der Zug _____ ?
2. Wegen des frischen Asphalts kann man diese Straße nicht _____ fahren.
3. Der Sprecher fuhr mit seiner Rede _____ .
4. Er _____ fuhr eine Baustelle auf der Straße.
5. Ich _____ fuhr seinen Namen nicht.

heraus-, herum-, her-, hinein-, hinunter-

6. Sie fuhren nutzlos im Kreis _____ .
7. Kannst du das Auto für mich aus der Garage _____ fahren?
8. Der Schiläufer fuhr den Berg _____ .
9. Fahr das Auto in die (= *into the*) Garage _____ .
10. Kannst du zu mir _____ fahren?

vor-, aus-, zusammen-, durch-, zurück-

11. Er fährt immer bei Rot _____ .
12. Der Chauffeur fährt die alte Dame jeden Sonntag _____ .
13. Zwei Autos fuhren auf der Autobahn _____ .
14. Wegen der vielen Kurven darf man auf dieser Bergstraße nicht _____ fahren.
15. Ich muß nach Hause _____ fahren.

ein-, hinüber-, los-, auf-, nieder-

16. Plötzlich fuhr er _____ und schrie mich an!
17. Hans muß das neue Auto zuerst _____ fahren.
18. Bald fahren alle Rennwagen _____ .
19. Um Gottes Willen! Fahr den Hund nicht _____ !
20. Wir fuhren zur anderen Seite des Flusses _____ .

GEDANKENPROBLEM: **By examining the verbs shown, determine the meaning imparted by the inseparable prefix. Use a dictionary for reference.**

a. *mißtrauen, mißverstehen, mißhandeln, mißbrauchen*
b. *entmutigen, entkernen, entlasten, entkleiden*
c. *verletzen, verbiegen, sich verlaufen, sich versprechen*
d. *zerschlagen, zerreißen, zerfetzen, zerbrechen*

What's wrong with these?

1. Mein bester Freund ankommt morgen mit dem Zug.
2. Friedrich betretete das Zimmer.
3. Bring deine Schmutzwäsche hier!
4. Wir gingen in ein deutsches Restaurant herein.
5. Erika armte Peter leidenschaftlich um.
6. Ein Blatt fiel auf meinen Kopf hinunter.

Verbs: Present Perfect, Past Perfect, and Future Tense

3

A. Survey of Verb Tenses

For reference, examples of the major tenses of German verbs are given below. The forms for the verbs **haben** *(to have)*, **sein** *(to be)*, and **werden** *(to become)* are also listed because of their importance for the formation of various tenses:

Future:

Ich **werde** meiner Schwester einen Brief **schreiben.**
I will write my sister a letter.

Present:

Ich **schreibe** meiner Schwester einen Brief.
I am writing my sister a letter.

Simple Past:

Strong verb:

Ich **schrieb** meiner Schwester einen Brief.
I wrote my sister a letter.

Weak verb:

Er **kaufte** einen neuen Mantel.
He bought a new coat.

Present Perfect (Past Perfect):

Strong verb with *haben* as auxiliary:

Ich **habe (hatte)** meiner Schwester einen Brief **geschrieben**.
I have (had) written my sister a letter.

Strong verb with *sein* as auxiliary:

Wir **sind (waren)** mit dem Zug nach Bonn **gefahren**.
We have (had) gone by train to Bonn.

Weak verb with *haben* as auxiliary:

Er **hat (hatte)** einen neuen Mantel **gekauft**.
He has (had) bought a new coat.

Weak verb with *sein* as auxiliary:

Ich **bin (war)** oft nach Stockholm **gereist**.
I have (had) often traveled to Stockholm.

PRESENT TENSE				SIMPLE PAST TENSE		
infinitive:	*haben*	*sein*	*werden*	*haben*	*sein*	*werden*
ich	habe	bin	werde	hatte	war	wurde
du	hast	bist	wirst	hattest	warst	wurdest
er, sie, es	hat	ist	wird	hatte	war	wurde
wir	haben	sind	werden	hatten	waren	wurden
ihr	habt	seid	werdet	hattet	wart	wurdet
sie, Sie	haben	sind	werden	hatten	waren	wurden

PAST PARTICIPLES:

| Ich habe **gehabt.** | Ich bin **gewesen.** | Ich bin **geworden.** |
| *I have had.* | *I have been.* | *I have become.* |

B. Present Perfect and Past Perfect Tenses

The basic structure of a typical German sentence in the present perfect tense is shown below:

Strong verb (infinitive: *schreiben*):

| | AUXILIARY | | PAST PARTICIPLE |
| Ich | habe | meiner Schwester einen Brief | **ge**schrie**ben.** |

English equivalent:

| | AUXILIARY | PAST PARTICIPLE | |
| *I* | *have* | *written* | *my sister a letter.* |

Weak verb (infinitive: *kaufen*):

| | AUXILIARY | | PAST PARTICIPLE |
| Er | hat | einen neuen Mantel | **ge**kauf**t.** |

English equivalent:

| | AUXILIARY | PAST PARTICIPLE | |
| *He* | *has* | *bought* | *a new coat.* |

The above examples show that German puts the past participle at the end of the clause in contrast to English. Both strong and weak verbs normally add a **ge-** prefix, but weak verbs have a **-t** suffix, strong verbs an **-en.**

The auxiliary verb in German can be either **haben,** as shown in the previous examples, or **sein** as seen in the example below:

Wir **sind** mit dem Zug nach Bonn gefahren.
We have gone (went) by train to Bonn.

The problem of deciding which auxiliary to use is discussed in section C.

Strong verbs may have a stem vowel in the past participle which is different from the infinitive stem and which may also be different from the stem vowel of the simple past:

INFINITIVE	SIMPLE PAST	PAST PARTICIPLE
schreiben	schrieb	geschrieben
to write	*wrote*	*written*
helfen	half	geholfen
to help	*helped*	*helped*

As with the forms of the simple past tense, the past participles of strong verbs must be memorized (consult the list of strong verbs on page 327–330 of this book).

You may recall from Chapter 1, section A, that certain weak verbs such as **arbeiten** *(to work)* and **regnen** *(to rain)* insert an **e** before endings in the present and simple past tense.

The same verbs also add an **e** before the final **-t** of the past participle:

INFINITIVE	PRESENT TENSE	SIMPLE PAST	PAST PARTICIPLE
arbeiten	Er arbeitet.	Er arbeitete.	Er hat gearbeitet.
to work	*He is working.*	*He worked.*	*He has worked.*
regnen	Es regnet.	Es regnete.	Es hat geregnet.
to rain	*It's raining.*	*It rained.*	*It has rained.*

Mixed verbs undergo the same stem changes in the past participle as they do in the simple past tense:

INFINITIVE	PRESENT TENSE	SIMPLE PAST	PAST PARTICIPLE
kennen	Ich kenne ihn.	Ich kannte ihn.	Ich habe ihn gekannt.
to know	*I know him.*	*I knew him.*	*I have known him.*
bringen	Er bringt es.	Er brachte es.	Er hat es gebracht.
to bring	*He is bringing it.*	*He brought it.*	*He has brought it.*

In English, we generally use the simple past tense to indicate an action that happened in the past and ended then, whereas the present perfect indicates an action that started in the past and has just stopped:

1. *I wrote her a letter last week. (simple past)*
2. *I have (just) written her a letter. (present perfect)*

German usually does not make this distinction in colloquial speech. Instead, German would use the present perfect tense to express both of the sentences above:

1. Ich **habe** ihr vorige Woche einen Brief **geschrieben.**
2. Ich **habe** ihr (eben) einen Brief **geschrieben.**

In formal writing, German would make the same distinction as English:

1. Ich **schrieb** ihr vorige Woche einen Brief.
2. Ich **habe** ihr (eben) einen Brief **geschrieben.**

However, with common verbs such as **haben, sein,** and the modals, many Germans do make the distinction in colloquial speech between simple past and present perfect:

Ich **war** vorige Woche im Krankenhaus.
I was in the hospital last week.

Ich **bin** diese Woche krank **gewesen.**
I have been sick this week.

The *past perfect* tense has basically the same function in German as in English and is formed analogously to English by putting the *auxiliary* in the *simple past* tense:

Klaus **hatte** Wien schon verlassen, als ich ankam.
Klaus had already left Vienna when I arrived.

COMPREHENSION CHECK: *Part A: Write the past participle of the following verbs.*

1. a. schreiben b. reisen c. singen d. machen e. arbeiten f. kosten
g. zeichnen h. atmen i. kennen j. nennen k. denken

Part B: Rearrange these groups of words into a meaningful sentence. Do not change any word within a group. Then rewrite the sentence in the past perfect tense.

2. Er/seine Autoschlüssel/verloren/hat.
3. Du/jemals nach Europa/geflogen/bist?

ANSWERS: 1. a. geschrieben b. gereist c. gesungen d. gemacht e. gearbeitet f. gekostet g. gezeichnet h. geatmet i. gekannt j. genannt k. gedacht 2. Er hat seine Autoschlüssel verloren. *past perfect:* Er hatte seine Autoschlüssel verloren. 3. Bist du jemals nach Europa geflogen? *past perfect:* Warst du jemals nach Europa geflogen?

C. The Auxiliary: When to Use *Haben* or *Sein*

The majority of German verbs use **haben** as the auxiliary in the present perfect and past perfect tense. Those that employ **sein** must fulfill *both* of the conditions listed below:

    1. The verb must be intransitive.

and

    2. The verb must show motion *or* change of condition.

An *intransitive* verb is one which cannot take a direct object (verbs that do take a direct object are called *transitive* verbs). As a general rule, an intransitive verb in English will be intransitive in German also. Therefore, you can usually determine whether a given German verb is intransitive by examining the equivalent English verb. To do this, form a simple sentence such as: *"He* VERB (simple past tense) *it."* If the resulting sentence makes sense, then the verb is transitive, if not, the verb is intransitive. For example, let us assume you want to know if *to see* and *to wait* are transitive or intransitive:

    He saw it.   **He waited it.*

The first sentence makes sense, therefore *to see* is a transitive verb. The second sentence does not, so *to wait* must be intransitive.

    The examples below show **sein** used as the auxiliary:

Ich **bin** ins Wasser gefallen.
I fell into the water.
(intransitive verb **fallen,** motion)

Wann **ist** sie gestorben?
When did she die?
(intransitive verb **sterben,** dramatic change of condition)

The next example illustrates a verb which is intransitive but shows no motion or change of condition. The auxiliary is therefore **haben:**

Ich **habe** lange geschlafen.
I slept for a long time.

A number of verbs of motion can be used either transitively or intransitively, in which case the auxiliary is **haben** or **sein** accordingly:

Er **ist** mit dem Auto nach München gefahren.
He went to Munich by car.
(intransitive)

Er **hat** das Auto nach München gefahren.
He drove the car to Munich.
(transitive, direct object: **das Auto**)

A few intransitive verbs take **sein** as an auxiliary for no apparent reason. The most common of these are:

bleiben *(to stay)*, **geschehen** *(to happen)*, **sein** *(to be)*

> Ich **bin** zu Hause geblieben.
> *I stayed at home.*

In addition, speakers in northern Germany generally use **haben** as the auxiliary for the verbs listed below, whereas speakers in southern Germany and Austria use **sein:**

liegen *(to lie)* (somewhere), **sitzen** *(to sit)*, **stehen** *(to stand)*

> Wo **haben** Sie gesessen? (northern Germany)
> Wo **sind** Sie gesessen? (southern Germany, Austria)
> *Where did you sit?*

Finally, if you are in doubt whether a verb takes **haben** or **sein,** a good German dictionary will provide this information.

COMPREHENSION CHECK: *Part A:*

1. Which of the following verbs, finden, fallen, schlafen, werfen, sterben, lachen, are intransitive?
2. Which of the verbs in question 1 show motion?
3. Which show change of condition?
4. Which would therefore have **sein** as the auxiliary?

Part B: Fill in the blank with the appropriate auxiliary form.

5. Wir _____ mit dem Zug nach Berlin gefahren.
6. Ich _____ einen Brief geschrieben.

> ANSWERS: 1. fallen, schlafen, sterben, lachen 2. fallen, werfen 3. sterben 4. fallen, sterben 5. sind 6. habe

D. Verbs with Separable or Inseparable Prefixes and Verbs Ending in -ieren: Past Participle Forms

Base verbs with *separable* prefixes form the past participle by attaching the prefix directly to the past participle of the base verb; verbs with *inseparable* prefixes do the same except that the **ge-** is omitted:

> Niemand hat einen Fotoapparat **mitgenommen.**
> *No one took along a camera.*
> (infinitive: **mitnehmen,** base verb: **nehmen,** past participle of base verb: **genommen**)

Ich habe es ihm **versprochen.**
I promised it to him.
(infinitive: **versprechen,** base verb: **sprechen,** past participle of base verb: **gesprochen**)

Note that **ge-** is itself an inseparable prefix. Therefore, the **ge-** prefix of a past participle may in fact be a part of the verb infinitive:

Das Haus hat ihm **gehört.**
The house belonged to him.
(infinitive: **gehören,** past participle: **gehört**)

As with verbs having inseparable prefixes, German verb infinitives ending in **-ieren** omit the **ge-** prefix in the past participle:

Diese Note hat mich **ruiniert!**
This grade has ruined me!
(infinitive: **ruinieren**)

Note: The stress of such verbs is always on **-iér-** e.g., **ruiniéren.**
The addition of a prefix to a base verb can change the meaning of the verb. As a result, the prefix can also affect whether the verb uses **haben** or **sein** as the auxiliary:

Meine Tante Elke **ist** angekommen.
My aunt Elke has arrived.
(infinitive: **ankommen,** auxiliary: **sein**)

Ich **habe** ein Paket von Tante Elke bekommen.
I have received a package from aunt Elke.
(infinitive: **bekommen,** auxiliary: **haben**)

COMPREHENSION CHECK: *Fill in the blank with the appropriate past participle of the verb given in parentheses.*

1.   Warum bist du _____? (weglaufen)
2.   Er hat krank _____. (ausschauen)
3.   Ich habe es nicht _____. (erwähnen)
4.   Die Tulpen sind im Laufe der Woche _____. (verblühen)
5.   Sein Benehmen hat uns _____. (schockieren)

ANSWERS: 1. weggelaufen   2. ausgeschaut   3. erwähnt   4. verblüht   5. schockiert

E. Future Tense

The basic structure of the future tense in German is as follows:

werden (present tense) . . . infinitive (end of clause)

Note: See section A for the complete conjugation of **werden.**

Here is an example:

> Ich **werde** einen Regenschirm **kaufen.**
> *I will buy an umbrella.*

When a sentence contains a modal, the structure of the sentence in the future tense is as follows:

---

werden *(present tense)* . . . *infinitive + modal (end of clause)*

To see how this works, consider first a sentence containing a modal in the *present* tense:

> Er **darf** nicht **kommen.**
> *He is not allowed to come.*

Now the same sentence is rewritten in the *future* tense:

> Er **wird** nicht **kommen dürfen.**
> *He will not be permitted to come.*

Separable prefixes are always joined to the base verb in the infinitive form and are therefore attached to the base verb in the future tense:

> Hoffentlich wird der Film bald **anfangen.**
> *Hopefully the film will begin soon.*

German uses the future tense less often than English, particularly when the idea of future is clear because of the presence of an adverb that indicates future tense. In such cases, the present tense is more likely. For example, in actual conversation the German sentence given above would more likely be stated as follows:

> Hoffentlich fängt der Film **bald** an.

The future tense is superfluous here because the adverb **bald** *(soon)* makes evident that the action will begin in the future.

The future tense of **werden** + infinitive is frequently used with **wohl** *(probably)* to indicate the likelihood of something taking place:

> Es wird **wohl** morgen regnen.
> *It will probably rain tomorrow.*

COMPREHENSION CHECK: *Rewrite these sentences in the future tense.*

1. Ich brauche deine Hilfe.
2. Du mußt langsamer fahren.
3. Er kommt mit.

German Core Vocabulary

This list contains all of the verbs in the exercises.

Note: For strong verbs, the past participle is given after the simple past form. For verbs with separable prefixes, only the past participle of the *base* verb is given.

ab.fahren (fährt), fuhr, gefahren	to depart	finden, fand, gefunden	to find
ab.lehnen	to refuse	fliegen, flog, geflogen	to fly
an.fangen (fängt), fing, gefangen	to begin	fliehen, floh, geflohen	to flee
an.kommen, kam, gekommen	to arrive	geben (gibt), gab, gegeben	to give
an.lügen, log, gelogen	to lie to (someone)	es gibt	there is/are
an.nehmen (nimmt), nahm, genommen	to accept	gefallen (gefällt), gefiel, gefallen	to please
		gehorchen	to obey
an.rufen, rief, gerufen	to call	genießen, genoß, genossen	to enjoy
auf.muntern	to cheer up	geschehen (geschieht), geschah, geschehen	to happen, to occur
aus.schauen	to look (like), to appear		
baden	to bathe	gewinnen, gewann, gewonnen	to win
beginnen, begann, begonnen	to begin	haben (hat), hatte, gehabt	to have
begleiten	to accompany	kapieren	to understand, to catch on
behaupten	to maintain		
bleiben, blieb, geblieben	to stay	klingeln	to ring
dementieren	to deny	kopieren	to copy
ein.schenken	to pour	kosten	to cost
entwerten	to invalidate	kriechen, kroch, gekrochen	to crawl
erkennen (*mixed verb*)	to recognize		
		lachen	to laugh
erscheinen, erschien, erschienen	to appear	laufen (läuft), lief, gelaufen	to run
erwähnen	to mention	riechen, roch, gerochen	to smell
essen (ißt), aß, gegessen	to eat	schlafen (schläft) schlief, geschlafen	to sleep
fallen (fällt), fiel, gefallen	to fall		

schockieren	*to shock*	verlieren, verlor, verloren	*to lose*
schreiben, schrieb, geschrieben	*to write*	verschwinden, verschwand, verschwunden	*to disappear*
sein (ist), war, gewesen	*to be*	waschen (wäscht), wusch, gewaschen	*to wash*
sehen (sieht), sah, gesehen	*to see*	weg.fliegen, flog, geflogen	*to fly away*
singen, sang, gesungen	*to sing*	weg.laufen (läuft), lief, gelaufen	*to run away*
spezialisieren	*to specialize*	werden (wird), wurde, geworden	*to become*
sterben (stirbt), starb, gestorben	*to die*	werfen (wirft), warf, geworfen	*to throw*
tanzen	*to dance*	zeichnen	*to draw*
teil.nehmen (nimmt), nahm, genommen	*to participate*	zerplatzen	*to burst*
um.rechnen	*to convert*	zurück.kommen, kam, gekommen	*to come back*
verblühen	*to fade*		
verlassen (verläßt), verließ, verlassen	*to leave*		

EXERCISE 1 (prerequisite: sections A–B, topic: formation of past participles for verbs without prefixes)

Fill in the blank with the correct form of the past participle for the verb given in parentheses.

1. Wir haben einen guten Film _____. (sehen)
2. Was hast du _____? (machen)
3. Ich habe lange auf ihn _____. (warten)
4. Meine Großeltern haben oft Pilze _____. (sammeln)
5. Niemand hat ihn gut _____. (kennen)
6. Die Gäste haben im schönsten Zimmer _____. (schlafen)
7. Wer hat diesen Brief _____? (öffnen)
8. Was haben deine Eltern von mir _____? (denken)
9. Wir haben die ganze Nacht _____. (tanzen)
10. Ich habe einen Fehler _____. (finden)

EXERCISE 2 (prerequisite: sections A–C, topic: deciding when to use **haben** or **sein** as the auxiliary)

Fill in the blank with the correct form of the auxiliary to indicate present perfect tense. Then rewrite the auxiliary to give the past perfect tense.

1. Er _____ das Auto gewaschen.
2. Ich _____ zum Geschäft gegangen.
3. Mein Goldfisch _____ gestorben!
4. Was _____ ihr zum Frühstück gegessen?
5. Der brave Sohn _____ seiner Mutter Blumen gebracht.
6. Warum _____ du zu Hause geblieben?
7. Das Baby _____ vom Wohnzimmer in die Küche gekrochen.
8. Wann _____ Sie Rechtsanwalt geworden?
9. Was _____ hier geschehen?
10. a. Der Pilot _____ das Flugzeug nach Frankfurt geflogen.
    b. Wir _____ mit einem Charterflugzeug nach Frankfurt geflogen.

EXERCISE 3 (prerequisite: sections A–C, topic: summary of sections A–C)

Rewrite these sentences in the present perfect tense.

1. Wir haben beim Fischen kein Glück.
2. Er läuft jeden Tag nach Hause.
3. Warum lachst du?
4. Zwei Ostdeutsche fliehen über die Grenze.
5. Ich reise nach Paris.
6. Das Haus brennt.
7. Riechen Sie etwas?
8. Wo arbeitet ihr?
9. Er ist traurig.
10. Das Telefon klingelt.

EXERCISE 4 (prerequisite: sections A–B and D, topic: formation of past participles for verbs with prefixes and **-ieren** verbs)

Supply the appropriate past participle of the verb in parentheses.

1. Warum hast du sein Angebot _____? (ablehnen)
2. Er hat seine Freundin nach Hause _____. (begleiten)
3. Die Vögel sind alle _____. (wegfliegen)
4. Ich habe den Preis in Dollar _____. (umrechnen)
5. Das Buch hat mir nicht _____. (gefallen)
6. Wir haben alles _____. (verbrennen)
7. Er hat sich auf die deutsche Kunst der Renaissance _____. (spezialisieren)
8. _____ sie *(they)* schon _____? (abfahren)
9. Die Maschine hat den Fahrschein _____. (entwerten)
10. Ihr habt eine Reise nach Italien _____! (gewinnen)

EXERCISE 5 (prerequisite: sections A–D, topic: summary of sections A–D)

Fill in the first blank with the appropriate auxiliary form for the present perfect tense. Insert in the second blank the correct past participle of the verb in parentheses.

1. Wann _____ du gestern _____? (zurückkommen)
2. Zu spät _____ wir seine wahren Absichten _____. (erkennen)
3. Was _____ er jetzt _____? (behaupten)
4. Du _____ mir nicht _____! (gehorchen)
5. Mein Mann _____ schon _____. (hinausgehen)
6. Er _____ das Gerücht _____. (dementieren)
7. _____ du deinen Aufsatz _____? (beginnen)
8. Der Ballon _____ plötzlich _____. (zerplatzen)
9. Ich _____ schrecklich _____. (ausschauen)
10. _____ ihr die richtige Adresse _____? (haben)

EXERCISE 6 (prerequisite: section E, topic: future tense)

Rewrite these sentences in the future tense.

1. Wir essen um 6 Uhr.
2. Meine Frau und ich gehen ins Kino.
3. Wann steht sie auf?
4. Du mußt dein Zimmer sauber machen!
5. Nehmt ihr am Wettbewerb teil?
6. Darf der Lehrer die Studenten mit ,,du'' anreden?
7. Es gibt im Winter viel Schnee.
8. Rufen Sie mich heute abend an?
9. Viele Leute besuchen diese Stadt.
10. Wer kann die Frage beantworten?

EXERCISE 7 (comprehensive)

Rearrange these groups of words into meaningful sentences. Put all verbs in the present perfect tense unless otherwise indicated. You will have to supply the auxiliary and change the infinitive to the past participle form.

1. Sein Rat/mir nicht viel/helfen.
2. Wir/über die Politik/reden.
3. Ich/ihn/ein bißchen/aufmuntern. *(past perfect)*
4. Was/Sie/mir heute/bringen?
5. Du/jemals in Norwegen/sein?
6. Unser Wirt/den Wein/einschenken. *(future)*

7. Wann/er/zum letzten Mal/baden?
8. Der Zug/ankommen. *(past perfect)*
9. Du/es endlich/kapieren?
10. Ich/nicht genug Zeit/haben.
11. Du/seit vorigem Jahr größer/werden.
12. Der Beamte/mich/auslachen.
13. Eine neue Auflage von Heine/soeben/erscheinen. *(past perfect)*
14. Viele Leute/seinen Vorschlag/annehmen/wollen. *(future)*
15. Du/die Ferien/genießen?

GEDANKENPROBLEM: The German sentence below is an example of the future perfect tense:

Ich werde schon gegessen haben, wenn du kommst.
I will have already eaten when you come.

In analogy to the example above, figure out how to say this English sentence in German:
The train will have departed already when you come.

What's wrong with these?

1. Ich habe gesehen diesen Film dreimal.
2. Warum hast du mich angelügt?
3. Das Geld hat verschwunden.
4. Ich habe den Hund ,,Wolf'' genennt.
5. Manche Freunde haben mich verlassen, aber du hast geblieben.
6. Wir haben das Buch gekopiert.
7. Die Oper hat um 7 Uhr geanfangen.
8. Wir werden müssen nach Hause gehen.

Review Exercises Chapters 1–3

EXERCISE 1

Fill in the blank with the correct present tense form of the verb given in parentheses. Then rewrite each sentence with the verb in the simple past tense and then in the present perfect tense.

1. Er _____ nachts. (arbeiten)
2. _____ ihr Hilfe? (brauchen)
3. In der Wüste _____ es selten. (regnen)
4. Er _____ gerne Pizza. (essen)
5. Was _____ er? (sehen)
6. Wann _____ der Film _____? (anfangen)
7. Wohin _____ er? (fahren)
8. Ich _____ schnell zur Uni fahren. (wollen) *(skip present perfect tense)*
9. Warum _____ du mich? (stoßen)
10. Sie (= *she*) _____ vielen Leuten. (helfen)
11. Wann _____ sie *(they)* _____? (aufstehen)
12. Du _____ hier nicht rauchen. (dürfen) *(skip present perfect tense)*

EXERCISE 2

*Fill in the blank with the correct imperative. With first names, use the **du**-form or **ihr**-form as appropriate; use the **Sie**-form with family names.*

1. Udo und Uschi, _____ sofort! (kommen)
2. Peter, _____ an zu spielen! (fangen)
3. Jörg, _____ dein Wort nicht! (brechen)
4. Franz, _____ das Buch! (lesen)
5. Frau Kranzmeyer, _____ mir nicht böse! (sein)
6. Martin, _____ bitte ein bißchen lauter! (reden)

EXERCISE 3

Rearrange these words into meaningful sentences. Write each sentence in the future, present, simple past, present perfect and past perfect tense making all necessary changes in the verb.

1. Er/den Vorschlag/annehmen.
2. Du/das nicht/begreifen.
3. Ich/die Zeitung/durchfliegen.
4. Wir/Chemie/studieren.

EXERCISE 4

Insert the correct prefix from the choices given.

1. Kannst du mir deinen Bleistift ＿＿＿ geben? (her, hin)
2. Wir fangen hier unten an und gehen dann den Berg ＿＿＿. (herauf, hinauf)
3. Kommen Sie ＿＿＿! (herein, hinein)
4. Bring mir meine Brieftasche aus dem Haus ＿＿＿! (heraus, hinaus)

What's wrong with these?

1. Er gingt langsam nach Hause.
2. Was gescheht hier?
3. Er zurückkommt morgen mit dem Zug.
4. Der Präsident hat es nicht gedementiert.
5. Ich habe nicht an Sie gedenkt.
6. Die Arbeiter tragten alles aus dem Haus hinaus.
7. Kinder, komm hier!
8. Hat sie schon weggegangen?
9. Mein Vater bringte mir ein Mikroskop.
10. Hast du gut geschlaft?
11. Ich müsse heute abend zu Hause bleiben.
12. Die ganze Klasse hat gemitkommen.
13. Wir haben so lange gewarten.
14. Ich werde besuchen meine Tante nächste Woche.

The German Case System

4

A. How to Determine the Case of a German Word

In German, adjectives must take certain endings depending on these three character-istics of the noun following the adjective:

gender, i.e., masculine, neuter, or feminine
number, i.e., singular or plural
case, i.e., nominative, accusative, dative, or genitive

The actual endings that occur are discussed in section B. This section deals with the preliminary problem of determining the gender, number and case of noun.

The gender of a noun can be looked up easily in a dictionary, and the number (singular or plural) is usually obvious from context or, if necessary, can also be looked up in a dictionary. The case of a noun, however, is not inherent in the noun itself but instead is determined by the grammatical function of the word in the sentence. Therefore you cannot simply look up the case of a noun. The relationship between the *case* of a German word and its *grammatical function* in the sentence is outlined in the table below:

case:	corresponds to:
nominative	subject in sentence
accusative	direct object in sentence
dative	indirect object in sentence
genitive	possessive, e.g., of + noun

The English sentence and German translation below illustrate the case elements:

SUBJECT   VERB   INDIRECT OBJECT   DIRECT OBJECT   POSSESSIVE

The man   gave   my father   a copy   of the book.

NOMINATIVE	VERB	DATIVE	ACCUSATIVE	GENITIVE
Der Mann	gab	meinem Vater	eine Kopie	des Buches.

The grammatical function of a word in an English sentence can be determined by asking a few questions with respect to the verb. The model English sentence above will be used as an example:

ask question:	answer:	corresponds to:
Who or what gave?	the man	subject
What did the man give?	a copy	direct object
To whom did the man give a copy?	my father	indirect object
The man gave a copy *of what?*	the book	possessive

COMPREHENSION CHECK: *Part A: In the sentences below, label the words shown in italics according to their function as subject, direct object, indirect object or possessive.*

1. *George* gave his *girlfriend* a *ring*.
2. *I* don't like the *tone* of your *voice!*
3. The *mayor* of our *town* greeted the *prime minister*.

Part B: The sentences that follow are German translations of the English sentences above. Label the case *of the words shown in boldface.*

4. **Georg** gab seiner **Freundin** einen **Ring**.
5. **Ich** habe den **Ton** deiner **Stimme** nicht gern!
6. Der **Bürgermeister** der **Stadt** bergrüßte den **Bundeskanzler.**

ANSWERS: 1. *George* subject, *girlfriend* indirect object, *ring* direct object   2. *I* subject, *tone* direct object, *voice* possessive   3. *mayor* subject, *town* possessive, *prime minister* direct object   4. **Georg** nominative, **Freundin** dative, **Ring** accusative   5. **Ich** nominative, **Ton** accusative, **Stimme** genitive   6. **Bürgermeister** nominative, **Stadt** genitive, **Bundeskanzler** accusative

B. Summary of German Adjective Case Endings

The following tables illustrate the most important facets of case endings in German (the endings are shown in boldface):

Der-words TABLE A

CASE	gender MASCULINE		NEUTER		FEMININE		PLURAL	
nominative	der	dieser	das	dieses	die	diese	die	diese
accusative	den	diesen	das	dieses	die	diese	die	diese
dative	dem	diesem	dem	diesem	der	dieser	den	diesen
genitive	des	dieses	des	dieses	der	dieser	der	dieser

Kein-words TABLE B

CASE	gender MASCULINE	NEUTER	FEMININE	PLURAL
nominative	kein	kein	keine	keine
accusative	keinen	kein	keine	keine
dative	keinem	keinem	keiner	keinen
genitive	keines	keines	keiner	keiner

Strong adjective endings TABLE C

CASE	gender MASCULINE	NEUTER	FEMININE	PLURAL
nominative	guter	gutes	gute	gute
accusative	guten	gutes	gute	gute
dative	gutem	gutem	guter	guten
genitive	guten	guten	guter	guter

Weak adjective endings: TABLE D

CASE	*gender* MASCULINE	NEUTER	FEMININE	PLURAL
nominative	gut**e**	gut**e**	gut**e**	gut**en**
accusative	gut**en**	gut**e**	gut**e**	gut**en**
dative	gut**en**	gut**en**	gut**en**	gut**en**
genitive	gut**en**	gut**en**	gut**en**	gut**en**

The adjective endings shown in the tables are used according to the following rules:

1. After a **der-**word, all successive adjectives take *weak* endings:

    Der gute Kuchen war zu teuer.
    The good cake was too expensive.
    (nominative masculine singular)

2. After **kein-**words *with* endings, all successive adjectives take *weak* endings:

    Ich habe keine gut**en** Filme gesehen.
    I didn't see any good films.
    (accusative masculine plural)

3. After **kein-**words with *no* endings (shown in italics in Table B), all successive adjectives take *strong* endings:

    Ein gut**er** Wagen kann viel kosten.
    A good car can cost a lot.
    (nominative masculine singular)

4. If the first adjective is neither a **der-**word or a **kein-**word, then it and all following adjectives take *strong* endings:

    Gut**er** alter Fritz!
    Good old Fritz!
    (nominative masculine singular)

    Viele gute Autos sind teuer.
    Many good cars are expensive.
    (nominative neuter plural)

5.   The most common **der**-words in addition to the definite article are:

alle	*all*	manche	*some, much*
dieser	*this*	solche	*such*
jeder	*each, every*	welche	*which*

All of these words, including the definite article, take the same endings as **dieser,** except **das** and **die** (see Table A). **All-, manch-, solch-,** and **welch-** are regular **der**-words only in the *plural,* in the singular, various possibilities exist (see Chapter 7, section F for a discussion on this).

6.   The **kein**-words are **kein** *(no, none),* **ein** *(a, one),* and all *possessive adjectives.*

mein	*my*	unser	*our*
dein	*your* (**du**-form)	euer	*your* (**ihr**-form)
sein	*his*	ihr	*their*
ihr	*her*	lhr	*your* (**Sie**-form) *(note capitalization)*
sein	*its*		

Unser usually drops the **e** in colloquial speech when an ending is added, **euer** always does this:

Was ist **unsere** Arbeit?   Das ist **eure** Arbeit.
                                      That is your work.

or

Was ist **unsre** Arbeit?
What is our work?

Here are some hints for remembering the adjective endings:

1.   When a **kein**-word has an ending, the ending is the same as that found on a **der**-word such as **dieser.**

2.   The strong adjective endings are also the same as those to be found on a **der**-word such as **dieser** except for the masculine and neuter genitive ending where the ending is **-en** and not the expected **-es** (see tables A and D).

3.   Learn the weak endings in terms of two groups, an **-e** group and an **-en** group (see Table D).

COMPREHENSION CHECK: *Fill in the blank with the correct case ending.*
The symbol D____ stands for the definite article. To simplify the exercise, the
answers all involve the nominative case. Some blanks must be left blank.

1.   D____ neu____ Student heißt Markus.
2.   Mein____ braun____ Notizbuch ist verschwunden.

3. Kein_____ ander_____ Frau hat es getan.
4. Zwei nett_____ jung_____ Männer haben mir geholfen.
5. Dies_____ billig_____ Restaurant serviert das beste Essen in der Stadt.
6. D_____ klein_____ Kinder haben geweint.
7. Einig_____ klein_____ Kinder haben geweint.
8. Manch_____ deutsch_____ Familien haben nur ein Kind.

ANSWERS: 1. Der neue 2. Mein braunes 3. Keine andere 4. nette junge
5. Dieses billige 6. Die kleinen 7. Einige kleine 8. Manche deutschen

C. Noun Endings: Dative Plural and Genitive Case

Most case endings in German involve adjectives, but nouns in the dative plural also have a case ending:

> *Nouns add -n in the dative plural unless the noun already ends in -n.*

The example below shows a plural noun in the accusative and then the same noun in the dative with the **-n** added:

Ich habe zwei **Autofahrer** gesehen.
I saw two motorists.

Ich gab zwei **Autofahrern** Auskunft.
I gave two motorists information.

Forgetting the dative plural **-n** is one of the most common mistakes with respect to the German case system:

*Du schuldest diesen **Männer** eine Erklärung!
You owe these men an explanation!
correct: Du schuldest diesen **Männern** eine Erklärung!

In the *genitive singular* case, most *masculine* and *neuter* nouns add **-(e)s** (the major exceptions to this rule are the weak nouns, discussed in Chapter 9, section D). Feminine and plural nouns do not add anything in the genitive. The exact form of the genitive ending is determined by the rules outlined below:

1. The **-es** ending is required when the noun ends in an **-s** sound, e.g., **-s, -ß, -x, -z, -sch, -st** (exception: words ending in **-mus,** see rule 5 below). Here are a few examples:

das Haus	*house*	des Hauses	*of the house*
das Gesetz	*law*	des Gesetzes	*of the law*
der Gast	*guest*	des Gastes	*of the guest*

2. For nouns ending in other sounds, words of one syllable usually add **-es,** words of more than one syllable generally add **-s:**

das Bett	*bed*	des Bett**es**	*of the bed*
der Sänger	*singer*	des Sänger**s**	*of the singer*

3. Nouns that end in **-ß** change this to **-ss** when the preceding vowel is short:

der Fluß	*river*	des Flu**sses**	*of the river* (*short* **u** *in* **Fluß**)
der Fuß	*foot*	des Fu**ß**es	*of the foot* (*long* **u** *in* **Fuß**)

4. Neuter nouns ending in **-nis** double the **s** before the **-es** ending (caution: some nouns ending in **-nis** are feminine):

das Zeugnis	*certificate*	des Zeugni**sses**	*of the certificate*

5. Masculine nouns ending in **-mus** add no ending at all:

der Soziali**mus**	*socialism*	des Soziali**mus**	*of socialism*

If you are unsure as to the appropriate genitive ending for a given noun, a good German dictionary will give you this information (for practice, look up all the examples above in your dictionary).

COMPREHENSION CHECK: *Fill in the blank with the correct adjective or noun endings. Not every blank need be filled. You may also have to change the noun stem.*

1. Das Zerbrechen ein_____ Glas_____ weckte mich.
2. Die Arbeit mein_____ Vater_____ war immer schwer.
3. Der Sportverein gab d_____ best_____ Läufer_____ (*plural*) Medaillen.
4. Sein Name war auf der dritten Seite d_____ Namensverzeichnis_____.
5. Diese Ruine ist die ehemalige Mauer d_____ Schloß_____.
6. Das ist das Resultat dein_____ Egoismus_____!

ANSWERS: 1. eines Glases 2. meines Vaters 3. den besten Läufern 4. des Namensverzeichnisses 5. des Schlosses 6. deines Egoismus

D. Dative Verbs

Many verbs can take dative objects in German:

Das gehört **dem** Mann da drüben.
That belongs to the man over there.

Was hast du **dem** Mann gesagt?
What did you say to the man?

Such verbs present no great problem because the corresponding English verb has the expected indirect object. However, a few verbs in German always take a dative object even though the corresponding English verb has a direct object:

Helfen Sie **dem** armen Mann!
Help the poor man!

The English verb gives no hint that the equivalent German verb requires the dative case. For this reason, you will simply have to memorize which verbs take the dative in German. For the time being, learn this short list of dative verbs (a more complete list is given in Chapter 22, section B):

antworten	*to answer*	glauben	*to believe*
begegnen	*to meet*	helfen	*to help*
danken	*to thank*	schaden	*to hurt*
folgen	*to follow*	schmeicheln	*to flatter*
gefallen	*to please*	trauen	*to trust*
gehorchen	*to obey*	verzeihen	*to forgive*

COMPREHENSION CHECK: *Fill in the blank with the correct adjective ending.*

1. Dieses Haus gehört ein_____ Freund meiner Familie.
2. Bernard glaubt sein_____ Frau nicht mehr.
3. Folgen Sie bitte dies_____ Mann!

ANSWERS: 1. einem 2. seiner 3. diesem

E. Pronouns

The German case system also affects pronouns. The table below gives the various forms in German and English:

Singular

CASE	1ST PERSON		*YOU* FAMILIAR		*YOU* POLITE		3RD PERSON					
nom.	ich	*I*	du	*you*	Sie	*you*	er	*he*	sie	*she*	es	*it*
acc.	mich	*me*	dich	*you*	Sie	*you*	ihn	*him*	sie	*her*	es	*it*
dat.	mir	*me*	dir	*you*	Ihnen	*you*	ihm	*him*	ihr	*her*	ihm	*it*

Plural

nom.	wir	*we*	ihr	*you*	Sie	*you*	sie	*they*
acc.	uns	*us*	euch	*you*	Sie	*you*	sie	*they*
dat.	uns	*us*	euch	*you*	Ihnen	*you*	ihnen	*them*

Note: Genitive pronouns also exist but rarely occur in present-day German.

You can easily become confused as to which pronoun to use in German. For example, the indirect object *her* corresponds to **ihr,** but the direct object *her* corresponds to **sie.** The only way to avoid this problem is to memorize each German pronoun according to its case and person without regard to the corresponding English pronoun.

In German and in English, a reflexive pronoun is any pronoun that refers back to the subject. The examples below illustrate the difference between a reflexive pronoun and a nonreflexive one:

> Er verletzte **sich.**
> *He hurt himself.*
> (reflexive pronoun)

> Er verletzte **ihn.**
> *He hurt him.*
> (i.e., He hurt some other man, nonreflexive pronoun)

The adverbs **selbst** or **selber** are often used with reflexive pronouns to give emphasis to the pronoun:

> Er verletzte sich **selbst (selber).**
> *He hurt himself.*
> (emphasis on *himself*)

Do not confuse **selbst (selber)** for the *-self* of the English reflexive pronoun, e.g., him*self*. The English reflexive pronoun would be wrong without the **-self,** but German **selbst (selber)** is simply an adverb that can be optionally added to give emphasis.

The correct reflexive pronoun to use in a given sentence is determined by the rule below:

---

*The reflexive pronoun that refers back to **Sie** and to all third-person pronouns is **sich.** The remaining reflexive pronouns are identical to the nonreflexive pronouns.*

Here are a few more examples of reflexive pronouns:

Ich wasche **mich** jeden Tag mit dieser Art von Seife.
I wash myself every day with this kind of soap.

Meine Kinder waschen **sich** auch mit dieser Seife.
My children wash themselves also with this soap.

Du willst nur **dir** selbst schmeicheln.
You only want to flatter yourself.
(dative reflexive)

COMPREHENSION CHECK: *Fill in the blank with the correct German pronoun as indicated by the English pronoun in parentheses:*

1. Sag _____ die Antwort! *(her)*
2. Wir verstehen _____ nicht. *(her)*
3. Können Sie _____ Ihre Telefonnummer geben? *(me)*
4. Sie wäscht _____ jeden Tag mit einer besonderen Seife. *(herself)*
5. Wäschst du _____ auch mit ihrer Seife? *(yourself)*

ANSWERS: 1. ihr 2. sie 3. mir 4. sich 5. dich

F. English Possessive *'s* and the German Genitive Case: a Comparison

As has already been seen, the genitive case in English is often equivalent to an English construction with *of:*

Was war der Name **des Schiffes?**
What was the name of the ship?

But the English possessive in the above example can also be expressed by the possessive *'s:*

What was the ship's name?

This second type of possessive construction is possible in German only with *names of people:*

Helgas Wohnung ist nicht groß.
Helga's apartment is not large.

German does not use an apostrophe to indicate possession as in English unless the name ends in an *s* sound:

Das ist Franz' Haus.
That is Franz' house.

Here is another example of a name used in the genitive case:

> Das ist **Goethes** Haus.
> *That is Goethe's house.*

In formal German, the genitive of the name can be put after the noun modified:

> Das ist das Haus **Goethes.**
> *That is the house of Goethe.*

When a genitive proper noun is preceded by the title **Herr** *(mister),* then the genitive form of the title must be used, namely **Herrn:**

> Wo ist **Herrn** Rahdes Büro?
> *Where is Mr. Rahde's office?*

Be careful to avoid mistakes such as this:

> *Unsere Sekretärins Vorschlag war ausgezeichnet.
> *Our secretary's suggestion was excellent.*

Since *secretary* is not a person's name, the correct German sentence must be stated as follows:

> Der Vorschlag unserer Sekretärin war ausgezeichnet.
> *The suggestion of our secretary was excellent.*

COMPREHENSION CHECK: *Translate these sentences into German.*

1. My brother's girlfriend is called Karin.
2. She read Mr. Henkel's letter. *(present perfect tense)*
3. That is Johann's book. *(Do this two ways.)*

ANSWERS: 1. Die Freundin meines Bruders heißt Karin. 2. Sie hat Herrn Henkels Brief gelesen. 3. Das ist Johanns Buch. *or* Das ist das Buch Johanns.

German Core Vocabulary

This list contains all the nouns and adjectives in the answer portion of the exercises.
Note: The plural of a given noun, if it exists, is listed immediately after the noun. Example: **der Anfang, ⁻e;** the plural has umlaut of the stem vowel plus **-e** ending, i.e., **Anfänge.** Another example: **Anhänger, -;** the plural is identical to the singular.

Learn the **der**-words and **kein**-words given on pages 54, the dative verbs on page 57, the pronouns on pages 57–58, and the following:

alt	*old*	ander	*other*
amerikanisch	*American*	der Anfang, ⁻e	*beginning*

die Arbeit, -en	work, job
der Arzt, ⸚e	doctor
das Ausmaß	extent
das Auto, -s	car
die Bank, -en	bank
der Baum, ⸚e	tree
die Beschreibung, -en	description
der Besitzer, -	owner
best	best
der Besucher, -	visitor
billig	cheap
bösartig	mean
braun	brown
der Brief, -e	letter
der Bub, -en	boy
deutsch	German
DM (= Deutsche Mark)	German mark (monetary unit)
der Dom, -e	cathedral
der Edelstahl	high-grade steel
der Egoismus	egotism
einig	several
die Eltern	parents
die Familie, -n	family
die Farbe, -n	color
der Film, -e	film
die Firma, Firmen (plural)	firm, company
der Fisch, -e	fish
das Fräulein, -	Miss, young lady
die Frau, -en	woman, wife
der Fremdenführer, -	tour guide
der Freund, -e	friend
frisch	fresh
der Gast, ⸚e	guest
das Gebäude, -	building
gebaut	built
geehrt	honored, dear (in letters)
das Glas, ⸚er	glass
groß	large
gut	good, well
der Hagel	hail
der Handschuh, -e	glove
das Haus, ⸚er	house
der Hund, -e	dog
die Jugend	youth
jung	young
der Kellner, -	waiter
das Kind, -er	child
das Kleid, -er	dress
klein	small
krank	sick
die Krawatte, -n	tie
der Läufer, -	runner
das Leben, -	life
der Lehrer, -	teacher
die Leute	people
die Lösung, -en	solution
die Luft	air
das Mädchen, -	girl
der Mann, ⸚er	man, husband
die Maschine, -n	machine
meist	most
mehrer	several
der Mensch, -en	person, human being
die Miete, -n	rent
modern	modern
die Möglichkeit, -en	possibility
das Namens- verzeichnis, -nisse	directory of names
nett	nice
neu	new
das Notizbuch, ⸚er	notebook
das Obst	fruit
die Person, -en	person
der Pessimismus	pessimism
die Polizei	police
praktisch	practical
der Preis, -e	price
der Reisepaß, ⸚sse	passport
das Restaurant, -s	restaurant
die Rose, -n	rose
rot	red
schlecht	bad
das Schloß, ⸚sser	castle
der Schüler, -	student, pupil
die Schwester, -n	sister
die Socke, -n	sock
der Soldat, -en	soldier
der Student, -en	student
der Teil, -e	portion, part
das Trinkgeld, -er	tip
der Vater, ⸚	father
das Verständnis	understanding
verstärkt	strengthened

die Verwendung, -en	*use*	wenig	*few, little*
viel	*much, many*	die Wohnung, -en	*apartment*
der Wagen, -	*car*	die Zeit, -en	*time*
der Wähler, -	*voter*	der Zusammenbruch	*collapse*
weiß	*white*		

EXERCISE 1 (prerequisite: section A, topic: identifying grammatical function in English)

Label each noun or pronoun in the English sentences below according to subject, direct object, indirect object, or possessive.

1. Mozart wrote some beautiful symphonies.
2. Can you give me the name of a good doctor?
3. I will not loan my rake to the neighbors!
4. We sent the bereaved family flowers.
5. Will you please show the customer the merchandise.
6. The teacher told his students an interesting story.
7. Mr. Gross could not overcome his feelings of anxiety.
8. I finally sold my car to someone.
9. Do you know him personally?
10. He married the daughter of a rich industrialist.

EXERCISE 2 (prerequisite: sections A–B; topic: identifying case in German)

Label each noun according to nominative, accusative, dative, or genitive case. Do this first on the basis of the grammatical function of the noun in the sentence as you did for English in the previous exercise. Then determine the case of the noun by examining the case ending of the preceding adjective or definite article. Make sure both answers agree.

1. Die Polizei braucht eine Beschreibung des Mannes.
2. Sie hat mir immer Socken geschenkt.
3. Ein Teil der Arbeit ist verlorengegangen.
4. Ein anderer Schüler hat mein Notizbuch gestohlen.
5. Der Besitzer unserer Wohnung hat die Miete erhöht.
6. Die Bank wird der Firma 10.000 DM ausleihen.
7. Der Student schrieb seinen Eltern einen Brief.
8. Alle Menschen wollen ein gutes Leben haben.
9. Mein Vater hat dem Kellner ein kleines Trinkgeld gegeben.
10. Ich habe den Anfang des Filmes nicht gesehen.

EXERCISE 3 (prerequisite: sections A–B, topic: German case endings)

Fill in the blanks with the necessary case endings. With some words, no ending is necessary where a blank occurs.

1. Sie mußte ihr_____ Wagen verkaufen.
2. Wir wollen d_____ frisch_____ Luft genießen.
3. Was hast du d_____ Frau gesagt?
4. Welch_____ neu_____ Film hast du gestern gesehen?
5. Er hat schlecht_____ Handschuhe gekauft.
6. Sie wollte kein_____ bösartig_____ Hund kaufen.
7. Sehr geehrt_____ Fräulein Hochmeister!
8. Mehrer_____ krank_____ Leute warteten auf den Arzt.
9. Dein_____ braun_____ Krawatte hängt dort.
10. D_____ meist_____ Gäste sind schon nach Hause gefahren.
11. D_____ Bub wollte d_____ Mädchen ein_____ rot_____ Rose geben.
12. All_____ billig_____ Wohnungen sind zu weit weg.
13. Ich esse gern frisch_____ Obst.
14. Mein_____ weiß_____ Kleid ist schmutzig.
15. Manch_____ modern_____ Häuser sind billig gebaut.

EXERCISE 4 (prerequisite: sections A–C, topic: adjective and noun case endings)

Fill in the blanks with any necessary case endings. The addition of the genitive ending may require a change in the noun stem.

1. Niemand schätzte die sarkastische Bemerkung unser_____ Gast_____.
2. Dies_____ klein_____, aber besser gebaut_____ Auto ist preiswerter.
3. Das war d_____ best_____ Zeit mein_____ Jugend_____.
4. Als ich mein_____ Arbeit verlor, verschwanden viel_____ alt_____ Freunde.
5. Was ist d_____ Farbe ein_____ deutsch_____ Reisepaß_____?
6. Das Schreien d_____ Leute_____ wurde lauter.
7. D_____ amerikanisch_____ Soldaten gaben einig_____ deutsch_____ Kinder_____ Süßigkeiten.
8. Wir müssen ander_____ praktisch_____ Lösungen finden.
9. D_____ Ausmaß sein_____ Verständnis_____ war leider nicht groß.
10. Ich schenkte mein_____ Vater_____ ein_____ Krawatte.
11. Wie hoch ist d_____ Preis ein_____ gut_____ Fisch_____?
12. D_____ Fremdenführer zeigte d_____ zwölf Besucher_____ d_____ Dom.
13. Das war d_____ Anfang mein_____ Pessimismus_____.
14. D_____ Verwendung verstärkt_____ Edelstahl_____ verhindert ein_____ Zusammenbruch d_____ Maschine_____.

EXERCISE 5 (prerequisite: sections A–D, topics: case endings, dative verbs)

Fill in the blanks with any necessary case endings.

1. D____ Mädchen half ein____ alt____ Frau____ über die Straße.
2. Gibt es kein____ ander____ Möglichkeiten?
3. Ich dankte mein____ Freunde____.
4. Hermann wollte d____ Lehrer____ *(singular)* schmeicheln.
5. D____ Hagel hat mein____ Bäume____ geschadet.
6. Unser____ Arbeit war nicht besonders schwierig.
7. Folgen Sie d____ weiß____ Auto dort vorne!
8. Ein____ krank____ Mann hat d____ Arzt angerufen.
9. Manch____ Kinder wollen ihr____ Eltern nicht gehorchen.
10. Er traut sein____ Gäste____ nicht mehr.
11. Man sieht wenig____ groß____ Gebäude in dieser Stadt.
12. Ich werde es dies____ bösartig____ Mann niemals verzeihen.
13. Dies____ Auto gefällt d____ meist____ Leute____.
14. Hoffentlich begegne ich dies____ nett____ Person____ wieder.

EXERCISE 6 (prerequisite: sections D–E, topic: dative verbs, personal and reflexive pronouns)

Fill in the blank with the appropriate form of the pronouns in parentheses (the pronouns are listed in the nominative case, but each sentence requires the accusative or dative). When a reflexive pronoun is intended, the parentheses will contain the equivalent English word.

1. Ich liebe ____ (du, sie = *she*, er)
2. Die Polizei hat ____ einen Strafzettel geschickt. (ich, er, sie = *she*)
3. Wascht ____, bevor ihr ins Bett geht. *(yourselves)*
4. Niemand hat ____ geglaubt. (wir, sie = *they*, du)
5. Die Kinder wollten ____ sehen. (er, ihr, wir)
6. Das Essen gefällt ____ sehr. (ich, er, sie = *she*)
7. Er hat ____ weh getan. *(himself)*
8. Unser Vertreter wird ____ besuchen. (Sie, er, sie = *they*)
9. Sie schaden nur ____ selbst. *(yourself)*
10. Dieser Mann hat ____ beleidigt! (ich, sie = *they*, wir)
11. Die Gäste haben ____ gedankt. (ich, Sie, wir)
12. Warum kratzt du ____ ständig? *(yourself)*
13. Antworte ____! (ich, wir, er)
14. Zwei Bergsteiger haben ____ verletzt. *(themselves)*
15. Wer hat ____ dieses hübsche Bild gegeben? (du, er, ihr)

EXERCISE 7

(prerequisite: section F, topic: English possessive *'s* and German genitive case)

Translate these sentences into German.

1. Did you find Eva's ring?
2. Lorenz' girl friend can't come.
3. Our class's teacher was sick.
4. Have you read the poems of Shakespeare? *(Put the name after the noun.)*
5. My wife's car needs gas.
6. That is Mr. Bollmann's house. *(Do this two ways.)*

EXERCISE 8

(comprehensive)

Translate into German.

1. I gave the old tomcat a fish.
2. The beginning of the book was interesting.
3. No one helped the little children.
4. I sold him a lawn mower.
5. Black Turkish coffee is strong.
6. The clothes of the poor man were dirty.
7. He bought several beautiful rugs.
8. We had to find her.
9. We measured the diameter of the circle.
10. Are all rich people really happy?
11. Where is Oskar's coat?
12. Can you forgive me?
13. The university's new president is named Gärtner.
14. Call me tonight.

GEDANKENPROBLEM: **Combine the following words into a meaningful sentence. Do not change any endings. Use all of the words and only these:**

die, ihren, alte, kleinen, Frau, Hund, verloren, hat.

What's wrong with these?

1. Einige modernen Filme sind langweilig.
2. Die große Häuser sind zu teuer.

3. Ich wollte Irmgard's neues Kleid sehen.
4. Einer alte Freund hat mich gestern besucht.
5. Kleinen Autos sind besser.
6. Sie mußte ihre Schwesters Kleider tragen.
7. Wann hast du ihm gesehen?
8. Glaubst du mich nicht?

Prepositions: Case Usage and General Meanings

5

A. German Prepositions: General Meanings

A preposition in German may take on a large number of meanings from the viewpoint of an English speaking person, but each preposition also has a few basic meanings which occur again and again and are therefore worth memorizing. These basic meanings are illustrated in this section. For easy reference, the prepositions are presented alphabetically and the case governed by the preposition is given in capital letters (the cases are discussed in section B).

Note: Two-way prepositions are listed in section C.

(An)statt   GENITIVE

meaning: *instead of*

(An)statt eines Hauses kauften wir eine Eigentumswohnung.
Instead of a house we bought a condominium.
Note: In colloquial speech, **statt** is more common than **anstatt**.

Aus   DATIVE

1. meaning: *from,* i.e., to stem from, originate from

Ich komme **aus den Vereinigten Staaten.**
I come from the United States.

2. meaning: *out of*

Herbert und Hanna liefen **aus dem Haus.**
Herbert and Hanna ran out of the house.

3. meaning: *made (out) of*

Diese Kette ist **aus Silber.**
This chain is made (out) of silver.

Außer   DATIVE

1. meaning: *except for*

Jeder schrieb die Hausaufgaben **außer ihm.**
Everyone wrote the assignments except for him.

2. meaning: *in addition to*

Außer einer Katze habe ich auch zwei Hunde.
In addition to a cat I also have two dogs.

Bei   DATIVE

1. meaning: *at, with* (usually at someone's house or at a business, emphasis on location)

Das Kind wohnt **bei seinem Onkel.**
The child lives with his uncle. (i.e., at his uncle's place)

Ich habe um drei Uhr einen Termin **beim Zahnarzt.**
I have an appointment at the dentist's at three o'clock.

2. meaning: *near*

Ich wohne **bei der Uni.**
I live near the university.

Bis   ACCUSATIVE

1. meaning: *as far as*

Die Schienen gehen nur **bis Erpersdorf.**
The tracks only go as far as Erpersdorf.

2. meaning: *until*

Ich muß **bis nächsten Freitag** arbeiten.
I have to work until next Friday.

Note: **Bis** must be followed by the preposition **an, in,** or **zu** when the object of the preposition is preceded by the definite article:

Er fuhr **bis zum Bahnhof.**
He went as far as (to) the train station.

In such sentences, **bis** functions as an adverb, the real preposition is the second one; it alone determines the case. The choice of **an, in** or **zu** is determined by the rules for these prepositions (compare this example to the first example under the heading for **zu**).

Durch   ACCUSATIVE

meaning: *through*

Max ritt **durch den Wald.**
Max rode through the forest.

Für   ACCUSATIVE

meaning: *for*

Ich habe diesen Spinat **für dich** gekocht.
I cooked this spinach for you.

Gegen   ACCUSATIVE

1. meaning: *against*

Die ganze Stadt war **gegen ihn.**
The whole city was against him.

2. meaning: *around, approximately (but no more than)*

Gegen 20.000 Zuschauer waren im Stadium.
There were approximately 20,000 spectators in the stadium (but no more than that).

Gegenüber   DATIVE

meaning: *opposite*

Note: This preposition can go *before or after the noun* it governs and *must go after pronouns*.

Eine unbekannte Person stand **ihm gegenüber.**
An unknown person stood opposite him.

Gegenüber der Schule war unser Lieblingskaffeehaus.

or

Der Schule gegenüber war unser Lieblingskaffeehaus.
Opposite the school was our favorite coffee house.

Mit   DATIVE

1. meaning: *with* (i.e., *together with,* compare with **bei**)

Ich will nicht **mit ihm** arbeiten.
I don't want to work with him.

2. meaning: *with* (i.e., *by means of*)

Ich schreibe nicht gern **mit** einem Bleistift.
I don't like to write with a pencil.

Nach   DATIVE

1. meaning: *after*

Nach elf Uhr am Abend will ich nur schlafen.
After eleven o'clock in the evening I only want to sleep.

2. meaning: *to* (countries and cities)

Wir sind während der Ferien **nach Österreich** gefahren.
During vacation we went to Austria.

3. meaning: *according to* (when **nach** follows the noun in question)

Diesem Artikel nach wird die Ökonomie bald besser werden.
According to this article the economy will soon get better.

Ohne   ACCUSATIVE

meaning: *without*

Ich kann diesen Aufsatz **ohne deine Hilfe** schreiben.
I can write this essay without your help.

Seit   DATIVE

meaning: *since* (that time), *for* (a given length of time).

The use of this preposition is discussed in detail in Chapter 11, sections B–C)

Trotz   GENITIVE

meaning: *in spite of*

Trotz vieler Probleme konnten wir das Schauspiel rechtzeitig aufführen.
In spite of many problems we were able to perform the play on time.

Um   ACCUSATIVE

1. meaning: *around*

Die Läufer sind dreimal **um das Feld** gelaufen.
The runners ran around the field three times.

2. *at* (time)

Der Film fängt **um sieben Uhr** an.
The film starts at seven o'clock.

Von   DATIVE

1. meaning: *from* (to drive from, receive from, etc.; compare with **aus**)

Ich habe einen Brief **von meiner Mutter** bekommen.
I received a letter from my mother.

2. meaning: *by* (written by, done by, etc.)

Diese Oper ist **von Mozart.**
This opera is by Mozart.

Während   GENITIVE

meaning: *during*

Während des Sommers bleiben wir auf dem Land.
During the summer we stay in the country.

Wegen   GENITIVE

meaning: *because of*

Wegen des Streiks waren alle Hotels geschlossen.
Because of the strike all hotels were closed.

Note: **Wegen** can be optionally put after the object of the preposition, particularly in formal German:

Des Streiks wegen waren alle Hotels geschlossen.

Zu   DATIVE

meaning: *to* (buildings and people; compare with **nach**)

Wie komme ich von hier **zum Bahnhof?**
How do I get from here to the train station?

Ich gehe nicht gern **zum Zahnarzt.**
I don't like to go to the dentist.

COMPREHENSION CHECK: *Fill in the blank with the correct German preposition as indicated by the English preposition in parentheses.*

1. Ich kann _____ ein Kissen nicht schlafen. *(without)*
2. Was haben Sie _____ des Krieges gemacht? *(during)*
3. Fahren wir dieses Wochenende _____ Berlin! *(to)*
4. Diese Vogelart stammt _____ Grönland. *(from)*
5. Wohnen Sie _____ ihren Eltern oder im Studentenheim? *(with)*
6. Ich wohne in einer kleinen Wohnung zusammen _____ zwei anderen Studentin-nen. *(with)*

ANSWERS: 1. ohne 2. während 3. nach 4. aus 5. bei 6. mit

B. German Prepositions and The Case System

With most prepositions in German, the words that serve as objects of the preposition must be in a particular case: accusative, dative, or genitive, depending on the preposition:

Mein Vater arbeitet **für den Staat.**
My father works for the state.
(accusative)

Wir müssen **zu einem anderen Geschäft** gehen.
We have to go to another store.
(dative)

Während des Filmes haben sie sich geküßt.
During the film they kissed each other.
(genitive)

Some prepositions can take either the accusative or dative case depending on the usage of the preposition in the sentence. These prepositions will be called *two-way prepositions* in this book. They are discussed in detail in section C of this chapter.

For reference, the most common German prepositions are listed below according to the case(s) they take:

Accusative:	bis, durch, für, gegen, ohne, um
Dative:	aus, außer, bei, gegenüber, mit, nach, seit, von, zu
Genitive:	(an)statt, trotz, während, wegen
Two-way:	an, auf, hinter, in, neben, über, unter, vor, zwischen

Prepositions are so often followed by the definite article that contracted forms have arisen with some prepositions. The most common of these are:

am = an dem	beim = bei dem	vom = von dem
ans = an das	im = in dem	zum = zu dem
aufs = auf das	ins = in das	zur = zu der

The noncontracted forms are most likely to occur when the definite article is being stressed, i.e., when it fulfills the function of the demonstrative adjective:

Sie wohnt in **dem** Haus.
She lives in that house.

COMPREHENSION CHECK: *Part A: Fill in the blanks with the correct case endings as required by the preceding preposition.*

1. Niemand kam zum Vortrag außer d_____ Mutter des Redners.
2. Wie kann man Suppe ohne ein_____ Löffel essen?
3. Wegen ein_____ einzig_____ Fehler _____ hat er eine schlechte Note bei der Prüfung bekommen.

Part B: Rewrite the preposition plus d_____ (i.e., the definite article) using the contracted form of the preposition:

4. Ich muß zu_____ d_____ Apotheke fahren.
5. Er ist bei_____ d_____ Arzt.

ANSWERS: 1. der 2. einen 3. eines einzigen Fehlers 4. zur 5. beim

C. Two-way Prepositions

Two-way prepositions use the accusative case when the verb indicates motion towards the object and the dative case when there is no motion:

Legen Sie das Geld **auf den Tisch.**
Put the money on(to) the table.
(motion toward table, accusative case)

Das Geld liegt **auf dem Tisch.**
The money is lying on the table.
(no motion toward table, dative case)

In the example that follows, the dative case is used even though the verb implies motion, because the motion is not toward the object of the preposition:

Der Schauspieler lief **auf der Bühne** herum.
The actor ran around on the stage.

Now compare the example above with the one below where the motion *is* directed toward the object of the preposition:

> Der Schauspieler lief **auf die Bühne,** als er sein Stichwort hörte.
> *The actor ran onto the stage when he heard his cue.*

Here are two more examples:

> Wir wanderten **in den Bergen.**
> *We wandered (around) in the mountains.*
> (motion, but not toward the mountains, therefore dative case)

> Wir wanderten **in die Berge.**
> *We wandered into the mountains (from outside).*
> (motion into the mountains, accusative case)

The meanings of the two-way prepositions are summarized here:

An

1. meaning: *on* (vertical surfaces, compare with **auf**)

dative: Dein Bild hängt immer noch **an der Wand.**
          Your picture is still hanging on the wall.

accusative: Häng mein Bild **an die Wand.**
              Hang my picture on the wall.

2. meaning: *at/to* (*at* when dative, *to* when accusative, used when going up to a border or any object limiting further progress)

dative: Elizabeth stand **am Fenster.**
          Elizabeth stood at the window.

accusative: Elizabeth ging **ans Fenster.**
              Elizabeth went to the window.

Auf

meaning: *on* (horizontal surfaces)

dative: Das Buch liegt **auf meinem Tisch.**
          The book is (lying) on my table.

accusative: Leg das Buch **auf meinen Tisch.**
              Lay the book on my table.

Hinter

meaning: *behind*

dative: Der Rechen liegt **hinter der Garage.**
          The rake is (lying) behind the garage.

accusative: Stellen Sie den Rechen **hinter die Garage.**
              Put the rake behind the garage.

In

meaning: *in*

dative: Die Gäste sitzen alle **im Wohnzimmer.**
              The guests are all sitting in the living room.

accusative: Die Gäste sind alle **ins Wohnzimmer** gegangen.
              The guests have all gone into the living room.

Neben

meaning: *next to, beside*

dative: Das Messer muß **neben dem Löffel** sein.
              The knife must be next to the spoon.

accusative: Sie müssen das Messer **neben den Löffel** legen.
              You have to put the knife next to the spoon.

Über

meaning: *over*

dative: Ein Warnungsschild hing **über der Sperre.**
              A warning sign hung over the barrier.

accusative: Das Pferd sprang **über die Sperre.**
              The horse jumped over the barrier.

Unter

1. meaning: *under*

dative: Ich habe meinen Kugelschreiber **unter dem Sessel** gefunden.
              I found my pen under the chair.

accusative: Mein Kugelschreiber fiel **unter den Sessel.**
              My pen fell under the chair.

2. meaning: *among* (always *dative* case with this meaning)

Unter den vielen Kunden war nur einer unzufrieden.
Among the many customers, only one was dissatisfied.

Vor

1. meaning: *in front of*

dative: Der Abfall liegt immer noch **vor dem Haus.**
              The garbage is still lying in front of the house.

accusative: Schmeiß den Abfall **vor das Haus!**
Throw the garbage in front of the house!

2. meaning: *before* (time) (always *dative* in this meaning)

Das war **vor meiner Zeit.**
That was before my time.

3. meaning: *ago* (always *dative* in this meaning, preposition *precedes* object)

Vor zwei Jahren wohnte ich in Deutschland.
Two years ago I lived in Germany.

Zwischen

meaning: **between**

dative: Der Vater saß **zwischen seinem Sohn und seiner Frau.**
The father sat between his son and his wife.

accusative: Der Vater setzte sich **zwischen seinen Sohn und seine Frau.**
The father sat down between his son and his wife.

One final comment: Do not try to make every preposition a two-way preposition. Consider the incorrect German sentence below:

*Fährst du **zu das Rathaus?**
Are you driving to the town hall?

The sentence clearly shows motion toward the object of the preposition, but **zu** is not a two-way preposition, therefore the dative case must be used, as always, with **zu.**

correct: Fährst du **zum Rathaus?**

COMPREHENSION CHECK: *Fill in the blank with the appropriate German words as indicated by the English words in parentheses. Use contracted forms of the preposition + definite article wherever possible.*

1. Wir sollen jetzt _____ Haus gehen. *(in the)*
2. Du hast eine Fliege _____ Kopf. *(on your)*
3. Wer sitzt _____? *(beside him)*
4. Setzen Sie sich _____. *(beside me)*
5. Sein Diplom hängt _____ Wand. *(on the)*
6. _____ war ich krank. *(two weeks ago)*

ANSWERS: 1. ins 2. auf deinem 3. neben ihm 4. neben mich 5. an der 6. Vor zwei Wochen

D. Da-Compounds

When the object of a preposition is a pronoun, the pronoun can only refer back to an animate object (living creature):

noun form: Ich bin **mit einem Freund** nach Düsseldorf gefahren.
                 I went with a friend to Düsseldorf.

pronoun form: Ich bin **mit ihm** nach Düsseldorf gefahren.
                 I went with him to Düsseldorf.

To express the same idea of preposition plus pronoun where the pronoun would refer to a thing, a **da**-compound must be used in German:

noun form: Ich bin **mit dem Autobus** nach Düsseldorf gefahren.
                 I went to Düsseldorf by bus.

da-compound: Ich bin **damit** nach Düsseldorf gefahren.
                 I went with it to Düsseldorf.

To form the **da**-compound of a preposition, add **da-** to prepositions that begin with a consonant, add **dar-** to prepositions that begin with a vowel.

Examples:

PREPOSITION	DA-COMPOUND
mit	damit
von	davon
aus	daraus
unter	darunter

COMPREHENSION CHECK: *Part A: Form a **da**-compound from these prepositions:*

1. vor **2.** zwischen **3.** an **4.** in

*Part B: Replace the prepositional phrase by a **da**-compound or by a preposition plus pronoun, whichever is appropriate.*

5.   Der Mann steht neben seiner Frau.
6.   Stellen Sie Ihre Schuhe auf die Matte!
7.   Es gibt keinen Grund für deinen Zorn.
8.   Setzen Sie sich neben Heinz!

ANSWERS: 1. davor 2. dazwischen 3. daran 4. darin 5. neben ihr 6. darauf 7. dafür 8. neben ihn

German Core Vocabulary

This list includes all adjectives and nouns used in the answer portion of the exercises.

der Abfallkorb, ⸚e	*garbage can*	nächst	*next*
die Apotheke, -n	*pharmacy*	die Nacht, ⸚e	*night*
arm	*poor*	die Nichte, -n	*niece*
der Bahnhof, ⸚e	*train station*	der Ofen, ⸚	*oven*
beid	*both*	österreichisch	*Austrian*
der Berg, -e	*mountain*	der Park, -s	*park*
das Bett, -en	*bed*	die Pfütze, -n	*puddle*
die Bibliothek, -en	*library*	das Problem, -e	*problem*
		die Prüfung, -en	*test*
der Boden, ⸚	*floor*	pur	*pure*
das Buch, ⸚er	*book*	das Rathaus, ⸚er	*city hall*
das Deutschland	*Germany*	der Rechtsanwalt, ⸚e	*lawyer*
der Dienstag, -e	*Tuesday*		
einfach	*simple*	der Regenmantel, ⸚	*raincoat*
ein paar	*a few*	das Rußland	*Russia*
einzig	*single*	der Schriftsteller, -	*writer*
der Fehler, -	*mistake*	der Sessel, -	*chair*
das Fenster, -	*window*	das Silber	*silver*
der Fernseher, -	*television set*	die Stadt, ⸚e	*city*
Frankfurt	*Frankfurt (city in Germany)*	die Studentin, -innen	*female student*
der Friseur, -e	*hairdresser*	die Stunde, -n	*hour, classroom hour*
furchtbar	*terrible*		
das Gebüsch, -e	*bush*	Stuttgart	*Stuttgart (city in Germany)*
das Geld	*money*		
das Geschäft, -e	*store*	die Szene, -n	*scene*
gewiß	*certain*	der Tag, -e	*day*
das Gras, ⸚er	*grass*	die Tante, -n	*aunt*
die Grenze, -n	*border*	die Tasche, -n	*bag, pocket*
die Großmutter, ⸚	*grandmother*	der Tee, -s	*tea*
der Hals, ⸚e	*neck*	der Teppich, -e	*rug*
die Häßlichkeit	*ugliness*	der Tisch, -e	*table*
die Hitze	*heat*	die Tür, -en	*door*
das Hotel, -s	*hotel*	die Uhr, -en	*watch, clock, o'clock*
die Jacke, -n	*jacket*		
das Kissen, -	*pillow*	der Verfasser, -	*author*
der Kleiderschrank, ⸚e	*clothes closet*	der Vorschlag, ⸚e	*suggestion*
		die Wand, ⸚e	*wall*
das Konzert, -e	*concert*	die Weinstube, -n	*wine tavern*
der Kopf, ⸚e	*head*	das Werkzeug, -e	*tool*
der Krieg, -e	*war*	das Wetter	*weather*
das Loch, ⸚er	*hole*	der Wind, -e	*wind*
der Löffel, -	*spoon*	der Wunsch, ⸚e	*wish*
die Matte, -n	*mat*	die Zeitung, -en	*newspaper*
der Mittwoch, -e	*Wednesday*	das Zimmer, -	*room*
die Mutter, ⸚	*mother*	der Zorn	*anger*

EXERCISE 1

(prerequisite: section A, topic: accusative, dative and genitive prepositions: basic meanings)

Fill in the blank with the correct German preposition as indicated by the English preposition in parentheses.

1. An dem Tag fuhren wir nur _____ Stuttgart. *(as far as)*
2. _____ Tee trinke ich auch Kaffee und Milch. *(in addition to)*
3. Monika mietete eine kleine Wohnung _____ dem Bahnhof. *(opposite)*
4. Ich will nächstes Jahr _____ Rußland fahren. *(to)*
5. Mein zweiter Wagen kommt _____ Deutschland. *(from)*
6. Rolf ging _____ seinem Hund spazieren. *(with)*
7. Ich will _____ acht Uhr aufstehen. *(at)*
8. _____ 50 Leute waren in der Vorlesung. *(around, approximately)*
9. Das Rathaus steht _____ der Bank. *(near)*
10. Ich fahre heute abend _____ Helga. *(to)*
11. Wir sind fünf Minuten _____ dem Anfang des Filmes angekommen. *(after)*
12. Mein Mann war _____ der Nacht wach. *(during)*
13. Wir flogen direkt _____ Frankfurt nach Athen. *(from)*
14. Wohnst du immer noch zusammen _____ Peter? *(with)*
15. Die Heizung funktioniert nicht _____ uns. *(at our place)*

EXERCISE 2

(prerequisite: sections A–B, topics: accusative, dative and genitive prepositions: basic meanings and case system)

Fill in the blank with the correct German preposition as indicated by the English preposition in parentheses. Supply also any necessary case endings. Where possible, use contracted forms of the preposition + definite article.

1. _____ ein_____ Jacke bekam ich einen Pullover. *(instead of)*
2. Warst du heute _____ d_____ Friseur? *(at)*
3. Ich habe dieses Andenken _____ mein_____ Nichte gekauft. *(for)*
4. Soll ich _____ mein_____ Auto fahren? *(with)*
5. _____ d_____ Kinder ist sie einige Jahre zu Hause geblieben. *(because of)*
6. Sie trug eine Perlenkette _____ d_____ Hals. *(around)*
7. Holen Sie bitte Ihren Paß _____ d_____ Tasche! *(out of)*
8. Ich bin leider _____ mein_____ Regenmantel hinausgegangen. *(without)*
9. Sie liebte ihn _____ sein_____ Häßlichkeit. *(in spite of)*
10. _____ einig_____ klein_____ Probleme_____ war die Reise ein Erfolg. *(except for)*
11. Mein bester Freund saß _____ _____. *(opposite me)*
12. Sie dürfen nur_____ nächst_____ Dienstag bleiben. *(until)*
13. Dieser Roman ist _____ ein_____ österreichisch_____ Schriftsteller. *(by)*
14. Diese Straße führt _____ d_____ schönst_____ Teil Deutschlands. *(through)*

15. Er arbeitet _____ d_____ Tag_____. *(during)*
16. Er machte seine letzten Schritte _____ _____ Weinstube. *(as far as to the)*
17. Die Radfahrer mußten _____ d_____ Wind fahren. *(against)*
18. Brigitte ging _____ ihr_____ Mutter. *(to)*
19. Dies_____ Verfasser _____ wird die Erde in den nächsten 30 Jahren wärmer werden. *(according to)*
20. Dieses Messer ist _____ pur_____ Silber. *(made out of)*

EXERCISE 3 (prerequisite: section C, topic: two-way prepositions)

Fill in the blanks with the correct German words corresponding to the English words in parentheses. Add any necessary case endings.

1. Ich habe zwei Kätzchen _____ ein_____ Gebüsch gefunden. *(behind)*
2. Dein Hemd hängt _____ Kleiderschrank. *(in the)*
3. Ein Stein fiel _____ Gras. *(on the)*
4. Mindestens haben wir ein Dach _____ d_____ Kopf. *(over)*
5. Jemand kommt _____ unser_____ Tür. *(to)* *(Do not use* **zu.***)*
6. Hast du die Hausaufgaben _____ d_____ Stunde geschrieben? *(before)*
7. Legen Sie Ihr Buch _____ d_____ ander_____ Bücher. *(beside)*
8. Kinder, kommt _____ Haus! *(in the)*
9. Ich mußte _____ Pfütze springen. *(over the)*
10. Warum hast du deine Spielsachen _____ Ofen geworfen? *(behind the)*
11. Er stellt seine Schuhe immer _____ Bett. *(in front of the)*
12. Das Dorf liegt _____ zwei groß_____ Berge_____. *(between)*
13. Sie werden Ihren Paß _____ Grenze brauchen. *(at the)*
14. Ich war endlich _____. *(among friends)*
15. Ich habe sie _____ Bibliothek getroffen. *(in front of the)*
16. Schnell, schieb es _____ Teppich! *(under the)*
17. Die Polizei fand die Pistole _____ _____. *(beside her)*
18. Stellen Sie den Sessel _____ d_____ Tisch und d_____ Fernseher! *(between)*
19. _____ welch_____ Hotel werden Sie übernachten? *(in)*
20. Das Flugzeug mußte dreimal _____ Stadt kreisen. *(over the)*

EXERCISE 4 (prerequisite: section D, topic: **da**-compounds)

Replace the prepositional phrase by a **da**-*compound or by a preposition plus pronoun, whichever is appropriate.*

1. Ich bin absolut gegen diesen Vorschlag.
2. Sie wohnt bei ihrer Tante.
3. Was sollen wir nach dem Konzert tun?
4. Außer Uschi hat jeder ein Wiener Schnitzel bestellt.

5. Ich habe heute einen Anruf von meinem Freund bekommen.
6. Die Schulgruppe ist ohne den Lehrer gefahren.
7. Sie können sich auf diesen Sessel setzen.
8. Mein alter Hut lag im Abfallkorb.
9. Stellen Sie sich hinter die anderen Leute!
10. Gehen Sie bitte durch diese Tür!

EXERCISE 5 (comprehensive)

This exercise has 5 sections. Each section has 5 prepositions to choose from. Within each section, fill in the blank with the preposition that best completes the meaning of the sentence. Use each preposition only once. The case endings after the blank should help you to decide which preposition to insert in any given sentence.

aus, in, um, zu, trotz

1. Ich ließ einen Zaun _____ mein neues Haus aufstellen.
2. Fahr schnell _____ deiner kranken Großmutter!
3. Der Dieb sprang _____ dem Fenster.
4. _____ dieser furchtbaren Hitze spielten wir den ganzen Nachmittag draußen.
5. Hermann ging _____ das Geschäft.

außer, bis, gegen, nach, statt

6. _____ jeder Prüfung bin ich müde.
7. Niemand war da _____ mir.
8. Ich bleibe _____ nächsten Mittwoch in Frankfurt.
9. Du heiratest diese Frau _____ den Wunsch deiner Mutter!
10. _____ eines Briefes bekam er in der Post bloß Rechnungen.

durch, für, gegenüber, vor, wegen

11. Das Postamt steht _____ dem Rathaus.
12. Er stellte die Milch _____ die Tür.
13. Jugendliche sollten den Film _____ gewisser Szenen nicht anschauen.
14. Wir sammeln Geld _____ arme Kinder.
15. Wir sind _____ mehrere kleine Städte gereist.

auf, mit, nach, während, zu

16. Meine Katze schläft immer _____ meinem Bett.
17. Ich werde _____ seinem Haus fahren.
18. Du solltest mich nicht _____ der Arbeit anrufen.
19. Dieser Zeitung _____ werden die Sozialisten bei der nächsten Wahl gewinnen.
20. Er konnte alles _____ ein paar einfachen Werkzeugen reparieren.

an, aus, bei, ohne, zwischen

21. Geh bitte _____ die Tür; jemand hat geklopft.
22. Ich saß _____ den beiden Gästen.
23. Meine Großeltern kamen _____ Deutschland.
24. Sie arbeitete _____ einem Rechtsanwalt.
25. Kann man wirklich _____ Geld glücklich sein?

EXERCISE 6 (comprehensive)

Translate into German.

1. Albrecht is descendent from an old rich family.
2. Her pen is lying beside it.
3. Do you have something against them?
4. I found my socks in the basement.
5. The train went from Hamburg to Bremerhaven.
6. A mother with two children sat opposite us.
7. Someone coughed constantly during the program.
8. Put the sofa beside the chair.
9. I stayed with my parents-in-law. (at their place)
10. The streetcar only goes as far as the city hall.
11. You are sitting on it.
12. Dieter had to stand in front of the class.
13. This painting is by Dürer.
14. We rented a small apartment behind the main building of the university.
15. Where were you two days ago?

GEDANKENPROBLEM: **Combine these words into a meaningful sentence. Do not change any endings. Use all of the words and only these.**

den, die, des, ihrem, durch, trotz, mit, Mann, Park, Frau, Wetters, gegangen, ist.

What's wrong with these?

1. Viele Papiere lagen auf den Boden.
2. Jeder hatte den Film gern außer für Jürgen.
3. Gehen Sie bitte in diesem Zimmer hinein!
4. Mein altes Auto ist hin; ich kann nicht mehr mit ihm fahren.
5. Das Gedicht ,,Die Schlesischen Weber'' ist bei Heine.
6. Nächste Woche fahren wir zu London.
7. Die Maus lief aus das Loch.
8. Ein junges Ehepaar kaufte das Haus gegenüber uns.

Prepositions: Less Common Meanings, Specific Meanings

A. Less Common Meanings of Prepositions

A number of prepositions have meanings beyond those listed in the previous chapter. These meanings are either less common than those given before or can only be used with a narrow range of words after the preposition. You may know some of these already as "idioms." Learn these additional meanings:

Aus

1. meaning: *for* (reason)

aus diesem Grund	aus vielen Gründen	aus welchem Grund
for this reason	*for many reasons*	*for what reason*

2. meaning: *out of* (emotion)

aus Angst	aus Mitleid	aus Eifersucht
out of fear	*out of pity*	*out of jealousy*

Außer

außer Atem	außer Betrieb	außer Gefahr
out of breath	*out of order*	*out of danger*

Bei

meaning: *on, with* (a person)

Hast du einen Kugelschreiber **bei dir?**
Do you have a pen on you (with you)?

Bis

von Kopf **bis** Fuß, von oben **bis** unten
from head to toe, from top to bottom

Durch

1. meaning: *divided by*

Zehn **durch** zwei ist fünf.
Ten divided by two is five.

2. durch Zufall
by chance, coincidence

In

1. meaning: *on* (plus definite article plus street name)

Ich wohnte **in der Mariahilferstraße.**
I lived on Mariahilfer Street.

2. meaning: *to* (plus definite article plus country of feminine gender)

Wir fahren **in die Schweiz, in die Tschechoslowakei, in die Türkei.**
We are going to Switzerland, to Czechoslovakia, to Turkey.

Note the accusative case after the preposition. If no motion is implied, the dative case is used:

Zürich liegt **in der Schweiz.**
Zurich is in Switzerland.

Mit

1. meaning: *by* (plus definite article plus means of transportation)

Fahren Sie **mit dem Zug?**
Are you going by train?

2. mit Gewalt: *by force*

Nach

1. Meiner (seiner) Meinung nach
2. *In my (his) opinion*

nach Hause
(to) home
(motion toward home)

Unter

unter vier Augen
in all confidentiality

Vor

vor allem
above all

Zu

1. meaning: *at, for* (when followed by important time events)

Ich will **zu Ostern (Weihnachten)** nach Hause fahren.
I want to go home for Easter (Christmas).

and

zu der (dieser) Zeit: *at that (this) time*

2. zu Hause
at home

3. zum Beispiel
for example

4. zu Fuß
on foot

COMPREHENSION CHECK: *Fill in the blank with the German equivalent of the English words in parentheses.*

1. Wir werden _____ fahren. *(by car)*
2. Der Patient ist _____. *(out of danger)*
3. Istanbul liegt _____. *(in Turkey)*
4. _____ bist du zu jung für ihn. *(in our opinion)*
5. Wir haben das Auto _____ gewaschen. *(from top to bottom)*

ANSWERS: 1. mit dem Auto 2. außer Gefahr 3. in der Türkei 4. Unserer Meinung nach 5. von oben bis unten

B. Specific Prepositions

In some cases, the choice of a preposition is determined very specifically by a certain word in the sentence. Such prepositions will be called *specific prepositions* and the word which determines the preposition will be referred to as the *dominant word*. Consider, for example, the sentence below:

> Ich bin **stolz auf** Ihre Arbeit.
> *I am proud of your work.*

The specific preposition is **auf** and the dominant word is **stolz.** Similarly, the dominant word in English is *proud* and the specific preposition is *of*. These prepositions are specific because they "go together" with the dominant word. As with the prepositions in the previous sections, these are often listed in textbooks as "idioms." Many specific prepositions are also two-way prepositions, as in the example above. Specific two-way prepositions do *not* alternate between accusative and dative regardless of whether there is motion or not. Instead, the case that follows the preposition is fixed on either the accusative or dative for a given dominant word. In other words, for two-way prepositions, the dominant word determines not only the specific preposition but also the case that follows it. In the example above, the two-way preposition **auf** is fixed on the accusative for the dominant word **stolz.** Of course, if a specific preposition is not a two-way preposition, it takes the case it always has.

A given dominant word may be used with two or more specific prepositions, each with a different meaning:

> a. Liesl **freute sich auf** das neue Fahrrad.
> *Liesl was looking forward to the new bicycle.*

> b. Liesl **freute sich über** das neue Fahrrad.
> *Liesl was happy with her new bicycle.*

The same principle holds true in English or most any language:

> *I am waiting for him.*
> *I am waiting on him.* (i.e., *I am serving him.*)

The dominant word can be an adjective, as with **stolz,** or a verb, as with **sich freuen,** or a noun, as in this example:

> Was war seine **Reaktion auf** deine Schwangerschaft?
> *What was his reaction to your pregnancy?*
> (dominant word **Reaktion,** specific preposition **auf** plus accusative case)

The dominant word is not necessarily before the preposition, as can be seen in the examples below where the dominant word is **erstaunt** *(astonished)* and the specific preposition is **über:**

> Wir waren alle **erstaunt über** seine Bemerkung.

or

> Wir waren alle **über** seine Bemerkung **erstaunt.**
> *We were all astonished at his remark.*

Specific prepositions will be discussed in more detail in the next section. You will understand the theory better if you have first had some practical experience in working with specific prepositions. Therefore memorize the list below. It gives some common dominant words and the dependent specific prepositions:

DOMINANT WORD	SPECIFIC PREPOSITION	CASE (IF TWO-WAY)	MEANING
arbeiten	an	dative	*to work on*
arm	an	dative	*poor in*
begeistert	von		*enthusiastic about*
beruhen	auf	dative	*to be based on*
Brief	an	accusative	*letter to*
denken	an	accusative	*to think of*
Eifersucht	auf	accusative	*jealousy of*
erstaunt	über	accusative	*astonished at*
fragen	nach		*to ask about*
glauben	an	accusative	*to believe in*
Interesse	an	dative	*interest in*
lachen	über	accusative	*to laugh about, at*
Reaktion	auf	accusative	*reaction to*
reich	an	dative	*rich in*
schuldig	an	dative	*guilty of*
Sehnsucht	nach		*longing for*
stolz	auf	accusative	*proud of*
verzichten	auf	accusative	*to do without, renounce*
warnen	vor	dative	*to warn about, against*
warten	auf	accusative	*to wait for*
zornig	auf	accusative	*angry at*

Note: Additional specific prepositions are left for you to discover in exercises 3–6.

COMPREHENSION CHECK: *Insert the correct specific preposition for the dominant word of the sentence. Add also any necessary adjective endings.*

1. Glaubst du _____ dies_____ Religion?
2. Ich war stolz _____ mein_____ Arbeit.
3. Niemand war begeistert _____ d_____ Idee.
4. Dieses Brot ist arm _____ wichtig_____ Vitaminen.
5. Er beschrieb seine Sehnsucht _____ d_____ Heimat.

ANSWERS: 1. an diese 2. auf meine 3. von der 4. an wichtigen 5. nach der

C. Distinguishing between General and Specific Prepositions

The basic function of a preposition, general or specific, is to connect two words in a sentence. As an example, look at this sentence:

> Wir **fuhren an** die **Grenze.**
> *We drove to the border.*

The general preposition **an** connects the verb **fahren** to the noun **Grenze** and has the meaning *to*.

Another example:

> Ich bin **stolz auf dich.**
> *I am proud of you.*

The specific preposition **auf** connects **stolz** to **dich.**

Since both general and specific prepositions perform the same function of connecting words, why then is the distinction important? To find out, consider this English sentence:

> *We are hoping for a miracle.*

If you translate this directly by looking up the words in the dictionary, you might get this:

> *Wir hoffen **für** ein Wunder.

The sentence is correct except for the preposition. The German preposition **für** does normally translate the English *for,* but only when the preposition is *general.* You should realize that the English sentence contains a specific preposition determined by the dominant word *to hope.* If you look up this verb in your dictionary, you should find **hoffen** plus **auf** plus accusative equals *to hope for.* Therefore the sentence would be translated correctly as follows:

> Wir hoffen **auf** ein Wunder.

The point is that the "meaning" of a preposition only applies to its use as a *general* preposition, whereas *specific* prepositions are rather *arbitrary* in any language, e.g., there is no guarantee that the English specific preposition *for* will correspond to **für** in German or vice versa. The same is true for any other preposition. Furthermore, the dictionary usually lists specific meanings under the *dominant word.* General prepositions, on the other hand, are more likely to be found under the preposition itself.

In reading, too, the distinction between general and specific prepositions can be important. Assume you encounter this sentence:

> Er warnte mich **vor** den anderen Kollegen, weil man ihnen nicht trauen kann.

Since the general preposition **vor** means *before* or *in front of,* you might therefore translate the sentence as follows:

*He warned me in front of the other colleagues because you can't trust them.

This translation doesn't make very good sense and in fact it is wrong. The problem is that **vor** is a *specific* preposition in this sentence with the dominant word **warnen.** Together they mean *to warn about.* The correct translation would be:

He warned me about the other colleagues because you can't trust them.

Unfortunately, the distinction between general and specific prepositions is not always clear-cut, but the rules and examples below should help you to identify a preposition as general or specific:

1. A preposition that connects the object of the preposition to another *noun* or *adjective* is a specific preposition. The noun or adjective is the dominant word:

Hab keine **Angst vor mir!**

or

Hab **vor mir** keine **Angst!**
Don't be afraid of me.

The object of the preposition is **mir,** the specific preposition **vor** connects this to the noun **Angst,** which is the dominant word.

2. If the preposition connects the object of the preposition to the *verb,* the preposition can be general or specific, but specific prepositions tend to have meanings which do not correspond to the literal (general) meaning:

Sie **starb an** einer schweren Erkältung.
She died of a severe cold.

The English preposition *of* does not really indicate possession in this sentence and she didn't die while hanging vertically onto an **Erkältung** either. For comparison, here is the same German preposition used generally, i.e., literally:

Das Bild hängt **an** der Wand.
The picture is hanging on the wall.

3. If the preposition connects the object of the preposition to a verb and you cannot decide if the preposition is general or specific, simply look up the verb *and* the preposition. The correct meaning should be listed under one of the two or both. *But check the verb first,* because this usually takes less time than looking up the preposition.

Although the total number of prepositions in German is small, the number of general and specific meanings which they can generate is huge. Through long exposure to the language you should learn all of these eventually, but until then you will be dependent on the dictionary, and the rules above will help you in that task.

COMPREHENSION CHECK: *Part A: Each sentence below contains a specific preposition. Find the dominant word.*

1. I was terribly envious of her.
2. I couldn't overcome my anger at him.
3. Der Jäger zielte auf das Reh.

Part B: Determine whether the preposition in these sentences is general or specific. If specific, identify the dominant word.

4. The joy over his return was great.
5. Niemand wird um ihn trauern.
6. Throw the money under the mattress.

ANSWERS: 1. envious 2. anger 3. zielte 4. specific, dominant word: joy 5. specific, dominant word: trauern 6. general

German Core Vocabulary

This list covers the following:

1. The dominant words and specific prepositions used in the exercises but not listed in section B.

2. All of the nouns and adjectives used in the answer portion of the exercises.

3. All of the words in the translation into German exercises.

Learn the meanings of the prepositions given on pages 84–86, the dominant words and specific prepositions on page 88, and the following:

achten auf + *acc.*	*to pay attention to, heed*	die Erziehung	*upbringing*
		das Essen	*meal*
das Angebot, -e	*offer*	faul	*rotten*
die Aufmerksamkeit	*attentiveness*	die Fehde, -n	*feud*
		feilschen um	*to haggle over*
der Bau	*construction*	der Flug, ⁼e	*flight*
der Betrieb, -e	*order, operation*	das Flugzeug, -e	*airplane*
böse auf + *acc.*	*angry at*	die Freundin, -innen	*girlfriend*
das Ei, -er	*egg*		
eifersüchtig auf + *acc.*	*jealous of*	froh über + *acc.*	*happy with*
		der Fuß, ⁼e	*foot*
die Enttäuschung, -en	*disappointment*	die Gefahr, -en	*danger*
		gefährlich	*dangerous*

gefaßt auf + acc.	prepared for	Ostern (plural)	Easter
der Geist	spirit, intellect	die Physik	physics
die Gewalt	force, violence	der Raufbold, -e	bully, tough guy
der Gewinner, -	winner	reagieren auf + acc.	to react to
der Grund, ¨e	reason		
die Hausaufgabe, -n	homework	die Rede, -n	speech
		die Religion, -en	religion
die Heilfähigkeit, -en	healing ability	das Resultat, -e	result
		riechen, roch, gerochen nach	to smell like
die Heimat, -en	homeland		
hoffen auf + acc.	to hope for	die Sache, -n	matter, thing
die Idee, -n	idea	der Sohn, ¨e	son
immer noch	still	das Studentenheim, -e	dormitory
das Jahr, -e	year		
kämpfen um	to fight for	das Talent, -e	talent
die Kleider	clothes	trauern um	to mourn for
die Krankheit, -en	disease	das Verbrechen, -	crime
der Kurs, -e	course	die Vergangenheit, -en	past
leiden, litt, gelitten an + dat.	to suffer from		
		der Verkäufer, -	seller, salesperson
lieber sollen	ought to, should rather	das Vitamin, -e	vitamin
		der Weihnachtsmann, ¨er	Santa Claus
die Meinung, -en	opinion		
das Mittagessen	lunch	zielen auf + acc.	to point at
der Morgenschlaf	morning sleep	der Zufall, ¨e	coincidence
müde	tired		
die Nachricht	news		

EXERCISE 1 (prerequisite: section A, topic: less common meanings of prepositions)

Fill in the blank with the German word(s) corresponding to the English word(s) in parentheses.

1. Ich gehe nur _____ mit ihm aus. *(out of pity)*
2. Wieviel Geld habt ihr _____? *(on you)*
3. Was ist 1707 _____ 3? *(divided by)*
4. _____ darfst du deinen Reisepaß nicht verlieren! *(above all)*
5. Wo waren Sie _____? *(at that time)*
6. _____ wollen Sie nicht kommen? *(for what reasons)*
7. Warum sind diese Automaten immer _____. *(out of order)*
8. Wir mußten die Tür _____ aufbrechen. *(by force)*
9. Gehen wir _____! *(on foot)*
10. Kann ich dir etwas _____ sagen? *(in all confidentiality)*
11. Wir sind _____ nach Salzburg gefahren. *(by bus)*
12. Julia wohnt _____. *(on Main Street)*

13. Wo wirst du ____ sein? *(for Christmas)*
14. Diese Gleichung ist ____ sehr nützlich. *(for example)*
15. Viele Touristen sind voriges Jahr ____ gefahren. *(to Switzerland)*
16. Ich habe es ____ gehört. *(by coincidence)*
17. ____ ist das das beste Restaurant in der Stadt. *(in her opinion)*
18. Er war ____ schmutzig. *(from head to toe)*
19. Nach dem Laufen waren wir alle ____. *(out of breath)*
20. Mein Onkel lebt immer noch ____. *(in Czechoslovakia)*

EXERCISE 2 (prerequisite: section B, topic: specific prepositions)

Supply the correct specific preposition in the sentences and, if necessary, the proper case ending. Use prepositional contractions where appropriate.

1. Werde nicht zornig ____ mir!
2. Hast du die Briefe ____ sein____ Freundin gelesen?
3. Ich fragte ihn ____ sein____ Vergangenheit.
4. Der Vater war stolz ____ sein____ Sohn.
5. Damals hat jeder ____ d____ Bau der Kirche gearbeitet.
6. Seine Eifersucht ____ d____ Haus seines Nachbarn wurde lächerlich.
7. In zehn Jahren werden wir ____ dies____ Sache lachen.
8. Wir mußten zwei Stunden ____ unser____ Flug warten.
9. Wir waren alle begeistert ____ d____ Essen.
10. Sein Haß beruht ____ ein____ alt____ Fehde.
11. Er war reich ____ Geist, aber arm ____ Geld.
12. Ich verzichte sehr ungern ____ mein____ Morgenschlaf.
13. Die Nazis waren ____ viel____ Verbrechen schuldig.
14. Die Reaktion der Presse ____ sein____ Rede war im allgemeinen positiv.
15. Jeder war ____ d____ Resultat des Experiments erstaunt.
16. Meine Sehnsucht ____ dir wird immer stärker!
17. Rudi glaubt immer noch ____ d____ Weihnachtsmann.
18. Niemand warnte den neuen Schüler ____ d____ Raufbold der Schule.
19. Ich dachte ____ dies____ Nacht in Paris.
20. Sein Interesse ____ d____ Physik kam nur allmählich.

EXERCISE 3 (prerequisite: sections B–C, topic: identifying specific prepositions in German)

Each German sentence below contains a specific preposition not *listed in section B. Identify the dominant word. Then translate the sentence into English.*

1. Er war eifersüchtig auf den Gewinner.
2. Wie haben sie auf diesen Vorschlag reagiert?

3. Warum bist du immer noch auf ihn böse?
4. Er leidet an einer gefährlichen Krankheit.
5. Ich war auf eine Enttäuschung gefaßt.

EXERCISE 4 (prerequisite: sections B–C, topic: identifying specific prepositions in English)

These English sentences each contain a specific preposition not *listed in section B. Identify the dominant word. Then translate into German.*

1. You are dependent on my help.
2. I am interested in this method. (put the word for *interested* at the end of your sentence)
3. We were curious about his new girlfriend.
4. I drink to your health!
5. His remark was an allusion to the country's economic problems.

EXERCISE 5 (prerequisite: sections B–C, topic: distinguishing between general and specific prepositions in German)

Each German sentence below contains either a general preposition or a specific preposition not *listed in section B. Label the preposition as to general or specific; if specific, identify the dominant word. Then translate into English.*

1. Dieses Zimmer riecht nach faulen Eiern.
2. Der Verkäufer wollte nicht um den Preis feilschen.
3. Sie ist durch das Gras gelaufen.
4. Du sollst lieber auf meine Meinung achten!
5. Ich wohne in einem Studentenheim.
6. Wo kann ich Sie während des Tages anrufen?
7. Wir hoffen auf gutes Wetter.
8. Nach dem Mittagessen waren wir alle müde.
9. Ich war über diese Nachricht sehr froh.
10. Sie mußte hinter ihrem Mann sitzen.

EXERCISE 6 (prerequisite: sections B–C, topic: distinguishing between general and specific prepositions in English)

These English sentences contain either a general preposition or a specific preposition not *listed in section B. Label the preposition as to general or specific and, if specific, identify the dominant word. Then translate into German.*

1. I will always insist on my right.
2. Will you please come with me?

3. We ask for your understanding.
4. I have to work until noon.
5. The letter lay on the floor.
6. The drug had no effect on him.
7. This rock consists primarily of calcium.
8. No one was there except for two small children.
9. She swears by this plan.
10. This thin coat gives you no protection from the cold.

EXERCISE 7 (comprehensive)

In the sentences below, insert the preposition which is logically and/or grammatically necessary for the sentence. All of the necessary prepositions have been used in previous exercises. Also complete any missing case endings.

1. Ich glaube nicht mehr _____ dich!
2. Unsere Meinungen beruhen meistens _____ unser_____ Erziehung.
3. Ich habe es _____ Zufall in der Zeitung gelesen.
4. Er mußte _____ d_____ Geld verzichten.
5. _____ dies_____ Grund will ich nie wieder eine Nacht in einer Pension verbringen.
6. Er schwört _____ d_____ Heilfähigkeit dieses Kräutertees.
7. Unser Baby ist _____ zwei Jahren geboren.
8. Wer ist dein_____ Meinung _____ der größte deutsche Dramatiker?
9. Ich war eigentlich _____ d_____ Film nicht begeistert.
10. Das Telefon war leider _____ Betrieb.
11. Ich bestehe _____ Ihrer Aufmerksamkeit!
12. Wirst du _____ Ostern zu Hause sein?
13. Er war _____ Kopf _____ Fuß pudelnaß.
14. Die Mutter war _____ d_____ Kleider ihrer Tochter entsetzt.
15. Ich habe kein Kleingeld _____ mir.
16. Wartest du _____ ein besseres Angebot?
17. Er ist bloß eifersüchtig _____ mein_____ Talent.
18. Sie ist _____ d_____ Flugzeug gekommen.
19. Er will nicht _____ sein_____ Hausaufgaben arbeiten.
20. Ich konnte die alte Tür nur _____ Gewalt öffnen.

GEDANKENPROBLEM: **Assuming the sentence below is correct, what does it mean? Assuming it is wrong, how would you correct it?**

Wie lange hast du auf dem Zug gewartet?

What's wrong with these?

1. Viele Leute glauben in Gespenster.
2. Ich bin wirklich stolz von dir.
3. Heute bin ich nicht bei Auto zu dir gefahren, stattdessen bin ich auf Fuß gekommen.
4. Arno war böse an mir.
5. Wir waren noch nicht aus Gefahr.
6. Sie war in diesem Kurs sehr interessiert.

Review Exercises Chapters 4–6

Fill in the blanks with the appropriate German word(s) and endings to complete the sentence. Where necessary, an English translation of the word(s) required is given in parentheses. No blanks are provided for possible noun endings, you must figure out for yourself which nouns need dative or genitive endings.

1. Kannst du es _____ verzeihen? *(me)*
2. Leg das Messer _____ d_____ Löffel. *(beside)*
3. Du sollst _____ d_____ Vorschlag achten.
4. Ist das dein Bild _____ d_____ Wand? *(on)*
5. Sie hat _____ dir gefragt.
6. Was wirst du am Ende d_____ Jahr tun?
7. Ich muß _____ Bahnhof fahren. *(to the)*
8. D_____ meist_____ Leute haben Eis gern.
9. Der Kugelschreiber lag _____ d_____ Tisch und d_____ Ofen. *(between)*
10. Ich wohne bei zwei ander _____ Männer.
11. Wir wollten nicht _____ d_____ Geld verzichten.
12. Wegen d_____ schlecht _____ Wetter sind wir zu Hause geblieben.
13. Dieser Ring ist _____ Gold. *(made out of)*
14. Einig_____ krank_____ Leute warteten _____ d_____ Arzt.
15. Ich habe großes Interesse _____ dies_____ Film.
16. Udo kommt _____ ein_____ groß_____ Stadt in Deutschland. *(from) (i.e., he grew up there)*
17. Der Briefträger brachte mein_____ Mutter ein_____ Brief.
18. Ich kann sehr gut _____ leben. *(without her)*
19. Sie ging _____ Arzt. *(to the)*
20. _____ waren auch einige Tassen gebrochen. *(in addition to the plates)*
21. Sein Benehmen beruht _____ sein_____ Egoismus.
22. Wie kannst du während d_____ Tag schlafen?
23. Sie ist _____ geboren. *(in Switzerland)*
24. An dem Tag sind wir nur _____ Hamburg gefahren. *(as far as)*

What's wrong with these?

1. Ich habe mehrere kleinen Kinder in einer Kneipe gesehen.
2. Jetzt habe ich keines Geld mehr.
3. Du mußt deinen Vater gehorchen!
4. Stellen Sie der Abfallkorb vor der Tür!
5. Wer ist das Kind's Mutter?
6. Mein Bruder wohnt gegenüber mich.
7. Dieses interessantes Buch ist bei Heinrich Böll.

8. Hast du jeden Tag von mir gedacht?
9. Für welchen Grund haben sie das getan?
10. Wo sind die siamesische Katzen?
11. Außer für das Obst war das Essen sehr gut.
12. Ich habe 2 Jahre auf diesem Buch gearbeitet!

Specific Problems of the German Case System, Unusual Adjectives, and Participles

7

A. Case Identification in Inverted Sentences and after *sein* and *werden*

Most German sentences begin with the subject, but it is also possible to *invert* the normal word order and begin the sentence with some other word. For example, the German sentence below begins with the direct object:

> **Diesen Film** will ich nicht sehen.
> *I don't want to see this film.*

In the next example, the sentence begins with the indirect object:

> **Ihr** habe ich eine Bluse geschenkt.
> *I gave her a blouse.*

In fact, nearly any element of a German sentence can be put before the verb. Inverted sentences occur for two main reasons:

1.   The inverted word is being emphasized:

> **Den Kaffee** kann ich nicht trinken!
> *I can't drink that coffee!*

2.   The inverted word creates a link back to a previous sentence:

> Bleibst du **heute abend** zu Hause? Nein, **heute abend** gehe ich ins Kino.
> *Are you staying home tonight? No, tonight I'm going to a movie.*

A famous, though somewhat facetious example of inverted word order is this sentence:

> Den Mann biß der Hund.
> *The dog bit the man.* (not **The man bit the dog.*)

Clearly, you must be able to recognize inverted word order in German in order to avoid misunderstandings.

If the sentence does begin with the subject, then the nouns and pronouns after the verb will be non-nominative *except* when the verb is any form of **sein** or **werden;** these verbs always connect words which are *both* nominative:

> **Er** ist ein intelligenter **Mensch.**　　　**Er** wird ein guter **Fotograph.**
> *He is an intelligent person.*　　　*He is becoming a good photographer.*
> (**er** and **Mensch** are both nominative)　　　(**er** and **Fotograph** are both nominative)

Be particularly careful to avoid mistakes such as this:

> *Das soll nur **einen Witz** sein.
> *That's only supposed to be a joke.*

The word **Witz** appears to be the direct object of the modal verb **sollen,** but in fact, the case of **Witz** is determined by the verb infinitive **sein,** thus, **Witz** must be in the nominative case:

> correct: Das soll nur **ein Witz** sein.

This rule may help you to avoid such mistakes:

When a German sentence contains a modal verb and an infinitive, the infinitive determines the case of the words in the sentence.

COMPREHENSION CHECK:　　*Fill in the blanks with any necessary adjective endings.*

1. Dies_____ gut_____ Freund vergesse ich niemals.
2. Er will d_____ neu_____ Bundeskanzler werden.
3. Sein_____ Feinde_____ hat er nicht verziehen.
4. Mein Vater war ein_____ äußerst streng_____ Mensch.

ANSWERS:　1. diesen guten　2. der neue　3. seinen Feinden　4. ein äußerst strenger

B. Case in Isolated Pronouns and in Word Fragments

Pronouns used in isolation in English are often in the nonsubject form:

> Who is there? *Me!*

In more refined English, the same sentence might be stated as follows:

Who is there? *I. (am there)*

The words in parentheses show that the pronoun is actually the subject of an understood sentence. Still, in colloquial speech, the form *me* would be more common in such a sentence. German, however, does *not* have an equivalent colloquial form. For example, the German translation of the English example above can only be this:

Wer ist da? **Ich.** (bin da)

In other words, when using pronouns in isolation in German, you must always complete the understood sentence in your mind to see what the case of the pronoun really is (any case is possible).

In English and German, words are often used as fragments with the remainder of the sentence understood (isolated pronouns are a special case of this). Here is an English example of sentence fragments:

Give him the check. *Who? The man in the black suit.*

If the fragmented sentences were written out in full, they would read as follows:

Give him the check. *Who(m) should I give the check to? Give the check to the man in the black suit.*

The German equivalent of the original fragmented sentences would be this:

Geben Sie ihm die Rechnung! **Wem? Dem Mann im schwarzen Anzug.**

The words **wem** and **dem Mann** must be in the dative case because that is the case they would have if the fragmented sentences were written out fully:

Geben Sie ihm die Rechnung. **Wem** soll ich die Rechnung geben? Geben Sie die Rechnung **dem Mann** im schwarzen Anzug!

A fragment might equally well occur within a sentence:

Geben Sie ihm, **dem Mann im schwarzen Anzug,** die Rechnung!

Both **ihm** and **dem Mann** function as the indirect object in the above example, therefore both take the dative case. Another way of looking at this sentence is that **ihm** and **dem Mann** are equivalent, the one is simply a redefinition of the other, so both take the same case.

COMPREHENSION CHECK: *Complete the sentence with the correct German word as indicated by the English word in parentheses.*

1. Welcher Student ist krank? _____. *(him)*
2. Was hast du schließlich gekauft? _____ Hut. *(a)*
3. Sie heiratete Helmut, _____ Freund der Familie. *(an old)*.
4. Sie mußte ihm, _____ Milchmann, 20 Mark geben. *(the)*

ANSWERS: 1. Er 2. Einen 3. einen alten 4. dem

C. Case in Expressions of Time and Measurement

In German, time expressions which refer to definite time periods are in the accusative case (unless preceded by a dative preposition):

Letzten Monat war ich in Frankreich.
Last month I was in France.

When the time is indefinite, the genitive case is used:

Eines Tages wirst du das bereuen!
Some day (one day) you will regret that!

Note: Though the German word **Nacht** is feminine, the genitive of indefinite time for this word is **eines Nachts** (by analogy to other time expressions, which are all masculine or neuter):

Eines Nachts verschwand das Eis aus dem Kühlschrank.
One night the ice cream disappeared from the refrigerator.

The accusative case is also used for words indicating measurement or extent:

Die Temperatur ist jetzt **einen Grad** höher als vor einer Stunde.
The temperature is now one degree higher than an hour ago.

Das kostet bloß **einen Schilling.**
That costs just one Schilling.

Hansi ist schon **einen Meter** groß.
Hansi is already one meter tall.

Note: **Meter** can be masculine or neuter in German. In this book, the masculine form will be used.

COMPREHENSION CHECK: *Add the necessary case endings.*

1. Nächst_____ Dienstag fahre ich nach Hause.
2. Diese Mauer ist ein_____ Zentimeter breit.
3. Ein _____ Morgen_____ wollte ich nicht mehr in die Arbeit gehen.

ANSWERS: 1. Nächsten 2. einen 3. Eines Morgens

D. The Indefinite Pronoun

The German word **man** is the usual equivalent of the English indefinite pronoun *one:*

Man sollte nicht rauchen.
One shouldn't smoke.

In actual conversation, *one* is hardly ever used in English in this sense, more common is *you:*

> *You* shouldn't smoke. (as a general principle)

In German if you write:

> **Du** solltest nicht rauchen.

it means:

> *You (an individual person) should not smoke.*

In other words, if the *you* in your sentence could be substituted by *one,* then **man** must be used in German.

Man, however, changes according to case, as shown in the table that follows:

Nominative:	man
Accusative:	einen
Dative:	einem
Genitive:	eines *(rarely occurs)*

Here is an example of the accusative form of **man:**

> Es freut **einen** nicht, wenn man krank ist.
> *It doesn't make one happy when one is sick.*

In the next example, the sentence has been restated using a dative verb:

> Es gefällt **einem** nicht, wenn man krank ist.
> *It doesn't make one happy when one is sick.*

A common mistake with **man** is referring back to it with the pronoun **er,** in analogy to English usage. In German, only **man** itself can refer back to **man:**

> *Wenn **man** müde ist, sollte **er** ins Bett gehen.
> *When one is tired, he (one) should go to bed.*
> correct: Wenn **man** müde ist, sollte **man** ins Bett gehen.

Finally, do not confuse **man** *(one)* with **Mann** *(man, i.e., male human being).*

COMPREHENSION CHECK: *Insert the correct form of the indefinite pronoun:*

1. In unserem Studentenheim darf _____ nach 12 Uhr am Abend keinen Lärm machen.
2. Das Leben macht _____ so.
3. Es wird _____ klar, daß vieles in Deutschland anders ist als in Amerika.
4. _____ kann die frische Luft genießen, wenn _____ auf dem Land wohnt.

ANSWERS: 1. man 2. einen 3. einem 4. man...man

E. Was für ein

The idiom **was für ein** is the most common German equivalent of the English expression *what sort (kind) of (a)*:

> **Was für ein** Mensch ist er?
> *What sort (kind) of a person is he?*

In the above example, **ein Mensch** is in the nominative case because it is the subject of the sentence; **für** does not function as a preposition in the idiom **was für ein** and has therefore no effect on the case of any following words. Here is another example:

> Bei **was für einer** Familie haben Sie gewohnt?
> *With what sort of family did you live?*

In this example, the case ending on **ein-** is determined by the dative preposition **bei.** Again, **für** has no effect on the case of the words following. Another example:

> Was für **einen** Handschuh hast du gefunden?
> *What kind of glove did you find?*

In this example, the adjective after **für** does take an accusative ending, but only because **Handschuh** is the direct object in the sentence.

When the noun following the idiom is plural, **was für** alone is used:

> **Was für Bücher** haben Sie gern?
> *What sort of books do you like?*

In colloquial German speech, the idiom **was für ein** is often split after the **was.** Thus:

> **Was für ein** Mensch ist er?

can become:

> **Was** ist er **für ein** Mensch?

In this form of the idiom also, **für** does not determine the case of any of the words following.

COMPREHENSION CHECK: *Insert the correct form of* **was für (ein)** *into the sentence.*

1. _____ Wagen ist das?
2. _____ Mantel haben Sie verloren?
3. _____ Kleider willst du kaufen?
4. Aus _____ Land stammt er?

ANSWERS: 1. Was für ein 2. Was für einen 3. Was für 4. was für einem

F. Unusual Adjectives

Viel/Wenig

These two adjectives have the usual adjective endings in the plural but do not normally take any endings in the *singular:*

> Wir haben **viel (wenig)** Zeit. (*not* *viele Zeit)
> *We have a lot of (little) time.*

In the genitive singular, these adjectives do take the usual adjective endings, but the genitive singular rarely occurs. In a few other situations, an adjective ending *may* be added but is never required except in the common saying: **Vielen Dank!** *(Thanks!).*

All

This adjective is a **der-**word but the ending is often dropped when followed by another **der-**word or **kein-**word:

> **All dieses** Wissen war zu nichts gut.
> *All this knowledge was useless.*

> **All meine** Freunde sind Deutsche.
> *All my friends are Germans.*

The ending on the **der-**word or **kein-**word following **all** is the same as if the **all** were not there. In a few situations **all** *may* have an ending when followed by a **der-**word or **kein-**word, but the ending is never required.

Solch/Welch

These adjectives function as **der-**words in the plural. In the singular, the situation is a little more complicated. For example, the English sentence below:

> *That is such a good idea!*

can be expressed in German as follows:

> 1. Das ist **solch eine gute Idee!**

or

> 2. Das ist **so eine gute Idee!**

In sentence 1, **solch** takes no ending, in sentence 2, it is replaced by the adverb **so.**

Sentence type 2 is more common in colloquial speech than type 1. In both types, the endings on the adjectives following **solch/so** are the same as if **solch/so** were not there.

The idea of *such a* can also be expressed as follows:

Ein solcher Mensch weiß, was er will.
Such a person knows what he wants.

This construction is less common than the previous two and can only be used when *no* adjective follows the **solch-** (the ending on **solch-** is the usual ending after **ein**). You can always replace this third possibility by one of the first two:

Solch ein Mensch weiß, was er will.

or

So ein Mensch weiß, was er will.

The adjective **welch-** has two possibilities in the singular:

1. **Welcher Mann** ist dein Vater?
   Which man is your father?

2. **Welch ein Mann!**
   What a man!

In sentence 1, **welch-** is simply a normal **der**-word. The construction in sentence 2 is used in exclamations. As such, **welch-** functions like **solch ein-.**

Dunkel/Teuer/Hoch

All adjectives that end in **-el,** such as **dunkel** *(dark),* drop the final **e** of the stem when an adjective ending is added:

Siehst du die **dunkle** Wolke da drüben?
Do you see the dark cloud over there?

Other common adjectives that fit in this category are:

edel	eitel	heikel	plausibel
noble	*vain*	*picky*	*plausible*

In similar fashion, the adjective **teuer** *(expensive)* also drops the **e** when an ending is added:

Es war ein **teures** Geschenk.
It was an expensive present.

Two other common adjectives that function like **teuer** are:

sauer	ungeheuer
sour	*enormous, frightful*

Finally, the adjective **hoch** *(high)* changes to **hoh-** when an adjective ending is added:

> Ich habe **hohe** Ansprüche.
> *I have high demands.*

Note: The second **h** in **hohe** is not pronounced.

COMPREHENSION CHECK: *Add any necessary adjective endings. In some cases you will have to change the stem of the adjective also:*

1. Ich hatte viel _____ Glück.
2. Wer sind all _____ dies _____ Leute?
3. Ich esse sehr gern sauer _____ Gurken.
4. Sie haben einfach wenig _____ Verstand.
5. Welch _____ ein _____ Tragödie!
6. Ein _____ edel _____ Mensch war er nicht.
7. Wo hast du ein _____ solch _____ Teppich gekauft?
8. Ein _____ hoch _____ Baum stand vor unserem Haus.

ANSWERS: 1. viel 2. all diese 3. saure 4. wenig 5. Welch eine 6. Ein edler 7. einen solchen 8. Ein hoher

G.Present and Past Participles as Adjectives

The word in italics in the English sentence below is an example of a *present participle*:

> I want to reserve a room with *running* water.

Present participles in English are formed by adding *-ing* to the verb infinitive; in German, present participles are formed by adding **-d** to the verb infinitive. Furthermore, when used as adjectives, present participles in German add the usual adjective endings. Thus, the German equivalent of the English example above would be:

> Ich will ein Zimmer mit **fließendem** Wasser vorbestellen.
> (verb infinitive: **fließen** *(to flow)*, present participle: **fließend** *(flowing)*, adjective ending **-em**)

You have already encountered *past participles* in the present and past perfect tenses. Past participles can also be used as adjectives in direct analogy to English, but, of course, in German they must add the usual adjective ending:

> Weak verb: Er wollte ein **gebrauchtes** Auto kaufen.
> *He wanted to buy a used car.*
> (verb infinitive: **brauchen** *(to use)*, past participle: **gebraucht** *(used)*, adjective ending: **-es**)

Strong verb: Die **gebratenen** Forellen waren köstlich.

The fried trout were delicious.

(verb infinitive: **braten** *(to fry)*, past participle: **gebraten** *(fried)*, adjective ending: **-en**)

COMPREHENSION CHECK: *Fill in the blank with the correct form of the present or past participle as indicated by the English word in parentheses.*

1. Er ist ein _____ Experte in seinem Fach. *(leading)*
2. Ich habe das _____ Geld niemals gefunden. *(lost)*
3. Willst du _____ Eier zum Frühstück haben? *(cooked, i.e., boiled)*
4. Ich kann dieses _____ Kind nicht mehr aushalten! *(screaming)*

ANSWERS: 1. führender 2. verlorene 3. gekochte 4. schreiende

German Core Vocabulary

This list covers the adjectives and nouns in the answer portion of the exercises as well as the vocabulary in the English translation exercise.

der Anzug, ¨e	*suit*	der Feind, -e	*enemy*
die Ausrede, -n	*excuse*	das Fieber, -	*fever*
beleuchten	*to light up, illuminate*	die Frechheit, -en	*impudence*
		der Freitag, -e	*Friday*
betäuben	*to anesthetize*	die Frucht, ¨e	*fruit*
betrügen, betrog, betrogen	*to deceive*	ganz	*whole*
		der Gedanke, -n	*thought*
das Bettuch, ¨er	*bed sheet*	das Genie, -s	*genius*
der Beweis, -e	*proof*	das Geschenk, -e	*present*
die Bluse, -n	*blouse*	das Gesicht, -er	*face*
das Brot, -e	*bread*	das Gewitter, -	*thunderstorm*
der Bundeskanzler, -	*Federal Chancellor*	das Glück	*luck*
die Chance, -n	*chance*	der Groschen, -	*groschen (Austrian coin)*
damals	*at that time*		
deprimieren	*to depress*	großartig	*fantastic*
dokumentieren	*to document*	die Gurke, -n	*pickle*
der Dollar, -s	*dollar*	das Haar, -e	*hair*
edel	*noble*	halb	*half*
der Ehemann, ¨er	*husband*	heikel	*picky, fussy*
die Ehre, -n	*honor*	herum.liegen, lag, gelegen	*to lie around*
eitel	*vain*		
erfolgreich	*successful*	hoch	*high*
die Erklärung, -en	*explanation*	hübsch	*pretty*
der Experte, -n	*expert*	der Hut, ¨e	*hat*
färben	*to dye*	der Kaffee, -s	*coffee*
die Fassung, -en	*version*	die Katze, -n	*cat*

kaufen	*to buy*	streng	*strict*
kennen.lernen	*to become acquainted with, to get to know*	die Suppe, -n	*soup*
		die Temperatur, -en	*temperature*
der Knoblauch	*garlic*	teuer	*expensive*
der Kriminal- roman, -e	*detective novel*	der Ton, ⸚e	*tone*
		die Tragödie, -n	*tragedy*
das Land, ⸚er	*country, land*	der Trost	*comfort*
der Lärm	*noise*	die Truppe, -n	*army, troop*
der Mantel, ⸚	*coat*	der Turm, ⸚e	*tower*
die Meile, -n	*mile*	die Überraschung, -en	*surprise*
der/das Meter, -	*meter*		
der Milchmann, ⸚er	*milkman*	die Übung, -en	*exercise*
der Morgen, -	*morning*	ungeheuer	*enormous*
nicht	*not*	die Untertasse, -n	*saucer*
die Niederlage, -n	*defeat*	verkennen *(mixed verb)*	*to not recognize (someone)*
noch nicht	*not yet*		
das Papier, -e	*paper*	die Verspätung	*lateness*
das Pech: Pech haben	*bad luck: to be unlucky*	der Verstand	*common sense*
		vorig	*last*
der Physiklehrer, -	*physics teacher*	der Vormittag, -e	*morning*
plausibel	*plausible*	der Wein, -e	*wine*
der Ring, -e	*ring*	das Werk, -e	*work*
das Schiff, -e	*ship*	wichtig	*important*
schneiden, schnitt, geschnitten	*to mince, to chop*	der Wissenschaftler,-	*scientist*
schön	*beautiful*	der Zahn, ⸚e	*tooth*
schwer	*severe, difficult*	der/das Zentimeter,-	*centimeter*
sofort	*immediately*		

EXERCISE 1   (prerequisite: section A, topic: understanding inverted sentences)

Translate into English.

1. Eine Ausrede für seine Verspätung hatte er nicht.
2. Meine Frau hatte ich damals noch nicht kennengelernt.
3. Die anderen Übungen hat er nicht gemacht.
4. Seinem Kind gab er 2 Dollar.
5. Uns gefiel er sofort.

EXERCISE 2   (prerequisite: section A, topic: case in inverted sentences and after **sein/werden**)

Fill in the blank with the correct ending.

1. Heinrich will ein____ reich____ Arzt werden.
2. Dies____ Wein habe ich nie gern gehabt.

3. Herr Schneider ist ein_____ sehr wichtig_____ Mensch.
4. Sein_____ klein_____ Schwester schenkte er eine Puppe.
5. Franz wird bestimmt ein_____ gut_____ Wissenschaftler sein.

EXERCISE 3 (prerequisite: section B, topic: case in isolated pronouns and word fragments)

Fill in the blank with the correct ending or with the appropriate German word as indicated by the English word in parentheses.

1. Welcher Mann hat Ihre Brieftasche gestohlen? _____! *(him)*
2. Wieviel Geld hast du bei dir? Nur ein_____ Dollar.
3. Wem hast du es gesagt? Ein_____ gut_____ Freund.
4. Ich habe Herrn Lenz, unser_____ Milchmann, gesehen.
5. Erst am Ende des Buches, ein_____ Kriminalromans, erfährt man den Namen des Mörders.
6. Meinen Mathematiklehrer konnte ich nicht verstehen, aber mein_____ Physik-lehrer schon.
7. Dieses Konzert hat mir sehr gut gefallen. Ja, _____ auch. *(me)*
8. Was wünschen Sie zu trinken? Ein_____ Kaffee, bitte.
9. Außer Wolf, mein_____ Hund, habe ich keine Freunde.
10. Haben Sie diese Frau gemeint? Nein, _____. *(her)*

EXERCISE 4 (prerequisite: section C, topic: case in expressions of time and measurement)

Fill in the blank with the appropriate ending.

1. Jed_____ Tag ging er in die Arbeit.
2. Wir sollten ein_____ Nacht_____ die Stadtlichter anschauen.
3. Das Wasser im Schwimmbecken ist nur ein_____ halb_____ Meter tief.
4. Irmgard mußte d_____ ganz_____ Tag im Bett bleiben.
5. Vorig_____ Freitag war ich im Kino.
6. Ein_____ Vormittag_____ fanden wir ein Baby vor dem Haus.
7. Das kostet genau ein_____ Dollar.
8. Ein_____ Tag_____ werde ich einen Porsche besitzen.
9. Wir waren nur ein_____ Meile weg von zu Hause, als das Auto zusammen-brach.
10. Sie kann ein_____ Ton höher als ich singen.

EXERCISE 5 (prerequisite: section D, topic: the indefinite pronoun)

Insert the correct form of the indefinite pronoun in the space provided. Then translate the sentence into English giving both the colloquial and formal form of the indefinite article.

1. _____ sollte das Schloß Schönbrunn sehen, wenn _____ in Wien ist.
2. Gesundes Essen schadet _____ niemals.
3. Das macht _____ immer traurig, wenn _____ das sieht.
4. Darf _____ an dieser Universität die Vorlesungen schwänzen?
5. Es gefällt _____ nicht, wenn _____ lange warten muß.

EXERCISE 6 (prerequisite: section E, topic: **was für ein**)

Fill in the blank with the correct form of **was für (ein)**.

1. _____ Fisch ist das?
2. _____ Sachen werden wir auf der Reise brauchen?
3. Mit _____ Mann hast du am Telefon geredet?
4. _____ Bluse habt ihr im Geschäft gesehen?
5. In _____ Restaurant sind Sie gegangen?
6. _____ Leute lesen diese Zeitung?
7. _____ Katze ist sie?
8. In _____ Haus haben Sie damals gewohnt?

EXERCISE 7 (prerequisite: section F, topic: unusual adjectives)

Insert any necessary adjective endings. In some cases it will be necessary to change the stem form of the adjective also.

1. War all____ dies____ Arbeit wirklich notwendig?
2. Wir haben billig____ und teuer____ Anzüge.
3. Welch____ Kind meinen Sie?
4. Ein____ solch____ Geschenk habe ich nicht erwartet.
5. Damals haben viel____ Leute viel____ Geld an der Börse verloren.
6. Das ist so ein____ Überraschung!
7. Du warst schon als Kind ein sehr heikel____ Mensch.
8. Haben Sie jemals anderswo solch____ hübsch____ Kleider gesehen?
9. Sie hatte wenig____ Chance, den Preis zu gewinnen.
10. Der Patient hatte hoch____ Fieber.
11. Hast du all____ d____ Suppe gegessen?
12. Das ist ein____ ungeheuer____ Frechheit!
13. Das war so ein____ gut____ Essen!

14. Welch_____ ein_____ schön_____ Mantel!
15. Ich warte immer noch auf ein_____ plausibel_____ Erklärung.
16. Die Bank hat all_____ unser_____ Sachen weggenommen.
17. Gestern gab es solch_____ ein_____ schwer_____ Gewitter!
18. Welch_____ ein_____ Niederlage!
19. Kann man so viel_____ Pech haben?
20. Die Auszeichnung war ein_____ hoch_____ Ehre.

EXERCISE 8 (prerequisite: section G, topic: present and past participles as adjectives)

Fill in the blank with the correct adjectival form of the verb infinitive given in parentheses. Use the past participle of the verb unless otherwise indicated.

1. Er konnte den _____ Zahn nicht mehr spüren. (betäuben)
2. Der _____ Ehemann ließ sich von seiner Frau scheiden. (betrügen)
3. Wir konnten das _____ Schiff aus einer Entfernung von einem Kilometer sehen. (beleuchten)
4. Es war ein _____ Gedanke. (deprimieren) *(use present participle)*
5. Der Richter verlangte _____ Beweise. (dokumentieren)
6. Ich steckte das _____ Brot in meine Einkaufstasche. (kaufen)
7. Haben Sie jemals eine _____ Untertasse gesehen? (fliegen) *(use present participle)*
8. Die _____ Früchte waren alle schon schlecht. (ankommen)
9. Er will nur auf frisch _____ Bettüchern schlafen. (waschen)
10. Ich wette, sie hat _____ Haar. (färben)
11. Was ist der _____ Preis für diesen Wein? (empfehlen)
12. Ich konnte mein Buch unter all den _____ Papieren nicht finden. (herumliegen) *(use present participle)*
13. _____ Knoblauch ist eine gute Zutat. (schneiden)
14. Haben Sie die _____ Werke Büchners gelesen? (sammeln)
15. Ich bin ein _____ Genie. (verkennen)

EXERCISE 9 (comprehensive)

Fill in the blank with any necessary endings or with the appropriate German word(s) as indicated by the English word(s) in parentheses.

1. Die Prüfung ist nächst_____ Freitag.
2. Seine Worte gaben mir wenig_____ Trost.
3. Mein_____ braun_____ Mantel kannst du Rudi geben.
4. Die _____ Truppen erlitten eine schwere Niederlage. *(attacking)*
5. Was wirst du bestellen? Vielleicht ein_____ Tee.
6. Wo sind all_____ mein_____ Sachen?
7. Die Polizei hat das _____ Geld nicht gefunden. *(stolen)*

8. Mach nicht _____ Gesicht! *(such a sour)*
9. Ein_____ Tag_____ werde ich mit dem Studium fertig sein.
10. Sie war eine sehr _____ Frau. *(vain)*
11. Dieses Buch ist die zweite, _____ Fassung. *(revised)*
12. _____ Ring hat er dir gekauft? *(what kind of a)*
13. _____ hat Vati nichts gegeben! *(me)*
14. Es hat kein_____Groschen gekostet.
15. Otto ist ein_____ erfolgreich_____ Wissenschaftler geworden.
16. Das Buch zeigt _____, wie _____ ein Auto reparieren kann. *(one)*
17. _____ ein großartig_____ Film! *(what a)*
18. Wer war zuerst hier? _____. *(me)*
19. 30 Grad Celsius ist in Deutschland eine sehr _____ Temperatur. *(high)*
20. Ich mietete eine Wohnung zusammen mit Elke, mein_____ best_____ Freundin.

EXERCISE 10 (comprehensive)

Translate into German.

1. I have little patience with you.
2. Can you smoke here? *(as a general principle)*
3. He wants to become the leader of the Social Democratic Party.
4. Our club is a thriving organization.
5. Where were you last month?
6. What kind of a reason is that?
7. The child did not want to be in a dark room.
8. Someone sent Gerhard, my brother, a letter.
9. My bed is one meter wide.
10. That is such an expensive sweater.
11. The captured wolf growled at us.
12. Where is all the sugar?
13. Do you have a pen? No, only a pencil.
14. One night my cat became pregnant.

GEDANKENPROBLEM: Native English speakers often say sentences like this:

My aunt is visiting my parents and I.

What is wrong with this sentence? Why would a person make such a mistake?

(HINT: it's called hypercorrection in linguistics.) **How would you correctly say the sentence in German?**

What's wrong with these?

1. Man muß viel arbeiten, wenn er erfolgreich sein will.
2. Ein Tag werde ich in einem großen Haus wohnen.
3. Es war vieler Lärm um nichts.
4. Wen hast du gesehen? Er!
5. Meine Großmutter hat jeder Dienstag Bohnen gekocht.
6. Ich muß Anton, mein Freund, anrufen.
7. Diese Kirche hat einen hochen Turm.
8. Mann muß vieles im Leben tun, was man nicht gefällt.
9. Bist du so groß wie ihn?
10. Er muß den Vater dieses Kindes sein.

Comparative and Superlative Adjectives and Adverbs

8

A. Formation of Comparative and Superlative Adjectives

Adjectives in German normally form the comparative and superlative by adding **-er** and **-st** respectively:

BASE FORM	COMPARATIVE	SUPERLATIVE
schnell	schnell**er**	schnell**st-**
fast	*faster*	*fastest*

A number of one-syllable adjectives, and the two-syllable adjective **gesund** *(healthy)*, add an umlaut to the stem in the comparative and superlative:

BASE FORM	COMPARATIVE	SUPERLATIVE
j**u**ng	j**ü**nger	j**ü**ngst-
young	*younger*	*youngest*

A listing of the adjectives which take an umlaut in the comparative and superlative is given below:

alt	*old*	hart	*hard*	lang	*long*
arg	*bad*	jung	*young*	scharf	*sharp*
arm	*poor*	kalt	*cold*	schwach	*weak*
dumm	*stupid*	klug	*clever*	schwarz	*black*
gesund	*healthy*	krank	*sick*	stark	*strong*
grob	*uncouth*	kurz	*short*	warm	*warm*

In addition, the following adjectives *may* be used with an umlaut in the comparative and superlative, but the umlaut is not required:

blaß   *pale*   naß   *wet*   schmal   *narrow*

A number of irregular adjectives also have an umlaut in the comparative and superlative (see section B).

Note: Other adjectives of one syllable, e.g., **bunt** *(colorful)*, **rasch** *(quick)*, **stolz** *(proud)*, etc., do *not* take an umlaut in the comparative and superlative.

The final sound of an adjective may affect the comparative and superlative ending:

---

*If the adjective ends in an **s, t,** or **d**-sound, an **e** is inserted before the **-st** of the superlative except when the adjective is a present participle.*

BASE FORM	COMPARATIVE	SUPERLATIVE
heiß	heißer	heißest-
hot	*hotter*	*hottest*
hart	härter	härtest-
hard	*harder*	*hardest*
entscheidend	entscheidender	entscheidend**st**- (present participle)
decisive	*more decisive*	*most decisive*

---

*If the base form of the adjective already ends in **e,** the comparative ending is only **-r**.*

BASE FORM	COMPARATIVE	SUPERLATIVE
weise	weiser	weisest
wise	*wiser*	*wisest*

A comparative and superlative adjective that precedes a noun must still add the usual adjective ending *after* the comparative or superlative ending:

Das war eine **klügere** Idee.
That was a cleverer idea.
(base form: **klug**, comparative: **klüger**, adjective ending: -e)

COMPREHENSION CHECK: *Part A: Give the comparative and superlative forms of the following adjectives.*

1.   a. friedlich   b. dumm   c. nett   d. müde   e. rasch   f. aufregend

Part B: Fill in the blank with the comparative form of the adjective in parentheses unless the superlative is indicated. Do not forget to add the adjective ending also.

2.   Gib mir bitte ein _____ Messer. (scharf)
3.   Karin ist der _____ Mensch in unserer Klasse. (klug) *(superlative)*
4.   Der _____ Mann hat gewonnen. (stark)
5.   Das waren die _____ Tage während der Reise. (heiß) *(superlative)*

ANSWERS: 1.a. friedlicher, friedlichst- b. dümmer, dümmst- c. netter, nettest- d. müder, müdest- e. rascher, raschest- f. aufregender, aufregendst- 2. schärferes 3. klügste 4. stärkere 5. heißesten

B. Irregular Comparative and Superlative Adjectives

The following adjectives have irregular comparative or superlative forms:

BASE FORM		COMPARATIVE		SUPERLATIVE	
groß	*large*	größer	*larger*	größt-	*largest*
gut	*good*	besser	*better*	best-	*best*
hoch	*high*	höher	*higher*	höchst-	*highest*
nah	*near*	näher	*nearer*	nächst-	*nearest, next*
viel	*much*	mehr	*more*	meist-	*most*

Note: **Meist-** must always be preceded by the definite article, in contrast to English *most:*

> **Die meisten** Leute besitzen heutzutage ein Auto.
> *Most people nowadays own a car.*

You will recall from the previous chapter that adjectives ending in -el, as well as **teuer, sauer,** and **ungeheuer,** drop the final -e of the stem when an adjective ending is added. These same adjectives also lose the e when the *comparative* ending is added, but not the superlative ending:

BASE FORM		COMPARATIVE		SUPERLATIVE	
dunkel	*dark*	dunkler	*darker*	dunkelst-	*darkest*
teuer	*expensive*	teurer	*more expensive*	teuerst-	*most expensive*

When an adjective ending is added to an adjective such as **teuer,** it can become difficult to distinguish the base form from the comparative. The difference can be seen in the examples that follow:

teuer	*expensive*	dictionary form
ein teurer Mantel	*an expensive coat*	base form
ein teurerer Mantel	*a more expensive coat*	comparative
der teuerste Mantel	*the most expensive coat*	superlative

COMPREHENSION CHECK: *Fill in the blank with the comparative form of the adjective given in parentheses unless the superlative is indicated.*

1. Die Arbeiter verlangten einen _____ Lohn. (hoch)
2. Wo ist die _____ Toilette? (nah) *(superlative)*
3. Er war ein _____ Mensch als ich. (edel)
4. Sie wollte die _____ Äpfel kaufen. (teuer)
5. Was ist das _____ Kaufhaus in Berlin? (groß) *(superlative)*

ANSWERS: 1. höheren 2. nächste 3. edlerer 4. teureren 5. größte

C. Comparative and Superlative Adverbs

The base form of adverbs in German is characterized by no ending at all:

base form: Er läuft **schnell.**
              He runs quickly.

The comparative of adverbs in German is formed by adding **-er.** The superlative consists of **am** plus the adverb with **-(e)sten** ending:

comparative: Er läuft schnell**er.**
              He runs more quickly.

superlative: Er läuft **am** schnell**sten.**
              He runs the fastest.

As with adjectives, adverbs in German insert an **e** in the superlative after an **s**-sound and after **t** or **d:**

Dieser Ofen kocht am heißesten.
This oven cooks the hottest.

Der Ostwind bläst am kältesten.
The east wind blows the coldest.

The German adverb **oft** *(often)* is irregular in the comparative and superlative:

BASE FORM	COMPARATIVE	SUPERLATIVE
oft	öfter	am öftesten
often	*more often*	*most often*

An irregular adverb of particular importance is **gern(e):**

gern(e)	lieber	am liebsten
like	*prefer*	*like most of all*

Note: **Gerne** is somewhat more formal than **gern.**

The examples that follow illustrate the usage of this adverb:

base form: Ich trinke **gern** Cola.
              I like to drink Coke.

comparative: Ich trinke **lieber** Cola.
                I prefer to (would rather) drink Coke.

superlative: Ich trinke **am liebsten** Cola.
                I like to drink Coke most of all.

The irregular adjectives listed in section B also serve as the basis for the adverbial forms. For example, the irregular *adjective* **viel** *(much)* has the comparative form **mehr** and the superlative form **meist-;** the *adverb* **viel** has the comparative form **mehr** and the superlative form **am meisten.** These are illustrated in the examples below:

base form: Er hat nicht **viel** geschlafen.
              He didn't sleep much.

comparative: Er hat gestern **mehr** geschlafen.
                He slept more yesterday.

superlative: Er hat vorgestern **am meisten** geschlafen.
                He slept the most the day before yesterday.

A common mistake with the superlative adverb in German is the use of the definite article in analogy to English:

    *Meine Katze springt **die höchste.**
    My cat jumps the highest.
    correct: Meine Katze springt **am höchsten.**

COMPREHENSION CHECK: *Fill in the blank with the comparative form of the adverb shown in parentheses unless the superlative is indicated.*

1.   Dieser Aufsatz war _____ geschrieben. (deutlich) *(superlative)*
2.   Können Sie _____ kommen? (oft)

3. Du hast immer _____ geredet! (laut) *(superlative)*
4. Ich will _____ zu Hause bleiben. (gern)
5. Dieses Messer schneidet _____. (gut)

ANSWERS: 1. am deutlichsten   2. öfter   3. am lautesten   4. lieber   5. besser

D. Problems with the Comparative and Superlative

In the comparative, the English word *than* is expressed by **als** in German:

> Warum ist mein Buch teurer **als** dein Buch?
> *Why is my book more expensive than your book?*

Do not use the German word **dann** to translate the *than* of the English comparative:

> *Ich bin jünger **dann** mein Bruder.
> *I am younger than my brother.*
> correct: Ich bin jünger **als** mein Bruder.

This mistake is easy to make because **dann** sounds like *than,* but in fact, **dann** is the equivalent of the English adverb *then:*

> Zuerst mußt du dir die Hände waschen, **dann** kannst du essen.
> *First you have to wash your hands, then you can eat.*

When two items are compared and found to be equal, German uses **so... wie,** often combined with **genau** or **eben** *(just):*

> Mein Buch ist **genauso teuer wie** dein Buch.
> *My book is just as expensive as your book.*

The problem here is that students tend to use the German **als** in sentences such as the above, in analogy to the English *as,* instead of the correct **so... wie:**

> *Diese Prüfung war genau **als** schwierig **als** die letzte Prüfung.
> *This test was just as hard as the last test.*
> correct: Diese Prüfung was **genauso** schwierig **wie** die letzte Prüfung.

The German word **als** is indeed equivalent to the English *as,* but only as an adverb, not in the comparative. The example below shows the correct use of **als:**

> **Als** junger Mann ging er nach Amerika.
> *As a young man he went to America.*

Note: German does not use the indefinite article after **als** in such sentences.

English generally forms the comparative with *more* when the adjective or adverb is long. German does *not* do this regardless of the length of the adjective or adverb; likewise with the superlative. Do not transfer this English pattern to German by using **mehr** or **meist:**

> *Sie ist eine **mehr fleißige** Studentin als Gabriele.
> *She is a more industrious student than Gabriele.*
> correct: Sie ist eine **fleißigere** Studentin als Gabriele.

> *Was ist der **meist interessante** Film des Jahres?
> *What is the most interesting film of the year?*
> correct: Was ist der **interessanteste** Film des Jahres?

But when the same item is being compared using two adjectives, German does use **mehr** corresponding to English *more* (an alternative to **mehr** in this sense is the German word **eher**):

> Ihre Bemerkung war **mehr blöd** als witzig.
> *Her comment was more silly than clever.*
> (i.e., there was only one comment)

Compare the example above with this one where **mehr** can *not* be used:

> Ihre Bemerkung war **blöder** als seine Bemerkung.
> *Her comment was more silly than his comment.*
> (i.e., two comments are being compared)

Finally, note the meaning of the comparative after **immer** and after **noch** as shown in the examples below:

> Er wurde **immer stärker.**
> *He became stronger and stronger.*
> (This is also equivalent to the English *more and more strong* and *ever stronger*)

> Das ist (sogar) **noch schlimmer.**
> *That is even worse.*

Note: **Sogar** is often added to this type of construction to give emphasis.

COMPREHENSION CHECK: *Fill in the blanks with the appropriate German word(s) as indicated by the English word(s) in parentheses.*

1. Sie kann ＿＿＿ gut tanzen ＿＿＿ er. *(just as... as)*
2. Sie müssen ＿＿＿ sein. *(more careful)*
3. Das angebliche Trauerspiel war ＿＿＿. *(more funny than sad)*
4. Das ist bis jetzt die ＿＿＿ Idee. *(most ridiculous)*
5. Es wird ＿＿＿. *(darker and darker)*
6. Seine letzte Geschichte war ＿＿＿ die erste. *(even more unbelievable than)*

ANSWERS: 1. genauso (ebenso)... wie 2. vorsichtiger 3. mehr lustig als traurig 4. lächerlichste 5. immer dunkler 6. (sogar) noch unglaublicher als

German Core Vocabulary

This list contains the adjectives, adverbs, and nouns used in the answer portion of the exercises.

Learn the adjectives on pages 115, which have an umlaut in the comparative and superlative, the irregular adjectives on page 117, and the following:

abstoßend	*revolting*	das Museum,	*museum*
am liebsten	*most preferred*	plural: Museen	
der Apfel, ∸	*apple*	naß	*wet*
der Arbeiter, -	*worker*	das Niveau, -s	*level*
aufregend	*exciting*	öde	*desolate*
der Augenblick, -e	*moment*	oft, öfter, am	*often, more often,*
bequem	*comfortable*	öftesten	*most often*
blaß	*pale*	das Pferd, -e	*horse*
deutlich	*clear*	der Plan, ∸e	*plan*
dunkel	*dark*	pompös	*pompous*
fleißig	*industrious*	die Quelle, -n	*source*
flexibel	*flexible*	rasch	*quick*
friedlich	*peaceful*	die Rasierklinge,	*razor blade*
die Gegend, -en	*region*	-n	
gern	*like*	schlau	*clever*
die Hälfte, -n	*half*	schlimm	*bad*
heiß	*hot*	schmal	*narrow*
die Karte, -n	*ticket*	schnell	*fast*
die Kartoffel, -n	*potato*	sensibel	*sensitive*
das Kaufhaus, ∸er	*department store*	spät	*late*
klar	*clear*	süß	*sweet*
kräftig	*powerful*	tief	*deep*
langsam	*slow*	die Toilette, -n	*toilet*
laut	*loud*	die Traube, -n	*grape*
lieber	*prefer*	tüchtig	*competent*
der Lohn, ∸e	*salary*	verlockend	*tempting*
die Mannschaft,	*team*	die Ware, -n	*merchandise*
-en		der Weg, -e	*way*
das Messer, -	*knife*	weise	*wise*
das Mitglied, -er	*member*	der Zug, ∸e	*train*

EXERCISE 1 (prerequisite: section A, topic: regular comparative and superlative adjectives)

Fill in the blank with the comparative form of the adjective in parentheses unless the superlative is indicated.

1. Gibt es keinen _____ Zug? (schnell)
2. Die _____ Leute leben auf der anderen Seite der Stadt. (arm) *(superlative)*

3. Mein zweites Kind war ein ＿＿＿ Kind als das erste. (schlimm)
4. Kauf diesmal nicht die ＿＿＿ Kartoffeln! (billig) *(superlative)*
5. Ein ＿＿＿ Pferd habe ich noch nie gesehen. (dumm)
6. Erika trug das ＿＿＿ Kleid. (hübsch) *(superlative)*
7. Der ＿＿＿ Student hat nicht die beste Note bekommen. (intelligent) *(superlative)*
8. Der ＿＿＿ Arbeiter mußte mit der Arbeit aufhören. (müde)
9. Die ＿＿＿ Angebote sind manchmal Betrügereien. (verlockend) *(superlative)*
10. Heute ist der ＿＿＿ Tag des Jahres. (lang) *(superlative)*
11. Meine ＿＿＿ Schwester ist Ärztin geworden. (alt)
12. Wir verkaufen nur das ＿＿＿ Brot. (frisch) *(superlative)*
13. Er wollte ein ＿＿＿ Leben führen. *(gesund)*
14. Diese Wüste ist die ＿＿＿ Gegend auf der Welt. (öde) *(superlative)*
15. Die ＿＿＿ Mannschaft hat gewonnen. (schlau)
16. Sie hatte ＿＿＿ Haar als ihre Schwester. (schwarz)
17. Die ＿＿＿ Kinder hatten Angst vor dem Donner. (jung)
18. Heute ist ein ＿＿＿ Tag als gestern. (klar)
19. Hast du jemals ein ＿＿＿ Gesicht gesehen? (abstoßend)
20. Fahren wir den ＿＿＿ Weg! (kurz) *(superlative)*
21. Die ＿＿＿ Menschen treiben Sport. (gesund) *(superlative)*
22. Dies ist ein ＿＿＿ Sessel. (bequem)
23. Er war der ＿＿＿ Vater im Krankenhaus. (stolz) *(superlative)*
24. Wir brauchen einen ＿＿＿ Wagen. (neu)
25. Die ＿＿＿ Leute sparen ihr Geld. (weise) *(superlative)*

EXERCISE 2 (prerequisite: section B, topic: irregular comparative and superlative adjectives)

Fill in the blank with the comparative form of the adjective in parentheses unless the superlative is indicated.

1. Der ＿＿＿ Mann hieß Alfred. (groß)
2. Was ist der ＿＿＿ Berg in Deutschland? (hoch) *(superlative)*
3. Ich habe niemals einen ＿＿＿ Mann gekannt. (sensibel)
4. Die Vögel haben die ＿＿＿ Trauben nicht gefressen. (sauer)
5. Ich brauche ＿＿＿ Geld. (viel)
6. Wien ist die ＿＿＿ Stadt in Österreich. (groß) *(superlative)*
7. Die ＿＿＿ Karten sind schon ausverkauft. (gut)
8. Das waren die ＿＿＿ Jahre in der Geschichte Englands. (dunkel) *(superlative)*
9. Unsere Waren sind auf einem ＿＿＿ Niveau. (hoch)
10. Wir müssen mit dem ＿＿＿ Zug fahren. (nah) *(superlative)*
11. Warum sollte man die ＿＿＿ Ware kaufen? (teuer)
12. Jetzt arbeiten wir nach einem ＿＿＿ Plan. (flexibel)
13. Das ＿＿＿ Essen gibt es in Italien. (gut) *(superlative)*

14. Ich kaufe meistens in den _____ Geschäften ein. (nah)
15. Er übernachtet immer in den _____ Hotels. (teuer) *(superlative)*

EXERCISE 3 (prerequisite: section C, topic: comparative and superlative adverbs)

Fill in the blank with the comparative form of the adverb in parentheses unless the superlative is requested.

1. Ich fahre _____ nach Griechenland, wenn ich Ferien habe. (oft) *(superlative)*
2. Sie müssen _____ arbeiten. (fleißig)
3. Im Schlaf atmet man _____. (tief) *(superlative)*
4. Klaus konnte einen Ball _____ schlagen als ich. (kräftig)
5. Was essen Sie _____? (gern) *(superlative)*
6. Kommen Sie bitte _____! (nah)
7. Wer hat _____ gehandelt? (weise) *(superlative)*
8. Von jetzt an werde ich _____ schlafen können. (oft)
9. Der Senator hat _____ gesprochen. (pompös) *(superlative)*
10. Das neugeborene Lamm hat unter der Kälte _____ gelitten. (arg) *(superlative)*
11. Ich kann Ihnen das Geld _____ geben. (spät)
12. Das Paket wird mit Luftpost _____ ankommen. (rasch) *(superlative)*
13. Manche Leute arbeiten _____ während der Nacht. (gern)
14. Bitte, fahren Sie _____! (langsam)
15. Sie hat eindeutig _____ gesungen. (gut) *(superlative)*

EXERCISE 4 (prerequisite: section D, topic: special problems)

Complete the sentences with the appropriate German word(s) as indicated by the English word(s) in parentheses.

1. Können Sie nicht _____ sein? *(more pragmatic)*
2. Diese Sitte ist _____. *(more American than European) (Note: Do not capitalize American and European in German.)*
3. Unsere Stadt wird _____. *(more and more beautiful)*
4. Was ist die _____ Quelle? *(most reliable)*
5. Vor dem Gewitter wurde der Himmel _____. *(ever darker)*
6. Diese Prüfung war schwieriger _____ die letzte. *(than)*
7. Meine Schulden werden _____. *(bigger and bigger)*
8. Ich will _____ ein Millionär sein. *(as rich as)*
9. Alle Konzertkarten sind dieses Jahr _____. *(even more expensive)*
10. Martin ist _____ Jörg. *(more energetic than)*
11. Unsere Sportler sind _____ die Russen. *(just as good as)*
12. Der Vater war _____ der Sohn. *(even more uncouth than)*

EXERCISE 5 (comprehensive)

Complete the sentences with the appropriate German word(s) as indicated by the English word(s) in parentheses.

1. Was ist das _____ Tier auf der Welt? *(most dangerous)*
2. Wie lebt die _____ Hälfte der Gesellschaft? *(richer)*
3. Ich wette, ich bin _____ als du. *(more tired)*
4. Wer hat den _____ Fisch gefangen? *(largest)*
5. Er war eine _____ Person als alle von uns. *(more noble)*
6. Wir haben die _____ Nächte im Februar. *(coldest)*
7. Das Schauspiel wurde _____. *(funnier and funnier)*
8. Tomaten haben jetzt einen _____ Preis. *(high)*
9. Mein neuer Kugelschreiber schreibt _____ der alte Kugelschreiber. *(better than)*
10. Wollen Sie _____ Tee oder Kaffee haben? *(rather)*
11. Sie war immer das _____ Mitglied der Familie. *(most intelligent)*
12. Diese Schweinerei war _____ als die erste. *(even more outrageous)*
13. Meine Brieftasche ist leider _____. *(more empty than full)*
14. Er konnte immer _____ laufen. *(the fastest)*
15. Ich brauche eine _____ Rasierklinge. *(sharper)*
16. _____ europäischen Museen haben eine Studentenermäßigung. *(most)*
17. Ich bin _____ er. *(just as clever as)*
18. Er geht nur mit den _____ Mädchen aus. *(prettiest)*
19. Albert kommt immer _____ von allen. *(the latest)*
20. Was waren die _____ Augenblicke des Filmes? *(most exciting)*

EXERCISE 6 (comprehensive)

Translate into German.

1. Otto told the shortest story.
2. His words were more noble than his deeds.
3. The lawn was more yellow than green.
4. You can see better through the clearer glass of this window.
5. Give me a more reasonable suggestion.
6. He became weaker and weaker.
7. Who can sing the softest?
8. That is a more expensive comb.
9. Most students want to learn a foreign language.
10. He writes the most suspenseful novels.
11. This problem is even more difficult than the last problem.
12. I prefer to sleep in a warm room.

What's wrong with these?

1. Was ist höcher, die Zugspitze oder Pikes Peak?
2. Er ist genau als groß als du.
3. Sie war das süßste Baby in der Schönheitskonkurrenz.
4. Nein, er ist wirklich mehr tüchtig als Sie.
5. Sie war das stölzeste Mädchen im Dorf.
6. Iß viel Gemüse, und du wirst gesunder bleiben.
7. Er ist ein stärker Mann dann alle anderen.
8. Er wird der nähste Bundeskanzler werden.
9. Die Glocke im Domturm läutet die lauteste.
10. Meiste Bücher in unserem Geschäft sind teuerer als 10 DM.

Adjectival Nouns, Adjective Fragments, and Weak Nouns

9

A. Adjectival Nouns: Introduction

In German, adjectives are often used as nouns:

> Die **Armen** werden ärmer und die **Reichen** reicher.
> *The poor get poorer and the rich richer.*

Such adjectival nouns are capitalized as nouns but take endings as if they were still adjectives. In the plural, as in the example above, one can see which adjective ending is appropriate by assuming an imaginary **Leute** *(people)* after the adjectival noun:

> **Die armen Leute** werden ärmer und **die reichen Leute** reicher.
> *The poor people get poorer and the rich people richer.*

The next example demonstrates *singular* adjectival nouns:

> Der **Reiche** gab dem **Armen** etwas Geld.
> *The rich man gave the poor man some money.*

The endings on the adjectival nouns become clear if one assumes an imaginary **Mann** after them:

> **Der reiche Mann** gab **dem armen Mann** etwas Geld.
> *The rich man gave the poor man some money.*

If an adjectival noun refers to a female, the imaginary noun would be **Frau:**

> Die **Reiche** (Frau) gab der **Armen** (Frau) etwas Geld.
> *The rich woman gave the poor woman some money.*

The previous examples have shown that a masculine or feminine adjectival noun is a shorthand form for the adjective plus **Mann, Frau** or **Leute.** In some cases, adjectival nouns have become so common that they are almost always used *instead of* the adjective plus **Mann, Frau** or **Leute.** A good example of this is the German word meaning *a German:*

> Er ist (ein) **Deutscher.**
> *He is a German.*

> Sie ist eine **Deutsche.**
> *She is a German.*

> Die **Deutschen** trinken oft Wein zum Essen.
> *The Germans often drink wine with their meals.*

Such adjectival nouns will be given in any good German dictionary as separate words. Here is a listing of the most common of these (the ending **-e(r)** indicates an adjectival noun):

Abgeordnet-e(r)	*elected representative*	Fremd-e(r)	*stranger, foreigner*
Angestellt-e(r)	*employee*	Gefangen-e(r)	*prisoner*
Beamt-e(r)	*public official*	Geliebt-e(r)	*lover*
Bekannt-e(r)	*acquaintance*	Verwandt-e(r)	*relative*
Delegiert-e(r)	*delegate*	Verwundet-e(r)	*wounded person*
Deutsch-e(r)	*(a) German*	Vorgesetzt-e(r)	*superior (at work)*
Erwachsen-e(r)	*adult*	Vorsitzend-e(r)	*chairman*

COMPREHENSION CHECK: *Fill in the blank with the proper adjectival noun formed from the adjective in parentheses. The intended number and gender of the adjectival noun are given when these are not clear from the sentence.*

1. Wer ist dieser _____? (dumm)
2. Helfen Sie dem _____! (fremd)
3. Hast du _____ gern? (blond) *(female, plural)*
4. Ein _____ hat Bestechungsgeld angenommen. (Abgeordnet-)
5. Ich habe den _____ beleidigt. (Beamt-)

ANSWERS: 1. Dumme   2. Fremden   3. Blonde   4. Abgeordneter   5. Beamten

B. Other Types of Adjectival Nouns

Aside from masculine and feminine adjectival nouns, *neuter* adjectival nouns can also be formed:

> Viele Leute wollen **das Häßliche** im Leben nicht sehen.
> *Many people do not want to see the ugliness in life.*

> Was war **das Schlimme** an seinem Benehmen?
> *What was the bad thing about his behavior?*

Note: The specific preposition **an** plus dative case is the equivalent of the English *about* in this type of construction.

The second example above shows that a German neuter adjectival noun may correspond to an *adjective* plus *thing* in English. Do not use **Ding** *(thing)* in German after neuter adjectival nouns in analogy to English:

> *__Das beste Ding__ am Gedicht war der Reim.
> *The best thing about the poem was the rhyme.*
> correct: **Das Beste** am Gedicht war der Reim.

Neuter adjectival nouns are often superlatives, as in the previous example. Adjectival nouns can also be formed from past or present participles:

> Die **Verleumdeten** werden sich rächen.
> *The slandered will take their revenge.*
> (past participle: **verleumdet** *slandered*, from infinitive: **verleumden** *to slander*)

> Das **Beleidigende** daran war die Art, wie er es sagte.
> *The insulting thing about it was the manner in which he said it.*
> (present participle: **beleidigend** *insulting*, from infinitive: **beleidigen** *to insult*)

The following is another important group of adjectival nouns:

---

*Adjectives used after the quantity words **etwas, nichts, viel** and **wenig** are neuter adjectival nouns.*

> Hast du **etwas Neues** gehört?
> *Did you hear something new?*

> Das ist **nichts Besonderes.**
> *That is nothing special.*

> Er hat **viel (wenig) Gutes** für unsere Stadt getan.
> *He has done much (little) good for our city.*

The **-es** ending on these adjectival nouns is the neuter singular *strong* ending for the *nominative* and *accusative*. When the adjectival noun is in the *dative* case, the ending is **-em:**

> Er hatte Angst vor etwas Unbeschreiblich**em.**
> *He was afraid of something indescribable.*

Finally, two special cases:

1. An adjective following **alles** is also a neuter adjectival noun but takes a *weak* adjective ending:

> Sie haben schon alles Billig**e** verkauft.
> *They have already sold everything cheap.*

2. **Ander-** *(other),* when used as an adjectival noun, is *not capitalized:*

> Ich habe etwas **a**nderes gemeint.
> *I meant something else.*

In principle, any adjective can be used as an adjectival noun, but in practical terms, certain adjectives are more frequently used in this manner than others. The adjectival nouns employed in this chapter should give you a sense of which adjectives are commonly used as adjectival nouns.

COMPREHENSION CHECK: *Fill in the blank with the appropriate adjectival noun formed from the adjective in parentheses.*

1. Das einzige ＿＿ an meinem alten Auto war das Radio. (gut)
2. Habe ich etwas ＿＿ gesagt? (falsch)
3. Wo liegt der ＿＿? (verletzt)
4. Jemand gab dem ＿＿ eine schmerzstillende Tablette. (leidend)
5. Das ＿＿ am Film war die Liebesszene. (interessant) *(superlative)*
6. Sie kann alles ＿＿ außer Fisch essen. (ander)

ANSWERS: 1. Gute 2. Falsches 3. Verletzte 4. Leidenden 5. Interessanteste 6. andere

C. Adjective Fragments

An adjective can be used without a noun following and still not be an adjectival noun:

> Udo kaufte sich einen grauen Mantel, und dann kaufte er seinem Vater **einen schwarzen.**
> *Udo bought himself a grey coat, and then he bought his father a black one.*

The word **Mantel** is clearly understood after **einen schwarzen.** The phrase **einen schwarzen** is an *adjective fragment* and the adjectives are *not* capitalized, as if the understood noun were there. By contrast, the sentence below contains a true adjectival noun:

> **Der Rothaarige** kaufte sich einen Mantel.
> *The red-haired man bought himself a coat.*

Der Rothaarige is an adjectival noun because it does not refer back to some specific word in this or a previous sentence, instead it stands for the concept: *a red-haired man.*

The ending on an adjective fragment is usually the same as the ending which would occur if the understood word were present. However, there is a complication when the fragment is a **kein-**word:

> **Kein**-words, when used as adjective fragments, take the same endings as **der**-words.

To see how this rule works, consider the example below:

> Hast du einen Kugelschreiber? Ja, hier ist ein**er**.
> *Do you have a pen? Yes, here is one.*

The word referred back to after **einer** is **Kugelschreiber.** The ending on **ein** is the same as that of a **der**-word, e.g., **dieser** Kugelschreiber. For comparison, here is the above example with the understood noun stated explicitly; **ein** is no longer an adjective fragment:

> Hast du einen Kugelschreiber? Ja, hier ist **ein** Kugelschreiber.
> *Do you have a pen? Yes, here is a pen.*

Here is another example of a **kein**-word used as an adjective fragment:

> Das kleine Buch ist **seines** und das große ist **meines.**
> *The little book is his and the big one is mine.*
> (understood word **Buch,** ending as in **dieses Buch**)

If the above sentences were written out fully, they would read like this:

> Das kleine Buch ist sein Buch und das große Buch ist mein Buch.
> *The little book is his book and the big book is my book.*

You can see from this example that the adjective fragments make the English and German sentences sound more natural.

Note: When used as adjective fragments in colloquial speech, the neuter forms of **kein**-words, i.e., **keines, deines, meines,** etc., are often contracted to **keins, deins, meins** etc.

In German, superlative adjectives frequently appear as fragments after **sein:**

> Von den acht Studenten war Ludwig **der beste** (Student).
> *Of the eight students, Ludwig was the best (student).*
> (adjective fragment **der beste,** understood noun **Student**)

The German sentence could also be written as follows with the same meaning:

> Von den acht Studenten war Ludwig **am besten.**

In the second example, the adjective fragment has been replaced by a superlative *adverb*. The adjective fragment can only be used when there is an understood word following it; the superlative adverb, on the other hand, can be used with or without an understood noun. For example, in the German sentence that follows, the superlative adverb alone is possible:

> Seine Romane sind interessant, aber seine Dramen sind **am interessantesten.**
> *His novels are interesting, but his dramas are the most interesting.*

You cannot meaningfully insert an understood noun after *interesting* in the English sentence, therefore the superlative adverb must be used in German.

COMPREHENSION CHECK: *Complete the sentences with the appropriate German words corresponding to the English words in parentheses.*

1. Wollen Sie das teure oder das billige Zimmer haben? Ich will _____. *(the cheap one)*
2. Haben Sie Verwandte in Deutschland? Ja, ich habe _____. *(one) (male)*
3. Ist das dein Regenschirm? Nein, das ist _____. *(his)*
4. Welches Ergebnis war _____? *(the best)*
5. Das Wiener Schnitzel ist nicht schlecht, aber das Rindsgulasch ist _____. *(best)*

ANSWERS: 1. das billige   2. einen   3. seiner   4. das beste *or* am besten   5. *only* am besten

D. Weak Nouns

In sections A–B we discussed adjectives that behaved like nouns. This section deals with a group of nouns that function very much like masculine adjectives with weak endings. For this reason, these nouns are usually referred to as *weak nouns*. They add **-(e)n** in all cases except the nominative singular. There are three types of weak nouns. The table below gives an example of each type:

		meaning		
	case	*person*	*ape*	*name*
Singular	nominative	Mensch	Affe	Name
	accusative	Mensch**en**	Affe**n**	Name**n**
	dative	Mensch**en**	Affe**n**	Name**n**
	genitive	Mensch**en**	Affe**n**	Name**ns**
Plural	all cases	Mensch**en**	Affe**n**	Name**n**

The weak endings can be summarized by the following rules:

> **Mensch**-*type: These weak nouns end in a consonant in the nominative singular (the dictionary form). They add* **-en** *in other cases.*

The majority of weak nouns can be recognized as being weak according to the following rule:

NOUN ENDING	EXAMPLE	
1. -e	Franzose	*Frenchman*
2. -at	Kandid**at**	*candidate*
3. -ant	Elef**ant**	*elephant*
4. -ent	Stud**ent**	*student*
5. -ist	Tour**ist**	*tourist*

The remaining weak nouns referring to living creatures are not recognizable on the basis of their form. The list below gives the most common of these·

Astronaut	*astronaut*	Katholik	*Catholic*
Astronom	*astronomer*	Komet	*comet*
Bär	*bear*	Lump	*scoundrel*
Fürst	*sovereign*	Mensch	*person*
Graf	*earl*	**Nachbar**	*neighbor*
Held	*hero*	Narr	*fool*
Herr	*gentleman*	Philosoph	*philosopher*
Kamerad	*comrade*	Prinz	*prince*

Note: **Herr** adds only **-n** in the singular, **-en** in the plural. **Nachbar** adds only **-n** in both the singular and plural. The table below shows the complete forms for these two nouns:

Singular	Nominative	Herr	Nachbar
	Accusative	Herr**n**	Nachbar**n**
	Dative	Herr**n**	Nachbar**n**
	Genitive	Herr**n**	Nachbar**n**
Plural	All cases	Herr**en**	Nachbar**n**

The third type of weak noun, represented by **Name,** is also not recognizable on the basis of its form. Only a few nouns belong in this category. These are listed here:

Buchstabe	*letter (on a page)*	Glaube	*belief*
Funke	*spark*	Name	*name*
Gedanke	*thought*	Wille	*will*

Finally, the neuter noun **Herz** *(heart)* is a somewhat irregular weak noun:

Singular	Nominative	das Herz
	Accusative	das Herz
	Dative	dem Herz**en**
	Genitive	des Herz**ens**
Plural	All cases	die Herz**en**

Weak nouns are relatively easy to understand but very hard to remember. A good German dictionary can tell you whether a given noun is weak (for practice, look up **Mensch, Affe,** and **Name** in your German dictionary).

COMPREHENSION CHECK: *Part A: Based on the form and meaning of the noun, determine which of the following* must *be weak nouns. You may assume that the remaining are* not *weak nouns.*

1. a. Hase *rabbit* b. Hund *dog* c. Assistent *assistant* d. Theologe *theologian* e. Bauer *farmer* f. Advokat *lawyer* g. Spezialist *specialist* h. Mechaniker *mechanic*

Part B: Fill in the blank with the correct form of the weak noun shown in parentheses.

2. Hast du jemals einen _____ gesehen? (Komet)
3. Er war ein guter _____. (Mensch)
4. Das ist das Haus eines _____ von mir. (Kollege)
5. Was ist die Folge dieses _____? (Gedanke)

ANSWERS: 1. a. weak b. not weak c. weak d. weak e. not weak f. weak g. weak h. not weak 2. Kometen 3. Mensch 4. Kollegen 5. Gedankens

German Core Vocabulary

This list includes the adjectives and nouns in the answer portion of the exercises. Note: Weak nouns are indicated by showing the genitive singular ending and the plural ending, e.g., **der Affe, -n, -n.**

Learn the adjectival nouns listed on pages 128, the weak nouns on pages 133–134, and the following:

der Affe, -n, -n	ape	das Lied, -er	song
ästhetisch	esthetic	der Löwe, -n, -n	lion
der Aufsatz, ⁻e	essay	lustig	funny
beleidigend	insulting	der Matrose, -n, -n	sailor
beunruhigend	upsetting, disturbing	merkwürdig	peculiar
		der Passant, -en, -en	passer-by
das Bier, -e	beer		
bissig	mean, sarcastic	der Pirat, -en, -en	pirate
der Bürokrat, -en, -en	bureaucrat	der Polizist, -en, -en	policeman
der Elefant, -en, -en	elephant	der Regenschirm, -e	umbrella
das Ergebnis, -nisse	result	der Russe, -n, -n	(a) Russian
		der Schuh, -e	shoe
falsch	false	die Straßenbahn, -en	streetcar
der Franzose, -n, -n	Frenchman		
		tot	dead
das Gefühl, -e	emotion, feeling	der Tourist, -en, -en	tourist
der Hase, -n, -n	rabbit		
das Hemd, -en	shirt	der Trottel, -	fool
interessant	interesting	der Türhüter, -	doorman
der Junge, -n, -n	boy	der Verkäufer, -	salesman
der Kerl, -e	guy	verliebt	in love
der Kollege, -n, -n	colleague	der Vogel, ⁻	bird
der König, -e	king	zeigen	to show
der Kunde, -n, -n	customer	der Zeuge, -n, -n	witness

EXERCISE 1 (prerequisite: section A, topic: basic adjectival nouns)

Fill in the blank with the appropriate adjectival noun formed from the adjective in parentheses.

1. a. Niemand kannte die _____. (tot) *(singular)*
    b. Die _____ schweigen. (tot)
2. a. Gestern habe ich zufällig einen alten _____ getroffen. (bekannt)
    b. Sie ist mit einigen _____ in die Berge gefahren. (bekannt)
3. a. Man hat den _____ ins Krankenhaus gebracht. (krank)
    b. Sie gab der _____ eine Tablette. (krank)
4. a. Er ist ein treuer _____. (angestellt)
    b. Die _____ hassen den Chef. (angestellt)
5. a. Der _____ konnte kein Deutsch verstehen. (fremd)
    b. Der Polizist gab dem _____ Auskunft. (fremd)
6. a. Sie ist meine _____. (geliebt)
    b. Ich habe ihn gestern mit seiner _____ gesehen. (geliebt)
7. a. Die _____ sind im allgemeinen sehr gastfreundlich. (deutsch)
    b. Was hat der _____ gesagt? (deutsch)
8. a. Ruth ist eine _____ von mir. (verwandt)
    b. Meine _____ kommen zu Besuch. (verwandt)
9. a. Der _____ hat all sein Geld verloren. (arm)
    b. Der Staat wollte den _____ kein Wohlfahrtsgeld mehr geben. (arm)
10. a. Martin ist unser neuer _____. (vorgesetzt)
    b. Martin ist der neue _____. (vorgesetzt)

EXERCISE 2 (prerequisite: section B, topic: other types of adjectival nouns)

Fill in the blank with the proper adjectival noun formed from the adjective in parentheses.

1. Die _____ haben sich geküßt. (verliebt)
2. Haben Sie nichts _____? (besser)
3. Alles _____ ist passiert, was nur passieren konnte. (schlecht)
4. Das _____ an ihm war sein Kostüm. (lustig) *(superlative)*
5. Er war nur am _____ im Leben interessiert. (ästhetisch)
6. Wollen Sie etwas _____ bestellen? (ander)
7. Das _____ war der Ton seiner Stimme. (beleidigend)
8. Ich habe heute etwas _____ gesehen. (merkwürdig)
9. Ich suche nach etwas _____. (billig)
10. Die Nachrichten haben wenig _____ berichtet. (interessant)
11. Das _____ an einem Gewitter ist natürlich der Blitz. (gefährlich)
12. Auf der Reise haben wir viel _____ gesehen. (schön)
13. Wir wünschen Ihnen alles _____. (gut)
14. Der Arzt hat nichts _____ festgestellt. (beunruhigend)

EXERCISE 3 (prerequisite: section C, topic: adjective fragments)

Fill in the blank with the German word(s) corresponding to the English word(s) in parentheses.

1. Susi hat braunes Haar, aber ihre Schwester hat _____. *(blond)*
2. Kleinschmidt ist ein guter Lehrer, aber Frenzl ist _____. *(the best)*
3. Peter hat ein neues Auto und ich habe _____. *(none)*
4. Ich ging mit der ältesten Schwester aus und mein Freund mit der _____. *(youngest)*
5. Mozarts Opern sind schön, aber seine Sinfonien sind _____. *(the most beautiful)*
6. Ich will ein helles Bier, und was willst du? _____. *(a dark one)*
7. Von den drei Studenten war Dietrich _____. *(the most intelligent)*
8. Wie viele Schüler waren gestern krank? Nur _____. *(one)*
9. Der Zug ist schneller als der Autobus, aber das Flugzeug ist _____. *(the fastest)*
10. Wessen Aufsatz ist das? _____. *(mine)*
11. Welche Schuhe sind _____? *(the widest)*
12. Der Mercedes ist teurer als der VW, aber der BMW ist _____. *(the most expensive)*

EXERCISE 4 (prerequisite: section D, topic: identifying weak nouns)

Put a check after each German noun that must be a weak noun on the basis of its form and meaning.

1. Optimist *optimist*	6. Käse *cheese*	11. Fabrikant *manufacturer*	16. Detektiv *detective*
2. Amateur *amateur*	7. Bürokrat *bureaucrat*	12. Revolutionär *revolutionary*	17. Diplomat *diplomat*
3. Professor *professor*	8. Knabe *boy*	13. Archäologe *archaeologist*	18. Verfasser *author*
4. Agent *agent*	9. Offizier *officer*	14. Sozialist *socialist*	19. Löwe *lion*
5. Biologe *biologist*	10. Bäcker *baker*	15. Vampir *vampire*	20. Kommandant *commandant*

EXERCISE 5 (prerequisite: section D, topic: usage of weak nouns)

Fill in the blank with each of the nouns in parentheses. Some of the nouns are weak, some are not.

1. Bedienen Sie bitte den _____! (Kunde, Mann, Herr)
2. Sie hat darüber mit einem _____ geredet. (Nachbar, Russe, Lehrer)

3. Er war ein junger _____. (Arbeiter, Franzose, Matrose)
4. Im Zoo haben wir viele _____ gesehen. (Affe, Leute, Löwe)
5. Die Prinzessin hat einen _____ geheiratet. (König, Graf, Prinz)
6. Die Stärke seines _____ war nicht groß. (Wille, Gefühl)
7. Ich werde diesen _____ fragen. (Polizist, Türhüter, Passant)
8. Niemand konnte das Geld des _____ finden. (Tourist, Herr, Pirat)
9. Wer ist dieser _____? (Kerl, Lump, Mensch)
10. Warum hast du einen _____ gekauft? (Elefant, Hase, Vogel)
11. Die Dummheit dieses _____ war unglaublich. (Trottel, Narr, Bürokrat)
12. Zwei _____ haben mich gestern angerufen. (Kollege, Verkäufer, Schüler)
13. Der Lehrer hat dem _____ die Prüfung gezeigt. (Junge, Student, Schüler)
14. Der Rhythmus des _____ war unregelmäßig. (Lied, Herz)
15. Wir haben einen _____ mit dem Fernrohr angeschaut. (Komet, Bär, Berg)

EXERCISE 6 (comprehensive)

Fill in the blank with the German word(s) corresponding to the English word(s) in parentheses.

1. Am Wochenende haben wir nichts _____ getan. *(special)*
2. Er hat dem _____ gedankt. *(messenger)*
3. Ein Schäferhund hat dem _____geholfen. *(blind man) (one word)*
4. Ich habe dort viele nette Leute kennengelernt, aber auch viele _____. *(bad ones)*
5. Die _____ trug ein rotes Tuch auf dem Kopf. *(old woman) (one word)*
6. Ich kann meinen _____ nicht aushalten. *(neighbor)*
7. Kannst du etwas _____ für mich tun? *(nice)*
8. Ich habe wenig _____ von diesem Artikel gelernt. *(new)*
9. Ich gebe dir mein Hemd, und du gibst mir _____. *(yours)*
10. Was ist der erste Buchstabe Ihres _____? *(name)*
11. Sein zweiter Film war _____. *(the best)*
12. Ein _____ hat einen Vortrag gehalten. *(delegate)*
13. Die Ketten des _____ waren aus Eisen. *(slave)*
14. Er wollte alles _____ haben. *(forbidden)*
15. Ich habe mehrere _____ in Frankfurt. *(acquaintances)*
16. Der Brunnen ist älter als das Rathaus, aber das Schloß ist _____. *(the oldest)*
17. Was Häuser betrifft, bin ich mit etwas _____ zufrieden. *(simple)*
18. Einige Bürger besuchten das Büro ihres _____ im Kongreß. *(representative)*
19. Das _____ daran war, ich hatte meinen besten Anzug an, aber ich war unrasiert. *(stupid thing)*
20. Fahr nicht mit dem _____! *(crazy one)*

EXERCISE 7 (comprehensive)

Translate into German.

1. My wife always eats the sour pickles, and I eat the sweet ones.
2. Who is that stranger?
3. The best thing about her was her smile.
4. I bought my nephew a teddy bear.
5. He is now the chairman of my company.
6. Everything else was too expensive.
7. Is that your dog? No, it's his.
8. I want to buy something unusual.
9. Have you read Heinrich Böll's "Letter to a Young Catholic"?
10. The first lecture was the most interesting.

GEDANKENPROBLEM: How would you say this in German?

One of my acquaintances (male) will visit me soon.

What's wrong with these?

1. Haben Sie nichts Besser?
2. Soll ich mit dieser Straßenbahn oder mit der Nächsten fahren?
3. Jeder lobte die Tapferkeit des Helds.
4. Das wesentliche Ding ist, daß du die Wahrheit gesagt hast.
5. Wo ist mein Mantel? Ich weiß es nicht, aber hier ist mein.
6. Niemand hat dem Zeuge geglaubt.
7. Es war seine Philosophie, nichts bissiges im Leben zu sagen.
8. Er wollte die gespannte Stimmung mit etwas Lustiges auflockern.
9. Sie untersuchte den Ursprung dieses Glauben.
10. Viele Deutscher haben am Anfang an Hitler geglaubt.

Review Exercises Chapters 7–9

EXERCISE

Fill in the blank as needed with the proper adjective ending or with the German words corresponding to the English words in parentheses.

1. Ein_____ Tag_____ werde ich eine Weltreise machen.
2. Wenn _____ viel_____ Bier trinkt, kriegt _____ einen Bierbauch. *(one)*
3. Er will ein_____ gut _____ Arzt werden.
4. Ist das ein _____ Wagen? *(more expensive)*
5. Meine Katze hat den _____ Fisch gefressen. *(thrown-away)*
6. Hier ist mein Zimmer, und da drüben ist _____. *(yours)*
7. Es tut mir leid, aber ich habe wenig_____ Zeit für Sie.
8. Wer will ins Kino gehen? _____! *(me)*
9. Ich fahre _____ mit dem Zug. *(rather)*
10. Er saß ein_____ Meter von ihr entfernt.
11. Ich wohne bei einem _____. *(German)*
12. Er ist immer noch _____ Kind. *(such a)*
13. _____ Leute wollen ihr eigenes Haus besitzen. *(most)*
14. Sie hat all_____ mein_____ Wein getrunken.
15. Welches Kleid ist_____? *(the cheapest)*
16. Welch_____ ein_____ Überraschung!
17. Ich bin ein Jahr _____ du. *(younger than)*
18. Sie ist sehr nett, aber ihr_____ Freund kann ich nicht aushalten.
19. Ich war _____. *(more surprised than angry)*
20. Wem hast du deinen Regenschirm gegeben? Mein_____ Vater.
21. Sie hat einen _____ geheiratet. *(Frenchman)*
22. Haben Sie jemals einen _____ gesehen? *(dancing bear)*
23. _____ Mann ist dein Vater? *(what kind of)*
24. Ulrike trug immer eine blaue Bluse und ihre Schwester _____. *(a brown one)*
25. Es trifft _____ schwer, wenn ein guter Freund stirbt. *(one)*
26. Die Schriften dieses _____ sind alle berühmt geworden. *(philosopher)*
27. Ich habe Klemenz, ein_____ alt_____ Freund, getroffen.
28. Was ist die _____ Stadt in Deutschland? *(oldest)*
29. Er hatte einen _____ Anzug an. *(dark)*
30. Du wirst _____. *(prettier and prettier)*
31. Er war _____ als sein Vetter. *(even more stupid than)*
32. Hast du etwas _____ gehört? *(new)*
33. Wo warst du letzt_____ Freitag?
34. Er lebte auf einem _____ Berg. *(high)*
35. Es war der _____ Film, den ich jemals gesehen hatte! *(most depressing)*

What's wrong with these?

1. Diese Prüfung war genauso schwierig als die Letzte.
2. Darf Mann hier rauchen?
3. Warum hast du diesen Mensch geheiratet?
4. Wir haben zu vieles Brot gegessen.
5. Ich wollte einen warmeren Mantel holen.
6. Sie ist keine dumme blonde.
7. Viele Erwachsener benehmen sich wie Kinder.
8. Das ist ein besser Wagen.
9. Konrad gab Herr Fink, der Fremdenführer, das Geld.
10. Hast du ein bißchen Geld bei dir? Nein, ich habe kein.
11. Wer wird den neuen Lehrer sein?
12. Ich habe heute etwas merkwürdig gesehen.
13. Was soll man tun, wenn er alles verloren hat?
14. Dieser Kurs wird jeder Tag mehr interessant.
15. Wer hat die Suppe bestellt? Ihn.
16. Das beste Ding am Essen war die Nachspeise.
17. Rolf ist größer dann Nina.
18. In dieser Mannschaft spielt Lothar der beste.

Passive Sentences

10

A. Basic Passive Sentences

For reference, the basic structure of passive sentences in English and German is shown in the illustrative sentences below. The German words in boldface indicate the tense of the sentence.

Present:

Das Haus **wird** vom Eigentümer verkauft.
The house is being sold by the owner.

Simple Past:

Das Haus **wurde** vom Eigentümer verkauft.
The house was sold by the owner.

Present Perfect (Past Perfect):

Das Haus **ist (war)** vom Eigentümer verkauft **worden.**
The house has (had) been sold by the owner.

Future:

> Das Haus **wird** vom Eigentümer verkauft **werden.**
> *The house will be sold by the owner.*

The main features of the passive in German and English can be summarized as follows:

1. The tense of a German passive sentence is determined entirely by the passive auxiliary **werden.** The only complication is that the past participle of **werden** in a passive sentence is **worden** and not the expected **geworden.**

2. The main verb of the sentence appears as a *past participle* in both English and German.

3. German puts the past participle of the main verb at the *end* of the clause but before the **worden** of the present (past) perfect tense and before the final **werden** of the future tense.

COMPREHENSION CHECK: *This exercise is based on the model German sentence shown here:*

> Das Auto wird gewaschen.
> *The car is being washed.*

Make changes in the model German sentence as required in the exercise that follows.

1. Beide Autos _____ gewaschen. *(insert correct form of **werden,** use present tense)*
2. Das Auto wird _____. *(insert correct form of new verb **reinigen**)*
3. Das Auto _____ gewaschen. *(simple past)*
4. Das Auto _____ gewaschen _____. *(present perfect)*
5. Das Auto _____ gewaschen _____. *(past perfect)*
6. Das Auto _____ gewaschen _____. *(future)*

ANSWERS: 1. werden 2. gereinigt 3. wurde 4. ist...worden 5. war...worden 6. wird...werden

B. Passive Sentences with Modal Verbs

A modal verb can be used in a passive sentence:

> Tennisschuhe **dürfen** nicht in der Kirche **getragen werden.**
> *Tennis shoes may not be worn in church.*

In such sentences, the modal is the conjugated verb and indicates the tense, which is usually present or simple past. Both tenses are shown in the examples below:

present tense: Meine alte Jacke **muß** weggeworfen werden.
                            My old jacket has to be thrown away.

simple past tense: Meine alte Jacke **mußte** weggeworfen werden.
                            My old jacket had to be thrown away.

The verb agrees with the modal in such sentences:

> Du **kannst** ersetzt werden!
> *You can be replaced!*

In all these sentences, the past participle and the passive infinitive **werden** remain fixed at the end of the sentence.

COMPREHENSION CHECK: *Make meaningful passive sentences by using the verb(s) shown in parentheses. You will have to supply **werden** where necessary. Use the present tense unless otherwise indicated.*

1. Das verschwundene Schiff _____ nicht gefunden werden. (können)
2. Die Hausaufgaben müssen _____ _____. (schreiben)
3. Ich _____ nur _____ _____. (wollen, respektieren)
4. Diese Rechnung _____ _____ _____. (müssen, bezahlen) *(simple past tense)*

ANSWERS: 1. kann 2. geschrieben werden 3. will... respektiert werden
4. mußte... bezahlt werden

C. The Usage of the Passive in English and German

A passive sentence is always an alternative form of some *active* sentence:

active: **Der Verkäufer** betrog **den Kunden.**
           The salesman cheated the customer.

passive: **Der Kunde** wurde **vom Verkäufer** betrogen.
           The customer was cheated by the salesman.

The passive switches the direct object of the active sentence into the subject position of the passive sentence and, in so doing, emphasizes what happened to the direct object. The subject of the active sentence becomes the object of a prepositional phrase and is de-emphasized as a result. In fact, the entire prepositional phrase could be deleted with little change in meaning:

> Der Kunde wurde betrogen.
> *The customer was cheated.*

In short, a passive sentence rearranges the emphasis of the equivalent active sentence, but both have the same basic meaning.

The object of the preposition in a passive sentence is called the *agent*. The preposition used before the agent in German can be **von** or **durch,** depending on the nature of the agent. The choice is determined by the general rule given below:

Use **von** when the agent is an animate noun (living creature), use **durch** when the agent is an inanimate noun (nonliving).

---

animate noun: Der Bericht wurde **von einem Assistenten** geschrieben.
The report was written by an assistant.

inanimate noun: Unser Dach wurde **durch Hagel** beschädigt.
Our roof was damaged by hail.

English uses the preposition *by* before the agent. For this reason, students often mistakenly use **bei** before the agent in a German passive sentence:

*Der Vorschlag wurde **bei** allen besprochen.
The suggestion was discussed by all.
correct: Der Vorschlag wurde **von** allen besprochen.

Consider the following active sentence in English:

active: *His grandmother gave him the sweater.*

The passive equivalent, based on the *direct object* of the active sentence, would be the following:

passive: *The sweater was given to him by his grandmother.*

The German equivalents of the above would be:

active: Seine Großmutter gab ihm **den Pullover.**
passive: **Der Pullover** wurde ihm von seiner Großmutter gegeben.

In English, one can also form a passive sentence based on the *indirect object* of the active sentence:

He was given the sweater by his grandmother.

By contrast, German does *not* allow passive sentences derived from the indirect object of the active sentence:

***Er** wurde den Pullover von seiner Großmutter gegeben.

The nearest German equivalent to the English passive sentence based on the indirect object would be the following:

Ihm wurde **dieser Pullover** von seiner Großmutter gegeben.

This sentence is the same as the German passive sentence based on the direct object.

Note that the indirect object has been shifted to the beginning of the sentence. The word **Pullover** is still the subject of the passive sentence, but the shift in word order has the effect of emphasizing the word **ihm.** English accomplishes the same task by making the indirect object of the active sentence the subject of a passive sentence. Here is another example:

1. Die Kirche gab vielen Leuten ein Gratisessen.
The church gave many people a free meal.
(active sentence)

2. Ein Gratisessen wurde vielen Leuten von der Kirche gegeben.
A free meal was given to many people by the church.
(passive sentence based on direct object in English and German)

3. Vielen Leuten wurde ein Gratisessen von der Kirche gegeben.
Many people were given a free meal by the church.
(English passive based on indirect object, German passive still based on direct object, **vielen Leuten** stressed)

Note that the verb in the third German sentence is singular because the subject is still **Gratisessen,** as in the second sentence. The verb in the third English sentence, however, is plural because the subject is *many people*.

As a practical example, let us assume you wanted to say the following English passive sentence in German:

He was sent a bill.

The closest German equivalent would be:

Ihm wurde eine Rechnung geschickt.

With practice, you will be able to say such sentences in German instinctively, but until then, you may find it easier to go through the process outlined below:

1. Rewrite the sentence as an active sentence with *they* as the subject:

They sent him a bill.

You should now realize that the subject of the English passive sentence is based on the *indirect object* of the equivalent active sentence.

2. Now rewrite the English passive sentence so that the subject is based on the *direct object* of the equivalent active sentence:

A bill was sent to him.

3. Translate this last sentence into German as you have done in previous sections:

Eine Rechnung wurde ihm geschickt.

4. Put the dative object of the German passive sentence at the beginning of the sentence in order to emphasize it:

Ihm wurde eine Rechnung geschickt.

You now have the closest German equivalent to the original English passive sentence.

Of course, if the English passive sentence had been based on the direct object, you would have stopped at step 3.

COMPREHENSION CHECK: *Part A: Fill in the blank with* **von** *or* **durch,** *as appropriate, and add any necessary adjective endings.*

1. Das Experiment wurde _____ ein_____ Fehler ruiniert.
2. Der Kranke wurde _____ ein_____ Arzt untersucht.

Part B: Find the closest German equivalent to the English passive sentence below by going through the four steps outlined in this section.

> *The best student was given a scholarship.*

ANSWERS: 1. durch einen 2. von einem *Part B: Step 1: They gave the best student a scholarship. Step 2: A scholarship was given to the best student. Step 3: Ein Stipendium wurde dem besten Studenten gegeben. Step 4: Dem besten Studenten wurde ein Stipendium gegeben.*

D. Impersonal Passive Sentences

A passive verb with **es** as the subject is often used to express a general activity, or an activity in which the agent is unknown. Such sentences are called *impersonal passives:*

general activity: Es wird hier nicht geraucht!
  There is no smoking here!

  Es wurde gegessen und getrunken.
  There was eating and drinking.

agent unknown: Es wurde gestern abend bei uns eingebrochen.
  There was a break-in at our place last night.

When impersonal passive sentences are expressed in their active equivalents, the subject is usually an indefinite pronoun. Compare the previous examples to the ones below:

> **Man** darf hier nicht rauchen!
> *One may not smoke here! (i.e., No smoking!)*
>
> **Man** aß und trank.
> *They ate and drank. (they = people in general)*
>
> **Jemand** ist gestern abend bei uns eingebrochen.
> *Someone broke into our place last night.*

The **es** subject of an impersonal passive sentence occurs only when the sentence begins with the subject:

> **Es** wurde irgendwo gesungen.
> *There was singing somewhere.*

The **es** disappears when some other word is put at the beginning of the sentence:

> **Irgendwo** wurde gesungen.
> *There was singing somewhere.*

Note that this sentence has no stated subject, but the verb agrees with **es,** as if it were still present in the sentence.

As was explained in the previous section, the indirect object, i.e., dative object, of an active sentence cannot be used as the subject of the equivalent passive sentence. Dative verbs, by definition, have dative objects. Therefore the object of a dative verb can never be used as the subject of a passive sentence:

active:	Man glaubte **ihnen** nicht.
	No one believed them.
incorrect passive:	***Sie** wurden nicht geglaubt.
	They were not believed.

But dative verbs can be used in passive sentences by forming an impersonal passive:

> **Es** wurde ihnen nicht geglaubt.
> *They were not believed.*

The dative object is usually put, for emphasis, at the beginning of the sentence, with subsequent loss of the **es** subject:

> **Ihnen** wurde nicht geglaubt.
> *They were not believed.*

COMPREHENSION CHECK: *Part A: Translate into English.*

1. Es wird nicht während der Prüfung gesprochen!
2. Uns wurde nicht gedankt.
3. Es wurde bis zwei Uhr getanzt.

Part B: Rewrite these active sentences as passive sentences. The agent should be dropped. Keep the same tense as the active sentence.

4. Man feiert oft in meinem Studentenheim.
5. Man gehorcht mir!
6. Man verzieh ihm niemals.

ANSWERS: 1. There is (to be) no talking during the test! 2. We were not thanked. 3. There was dancing until 2 o'clock. 4. Es wird oft in meinem Studentenheim gefeiert. *or* In meinem Studentenheim wird oft gefeiert. 5. Es wird mir gehorcht! *or*

Mir wird gehorcht! 6. Es wurde ihm niemals verziehen. *or* Ihm wurde niemals verziehen.

E. Distinguishing between True and False Passive

Note the verb forms in the German and English examples that follow:

1. Mein altes Auto **war** schon **beschädigt.**
   My old car was already damaged.

2. Mein altes Auto **wurde** durch einen Stein **beschädigt.**
   Mv old car was damaged by a rock.

Both English sentences have the same verb form but the German sentences have different auxiliary verbs. The verb form based on the auxiliary **werden** is called the *true* passive, the verb form based on **sein** is the *false* passive. The distinction between the true and false passive can be explained as follows: In the first sentence, the *condition* of the car is being described. This is analogous to saying, the car was green. German uses the *false* passive to indicate the idea of condition. By contrast, in the second sentence, something *happened* to the car and this change was brought about by an agent, in this case a rock. German uses the *true* passive to indicate that an occurrence, a change, has taken place.

A given German sentence may be grammatically correct with either **sein** or **werden** as the auxiliary verb, but the meaning will be slightly different depending on the verb form used:

false passive: Das Bild **war** verkauft.
                The picture was sold. (i.e., someone had bought the picture, it was sold already)

true passive: Das Bild **wurde** verkauft.
                The picture was sold. (i.e., someone sold the picture at that time)

One distinguishing feature of a true passive sentence is that there is an agent, even though the agent may not be explicitly stated:

Das Bild wurde **von Herrn Lunzer** verkauft.
The picture was sold by Mr. Lunzer.

COMPREHENSION CHECK: *Decide whether the sentences below involve true or false passive and then fill in the blank with the appropriate German auxiliary verb. The desired tense is given in parentheses.*

1. Ein Ball _____ durch das Fenster geworfen. *(simple past)*
2. _____ die Kleider gewaschen, die du anhast? *(present)*
3. Ich habe sie angerufen, aber die Nummer _____ besetzt. *(simple past)*
4. Kann dieses Problem gelöst _____?

ANSWERS: 1. wurde 2. Sind 3. war 4. werden

German-English Vocabulary

ab.schicken	to send off
ändern	to change
angeblich	supposedly
an.haben (hat), hatte, gehabt	to have on, to wear
an.malen	to paint
die Antwort, -en	answer
auch	also
auf.führen	to perform
auf.passen	to watch out, to pay attention
der Ball, ⸚e	ball
bauen	to build
beherrschen	to control
beißen (beißt), biß, gebissen	to bite
beschädigen	to damage
beschließen, beschloß, beschlossen	to agree upon, to decide
besetzt	busy
bezahlen	to pay
der Blitz	lightning
braten (brät), briet, gebraten	to roast
der Dankzettel, -	thank-you note
das Denkmal, ⸚er	monument
deshalb	therefore
ein.laden (lädt), lud, geladen	to invite
des Ende, -n	end
entdecken	to discover
die Ente, -n	duck
erobern	to conquer
erreichen	to reach
erwünschen	to desire, to wish for
erziehen, erzog, erzogen	to raise
das Experiment, -e	experiment
feiern	to celebrate
das Feuer, -	fire
feuern	to fire
die Frage, -n	question
füttern	to feed
genug	enough
das Gesetz, -e	law
die Gesundheit	health
hier	here
impfen	to immunize
informieren über + acc.	to inform about
irgendwo	somewhere
jemand	someone
jetzt	now
der Kinderchor, ⸚e	children's choir
die Kirche, -n	church
klatschen	to clap
kochen	to cook
der Koffer, -	suitcase
der Kommunist, -en, -en	communist
die Kreditkarte, -n	credit card
langweilig	boring
lehren	to teach
lieben	to love
die List, -en	subterfuge
lösen	to solve
morgen	tomorrow
nicht mehr	no longer
nie (mals)	never
die Nummer, -n	number
nur	only
der Patient, -en, -en	patient
photographieren	to photograph
die Rechnung, -en	bill
der Reichstag	(German) parliament
reparieren	to repair
respektieren	to respect
der Roman, -e	novel
ruinieren	to ruin
schon	already
schreien, schrie, geschrien	to scream
die Schule, -n	school
die Schwierigkeit, -en	difficulty
die Sehenswürdigkeit, -en	tourist sight
die Sinfonie, -n	symphony
stecken: in Brand stecken	to set on fire
stehen.bleiben, blieb, ist stehengeblieben	to stop

stehen, stand, ist/hat gestanden	to stand, to be (somewhere)	weg.werfen (wirft), warf, geworfen	to throw away
trinken, trank, getrunken	to drink	weinen	to cry
um.werfen, warf, geworfen	to knock over	weiter.fahren (fährt), fuhr, ist weitergefahren	to continue on
untersuchen	to examine	wer	who
verletzen	to injure	wiederholen	to repeat
versteigern	to auction off	wie	how
vorbereiten	to prepare	zählen	to count
während	while	zerbrechen (zerbricht), zerbrach, ist zerbrochen	to shatter
wann	when		
warum	why		
das Wasser	water		
wecken	to wake (someone) up	zerstören	to destroy
weg	away	zusammen.mischen	to mix together

EXERCISE 1 (prerequisite: section A, topic: reading basic passive sentences)

Translate into English.

1. Alle Sehenswürdigkeiten wurden von den Touristen fotographiert.
2. Eine Sinfonie wird gespielt.
3. Herr Meyer, Sie sind gefeuert worden!
4. Die Geschenke werden aufgemacht werden.
5. Das Experiment wurde wiederholt.
6. Dieses Gebäude war schon vor dem Krieg gebaut worden.
7. Hier wird Deutsch gesprochen.
8. Ein neuer Komet ist von einem Astronomen entdeckt worden.

EXERCISE 2 (prerequisite: section A, topic: verb-subject agreement in basic passive sentences)

Exchange the subject of each sentence with the word(s) in parentheses. Keep the tense of the sentence.

1. Warum wurde ich nicht darüber informiert? (wir, sie = *she*)
2. Er wird niemals eingeladen werden. (ich, wir)
3. Sind Sie schon geimpft worden? (du, er)
4. Man wird oft mißverstanden. (ihr, wir)
5. Die Dankzettel sind schon geschrieben worden. (der Brief)
6. Er wurde als Kind oft geschlagen. (du, ich)
7. Ein Gefangener war erschossen worden. (zwei Gefangene)
8. Das Kind wird von der Mutter erzogen. (die Kinder)

9. Warum bin ich nicht erwähnt worden? (wir, ihr)
10. Mein Koffer wurde gestohlen. (all meine Koffer)

EXERCISE 3 (prerequisite: section A, topic: tenses of basic passive sentences)

Change the tense of the verb to the tense(s) in parentheses.

1. Eine neue Sinfonie wird aufgeführt. *(simple past, present perfect, future)*
2. Dieses Denkmal wird oft fotografiert. *(present perfect, simple past, past perfect)*
3. Eine Antwort wird erwünscht. *(future)*
4. Renate wurde von einem Hund gebissen. *(present, present perfect)*
5. Der rote und der weiße Wein wurden zusammengemischt. *(present, future)*

EXERCISE 4 (prerequisite: section A, topic: basic passive sentences, comprehensive)

Using the verb and tense shown in parentheses, complete each sentence so that it forms a passive sentence. You will also have to supply all necessary auxiliary verbs.

1. Nur die besten Sachen _____ in unserem Geschäft _____. (verkaufen, *present tense*)
2. _____ meine Kreditkarte in Deutschland _____ _____? (annehmen, *future*)
3. Das Geld _____ _____ _____. (stehlen, *past perfect*)
4. Wie lange _____ dieser Fisch _____? (kochen, *simple past*)
5. In Deutschland _____ viel Bier _____. (trinken, *present*)
6. Paß auf! Du _____ _____ _____! (warnen, *present perfect*)
7. Das Haus _____ _____ _____. (reinigen, *past perfect*)
8. Diese Romane _____ von Thomas Mann _____. (schreiben, *simple past*)
9. Der Brief _____ schon _____ _____. (abschicken, *present perfect*)
10. Sie _____ oft von ihrem Sohn _____. (besuchen, *present*)
11. Diese beiden Sessel _____ _____ _____. (versteigern, *future*)
12. Mein Auto _____ _____. (reparieren, *present*)

EXERCISE 5 (prerequisite: section B, topic: passive sentences with modal verbs)

Fill in the blanks using the appropriate forms of the verbs in parentheses. Assume present tense unless otherwise indicated.

1. Die Frage _____ sofort _____ werden. (müssen, beantworten)
2. Der Patient _____ nicht mehr _____ werden. (können, retten) *(simple past)*
3. Das _____ nicht vergessen _____! (dürfen, werden)
4. Diese Schwierigkeit _____ _____ werden. (sollen, vermeiden)

5. Alle Waren _____ _____ werden. (müssen, zählen) *(simple past)*
6. _____ das vor den Kindern _____ werden? (dürfen, sagen)
7. Wann _____ die Katzen _____ werden? (sollen, füttern)
8. Das Kind _____ nur von den Eltern _____ werden. (wollen, lieben)
9. Diese Bücher _____ nicht _____ werden. (dürfen, lesen) *(simple past)*
10. Meine Verwandten müssen auch zur Hochzeit _____ _____. (einladen, werden)
11. Diese Tür _____ nicht _____ werden. (können, öffnen)
12. Das alte Kleid _____ _____ werden. (müssen, wegwerfen) *(simple past)*
13. Wann _____ Sie _____ werden? (wollen, wecken)
14. Welche Sinfonie _____ jetzt gespielt _____? (sollen, werden)

EXERCISE 6 (prerequisite: section C, topic: deciding between **von** or **durch** before the agent)

*Fill in the blank with **von** or **durch**, as appropriate, and add any necessary adjective endings.*

1. Er wurde _____ Blitz verletzt.
2. Dieses Buch wurde _____ Goethe geschrieben.
3. Unser Auto wurde _____ Hagel beschädigt.
4. Es wurde _____ Zufall entdeckt.
5. Der große Baum vor unserem Haus wurde _____ ein_____ stark_____ Wind umgeworfen.
6. Die Lieder wurden _____ ein_____ deutsch_____ Kinderchor gesungen.
7. a. Der Reichstag wurde im Jahre 1933 _____ Feuer zerstört.
   b. Der Reichstag war angeblich _____ Kommunisten in Brand gesteckt worden.
8. Die Stadt wurde _____ List erobert.

EXERCISE 7 (prerequisite: section C, topic: determining whether a passive sentence in English is based on the direct or indirect object of the active sentence)

Rewrite the English passive sentences below as active sentences. Then state whether the passive sentence is based on the direct or the indirect object of the equivalent active sentence.

1. I was given two weeks notice.
2. My sister was awarded a scholarship.
3. The prisoner was removed from the courtroom.
4. Two chickens were slaughtered.
5. The bread was cut into many pieces.
6. A bald eagle was spotted yesterday.
7. We were told an entirely different story.
8. I was sent to Africa.
9. The house was painted in three hours.
10. The business was sold stolen goods.

EXERCISE 8 (prerequisite: section C, topic: creating passive sentences in German based on direct or indirect objects)

Determine whether the English passive sentences below are based on the direct or the indirect object of the equivalent active sentence. Then translate into German.

1. The poor mother was given no rest.
2. The library was dedicated to the former mayor.
3. The child was told a story.
4. We are forbidden much.
5. The plan was shown to us.
6. All workers were told the bad news.
7. She was denied a visa.
8. The meal is being brought out.
9. He was found under a bridge.
10. I will be loaned *20,000* DM. (*note: German numbers use a period where English has a comma and vice versa.*)

EXERCISE 9 (prerequisite: section D, topic: understanding impersonal passive sentences)

Translate into English.

1. Es wurde geschrien.
2. Ihm wird nicht mehr geglaubt.
3. Die Schule war für die Kinder langweilig, aber nach der Schule wurde gespielt.
4. Seiner Gesundheit wurde geschadet.
5. Die Reisenden waren alle müde und deshalb wurde geschlafen.
6. Wir sind lange genug stehengeblieben, jetzt wird weitergefahren!

EXERCISE 10 (prerequisite: section D, topic: creating German impersonal passives)

Rewrite these active sentences as passive sentences. The agent should be dropped. Keep the same tense as the active sentence.

1. In der Kirche singt man oft.
2. Jemand folgt uns.
3. Am Ende des Konzerts klatschte man begeistert.
4. Man half dem Kranken.
5. Jemand weint irgendwo.
6. Man wird vielen Leuten danken.

EXERCISE 11

(prerequisite: section E, topic: understanding the distinction between true and false passive)

Each sentence below is correct using the two auxiliary verbs shown. Explain the difference in meaning in each case.

1. Das Haus war/wurde mit weißer Farbe angemalt.
2. Er war/wurde schlecht auf die Prüfung vorbereitet.
3. Mein Fernseher ist/wird repariert.
4. Das Glas war/wurde zerbrochen.
5. Das Zimmer war/wurde gereinigt.

EXERCISE 12

(prerequisite: section E, topic: choosing between true and false passive)

Fill in the blank with one of the two auxiliaries shown in parentheses. Only one of these is grammatically correct and/or logically plausible.

1. Diese Tür _____ die ganze Zeit geschlossen, während wir weg waren. (war/wurde)
2. Die Koffer _____ ins Zimmer gebracht. (waren/wurden)
3. Der Plan _____ schon beschlossen und kann deshalb nicht mehr geändert werden. (ist/wird)
4. Das Essen _____ in den Abfallkorb geworfen. (war/wurde)
5. Das Gebäude, in dem wir jetzt sind, _____ im Jahre 1485 gebaut. (war/wurde)
6. Dieser Kurs wird von einem neuen Lehrer gelehrt _____. (sein/werden)
7. _____ die Ente gebraten? Ja, sie steht schon auf dem Tisch. (ist/wird)
8. Die Rechnung _____ bezahlt, aber ich wußte nicht, wer sie bezahlt hatte. (war/wurde)

EXERCISE 13

(comprehensive)

Translate into German. Use a true passive or false passive verb as needed in each sentence.

1. He was attacked by two men.
2. There was much singing.
3. The city was destroyed by an earthquake.
4. This theory can easily be proved.
5. We have not been served.
6. I was not believed.
7. That is simply not done.
8. This store is closed.

9. He was given a gold watch.
10. Many people were killed by this disease.
11. A new mayor will be chosen.
12. She was told nothing.
13. The car was apparently stolen.
14. Our teacher is constantly being flattered.

GEDANKENPROBLEM: **Figure out how to say this sentence in German:**

He could no longer be believed.

What's wrong with these?

1. Dein Mantel hat gefunden worden.
2. Die Gesetze wurden nicht gehorcht.
3. Das Pferd konnte nicht sein beherrscht.
4. Morgen wird meinen Wagen verkauft werden.
5. Er wurde keine Chance gegeben.
6. Der Teppich wurde beschädigt bei Wasser.

Special Problems of German Verbs

11

A. Progressive Verb Tenses in English: German Equivalents

English has a number of verb forms characterized by a form of *to be* plus a verb with an *-ing* ending. These are called *progressive* verb tenses. The list below gives three examples:

present progressive tense:	1. He *is* work*ing* and may not be disturbed.
simple past progressive:	2. He *was* work*ing* and did not want to be disturbed.
future progressive:	3. He *will be* work*ing* soon.

German does *not* have progressive verb tenses; the above sentences would normally be expressed in German using the present, simple past (or present perfect), and future tenses respectively:

1. Er **arbeitet** und darf nicht gestört werden.

2. Er **arbeitete** und wollte nicht gestört werden.

3. Er **wird** bald **arbeiten.**

Do not try to mimic the English progressive verb tenses in German by using a form of **sein** plus the verb infinitive:

*Wer ist singen?	*Bist du kommen?
Who is singing?	*Are you coming?*
correct: Wer singt?	correct: Kommst du?

The English progressive tenses indicate an action which is, was, or will be continuing to take place. For example, consider this sentence:

He is working and may not be disturbed.

It implies that the process of working is not completed at this time. Although German has no progressive tenses as such, the idea of continuing action shown in the English sentence can be roughly conveyed in German as follows:

Er **ist beim Arbeiten** und darf nicht gestört werden.

In this sentence, **Arbeiten** is a neuter noun formed from the verb infinitive **arbeiten.** The simple past tense of the German sentence would be as follows:

Er **war beim Arbeiten** und wollte nicht gestört werden.
He was working and did not want to be disturbed.

And the future tense:

Er **wird** wohl **beim Arbeiten sein.**
He will probably be working.

An alternative to the construction **sein** + **beim** + neuter infinitive is the word **gerade;** it adds the meaning of *just (now)* in the present tense and *just (then)* in the simple past and future tense. In so doing, it also conveys the idea of the English progressive tense:

Er **arbeitet gerade** und darf nicht gestört werden.
He is working just now and may not be disturbed.

Er **arbeitete gerade** und wollte nicht gestört werden.
He was just then working and did not want to be disturbed.

To emphasize the idea of progressive tense even more in German, both constructions, i.e., **sein** + **beim** + neuter infinitive *and* **gerade,** can be employed:

Er **ist gerade beim Arbeiten** und darf nicht gestört werden.
He is working just now and may not be disturbed.

There is, however, a difference in style between these German constructions and the English progressive tenses. In English, the progressive tense *must* be used whenever the verb indicates continuing action. In German, these *special* constructions are used only to *emphasize* the idea of continuing action. In most cases, German uses simply the present tense, simple past or future tense, to translate English progressive tenses. For that reason, you should be able to recognize the meaning of such sentences when they occur. However, you should not attempt to say them until your **Sprachgefühl** for German, i.e., feeling for the language, is more developed.

COMPREHENSION CHECK: *Part A: Translate these sentences into German.*
Do not use the special constructions shown in this section, i.e., **gerade** *or* **sein** +
beim + *neuter infinitive.*

1. Is the baby sleeping?
2. Two men were repairing the car.
3. We will be waiting for you.

Part B: Translate into English.

4. Er war gerade beim Reden, als *(when)* sie ihn unterbrach.
5. Kann Erich mit uns spielen? Nein, er ist beim Lernen.
6. Sie *(they)* werden wohl beim Essen sein, wenn ich komme.

ANSWERS: 1. Schläft das Baby?   2. Zwei Männer reparierten das Auto. *or* Zwei Männer haben das Auto repariert.   3. Wir werden auf Sie warten.   4. He was just then
talking when she interrupted him.   5. Can Erich play with us? No, he is learning (i.e,
studying).   6. They will probably be eating when I come.

B. Conflicting Verb Tenses in English and German

The *progressive present perfect* tense in English indicates an action that began in the
past and is continuing into the present. The German equivalent is generally a verb in
the *present* tense.

> Ich **studiere** Deutsch seit zwei Jahren.
> *I have been studying German for two years.*

An additional problem with such sentences is that the time expression is introduced
by the preposition **seit** (plus dative case), whereas English often has the preposition
for. Do *not* write such sentences in German using the present perfect tense and do
not use **für** as the preposition before the time expression:

> *Ich **habe für** eine Woche an dieser Idee **gearbeitet.**
> *I have been working on this idea for a week.*
> correct: Ich **arbeite seit** einer Woche an dieser Idee.

The adverb **schon** is often added in such sentences for emphasis:

> Ich arbeite **schon** seit einer Woche an dieser Idee.
> *I have been working on this idea for a week.*

The preposition **seit** may also correspond to English *since* in these sentences:

> Er arbeitet **seit** sieben Uhr.
> *He has been working since seven o'clock.*

The progressive present perfect tense is often used in connection with the idea of *how long*. In German, this is indicated as follows:

Wie lange studieren Sie **schon** Deutsch?
How long have you been studying German?

The answer would take this general form:

Ich studiere Deutsch **schon lange.**

or

Ich studiere Deutsch **(schon) seit langem.**
I have been studying German for a long time.

Sometimes English uses just the present perfect tense, not the *progressive* present perfect to indicate an action that began in the past and is continuing into the present. Here, German again uses the present tense:

Ich **kenne** ihn (schon) seit vielen Jahren.
I have known him for many years.

COMPREHENSION CHECK:

Part A: Translate into English.

1. Er schläft seit heute früh.
2. Wie lange fahren wir schon?
3. Er sitzt seit einer Stunde auf diesem Stuhl.

Part B: Translate into German.

4. We have been driving for eight hours.
5. I have studied German for a year.
6. One fork has been missing since yesterday.

ANSWERS: 1. He has been sleeping since this morning. 2. How long have we been driving? 3. He has been sitting on this chair for an hour. 4. Wir fahren seit acht Stunden. 5. Ich studiere Deutsch seit einem Jahr. 6. Eine Gabel fehlt seit gestern.

C. The Problem of *for* Plus Time Expression

As shown in the previous section, the English *for* is translated by the German **seit** specifically, when the verb expresses an action that began in the past and continues into the present. However, when the action of the verb is entirely in the past, present, or future, German generally uses no preposition at all where English has *for:*

Bleiben wir ein paar Stunden hier.
Let's stay here for a few hours.

Er blieb zwei Stunden zu Hause.
He stayed at home for two hours.

Do not use **für** in such sentences:

*Sie wird **für** drei Stunden arbeiten.
She will work for three hours.
correct: Sie wird drei Stunden arbeiten.

Lang may be added to this type of sentence to give emphasis to the length of time involved:

Ich mußte zwei Tage **lang** im Flughafen warten!
I had to wait for two days in the airport!

In the example above, the time expression indicates how long the action of the verb took place. However, sometimes the time expression does *not* refer to the activity expressed by the verb. In such sentences, German does use **für** where English has *for*:

Laß die Katze **für** die Nacht hinaus!
Put the cat out for the night.

To understand the necessity for **für** in this example, consider this: you do not need the entire night to put the cat out, rather you put the cat out and then it stays there *for the night*. Thus, the time element does not actually indicate the length of the verbal activity, and German shows this fact through the preposition **für.** Here are two more examples. In the first, **für** must be used, in the second, **für** must not be used:

Der Angeklagte wurde **für drei Wochen** freigelassen.
The accused was released for three weeks.
(Note: It did not take three weeks to release him.)

Ich mußte **einige Stunden** lang auf dem harten Boden sitzen.
I had to sit on the hard floor for several hours.
(Note: The process of sitting lasted several hours.)

Another common occurrence of *for* plus the time expression in English is in constructions such as *for the first time, for the last time,* etc. The German equivalent for this is **zu** plus the time expression **Mal** *(time period):*

Ich verstehe dieses Problem **zum ersten Mal.**
I understand this problem for the first time.

Clearly, you should not use **für** in such sentences, nor can you substitute **Zeit** *(time)* instead of **Mal:**

*Jetzt hast du mich **für** die zweite **Zeit** gestört!
Now you have bothered me for the second time!
correct: Jetzt hast du mich **zum** zweiten **Mal** gestört!

COMPREHENSION CHECK: *Decide whether to use **für, seit, zum** or no preposition at all in the sentences below. To clarify the intended meaning of the German sentence, an English translation of each is given.*

1. Fahren wir _____ das Wochenende in die Berge.
Let's go to the mountains for the weekend.
2. Er schnarchte _____ sechs Stunden lang.
He snored for six hours.
3. Die Kinder spielen _____ zwei Stunden.
The children have been playing for two hours.
4. Wann hast du ihn _____ letzten Mal gesehen?
When did you see him for the last time?

ANSWERS: 1. für 2. *nothing* 3. seit 4. zum

German-English Vocabulary

ab.waschen (wäscht), wusch, gewaschen	to wash (dishes)	der Monat, -e	month
		die Mutti, -s	mom
		das Projekt, -e	project
auf.geben (gibt), gab, gegeben	to give up	rauchen	to smoke
		der Strom	electricity
aus.fallen (fällt), fiel, gefallen	to go out, to cease to operate	der Stuhl, -̈e	chair
		das Telefon, -e	telephone
bestimmt	for sure, certainly	üben	to practice
die Bundesbahn, -en	Federal Railway	übernachten	to spend the night
		die Universität, -en	university
duschen	to take a shower	unterbrechen (unterbricht), unterbrach, unterbrochen	to interrupt
fern.sehen (sieht), sah, gesehen	to watch television		
frei.lassen (läßt), ließ, gelassen	to free, to release		
		verbannen von	to expel from
der Fußball	soccer	der Verteidigungs- minister, -	defense minister
gerade	just now		
heute früh	this morning	vorgestern	day before yesterday
der Klavierspieler, -	piano player	die Vorlesung, -en	lecture
die Küche, -n	kitchen	wohl	probably
das Mal, -e	time (period)		

EXERCISE 1 (prerequisite: section A, topic: progressive verb tenses in English, German equivalents)

*Translate into German. Do not use the special constructions shown in section A, i.e., **gerade** or **sein** + **beim** + neuter verb infinitive.*

1. Why are you standing here?
2. It was raining.

3. Is this train going to Koblenz?
4. She was running.
5. We will be watching television.
6. Were you laughing or crying?

EXERCISE 2 (prerequisite: section A, topic: understanding German sentences with **gerade, sein + beim +** neuter infinitive, or both)

Translate into English.

1. Mutti ist bestimmt in der Küche beim Abwaschen.
2. Er schreibt gerade einen Brief.
3. Wir werden wohl beim Kochen sein, wenn du kommst.
4. Wir haben gerade ferngesehen, als der Strom ausgefallen ist.
5. Ich war gerade beim Duschen, als das Telefon klingelte.
6. Ist sie beim Lesen?

EXERCISE 3 (prerequisite: section B, topic: conflicting verb tense in English and German, passive knowledge)

Translate into English.

1. Er ist seit zwei Monaten der deutsche Verteidigungsminister.
2. Ein fremder Mann steht schon seit zehn Minuten vor unserem Haus.
3. Wie lange schläft sie schon?
4. Ich warte schon seit einer Stunde auf ihn.
5. Mein Vater arbeitet seit zwanzig Jahren bei der Bundesbahn.
6. Meine Freundin ist seit vorgestern auf mich böse.

EXERCISE 4 (prerequisite: section B, topic: conflicting verb tense in English and German, active knowledge)

Translate into German.

1. This tree has been growing for one hundred years.
2. How long have you known him?
3. I have known him for a long time.
4. It has been raining since seven o'clock.
5. Nora has been crying for an hour.
6. My cat has been sick for three days. (put the German word for *sick* at the end of the sentence)

EXERCISE 5 (prerequisite: section B–C, topic: *for* plus time expression)

Fill in the blank with the appropriate German words as indicated by the English words in parentheses. With a few sentences, a translation of the verb is also given in parentheses in order to clarify the intended meaning of the sentence.

1. Der Klavierspieler übte jeden Tag _____. *(for four hours)*
2. Er geht *(has been going)* _____ zu diesem Arzt. *(for several months)*
3. Ich sage es dir _____! *(for the third time)*
4. Wir gingen _____ in den Park. *(for a few hours)*
5. _____ spiele ich gern Fußball. *(for many years)*
6. Hugo schwamm _____ lang. *(for fifteen minutes)*
7. Ich habe _____ an diesem Projekt gearbeitet. *(worked) (for three years)*
8. Die Universität hat ihn _____ von allen Vorlesungen verbannt. *(for one semester)*
9. Wir wollen _____ in diesem Hotel übernachten. *(for one night)*
10. Er hat das Rauchen _____ aufgegeben. *(for always)*
11. Wir laufen *(have been running)* _____. *(for an hour)*
12. Die Arbeiter bauen *(have been building)* dieses Gebäude _____. *(for six months)*

EXERCISE 6 (comprehensive)

Translate into German. Do not use the special constructions shown in section A.

1. He has been talking since nine o'clock this morning.
2. I was thinking of you.
3. We rented a mountain cabin for a week.
4. She has been working for five days on this report.
5. Are you coming or not?
6. They laughed for ten minutes.
7. Our son will be visiting us soon.
8. When did you see this movie for the first time?
9. I have lived here for many years.
10. They slept for twelve hours.
11. How long have you been waiting?
12. My notebook was lying on the table.

GEDANKENPROBLEM: **All of the verbs in group A below would have *für* before the time expression, the verbs in group B would not. Why?**

a. *aufgeben, freilassen, verbannen, verlassen*
b. *arbeiten, bleiben, sitzen, spielen*

What's wrong with these?

Note: To help clarify the intended meaning of each sentence, an English translation is given.

1. Es schneite für drei Tage lang.
   It snowed for three days.
2. Ich habe schon für zwei Stunden auf den Arzt gewartet.
   I have been waiting for the doctor for two hours.
3. Meine Eltern werden schon sein schlafen, wenn ich nach Hause komme.
   My parents will already be sleeping when I come home.
4. Ich habe diesen Berg eben für die zweite Zeit bestiegen.
   I have just climbed this mountain for the second time.

Problems of German Word Order

12

A. The Verb in Second Position Rule

The fundamental rule of German word order is that the first verb in a main clause is in second position:

> Gestern **bin** ich in die Stadt gegangen.
> *Yesterday I went to town.*

However, second position does not necessarily mean second word:

> Der Professor **kam** in den Vorlesungssaal.
> *The professor came into the lecture hall.*

In this sentence, second position occurs immediately after the noun phrase **der Professor;** the noun phrase functions as one *grammatical unit*. The rule regarding the position of the verb will therefore be restated as follows:

> *The first verb in a main clause follows immediately after the first grammatical unit.*

The list below shows the types of elements that can function as one grammatical unit in German:

Noun phrase:

Der Professor kam in den Vorlesungssaal.
The professor came into the lecture hall.

Adverb of time, manner, *or* place:

Gestern habe ich in der Bibliothek das richtige Buch gefunden.
Yesterday I found the right book in the library.
(adverb of time)

Vorsichtig öffnete er das Paket.
He opened the package carefully.
(adverb of manner)

Dort haben wir in einem billigen Hotel übernachtet.
We spent the night there in a cheap hotel.
(adverb of place)

Noun phrase + genitive object:

Das Auto meines Nachbarn wurde beschlagnahmt.
My neighbor's car was confiscated.

Noun phrase + prepositional phrase:

Das Haus um die Ecke gehört dem Bürgermeister.
The house around the corner belongs to the mayor.

Adverbs directly modifying a noun phrase:

Sogar Herr Frenzke hatte den Film gern.
Even Mr. Frenzke liked the film.

English, in contrast to German, allows more than one grammatical unit before the verb. This may lead you to write an incorrect German sentence:

*Gestern in der Bibliothek ich habe das richtige Buch gefunden.
Yesterday in the library I found the right book.
correct: Gestern habe ich in der Bibliothek das richtige Buch gefunden.

Notice that the English sentence has three grammatical units before the verb: an adverb of time, a prepositional phrase functioning as an adverb of place, and a pronoun, i.e, noun phrase. The correct German sentence can have any of these before the verb, but no more than one.

Here is another example. The sentence below contains *only one* grammatical unit before the verb:

> **Gestern um zwei Uhr** bin ich in die Stadt gefahren.
> *Yesterday at two o'clock I went to town.*

The phrase **gestern um zwei Uhr** is one extended adverb of time and functions therefore as one grammatical unit.

In English, a word before the verb may be marked off by a comma as a stylistic device:

> *Yesterday, I went to town.*

Do not use the comma in the equivalent German sentence:

> *****Gestern,** ich bin in die Stadt gefahren.

or

> *****Gestern,** bin ich in die Stadt gefahren.
> correct: **Gestern** bin ich in die Stadt gefahren.

Similarly, do not mark off words after the verb with commas:

> *Der Mantel war, **jedoch,** zu teuer.
> *The coat was, however, too expensive.*
> correct: Der Mantel war **jedoch** zu teuer.

In three types of sentences the German verb does not, on the surface, appear to be in second position:

1.   After the interjections **ach, ja,** or **nein:**

> **Ach,** das klingt wirklich furchtbar!
> *Oh, that sounds really terrible!*

These interjections function as miniature sentences, therefore the second word is actually the beginning of a new sentence.

2.   After conjunctions, e.g., **aber** *(but),* **oder** *(or),* **und** *(and),* **entweder... oder** *(either . . . or),* **sondern** *(rather):*

> Hermann ist mein Bruder, **und Ilse ist** meine Schwester.

Conjunctions connect sentences; they are not a part of the sentences themselves and therefore do not count as a grammatical unit in those sentences.

3.   When the second grammatical unit restates the first:

> Unser Professor, **Doktor Lehmann,** kam in den Vorlesungssaal.
> *Our professor, Doctor Lehmann, came into the lecture hall.*

Note that German *does* use commas in this last type of sentence. For the sake of contrast, consider the incorrect sentence below:

*Unser Professor, **meiner Meinung nach,** ist sehr kompetent.
Our professor, in my opinion, is very competent.
correct: Unser Professor ist **meiner Meinung nach** sehr kompetent.

The second grammatical unit does not restate the first, therefore only one of these can precede the verb.

COMPREHENSION CHECK: *Rearrange the word groups into meaningful sentences. Do not change any words. The first word(s) listed should begin the sentence.*

1. Vielleicht/nächste Woche/es/wird/regnen.
2. Das älteste Gebäude/unserer Universität/mußte/niedergerissen/werden.
3. Nur/eine Person/kann/helfen/lhnen.
4. Bald/in unserer Stadt/wir/werden/haben/einen Park.
5. Eine neue Methode/für diese Operation/wurde/entwickelt.
6. Manchmal/ich/will/einfach/im Bett/bleiben.

ANSWERS: 1. Vielleicht wird es nächste Woche regnen. 2. Das älteste Gebäude unserer Universität mußte niedergerissen werden. 3. Nur eine Person kann Ihnen helfen. 4. Bald werden wir in unserer Stadt einen Park haben. 5. Eine neue Methode für diese Operation wurde entwickelt. 6. Manchmal will ich einfach im Bett bleiben.

B. Word Order in the Middle Field

The middle field in German is the part of the sentence after the first verb and before the verb(s) at the end of the sentence (if no end verbs are present then the middle field extends to the end of the sentence). For example, the middle field of the sentence below is marked in boldface:

Ich muß **meinen Eltern bald einen Brief** schreiben.
I have to write my parents a letter soon.

Word order in the middle field often differs from that in the corresponding English sentence. A good example of this is the time-manner-place rule, namely:

In German, grammatical units indicating time, manner, and place, when they occur in the middle field, are normally in that order.

Geh sofort nach Hause! (time, place)
Go home immediately! (place, time)

Wir fuhren mit dem Zug in die Schweiz. (manner, place)
We went to Switzerland by train. (place, manner)

Note that the English sentences reverse the order of the elements in the middle field.

Other examples where German word order in the middle field is different from that of English are listed below:

1. Predicate adjectives and predicate nominatives usually go to the end of the middle field in German:

   Ich bin ihm trotz seiner Entschuldigung immer noch **böse.**
   I am still angry at him in spite of his apology.

   Er wird nächsten Monat **Bundeskanzler** werden.
   He will become federal chancellor next month.

If the predicate adjective or nominative is a *dominant* word determining a prepositional phrase, the prepositional phrase can go before or after the dominant word:

   Ich bin **stolz auf dich.**

or

   Ich bin **auf dich stolz.**
   I am proud of you.

2. When a prepositional phrase is determined by a *dominant verb,* the prepositional phrase tends to go to the end of the middle field:

   Sie **arbeitet** seit einer Woche **an ihrem Aufsatz.**
   She has been working on her essay for a week.

3. When the subject of the sentence appears directly beside a pronoun, the pronoun often goes first:

   Morgen bringt **mir** der Milchmann die Milch.
   Tomorrow the milkman will bring me the milk.

This can even occur if two pronouns are present:

   Morgen bringt **es mir** mein Onkel.
   Tomorrow my uncle will bring it to me.

The above rule includes the reflexive pronoun **sich:**

   Wo erkälteten **sich** die Kinder?
   Where did the children catch cold?

Some aspects of German word order in the middle field are similar to word order in English:

1. If the direct and indirect object are both pronouns, the direct object goes first:

   Gib es ihr.
   Give it to her.

2. If either the direct or indirect object is a pronoun, the pronoun goes first:

Gib ihr das Buch.
Give her the book.
(indirect object first)

Gib es der Frau.
Give it to the woman.
(direct object first)

3. If both the direct and indirect object are nouns, the indirect object goes first:

Gib der Frau das Buch.
Give the woman the book.

4. When the subject is a pronoun after the verb, it precedes the direct and indirect object:

Morgen gebe **ich** der Frau das Buch.
Tomorrow I will give the woman the book.

None of the rules listed in this section are absolutes; they merely represent the most likely pattern. Deviations from these rules are discussed in the next section.

COMPREHENSION CHECK: *Assemble these groups of words into meaningful sentences. The first word(s) listed should begin your sentence.*

1. Du/mußt/sein/am Bahnhof/um zehn Uhr.
2. Die Ökonomie/schlecht/ist/jetzt.
3. Bist/du/erstaunt/über meinen Entschluß?
4. Er/glaubt/bestimmt/an diese Religion.
5. Wann/hat/geschickt/dein Freund/dir/diesen Brief?
6. Ich/mußte/bezahlen/500 DM/diesem Geschäft.

ANSWERS: 1. Du mußt um zehn Uhr am Bahnhof sein.   2. Die Ökonomie ist jetzt schlecht.   3. Bist du erstaunt über meinen Entschluß? *or* Bist du über meinen Entschluß erstaunt?   4. Er glaubt bestimmt an diese Religion.   5. Wann hat dir dein Freund diesen Brief geschickt?   6. Ich mußte diesem Geschäft 500 DM bezahlen.

C. Variations from Normal Word Order

German allows a great deal of flexibility in the order of words in the middle field. In general, the grammatical unit at the *end* of the middle field is being emphasized. For example, notice how two different questions can produce two answers which differ only in the word order:

first question:	**Was** haben Sie heute gesehen? *What did you see today?*
answer:	Wir haben heute **das Mozartdenkmal** gesehen. *We saw the Mozart monument today.*
second question:	**Wann** haben Sie das Mozartdenkmal gesehen? *When did you see the Mozartdenkmal?*
answer:	Wir haben das Mozartdenkmal **heute** gesehen. *We saw the Mozart monument today.*

In these sentences, the key words, that is, the words which answer the question, are put at the end of the middle field for emphasis. Alternatively, as with English, German may emphasize a word simply by a rise in intonation and no change in word order.

In the previous section, various rules were given which put certain types of grammatical units at the end of the middle field, e.g., predicate adjectives. Looking at these rules from the viewpoint of this section, a predicate adjective tends to go to the end of the middle field because it is the most important grammatical unit there. When that importance no longer holds, however, the rules are changed. For example, the indirect object usually goes before the direct object when both are nouns. But consider the sentence below:

Er gab das Fahrrad **meiner Schwester** (und nicht meinem Bruder).
He gave the bicycle to my sister (and not to my brother).

The change in word order from the norm is necessitated by the need to emphasize **Schwester.** The above sentence might be in answer to this question:

Wem gab er das Fahrrad?
To whom did he give the bicycle?

This section can only give you a sense of how German word order is used for emphasis. As with the last section, the rules discussed here are not absolute.

COMPREHENSION CHECK: *Rearrange the groups of words into meaningful sentences so as to form an answer to the German sentence given. The first word listed should begin the sentence and the word that specifically answers the question should be emphasized.*

1. Wem geben Sie meistens ihre Stimme?
   Ich/den Sozialdemokraten/gebe/meine Stimme.
2. Wann hat er ihr den Ring geschenkt?
   Er/hat/geschenkt/den Ring/voriges Jahr/ihr.
3. Wem hast du unser Geheimnis gesagt?
   Ich/habe/gesagt/nur ihm/unser Geheimnis.

D. The Position of *Nicht* in the Middle Field

The German word **nicht** *(not)* can go almost anywhere in the middle field, but in the simplest case, **nicht** goes after any objects and *specific* time expressions and before everything else. The example that follows shows **nicht** after the indirect and direct object of the sentence:

> Ich konnte meinem Lehrer den Aufsatz **nicht** einreichen.
> *I was not able to hand in the essay to my teacher.*

In the next example, **nicht** is seen *after* a specific time expression but *before* a non-specific time expression:

> Du darfst morgen **nicht** lange schlafen.
> *You can't sleep for a long time tomorrow.*

However, **nicht** always goes before a word specifically negated, regardless of the rule just given:

> Sie hat **nicht mich** gern, sondern dich!
> *She doesn't like me, she likes you!*

Note: The word specifically negated is *stressed* in English (say the English sentence in the previous example to yourself).

Here is another example in which **nicht** is in its "normal" position:

> Warum haben Sie ihm den Vertrag **nicht** geschickt?
> *Why didn't you send him the contract?*

In this example, the **nicht** comes after the objects and negates the verb. Compare the example to the one below:

> Warum haben Sie ihm **nicht den Vertrag** geschickt?
> *Why didn't you send him the contract? (i.e., instead of what you did send)*

The sentence has the same translation in English, but the emphasis is on *contract*.

COMPREHENSION CHECK: *Each of the sentences below has the following English translation:*

> *Didn't you call him from the hotel last night?*

Identify the emphasized word(s) in each sentence.

1. Hast du ihn gestern abend vom Hotel nicht angerufen?
2. Hast du ihn gestern abend nicht vom Hotel angerufen?

3. Hast du ihn nicht gestern abend vom Hotel angerufen?
4. Hast du nicht ihn gestern abend vom Hotel angerufen?
5. Hast nicht du ihn gestern abend vom Hotel angerufen?

ANSWERS: 1. angerufen 2. vom Hotel 3. gestern abend 4. ihn 5. du

German-English Vocabulary

ab.sagen	to call off	die Grippe, -n	flu
angewiesen auf + acc.	dependent on	die Gruppe, -n	group
		halten: jemanden	to hold: to
die Angst, ⁻e	fear	für etwas halten	consider
die Antwort, -en auf + acc.	answer to	(hält), hielt, gehalten	someone to be something
auf alle Fälle	no matter what	heiraten	to marry
ausgerechnet (mir)	(to me) of all persons	heute	today
		die Hilfe	help
die Auszeichnung, -en	commendation	hoffentlich	hopefully
		holen	to get, to fetch
bald	soon	immer	always
die Banane, -n	banana	interessieren für (reflexive)	to be interested in
beichten	confess		
bekommen	to get, to receive	kompliziert	complicated
besonders	especially	die Kunst, ⁻e	art
bestrafen	to punish	Kurs: einen Kurs machen	course: to take a course
die Bombe, -n	bomb		
der Chef, -s	boss	lange	a long time
das Darleihen, -	loan	leider	unfortunately
das Dorf, ⁻er	village	liefern	to deliver
dort	there	leise	softly
engstirnig	narrow-minded	manchmal	sometimes
erinnern an + acc. (reflexive)	to remember	meinen	to mean
		meistens	mostly, usually
der Entschluß, ⁻sse	decision	die Methode, -n	method
entweder... oder	either... or	der Mittag, -e	noon
erklären	to explain	möglich	possible
erkranken an + dat.	to become sick with	nieder.reißen, riß, gerissen	to tear down
erzählen	to tell	die Ökonomie, -n	economy
etwas	some	die Operation, -en	operation
fertig	finished	die Presse, -n	press
freiwillig	voluntarily	das Prinzip, plural Prinzipien	principle
das Geheimnis, -nisse	secret		
		scheu bei	shy with
die Geschichte, -n	story	schicken	to send
gestern abend	yesterday evening, last night	schulden	to owe
		selbst	even
glücklich	happy	selten	seldom

der Sommer, -	summer	der Vertreter, -	representative
der Sozialdemokrat, -en, -en	social democrat	vieles	much
		vielleicht	perhaps
spazieren.gehen, ging, gegangen	to take a walk	vor allem	above all
		vorsichtig	carefully
die Stellage, -n	shelf	vor.stellen (reflexive)	to imagine
die Stimme, -n	vote	die Wahrscheinlichkeit, -en	probability
die Sünde, -n	sin		
die Tochter, ⁓	daughter	wahrscheinlich	probably
traurig	sad	Weihnachten	Christmas
treffen (trifft), traf, getroffen	to meet	wem (dative)	to whom
		wieder	again
tun, tat, getan	to do	Wien	Vienna
überhaupt nicht	not at all	die Woche, -n	week
übermorgen	day after tomorrow	die Zentralbank, -en	Central Bank
um.bringen (mixed verb)	to kill, to murder		
		zweit	second
versprechen (verspricht), versprach, versprochen	to promise		

EXERCISE 1 (prerequisite: section A, topic: verb in second position rule)

Rearrange the groups of words into meaningful sentences. The first word(s) listed should go first in your sentence.

1. Morgen/wir/fahren/nach Hause.
2. Übermorgen/hoffentlich/ich/bin/in Europa.
3. Die Gründe/dafür/sind/kompliziert.
4. Heute/im Bahnhof/wurde/gefunden/eine Bombe.
5. Die Antwort/auf diese Frage/steht/nicht im Buch.
6. Am Ende/des Sommers/sie/war/immer/traurig.
7. Selbst/Oskar/ist/gekommen.
8. Entweder/ist/es/heiß/oder/bin/ich/krank.
9. Herr Helm/unser Vertreter/wird/anrufen/Sie.
10. Gerade/in dem Augenblick/er/ist/gekommen.
11. Nein/du/darfst nicht/hinausgehen.
12. Das Konzert/leider/wurde/abgesagt.
13. Vor allem/ich/brauche/das Geld.
14. Neben den Äpfeln/in der zweiten Stellage/Sie/werden/finden/die Bananen.
15. Selbst/eine Nacht/in diesem Hotel/war/uns zu teuer.

EXERCISE 2 (prerequisite: section B, topic: word order in the middle field)

Form meaningful sentences using these groups of words. The first group should begin the sentence.

1. Ich/glücklich/werde/sein/nie wieder.
2. Er/fährt/nach Hause/bald.
3. Stell das Glas/vorsichtig/auf den Tisch.
4. Ich/habe/ein neues Kleid/versprochen/meiner Tochter.
5. Er/soll/werden/nächste Woche/Vater.
6. Hoffentlich/wird/die Zentralbank/mir/das Darleihen/geben.
7. Wirst/du/ihm/es/sagen?
8. Ich/bin/fertig/jetzt.
9. Der Chef/hat/gegeben/Herrn Klein/eine zweite Chance.
10. Klara/war/von der Idee/begeistert.
11. Sie/hat/gewartet/auf ihn/den ganzen Tag.
12. Sprechen Sie/bitte/leise/in der Bibliothek.
13. Er/schuldet/etwas Geld/mir.
14. Du/bist/dafür/zu jung.
15. Ich/kann mich/an seinen Namen/nicht mehr/erinnern.

EXERCISE 3 (prerequisite: section C, topic: word order for emphasis)

Underline the German words being emphasized. Then translate the sentence into English.

1. Erzählen Sie die Geschichte den Kindern.
2. Warum mußte er diese Arbeit ausgerechnet mir geben?
3. Er interessiert sich für die moderne Kunst seit mehreren Jahren.
4. Er hat seine Sünden dem Fremden gebeichtet.
5. Mein Mann achtete auf meine Meinung fast überhaupt nicht.
6. Sie werden dort um elf Uhr am Abend ankommen.
7. Warum bist du immer scheu bei mir?
8. Stell dir vor, sie haben die Auszeichnung ihm gegeben!

EXERCISE 4 (prerequisite: sections A–C, comprehensive)

Rearrange these word groups into meaningful sentences. Words in boldface should be put in emphasized position, otherwise use standard word order. Your sentence should begin with the first word group listed.

1. Wann/fährst/du/nach Hause/heute?
2. In zwei Stunden/ich/bin/fertig.
3. Ich/sehr müde/bin/nach dieser Arbeit.

4. Diesen Pullover/hat/**meine Großmutter**/mir/zu Weihnachten/geschickt.
5. Die meisten Leute/in diesem Dorf/sind/engstirnig.
6. Besonders/Ulrike/wollte/sehen/das Schloß.
7. Wir/liefern/alles/unseren Kunden.
8. Der Wissenschaftler/hat/**der Presse**/erklärt/das Prinzip.
9. In Deutschland/wir/sind/spazierengegangen/oft.
10. Er/ist/angewiesen/auf das Geld/seiner Frau.
11. Das Buch/ein Kriminalroman/war besonders/interessant.
12. Voriges Jahr/zu dieser Zeit/wir/waren/in Holland.
13. Ich/auf alle Fälle/**ihn**/will/heiraten.
14. Er/selten/erkrankte/an der Grippe.
15. Ich/in München/habe/getroffen/**meinen alten Freund.**

EXERCISE 5 (prerequisite: section D, topic: position of **nicht**)

*Negate each sentence with **nicht** in at least two different places in the middle field. Be prepared to explain the difference in meaning in both cases.*

1. Wir sind mit einer Gruppe durch Europa gereist.
2. Hast du meine Schuhe unter dem Bett gesehen?
3. Er wurde gestern bestraft.
4. Viele Studenten haben diesen Kurs freiwillig gemacht.
5. Ich habe dich gemeint.
6. Wir halten ihn für einen Narren.
7. Sie hat ihn aus Angst umgebracht.
8. Er dankte dem jungen Mann für seine Hilfe.
9. Wir haben unsere Koffer in Mexiko verloren.
10. Ich habe lange geschlafen.

EXERCISE 6 (comprehensive)

*Redo exercise 4, this time adding **nicht** to each sentence. Be prepared to explain the meaning of the sentence depending on where you decide to put the **nicht** (assuming there is a choice).*

EXERCISE 7 (comprehensive)

Translate into German. Emphasized words are in italics.

1. I was, nevertheless, not certain.
2. Children become adults so quickly!
3. We will buy a new car *very soon*.
4. Were you in Poland during the war?
5. They can't come today.

6. Our team lost again last night.
7. Unfortunately, his invention, a new mousetrap, was too expensive.
8. No, I showed *no one* the money.
9. He asked about you yesterday.
10. I don't want *this* table.
11. Even I became seasick during the trip.
12. Sometimes she doesn't wait for me.
13. Why did the doctor send us this bill?
14. As a consequence, we need better schools.

GEDANKENPROBLEM: **Explain what is going on in the German sentence below:**

Ich habe ihn nicht gehaßt, aber geliebt habe ich ihn auch nicht.

What's wrong with these?

1. Der neue Chef, in aller Wahrscheinlichkeit, wird vieles ändern.
2. Vielleicht, wir können es für Sie tun.
3. Heute zu Mittag im Park habe ich mein Geld verloren.
4. Entweder Traudi kann das Essen für uns holen, oder werde ich es tun.
5. Wahrscheinlich in Wien wir werden ein gutes Wiener Schnitzel bekommen.
6. Wir wollten kommen, aber es war, leider, nicht möglich.

Review Exercises Chapters 10–12

EXERCISE 1

Translate these sentences into German. Use standard word order unless a word is emphasized in italics.

1. A watch was found by a student.
2. She was writing a letter.
3. No, I didn't see her today.
4. Many cities were annihilated by the blitzkrieg.
5. After the main dish, the dessert was, unfortunately, a disappointment.
6. When were you in Germany for the first time?
7. The stranger could not be understood.
8. Where did his parents find him?
9. The package will soon be opened.
10. He has been painting the house for three hours.
11. After the storm, the house was damaged.
12. We didn't order *that!*
13. You were told everything.
14. How long have you been standing here?
15. Above all, this accomplishment must be rewarded.
16. She was finally forgiven.
17. Why did you tell *her* that?
18. In this fraternity, there is always a lot of drinking. *(use a passive construction)*
19. Hanna hoped for his return for many years.
20. The plan had been changed.
21. They have been working since noon.
22. I owe *the bank* the money, not the homeowner.
23. I want a job for the summer.
24. Have you been given a copy of the test?

What's wrong with these?

1. Unser Essen war leider vom Hund gefressen.
2. Die Prüfung wird, hoffentlich, nicht schwer sein.
3. Er saß für zwei Stunden auf dem Boden.
4. Der Ball wurde bei einem kleinen Kind geworfen.
5. Sie waren spielen Fußball.
6. Eines Tages, bestimmt, ich werde dem Chef meine Meinung sagen!
7. Beethovens neunte Sinfonie hat so oft gespielt worden.
8. Vor allem, du darfst deinen Regenschirm nicht vergessen.
9. Morgen ich bin für das letzte Mal Student.
10. Wurdest du für deine Hilfe gedankt?
11. Sie hat für eine Stunde geschlafen und soll in zwei Stunden geweckt sein.
12. Die Touristen waren gezeigt das Schloß.

Subordinate Clauses

13

A. Introduction to Subordinate Clauses

For reference, all of the subordinate conjunctions used in this chapter are listed here:

als	*as, while*	nachdem	*after*
bevor	*before*	obgleich	*although*
bis	*until*	obwohl	*although*
da	*since (for that reason)*	seitdem	*since (that time)*
		sobald	*as soon as*
daß	*that*	solange	*as long as*
ehe	*before*	während	*while*
es sei denn, daß	*unless*	weil	*because*
falls	*in case*	wenn	*if, when*
indem	*by (doing something)*		
je... desto (um so)	*the... the*		

In addition to the above, the following interrogative words also function as subordinate conjunctions when used in indirect questions:

ob	*if, whether*	wem *(dative)*	*who(m)*	wie	*how*
wann	*when*	wen *(accusative)*	*who(m)*	wieso	*why*
warum	*why*	wer *(nominative)*	*who*	wieviel	*how much*
was	*what*	wessen *(genitive)*	*whose*	wo	*where*

The subordinate conjunctions **ehe** and **obgleich** are more formal than **bevor** and **obwohl** respectively, but otherwise are identical in meaning and usage. The rules outlined below explain the main features of sentences with subordinate conjunctions:

1. The conjugated verb in the subordinate clause must go to the end of the clause:

    Ich habe nichts gegessen, weil ich abnehmen **muß.**
    I didn't eat anything, because I have to lose weight.

2. If the subordinate clause is the first part of the sentence, then the second part (the main clause) must begin with the conjugated verb of that clause:

    Solange du nicht um Verzeihung bittest, **werde** ich nicht mit dir reden.
    As long as you don't ask for forgiveness, I will not talk to you.

Note: In effect, the entire subordinate clause functions as the first element of the sentence, hence the verb in the main clause is in second position.

3. If the verb at the end of the subordinate clause has a separable prefix, then the prefix is attached to it:

    Wir gingen in ein Restaurant, bevor der Film **anfing.**
    We went to a restaurant before the movie began.

4. The subordinate clause must be separated from the main clause by a comma (see examples above).

The meanings of the subordinate conjunctions **indem** and **je... desto (um so)** may not be clear to you from the short translation given in the previous list. The examples below should clarify the meanings:

Indem

Indem sie mit dem Fahrrad fuhr, blieb sie fit.
By riding her bicycle, she stayed fit.

Er sparte das Geld für das Haus, indem er auch abends arbeitete.
He saved the money for the house by also working evenings.

Je... Desto (Um So)

Je früher wir morgen aufstehen, **desto (um so)** früher kommen wir an.
The earlier we get up tomorrow, the earlier we'll arrive.

Je länger ich den Stoff studiere, **desto (um so)** besser begreife ich ihn.
The longer I study the material, the better I understand it.

Desto is slightly more common than **um so,** but either can be used.

The German word **denn** has basically the same meaning as **weil,** but in spite of that fact, **denn** does not function as a subordinate conjunction, i.e., **denn** does not make the verb go to the end of the clause:

> Unser Wagen konnte nicht weiterfahren, **denn** der Tank **war** leer.
> *Our car could not go any farther, because the tank was empty.*

In fact, **denn** is a *coordinating* conjunction and thus functions like **und, aber, oder,** etc. As a result, **denn** does not count as the first element in a clause. In the example above, **der Tank** is the first element, and the verb comes after.

A common mistake with subordinate clauses is using the infinitive form of the verb rather than the conjugated verb:

> *Der Arzt muß in der Nähe eines Telefons bleiben, weil es zu jeder Zeit einen Notfall geben **können.**
> *The doctor has to stay near a telephone because there can be an emergency at any time.*
> correct: Der Arzt muß in der Nähe eines Telefons bleiben, weil **es** zu jeder Zeit einen Notfall geben **kann.**

This mistake occurs because it is easy to forget the connection between the subject and the verb when they are so far apart from each other.

COMPREHENSION CHECK: *Part A: Insert in the blank the German subordinate conjunction which corresponds to the English word in parentheses.*

1. Herr Fischer paßte auf das Baby auf, _____ seine Frau von der Arbeit zurückkam. *(until)*
2. Ich lasse den Schlüssel unter der Matte, _____ du ins Haus gehen willst. *(in case)*

Part B: Rearrange these words into meaningful sentences. The break between the subordinate and main clause is indicated by the two slashes.

3. Während/du/kaufst/die Fahrkarten//ich/hole/die Koffer.
4. Daß/er/ist/ein schlechter Mensch//ich/kann/nicht/glauben.
5. Sobald/die Kinder/stehen/auf//sie/müssen/das eigene Bett/machen.

Part C: Insert in the blank the correct present-tense form of the verb in parentheses.

6. Ich muß jetzt lernen, weil ich morgen auf der Uni eine schwere Prüfung _____. (haben)

ANSWERS: 1. bis   2. falls   3. Während du die Fahrkarten kaufst, hole ich die Koffer.   4. Daß er ein schlechter Mensch ist, kann ich nicht glauben.   5. Sobald die Kinder aufstehen, müssen sie das eigene Bett machen.   6. habe

B. Interrogative Words Used as Subordinate Conjunctions

The interrogative words listed in section A serve as subordinate conjunctions when used in indirect questions. As with any subordinate clause, the verb goes to the end of the clause in indirect questions, and the main clause is separated from the subordinate clause by a comma. The examples below illustrate the differences between a direct and an indirect question:

direct question: **Warum hat** er das getan?
                       Why did he do that?

indirect question: Weiß irgendjemand, **warum** er das getan **hat?**
                       Does anyone know why he did that?

direct question: **Wo kann** ich das Meldeamt finden?
                       Where can I find the bureau of registry?

indirect question: Können Sie mir sagen, **wo** ich das Meldeamt finden **kann?**
                       Can you tell me where I can find the bureau of registry?

Whether the question is direct or indirect, **wer** (nominative), **wen** (accusative) and **wem** (dative) reflect the case of the interrogative pronoun in the clause. An example of each is shown below in indirect questions:

nominative: Weißt du, **wer** er ist?
              Do you know who he is?

accusative: Weißt du, **wen** ich gesehen habe?
              Do you know who(m) I saw?

dative: Weißt du, **wem** er das Geld gegeben hat?
              Do you know who(m) he gave the money to?

Wessen is the genitive form of the interrogative pronoun; it corresponds to English *whose* in direct and indirect questions:

genitive: Jeder weiß, **wessen** Frau sie ist.
              Everyone knows whose wife she is.

COMPREHENSION CHECK: *Part A: Fill in the blank with the German interrogative word that corresponds to the English word in parentheses.*

1.   Wissen Sie, _____ der Bahnhof liegt? *(where)*
2.   Der Polizist fragte, _____ mein Geld gestohlen hatte. *(who)*
3.   Niemand weiß, _____ er gemeint hat. *(who)*

Part B: Rearrange the groups of words in the second part of the sentence so as to form a meaningful indirect question.

4.   Ich kann nicht begreifen, warum/er/ist/auf mich/zornig.

5.   Adam wollte seiner Frau nicht sagen, wieviel Geld/er/hatte/verspielt.

ANSWERS: 1. wo   2. wer   3. wen   4. warum er auf mich zornig ist   5. wieviel Geld er verspielt hatte.

C. *Als, Ob, Wann,* and *Wenn*

The meanings of the subordinate conjunctions **als, ob, wann,** and **wenn** pose a number of problems. They translate the English subordinate conjunctions *when, when(ever), if,* and *whether,* but the relationship between the German words and the English words is complicated. The chart below summarizes this relationship.

ENGLISH	GERMAN	USAGE
	als	past tense only, never in the meaning of *whenever*
when	wenn	present and future tenses only
	wann	all tenses, must be used in direct and indirect questions
when(ever) —	wenn	all tenses
if, whether —	wenn	all tenses, never in the meaning of *whether*
whether —	ob	all tenses

Note: *Whenever* is often shortened to *when* in English and the word *if* is often used in the meaning of *whether.* In German, these meanings must be kept distinct from each other.

Examples:

Ich war unter der Dusche, **als** die Türglocke geläutet hat.
I was in the shower when the doorbell rang.
(meaning: *when,* past tense only, one time occurrence)

Wenn das Seminar aus ist, sag es mir.
When the seminar is over, tell me.
(meaning: *when,* used in present and future tenses)

Wißt ihr, **wann** das Seminar aus ist?
Do you know when the seminar is over?
(meaning: *when,* must be used in all direct and indirect questions and only then)

184   SUBORDINATE CLAUSES

Ich war immer unter der Dusche, **wenn** die Türglocke geläutet hat.
I was always in the shower when(ever) the doorbell rang.
(meaning: *when* in the sense of *whenever*, i.e., an action that occurs repeatedly, any tense)

Wenn das wahr ist, können Sie weggehen.
If that is true, you can leave.
(meaning: *if*, cannot be used in the meaning of *whether*)

Könnt ihr mir sagen, **ob** das wahr ist?
Can you tell me if (whether) that is true?
(meaning: *if*, *whether*, must be used when *whether* could be substituted for *if*)

COMPREHENSION CHECK: *Fill in the blank with the correct German subordinate conjunction corresponding to the English word in parentheses.*

1. Die Nachbarn sind neugierig, _____ die neue Mieterin anständig ist. *(if)*
2. _____ der Lehrer ins Klassenzimmer kam, mußten alle Schüler immer aufstehen. *(when)*
3. _____ ich das Stipendium bekomme, kann ich auf der Uni Biologie studieren. *(if)*
4. Die Nazis kamen an die Macht, _____ mein Vater zwanzig Jahre alt war. *(when)*
5. Die Bevölkerung wird froh sein, _____ der Wahlkampf endlich vorbei ist. *(when)*
6. Wissen Sie, _____ Ihr Kind geimpft wurde? *(when)*

ANSWERS: 1. ob 2. Wenn 3. Wenn 4. als 5. wenn 6. wann

D. *After, Before, Since, That:* German Equivalents

The English words *after*, *before*, and *since* have a number of German equivalents depending on whether the word is a subordinate conjunction, preposition, or an adverb. In the case of *since*, the exact *meaning* of the word also makes a difference. The chart below summarizes the various possibilities and the examples after the table show each form in an actual sentence.

SUBORDINATE CONJUNCTION		PREPOSITION		ADVERB	
German	*English*	*German*	*English*	*German*	*English*
bevor	*before*	vor	*before*	vorher	*before*
nachdem	*after*	nach	*after*	nachher	*afterward*

SUBORDINATE CONJUNCTION		PREPOSITION		ADVERB	
German	*English*	*German*	*English*	*German*	*English*
seitdem	*since* (time)	seit	*since*	seitdem	*since then*
da	*since* (reason)	——	——	——	——

before:

Putz dir die Zähne, **bevor** du zu Bett gehst!
Brush your teeth before you go to bed.
(subordinate conjunction)

Ich habe sie mir **vorher** geputzt.
I brushed them before (earlier).
(adverb)

Du mußt **vor** elf Uhr wieder zu Hause sein.
You have to be back home before eleven o'clock.
(preposition)

after, afterward:

Nachdem wir am Abend gegessen haben, machen wir gewöhnlich einen Spaziergang.
After we have eaten in the evening, we usually take a walk.
(subordinate conjunction)

Nach dem Abendessen machen wir gewöhnlich einen Spaziergang.
After dinner we usually take a walk.
(preposition)

Nachher haben wir einen Spaziergang gemacht.
Afterward we took a walk.
(adverb)

since, since then:

Seitdem unsere Katze gestorben ist, ist unser Haus voll von Mäusen.
Since our cat died, our house is full of mice.
(meaning: *since that time,* subordinate conjunction)

Da unsere Katze gestorben ist, ist unser Haus voll von Mäusen.
Since our cat died, our house is full of mice.
(meaning: *for that reason, because,* subordinate conjunction)

Seit dem Tod unserer Katze ist unser Haus voll von Mäusen.
Since the death of our cat, our house is full of mice.
(preposition)

Vor drei Monaten ist unsere Katze gestorben. **Seitdem** ist unser Haus voll von Mäusen.
Three months ago our cat died. Since then our house has been full of mice.
(adverb)

The English word *that* also presents some problems. When used as a subordinate conjunction, the German equivalent is **daß;** when used as a demonstrative pronoun, the equivalent is **das:**

Ich wußte, **daß** er kommen wollte.
I knew that he wanted to come.
(subordinate conjuction)

Ich wußte **das.**
I knew that.
(demonstrative pronoun)

To distinguish between the two, note that the demonstrative pronoun can be replaced by *it* in English or **es** in German with little change in meaning:

Ich wußte **es.**
I knew it.

But this cannot be done with the subordinate conjunction.

Finally, *in English,* the subordinate conjunction *that* can be combined with other subordinate conjunctions:

*I found it strange **that whenever** my uncle came to visit, my father always disappeared.*

In German, by contrast, **daß** cannot be combined directly with other subordinate conjunctions:

*Ich fand es merkwürdig, **daß wenn** mein Onkel zu Besuch kam mein Vater immer verschwand.

In principle, this problem can be solved in the following fashion:

correct: Ich fand es merkwürdig, **daß, wenn** mein Onkel zu Besuch kam, mein Vater immer verschwand.

In other words, the sentence is resolved into two subordinate clauses. However, this German sentence sounds somewhat awkward. A better solution is to completely separate the two subordinate clauses:

correct: Ich fand es merkwürdig, **daß** mein Vater immer verschwand, **wenn** mein Onkel zu Besuch kam.

COMPREHENSION CHECK: *Fill in the blank with the German word corresponding to the English word in parentheses.*

1. a. Nach acht Stunden war er so hungrig, _____ er mehrere Wiener Schnitzel aß. *(that)*
   b. Warum hast du _____ gesagt? *(that)*
2. a. Wo haben Sie _____ gewohnt? *(before)*
   b. _____ Sie die Prüfung beginnen, will ich zuerst einige Anweisungen geben. *(before)*
3. a. _____ ich eine neue Brille gekriegt habe, kann ich viel besser sehen. *(since) (that time)*
   b. Wir haben das Restaurant verlassen, _____ das Essen zu teuer war. *(since) (because)*

ANSWERS: 1. a. daß b. das 2. a. vorher b. Bevor 3. a. Seitdem b. da

German-English Vocabulary

Learn the subordinate conjunctions listed on page 180, the words given in the table on pages 185–186, and the following:

die Abreise, -n	departure
die Ahnung, -en	idea
anständig	respectable
die Anweisung, -en	direction
der Aufenthalt, -e	stay
auf.passen auf + acc.	to take care of
aus.brechen (bricht), brach, gebrochen	to begin, to break out
das Baby, -s	baby
der Befehl, -e	command
beschlagnahmen	to confiscate
beschreiben, beschrieb, beschrieben	to describe
bestimmen	to determine
die Bevölkerung, -en	population
die Biologie	biology
bloß	merely
die Brille, -n	eyeglasses
der Bürgermeister, -	mayor
chemisch	chemical
dick	thick
drinnen	inside
eigen	own
der Empfang, ⁻e	reception
endlich	finally
Entschuldigung!	Excuse me.
erfahren (erfährt), erfuhr, erfahren	to find out, to learn
erraten (errät), erriet, erraten	to guess
erröten	to blush
erst	first
die Fahrkarte, -n	ticket
das Fahrrad, ⁻er	bicycle
das Gegenteil, -e	opposite
die Geige, -n	fiddle
die Geschäftsreise, -n	business trip
die Geschwindigkeit, -en	speed
graduieren	graduate
die Großeltern	grandparents
gültig	valid
hungrig	hungry
die Information	information
jemals	ever
das Kino, -s	movie house
ins Kino gehen	to go to the movies
das Klassenzimmer, -	classroom
die Krankenschwester, -n	nurse
kriegen	to get
läuten	to ring
leben	to live
ledig	single, unmarried
liegen, lag, hat/ist gelegen	to lie (somewhere), be (somewhere)
die Macht, ⁻e	power
an die Macht kommen	to come to power
die Mieterin, -innen	(female) renter
mindestens	at least
munter	awake
Nähe: in der Nähe	nearby
neugierig	curious
Neuschwanstein	name of a famous castle in Bavaria
niemand	no one
die Note, -n	grade
(das) Österreich	Austria
passieren (aux. sein)	to happen
regeln	to control
der Reisescheck, -s	traveler's check
die Republik, -en	republic
ruhen	to rest
der Schaden, ⁻	damage
der Schlüssel, -	key
selber	yourself, himself, myself, etc.

das Stipendium, plural Stipendien	scholarship	verhandeln	to deal
		verspielen	to lose at play
stur	stubborn	verstehen, verstand, verstanden	to understand
die Tablette, -n	pill		
die Telefon-nummer, -n	telephone number	vorbei	over
		der Vortrag, ⸚e	talk, lecture
die Theorie, -n	theory	der Wahlkampf, ⸚e	political campaign
der Überstundenlohn, ⸚e	overtime pay	der Wecker, -	alarm
		weg.ziehen, zog, gezogen	to move away
unabhängig	independent		
unbekannt	unknown	die Welt, -en	world
unerwartet	unexpectedly	wirklich	really
die Uni, -s (colloquial expression)	university	der Witz, -e	joke
		zuerst	first
		zufrieden	content
verhaften	to arrest		

EXERCISE 1 (prerequisite: section A, topic: subordinate conjunction meanings)

Fill in the blank with the German subordinate conjunction corresponding to the English subordinate conjunction in parentheses.

1. _____ seine Kreditkarte noch gültig war, lebte er wie ein König. *(as long as)*
2. _____ Rom brannte, spielte Nero Geige. *(while)*
3. Wir werden den Empfang drinnen halten, _____ es morgen regnet. *(in case)*
4. Ich werde nächsten Sommer in der Bibliothek arbeiten, _____ ich eine bessere Arbeit kriegen kann. *(unless)*
5. Ich werde nicht ruhen, _____ ich ihn gefunden habe! *(until)*
6. _____ es sehr heiß war, hatte er einen dicken Pullover an. *(although)*
7. _____ mehr Sie lernen, _____ besser wird Ihre Note sein. *(the... the)*
8. Wußtest du, _____ der Bürgermeister verhaftet wurde? *(that)*
9. _____ wir die Ergebnisse haben, werden wir Sie anrufen. *(as soon as)*
10. _____ man die Temperatur regelt, kann man die Geschwindigkeit der chemischen Reaktion bestimmen. *(by)*

EXERCISE 2 (prerequisite: section A, topic: word order in subordinate clauses)

Rearrange the word groups into meaningful sentences. The two slashes indicate the break between the subordinate and the main clause.

1. Ich/habe/drei Stunden/gewartet//bis/er/ist/endlich/gekommen.
2. Je/älter/ich/werde//desto/weniger/ich/verstehe/die Jugend.
3. Während/der Lehrer/hat/geredet//einige Studenten/geschlafen/haben.
4. Sie/lief/aus dem Haus//sobald/das Feuer/brach/aus.

5. Sie/immer/kommt//es sei denn, daß/sie/ist/krank.
6. Falls/etwas/passiert/Sie/können/erreichen/mich/mit dieser Telefonnummer.
7. Indem/Sie/errötet/sind//Sie/haben/mir/gezeigt//daß/Sie/haben/gelogen.
8. Ich/habe/ihn/nie/gesehen//denn/ich/war/damals/noch nicht auf der Welt.
9. Ich/bleibe/lieber/ledig//ehe/ich/heirate/ihn.
10. Obgleich/sie/war/verletzt//wir/froh/waren//daß/sie/war/mindestens nicht tot.

EXERCISE 3 (prerequisite: section B, topic: interrogative words used in indirect questions)

Fill in the blank with the German interrogative word corresponding to the English word in parentheses.

1. Hast du gesehen, _____ dich geschlagen hat? *(who)*
2. Kann mir jemand erklären, _____ alle Geschäfte geschlossen sind? *(why)*
3. Der Unbekannte fragte mich, _____ man zum Bahnhof fahren kann. *(how)*
4. Können Sie mir sagen, _____ er die Information gegeben hat? *(whom)*
5. Niemand konnte erraten, _____ Aufsatz der beste war. *(whose)*
6. Ich wollte bloß fragen, _____ ich kommen muß. *(when)*
7. Wir haben niemals erfahren, _____ er beleidigt hat. *(who)*
8. Hast du verstanden, _____ sie gemeint hat? *(what)*

EXERCISE 4 (prerequisite: section B, topic: word order in indirect questions)

Rearrange the groups of words in the second part of the sentence so as to form an indirect question.

1. Es war uns nicht klar, warum/er/wollte/reden/mit niemandem.
2. Jeder wollte sofort wissen, wen/er/hatte/geheiratet.
3. Können Sie mir beschreiben, wie/sie/schaut/aus?
4. Es gibt viele Theorien, warum/er/ist/eines Tages/verschwunden.
5. Hast du eine Ahnung, wieviel/das alles/wird/kosten?

EXERCISE 5 (prerequisite: section C, topic: **als, ob, wann, wenn**)

Insert in the blank the appropriate German subordinate conjunction as indicated by the English word in parentheses.

1. Das Kind war zwei Jahre alt, _____ die Großeltern ihn zum ersten Mal gesehen haben. *(when)*
2. Entschuldigung, können Sie mir sagen, _____ der Zug aus Berlin ankommt? *(when)*
3. Laß Klaudia von mir grüßen, _____ du sie siehst. *(when)*
4. Niemand weiß, _____ er immer noch lebt. *(if)*

5. _____ du willst, helfe ich dir. *(if)*
6. Herr Lenz lachte niemals, _____ jemand einen Witz erzählte. *(when)*
7. Ich war heute schon munter, _____ der Wecker geläutet hat. *(when)*
8. Der Chef hat uns nicht gesagt, _____ er mit unserer Arbeit zufrieden war. *(if)*
9. _____ das Kind seine Suppe aß, machte es immer so viel Lärm. *(when)*
10. Frage die Krankenschwester, _____ der Arzt zurückkommt. *(when)*
11. Tue es selber, _____ du glaubst, du kannst es besser. *(if)*
12. _____ ich dir einen Befehl gebe, gehorchst du! *(when)*

EXERCISE 6 (prerequisite: section D, topic: *after, before, since, that*)

Insert in the blank the correct German word as indicated by the English word in parentheses.

1. a. Maria weinte, _____ ihre beste Freundin weggezogen war. *(after)*
   b. _____ jeder Vorlesung mußte er sein Glas Wein haben. *(after)*
2. a. _____ Sie Ihre Rechnung nicht bezahlt haben, müssen wir Ihre Koffer beschlagnahmen. *(since, because)*
   b. _____ ich diese Tabletten nehme, ist mein Fieber nicht mehr so hoch. *(since)* *(that time)*
3. a. Er war _____ scheu, aber jetzt ist er gerade das Gegenteil. *(before)*
   b. Wir stehen jetzt _____ dem ältesten Gebäude der Stadt. *(before)*
4. a. Gestern hatten wir ein Gewitter. _____ sind wir ohne Strom. *(since then)*
   b. _____ diesem Gewitter haben wir keinen Strom. *(since)*
5. a. Sie wollen doch nicht _____ kaufen! *(that)*
   b. Wir erfuhren, _____ der Dom vor 800 Jahren gebaut worden war. *(that)*
6. a. Ich habe Inge angerufen, und _____ sind wir ins Kino gegangen. *(afterward)*
   b. _____ ich Inge angerufen hatte, wollte sie nicht mehr mit mir ins Kino gehen. *(after)*
7. a. Einer von uns muß die Reiseschecks _____ der Abreise kaufen. *(before)*
   b. Ich muß die Katze immer aus dem Zimmer werfen, _____ ich das Bett mache. *(before)*
8. a. Ich bin nicht gekommen, _____ ich an dem Tag krank war. *(since, because)*
   b. Österreich ist _____ 1955 wieder eine unabhängige Republik. *(since)*

EXERCISE 7 (comprehensive)

This exercise is divided into three sections. Complete each sentence with one of the words given at the top of the section. Use each word only once.

das, daß, während, was, wie

1. Es ist klar, _____ wir ihm nicht trauen können.
2. Wo waren Sie, _____ wir alle gearbeitet haben?

3. _____ darfst du nicht vergessen!
4. Können Sie verstehen, _____ er sagen will?
5. Erzählen Sie uns, _____ Ihr Aufenthalt in Zürich war.

nach, nachdem, solange, wen, wer

6. Ich will bloß wissen, _____ du gesehen hast.
7. _____ sie stur bleiben, werden wir nicht mit ihnen verhandeln.
8. Was wirst du tun, _____ du graduiert bist?
9. Weißt du, _____ sie war?
10. _____ dieser Prüfung bin ich mit der Schule fertig.

als, vor, vorher, wann, wenn

11. Der Bub war zwölfe Jahre alt, _____ er sein erstes Fahrrad bekam.
12. Kannst du mir sagen, _____ der Vortrag anfangen soll?
13. Sind Sie jemals _____ hier gewesen?
14. Dieses Gebäude gab es schon _____ dem Krieg.
15. Ich bekam immer ein Geschenk, _____ mein Vater von einer Geschäftsreise nach Hause kam.

EXERCISE 8 (comprehensive)

Translate into German.

1. I bought a new suit although I didn't really need it.
2. Can you tell me whose house that is?
3. She doesn't want any other dessert since *(time)* she has eaten *Sachertorte*.
4. Think before you talk.
5. I don't believe that he trusts us.
6. Since (because) you worked the most, you will receive a raise.
7. I know who we must help.
8. After I found the body I called the police.
9. The more I ate, the hungrier I became.
10. I don't know if he drove away yesterday or the day before yesterday. *(simple past)*
11. The plan was rejected because it was too impractical.
12. We will have to confiscate your car unless you pay this bill.
13.a. Do you know when the watch was stolen?
    b. Where were you when the watch was stolen?
14. We hope that as soon as she comes she can give us the answer.

What's wrong with these?

1. Können Sie mir sagen, wenn der Zug nach Hannover abfährt?
2. Ehe ich es vergesse, ich will Ihnen schnell meine Telefonnummer geben.
3. Wir sind bevor Weihnachten immer noch zu Hause.
4. Melde dich bei uns sobald du bist angekommen.
5. Wenn ich sieben Jahre alt war, besuchte meine Familie zum ersten Mal Neuschwanstein.
6. Zuerst gingen wir ins Kino, nachdem gingen wir tanzen.
7. Ich kann nicht glauben das sie wirklich kommen wird.
8. Jetzt ist sie Krankenschwester, bevor war sie Studentin.
9. Weil das Gewitter kam unerwartet, gab es viel Schaden.
10. Nach ich hungrig wurde, entdeckte ich ein kleines Restaurant in der Nähe.
11. Sie verstehen, daß obwohl Sie fünfzig Stunden gearbeitet haben, Sie werden keinen Überstundenlohn bekommen.
12. Solange ich diese Erkältung haben, muß ich zu Hause bleiben.

Subjunctive

14

A. Present Subjunctive: *Haben, Sein,* and *Werden*

All of the verb forms used previously in this book have been in the *indicative*. This chapter will show how the same verbs can be used in the *subjunctive*. The subjunctive is employed primarily to express the idea that something would happen if something else happened (i.e., an if-then situation):

> Wenn er derselbe Mann **wäre**, (dann) **würde** ich ihn **erkennen.**
> *If he were the same man, (then) I would recognize him.*

As a basic definition, a sentence in the subjunctive consists of a **wenn-**clause (*if-*clause) and a **dann-**clause (*then-*clause). The **dann** itself is often omitted just as the *then* in the equivalent English clause is not necessary. The example above illustrates the *present subjunctive*. The verb in a present subjunctive sentence may appear to be a past tense verb, but the action refers to something that would happen *now* if something else would happen *now,* hence the term present subjunctive. The **dann-**clause can also be put before the **wenn-**clause:

> Ich würde ihn erkennen, **wenn** er derselbe Mann wäre.
> *I would recognize him if he were the same man.*

From the information provided in the previous chapter, it is clear that the **wenn-**clause is a subordinate clause, whereas the **dann-**clause serves as the main clause (note the position of the verbs in the examples above). Questions are formed in the present subjunctive as with any sentence containing a subordinate and a main clause:

> Würdest du ihn erkennen, wenn er derselbe Mann wäre?
> *Would you recognize him if he were the same man?*

The subjunctive verb itself can be a single-word form, e.g., **wäre,** or a form of **würde** plus infinitive. For the purposes of this section and the next, the single-word form will always be used in the **wenn**-clause, and **würde** plus infinitive in the **dann**-clause. The table below shows the complete conjugation for **haben, sein,** and **werden** in the present subjunctive:

Present Subjunctive

infinitive:	haben	sein	werden
ich	hätte	wäre	würde
du	hättest	wärest	würdest
er, sie, es	hätte	wäre	würde
wir	hätten	wären	würden
ihr	hättet	wäret	würdet
sie, Sie	hätten	wären	würden

Here is an example of **haben** in the present subjunctive:

> Wenn ich das Geld **hätte, würde** ich ein Sommerhaus kaufen.
> *If I had the money, I would buy a summer house.*

Modal verbs and **wissen** are the same in the present subjunctive as in the simple past indicative, except that the stem vowel is umlauted for **wissen** and also for the modals if the infinitive form has an umlaut.

Present Subjunctive   Modal Verbs and *Wissen*

Infinitive	Dürfen	Können	Mögen	Müssen	Sollen	Wollen	Wissen
ich	dürfte	könnte	möchte	müßte	sollte	wollte	wüßte
du	dürftest	könntest	möchtest	müßtest	solltest	wolltest	wüßtest
er, sie, es	dürfte	könnte	möchte	müßte	sollte	wollte	wüßte
wir	dürften	könnten	möchten	müßten	sollten	wollten	wüßten
ihr	dürftet	könntet	möchtet	müßtet	solltet	wolltet	wüßtet
sie, Sie	dürften	könnten	möchten	müßten	sollten	wollten	wüßten

Here are two examples of modal verbs used in the present subjunctive:

> Wenn ich dir das Geld geben **könnte,** würde ich es tun.
> *If I could give you the money I would do it.*

> Wir würden nicht kommen, wenn wir es nicht wirklich **wollten.**
> *We wouldn't come, if we didn't really want to.*

Consider the English example below:

> *My dog* would *always come when(ever) I called him.*

This type of construction is *not* a present subjunctive form in German, even though the English sentence uses *would*. Note that the sentence does not express an if-then situation. Furthermore, the verbs actually express a past action. To be precise, English often uses *would* plus the infinitive to convey the idea of a past action that happened *habitually*. By contrast, German does *not* use **würde** to indicate habitual past action. Instead, the past tense is used, therefore a direct translation of the above into German would be false:

> *Mein Hund **würde** immer **kommen,** wenn ich ihn rief.
> correct: Mein Hund **kam** immer, wenn ich ihn rief.

Compare the two English sentences below:

> A. *If I* had *time, I would come.*   B. *Whenever I* had *time, I would come.*

The verb forms are identical in both sentences, but sentence A describes an if-then situation while sentence B describes a past action. The correct German equivalents would be:

> A. Wenn ich Zeit **hätte,** würde ich kommen.   B. Wenn ich Zeit **hatte,** kam ich.

Because English generally uses the same verb for the present subjunctive and the simple past tense, students often confuse the two and use a simple past tense form in German when, in fact, a present subjunctive is required:

> *Ich würde Ihnen helfen, wenn ich **konnte.**
> *I would help you if I could.*

> correct: Ich würde Ihnen helfen, wenn ich **könnte.**
> (if-then situation, present subjunctive)

For comparison, here is the same verb used correctly as a past tense verb:

> Ich **konnte** ihm damals nicht helfen.
> *I couldn't (was not able to) help him at that time.*
> (past tense occurrence)

COMPREHENSION CHECK: *Insert the correct present subjunctive form of the verb given in parentheses into the **wenn**-clause. Use the appropriate form of **würde** in the **dann**-clause.*

1. Wenn ich die Gelegenheit _____, dann _____ ich nach Rom fahren. (haben)
2. Wenn er _____, wie ich gelitten habe, _____ er nicht so lachen! (wissen)
3. Wenn du fleißiger _____, _____ du mehr verdienen. (sein)
4. _____ Sie zu Ostern nach Florida fahren, wenn Sie _____? (dürfen)

ANSWERS: 1. hätte...würde   2. wüßte...würde   3. wärest, wärest
4. würden...dürften

B. Present Subjunctive: Weak, Strong, and Mixed Verbs

For *weak* verbs, the single-word form of the present subjunctive is the same as the simple past indicative (as in English):

Wenn ich das Essen **kochte,** würde ich es verbrennen.
If I cooked the meal, I would burn it.

For *strong* verbs, the single-word form uses the same stem as the simple past indicative of the verb, but with an umlaut if possible and with subjunctive endings. The table below shows the present subjunctive for two typical strong verbs, **kommen** and **fallen.** For your reference, the simple past indicative stem of **kommen** is **kam;** for **fallen** it is **fiel.** The subjunctive endings are shown in boldface:

Present Subjunctive   Strong Verbs

infinitive	*kommen*	*fallen*
ich	käm**e**	fiel**e**
du	käm**est**	fiel**est**
er, sie, es	käm**e**	fiel**e**
wir	käm**en**	fiel**en**
ihr	käm**et**	fiel**et**
sie, Sie	käm**en**	fiel**en**

Here are two examples of these particular strong verbs used in the present subjunctive:

Wenn er **käme,** würden wir ihn begrüßen.
If he came, we would welcome him.

Wenn du **fielest,** würdest du dich verletzen.
If you fell, you would hurt yourself.

For *mixed* verbs, the single-word form of the present subjunctive is the same as the indicative simple past, except that the **e** of the infinitive stem does not change to **a** (in effect this is an umlaut). For the irregular mixed verbs **bringen** and **denken,** the **a** of the indicative simple past has an umlaut in the present subjunctive. For reference, the full conjugations of **nennen, bringen,** and **denken** in the present subjunctive are given here:

Present Subjunctive   Mixed Verbs

infinitive	*nennen*	*bringen*	*denken*
ich	nennte	brächte	dächte
du	nenntest	brächtest	dächtest

infinitive	nennen	bringen	denken
er, sie, es	nennte	brächte	dächte
wir	nennten	brächten	dächten
ihr	nenntet	brächtet	dächtet
sie, Sie	nennten	brächten	dächten

The example that follows shows a mixed verb used in the present subjunctive:

> Jeder Läufer würde Muskelkater kriegen, wenn er zu lange **rennte.**
> *Every runner would get muscle cramps if he ran too long.*

COMPREHENSION CHECK: *Insert the correct present subjunctive form of the verb given in parentheses into the **wenn**-clause. Use the appropriate form of **würde** in the **dann**-clause.*

1. _____ du mit ihr sprechen, wenn sie dich _____? (anrufen)
2. Wenn wir diese Frau wirklich _____, _____ wir es Ihnen sagen. (kennen)
3. Er _____ mir hoffentlich danken, wenn ich das für ihn _____. (machen)

ANSWERS: 1. Würdest… anriefe 2. kennten, würden 3. würde… machte

C. Deciding When to Use *würde* Plus Infinitive

In principle, any present subjunctive verb in German can be replaced by **würde** plus the infinitive and vice versa:

> Wenn wir mit dem Zug **führen, kämen** wir um elf Uhr **an.**

or

> Wenn wir mit dem Zug **fahren würden, würden** wir um elf Uhr **ankommen.**
> *If we went by train, we would arrive at eleven o'clock.*

In a given sentence, either the single-word form or **würde** plus the infinitive is stylistically preferred depending on the type of verb and whether it occurs in the **wenn**-clause or the **dann**-clause. The table that follows summarizes the likely possibilities:

VERB TYPE	WENN-CLAUSE	DANN-CLAUSE
haben, sein, modals and *wissen*	single-word most likely	single-word most likely
other strong verbs and mixed verbs	single-word or **würde** possible	single-word possible **würde** likely
weak verbs	**würde** likely single-word possible	**würde** very likely single-word slightly possible

A simplified rule for the same problem is this:

> Use the single-word form with **haben, sein,** the modals, and **wissen;** use **würde** plus the infinitive for everything else.

In other words, use single-word forms for the verbs discussed in section A and **würde** plus the infinitive for those discussed in section B.

COMPREHENSION CHECK: *Rearrange these groups of words into meaningful sentences and write the verb in the present subjunctive. The division between the* **wenn**-*clause and the* **dann**-*clause is indicated by two slashes. Using the simplified rule given in this section, decide whether the verb in each clause should use the single-word form or* **würde** *plus the infinitive.*

EXAMPLE:
Wenn/ich/fliegen//dann/haben/ich/mehr Zeit.
ANSWER: Wenn ich fliegen würde, dann hätte ich mehr Zeit.

1.   Wenn du gescheit/sein//studieren/du öfter.
2.   Wenn/Sie mir/helfen//sein/ich dankbar.
3.   Wenn er/können//kaufen/er alles im Geschäft.
4.   Die Bohnen/kochen/schneller//wenn du einen Druckkochtopf/verwenden.

ANSWERS: 1. Wenn du gescheit wärest, würdest du öfter studieren.   2. Wenn Sie mir helfen würden, wäre ich dankbar.   3. Wenn er könnte, würde er alles im Geschäft kaufen.   4. Die Bohnen würden schneller kochen, wenn du einen Druckkochtopf verwenden würdest.

D. Past Subjunctive

The *past subjunctive* is generally used to state that something would have happened if something else had happened. It is formed in German by putting the auxiliary, **haben** or **sein,** in the present subjunctive tense together with the past participle of the verb:

Wenn ich genug Geld **gehabt hätte, hätte** ich es **gekauft.**
If I had had enough money, I would have bought it.

Wenn du **geflogen wärest, wärest** du früher **angekommen.**
If you had flown, you would have arrived earlier.

When a *modal* verb is used in the past subjunctive with another verb, then the sentence has a double infinitive:

Wenn der Hund nicht ständig gebellt hätte, hätte ich besser **arbeiten können.**
If the dog had not constantly been barking, I would have been able to work better.

If the double infinitive arises in the **wenn-**clause, the auxiliary verb does *not* go all the way to the end of the clause; instead it goes *before* the double infinitive:

Es wäre schade gewesen, wenn wir dich nicht **hätten** sehen können.
It would have been a pity, if we had not been able to see you.

Normally, subjunctive verbs are used in *if-then* type sentences. **Sollen,** however, when used as a past subjunctive, does not follow this pattern:

Er hätte gestern arbeiten sollen.
He should have worked yesterday.

In contrast to English, which employs *would* in the *then*-clause of the past subjunctive, a German past subjunctive sentence does not contain **würde;** i.e., do not translate the English past subjunctive literally into German:

*Ich **würde haben** die Zeitung **gelesen,** wenn ich sie gehabt hätte.
I would have read the newspaper if I had had it.
correct: Ich **hätte** die Zeitung **gelesen,** wenn ich sie gehabt hätte.

COMPREHENSION CHECK: *Rearrange these groups of words so as to form meaningful sentences. Rewrite the verb infinitive in the past subjunctive tense. The two slashes indicate the break between the **wenn**-clause and the **dann**-clause.*

1. Wenn er besser/singen//er den Preis/gewinnen.
2. Wenn du da/sein//du etwas Besonderes/sehen.
3. Wir/nach Wien/fahren/können//wenn wir mehr Zeit/haben.
4. Er/das nicht/tun/sollen.
5. Wenn wir mit dem Chef/sprechen/dürfen//wir zufrieden/sein.

ANSWERS: 1. Wenn er besser gesungen hätte, hätte er den Preis gewonnen. 2. Wenn du da gewesen wärest, hättest du etwas Besonderes gesehen. 3. Wir hätten nach Wien fahren können, wenn wir mehr Zeit gehabt hätten. 4. Er hätte das nicht tun sollen. 5. Wenn wir mit dem Chef hätten sprechen dürfen, wären wir zufrieden gewesen.

E. Alternative Uses of the Subjunctive

The subjunctive is frequently used in wishes:

Wenn er nur **käme!**

or

Wenn er nur **kommen würde!**
If only he would come!

The same sentence can be restated in the past subjunctive:

Wenn er nur **gekommen wäre!**
If only he had come!

Another way to express a wish is by using the present subjunctive of **mögen:**

Ich **möchte** bitte einen kleinen Kaffee (haben).
I would like (to have) a small coffee.

The subjunctive frequently occurs after **als** or **als ob** *(as if):*

Mein Stubenkamerad tut immer so, **als ob** er viel studieren **würde.**

or

Mein Stubenkamerad tut immer so, **als würde** er viel studieren.
My roommate always acts as if he studied a lot.

Note the difference in the position of the verb depending on whether **als** or **als ob** is used.

An alternative to the **wenn-**clause is to put the verb in first position and omit the **wenn:**

Hätte ich das Geld, dann würde ich viel reisen. = Wenn ich das Geld hätte, dann würde ich viel reisen.
If I had the money, I would travel a lot.

This subjunctive construction with the verb in first position is very formal and should be used with discretion.

Finally, a subjunctive sentence may combine present subjunctive in one clause with past subjunctive in the other. In this, German functions like English:

Wenn Sie die Frage **verstanden hätten, könnten** Sie jetzt die richtige Antwort geben.
If you had understood the question, you could now give the correct answer.

COMPREHENSION CHECK: *Translate into English.*

1. Wäre er älter, dann dürfte er Auto fahren.
2. Er stand da, als könnte er nicht reden.
3. Wenn es nur wahr wäre!
4. Was möchten Sie bestellen?
5. Sie schaute aus, als ob sie Hunger hätte.

ANSWERS: 1. If he were older, then he would be permitted to drive a car. 2. He stood there as if he could not speak. 3. If only it were true! 4. What would you like to order? 5. She looked as if she were hungry.

F. The "Subjective" Use of the Modals

Modal verbs are often used to express conjecture or uncertainty:

> Dieses Restaurant **soll** gut sein.
> *This restaurant is supposed to be good.*

> Er **muß** es sein.
> *He must be the one.*

> Es **mag (kann)** wahr sein.
> *It may be true.*

When used in this fashion, modal verbs are said to show the *subjective* mode, i.e., the verb expresses a subjective appraisal on the part of the speaker about the certainty or uncertainty of something. In the examples above, the verbs were in the indicative tense in both English and German and the two languages were essentially analogous.

To indicate more doubt or uncertainty, English and German would use the subjunctive:

> Es **sollte** möglich sein.
> *It should be possible.*

> Es **müßte** möglich sein.
> *It ought to be possible.*

> Es **könnte** möglich sein.

or

> Es **dürfte** möglich sein.
> *It could (might) be possible.*

In these examples, the subjective of the German modals is the same as the present subjunctive. In the past tense, however, German modals, used subjectively, are *not* equivalent to German past subjunctive verb forms. Instead, special subjective forms are employed:

> Er **mag (kann)** es **getan haben.**
> *He may have done it.*

> Er **muß** es **getan haben.**
> *He must have done it.*

Even more uncertainty can be expressed by putting the modal into the present subjunctive:

> Er **dürfte** es getan haben.

or

> Er **könnte** es getan haben.
> *He could (might) have done it.*

> Er **müßte** es getan haben.
> *He must (perhaps) have done it.*

Not every modal can be used subjectively; in your own writing you should follow the patterns outlined above. In addition, the modals **sollen** and **wollen,** when in the past subjective, have unusual meanings:

> Er **soll** es **getan haben.**
> *He is said to have done it.*

> Er **will** es **getan haben.**
> *He claims to have done it.*

You must be able to distinguish between past *subjunctive* and past *subjective* of modals. Consider these examples:

> Er **kann** es **getan haben,** aber wer weiß, ob er es wirklich getan hat?
> *He could have done it, but who knows if he really did?*
> (past subjective, indicates conjecture)

> Er **hätte** es **tun können,** wenn er die Chance gehabt hätte.
> *He could have done it if he had had the chance.*
> (past subjunctive, i.e., he would have been able to do it, if etc., indicates if-then situation)

COMPREHENSION CHECK: *Fill in the blank with the appropriate German word(s) corresponding to the English word(s) in parentheses.*

1.   Das ____ sein. *(may)*
2.   Du ____ recht haben, aber ich bin nicht davon überzeugt. *(might)*
3.   Er ____ der Dieb ____, aber ich glaube nicht, daß wir es beweisen können. *(could have been)*
4.   Er ____ einmal ein berühmter Sportler ____. *(is said to have been)*
5.   Sie ____ einen Mercedes ____. *(claims to have had)*

ANSWERS: 1. mag (kann) 2. könntest (dürftest) 3. mag (kann)...gewesen sein 4. soll...gewesen sein   5. will...gehabt haben.

German-English Vocabulary

als ob	*as if*	aus.lachen	*to laugh at*
anders	*differently*	Auto fahren (fährt), fuhr, gefahren	*to drive a car*
an.schreien, schrie, geschrien	*to scream at*		
die Anschuldigung, -en	*accusation*	bereit	*ready*
		bereuen	*to regret*
an.sehen (sieht), sah, gesehen	*to look at*	beruhigt	*reassured*
		berühmt	*famous*
auch wenn	*even if*	beschäftigt	*busy*
auf.hören	*to stop*	besonders	*special, especially*
Ausflug: einen Ausflug machen	*to go for a drive*	bestellen	*to order*
		die Blume, -n	*flower*

die Bohne, -n	bean	die Panne, -n	breakdown
dankbar	grateful, thankful	der Preis, -e	prize
dann	then	raufen	to fight
dauern	to last	recht haben	to be right
der Dichter, -	poet	rechtzeitig	on time
der Dieb, -e	thief	die Reihe, -n	row
draußen	outside	scheinen, schien,	to seem
die Droge, -n	drug	geschienen	
der Druckkochtopf, ̈e	pressure cooker	schneien	to snow
die Dummheit, -en	stupidity	so (et)was	such a thing
ein bißchen	a little	sowieso	anyway
einmal	once	das Spiel, -e	game
erhalten (erhält), erhielt, erhalten	to receive	der Sportler, -	athlete
		staunen	to be astonished
die Erkältung, -en	cold	der Stein, -e	rock
erlauben	to allow	Stelle: an seiner (deiner) Stelle sein	to be in his (your) place
erleben	to experience		
ersticken	to suffocate	stimmen	to be correct
im Keim ersticken	to nip in the bud	stürzen	to stumble
		die Tasse, -n	cup
die Geduld	patience	der Teller, -	plate
der Gefallen, -	favor	trotzdem	just the same, in spite of that
die Gelegenheit, -en	opportunity		
		überzeugt von	convinced of
geraten (gerät), geriet, geraten in + acc.	to get into	umgekehrt	reversed
		verdienen	to earn
		verlangen	to demand
gescheit	clever	das Versicherungs- geld	insurance money
gleich	immediately		
hinter	back	verwenden	to use
hören auf + acc.	to listen to (someone's advice)	vor.kommen, kam, gekommen	to seem
		wachen	to be awake
Hunger haben	to be hungry	wagen	to dare
husten	to cough	wahr	true
irgendwann	sometime	die Wahrheit	truth
der Kater, -	tomcat	weg.fahren (fährt), fuhr, gefahren	to drive away, to go away
die Klasse, -n	class		
leicht	easy	weg.stellen	to put away
miteinander	with each other	der Wert, -e	value
nebenan	next door	das Wort, -e	word
nieder.brennen (mixed verb)	to burn down	zu.nehmen (nimmt), nahm, genommen	to gain weight
nochmal	again		
der Opernsänger, -	opera singer		

EXERCISE 1 (prerequisite: section A, topic: present subjunctive: **haben, sein,** modals and **wissen**)

*Fill in the blank in the **wenn**-clause with the present subjunctive form of the verb in parentheses. Add the necessary form of **würde** to the **dann**-clause.*

1. Wenn du Hunger _____, _____ du auch das essen. (haben)
2. Wenn die Kinder schon bereit _____, _____ wir wegfahren. (sein)
3. Wenn ich _____, _____ ich hier rauchen. (dürfen)
4. Ich _____ das nicht tun, wenn ich an seiner Stelle _____. (sein)
5. Er _____ den Aufsatz schreiben, wenn er ihn schreiben _____. (müssen)
6. Wenn wir gutes Wetter _____, _____ wir einen Ausflug machen. (haben)
7. Sie *(she)* _____ mit mir ausgehen, wenn sie nicht immer so beschäftigt _____. (sein)
8. Wenn ihr alles haben _____, was _____ ihr wollen? (können)
9. Wenn du nur _____, wie ich dich liebe, _____ du mich nicht verlassen! (wissen)
10. Wenn er ein Fieber _____, _____ ich den Arzt anrufen. (haben)

EXERCISE 2 (prerequisite: section B, topic: present subjunctive: strong, weak, mixed verbs)

*Fill in the blank in the **wenn**-clause with the present subjunctive form of the verb in parentheses. Add the necessary form of **würde** to the **dann**-clause.*

1. Es _____ nicht so lange dauern, wenn wir _____. (fliegen)
2. Auch wenn wir seine Hilfe _____, _____ wir ihn nicht darum bitten. (brauchen)
3. Wenn er meinen Brief _____, _____ er das Problem besser verstehen. (lesen)
4. Wenn unser Haus _____, _____ wir all unsere Sachen verlieren. (niederbrennen)
5. Du _____ besser tanzen, wenn du mehr _____. (üben)
6. Wenn wir diese Idee im Keim _____, _____ sie vielleicht für immer verschwinden. (ersticken)
7. Meine Frau _____ staunen, wenn ich ihr Blumen _____. (bringen)
8. Wenn Sie ihn _____, _____ Sie es bereuen. (heiraten)
9. Ich _____ das Angebot annehmen, wenn ich es _____. (erhalten)
10. Wenn wir ihn besser _____, _____ wir ihn besuchen. (kennen)

EXERCISE 3 (prerequisite: section C, topic: deciding when to use **würde** plus infinitive)

Rearrange the groups of words so as to form meaningful sentences and rewrite the verb infinitives in the present subjunctive. On the basis of the simplified rule given in section C, decide whether to use the single-word form of the present subjunctive or würde plus *infinitive. The division between the* **wenn-***clause and the* **dann-***clause is indicated by two slashes.*

1. Wenn du die Teller gleich nach dem Essen/abwaschen//sein/die Arbeit leichter.
2. Wenn Sie/wollen//dürfen/Sie noch eine Tasse Tee/haben.
3. Du/machen/solche Fehler nicht//wenn du vorher/denken.
4. Ich/haben/das Geld nicht bei mir//wenn/ich der Dieb/sein.
5. Wenn er nicht so viel/essen//zunehmen/er nicht so viel.
6. Viele Leute/nennen/sich selbst anders//wenn sie/können.
7. Wenn man ihnen das/erlauben//verlangen/Sie bald mehr.
8. Ich/kriegen/sowieso nicht viel für das Haus//wenn ich es/verkaufen.
9. Wenn du den Aufsatz nochmal schreiben/müssen//was/machen/du anders?
10. Du/ihm/verzeihen//wenn er/sein Zimmer jetzt/reinigen.

EXERCISE 4   (prerequisite: section D, topic: past subjunctive)

Rearrange these groups of words into meaningful sentences. Rewrite the verbs in the past subjunctive. The dividing line between the **wenn-***clause and the* **dann-***clause is indicated by two slashes.*

1. Wenn er das Geld/finden//er/reich/werden.
2. Das Wetter/schlecht/sein//wenn ich/kommen.
3. Ich die Wahrheit/erfahren//wenn ich dich/anrufen?
4. Ich/ihn/fragen/sollen.
5. Wir/lachen//wenn wir es/wagen.
6. Die Kinder/draußen/spielen/wollen//wenn es vorher/schneien.
7. Wie/man das Problem/lösen//wenn die Werte von x and y umgekehrt/sein?
8. Ich/sie/heiratet//wenn sie ja/sagen.
9. Wenn der Dichter nicht im Krieg/sterben//er/viel mehr/schreiben.
10. Es/nett/sein//wenn du mich/besuchen/können.

EXERCISE 5   (prerequisite: section E, topic: alternative uses of the subjunctive)

Translate into English.

1. Wenn das Baby nur mehr essen würde!
2. Könnte er bloß reden, dann würden wir die Wahrheit erfahren!
3. Wenn du damals öfter geschrieben hättest, wäre ich dir jetzt nicht böse.
4. Er hustet, als hätte er eine schwere Erkältung.
5. Hätte er auf mich gehört, dann wäre er nicht in Schwierigkeiten geraten.
6. Ich möchte ein kleines Bier.
7. Er sah den Fernseher an, als ob er so etwas nie vorher gesehen hätte.
8. Wenn ich ihn damals kennengelernt hätte, könnte ich Ihnen jetzt sagen, wie er aussieht.

9. Wenn ich bloß nicht krank geworden wäre!
10. Es schien mir, als wollte er mit dem Spiel niemals aufhören.

EXERCISE 6 (prerequisite: section F, topic: modal verbs and the subjective mode)

Fill in the blank(s) with the German words corresponding to the English word(s) in parentheses.

1. _____ seine Anschuldigungen wahr sein? *(could)*
2. _____ ich Sie um einen Gefallen bitten? *(might)*
3. Es _____ eine Möglichkeit geben, das zu tun. *(ought)*
4. Diese Droge _____ dem Patienten helfen. *(should)*
5. Er _____ schon zu Hause sein. *(might)*
6. Jemand _____ Ihren Hund schon _____. *(may have found)*
7. Sie _____ seine Geliebte _____. *(is said to have been)*
8. Ein Stein _____ das Fenster _____. *(must have broken)*
9. Das Pferd _____ das Rennen _____, wenn es nicht gestürzt wäre. *(might have won)*
10. Mein Nachbar _____ einen Löwen _____. *(claims to have killed)*

EXERCISE 7 (comprehensive)

Translate into English.

1. Wenn du diesen Film sähest, würdest du ihn niemals vergessen.
2. Ich hätte Schnitzel bestellt, wenn sie es gehabt hätten.
3. Wir wären rechtzeitig angekommen, wenn das Auto keine Panne gehabt hätte.
4. Wärest du beruhigt, wenn ich dich nach Hause begleitete?
5. Hätte sie mehr Geduld, dann würde sie vielleicht die Kinder nicht so oft anschreien.
6. Es könnte stimmen.
7. Es kam mir vor, als hätte ich all das irgendwann vorher erlebt.
8. Jemand soll das Haus nebenan gekauft haben.
9. Wenn man nur wieder jung werden könnte!
10. Würden sie den Brief morgen kriegen, wenn ich ihn heute schickte?
11. Ich hätte meine Schuhe finden können, wenn du sie nicht weggestellt hättest.
12. Er will eine fliegende Untertasse gesehen haben.
13. Was tätest du, wenn du keine Arbeit hättest?
14. Der alte Kater mag ein bißchen dumm gewesen sein, aber wir liebten ihn trotzdem.
15. Wenn ich nur hätte sprechen dürfen!
16. Die ganze Klasse sah ihn an, als ob er eine große Dummheit gesagt hätte.

EXERCISE 8 (comprehensive)

Translate into German.

1. What would you do if you won one million DM?
2. If you had gone to Germany last summer, you would have had bad weather.
3. I would be so happy if I could hear your voice.
4. It would have been difficult, but we could have done it.
5. Even if I knew her, I wouldn't introduce her to you.
6. If only they would obey me!
7. He would come by bicycle if he had one.
8. She may have solved the problem.
9. It was as if he had never been born.
10. Everyone would have laughed if they had seen me in this ridiculous costume.
11. He is said to have murdered his wife.
12. Might I speak with you?
13. He would always become sad when he drank.
14. If only I had been able to sleep longer!
15. We would like to order now.

GEDANKENPROBLEM: Consider first the two passive sentences shown here:

Er wird geliebt.   Ich bin eingeladen worden.
He is loved.   *I have been invited.*

Now translate the sentences below into German. In other words, write a passive sentence in the subjunctive mode:

He would be loved, if he were not such a tyrant.
I would have come if I had been invited.

What's wrong with these?

1. Wenn sie nur wußte, was ich damals für sie getan habe!
2. Wenn du hättest meine Worte wirklich verstanden, du hättest mich nicht ausgelacht.
3. Der Soldat schlief, während er wachen sollen hätte.
4. Wir würden haben bekommen mehr Geld für das Experiment, wenn die ersten Ergebnisse besser gewesen wären.
5. Der Opernsänger hätte lauter singen sollen, denn niemand könnte ihn in den hinteren Reihen hören.
6. Mein Bruder und ich würden oft miteinander raufen, als wir Kinder waren.

Quote Subjunctive

15

A. Present Q-Subjunctive: Introduction

Quoting someone directly in German is similar to the same process in English:

> Er sagte: ,,Ich bin einundzwanzig Jahre alt.''
> *He said, "I am twenty-one years old."*

The difference between the English and German direct quote is one of punctuation: German uses a colon before the quote, English a comma. In German, the first quotation marks are written at the bottom of the line.

However, if a statement is quoted indirectly, a special subjunctive form is often used in formal German for which English has no equivalent:

> Er sagte, er **sei** einundzwanzig Jahre alt.
> *He said he was twenty-one years old.*

The indirect quote must be preceded by a comma in German. Indirect quotes are often introduced by **daß** or some other subordinate conjunction, in which case the verb goes to the end of the clause as usual:

> Er sagte, **daß** er einundzwanzig Jahre alt **sei.**
> *He said that he was twenty-one years old.*

This *quote* subjunctive will be referred to as *q-subjunctive* for short. The sentence above uses the *present q-subjunctive* of the verb **sein** because the original statement is in the present tense. To avoid confusion, the subjunctive discussed in the previous chapter will hereafter be referred to as the *if-then subjunctive.*

For reference, the present q-subjunctive forms for **haben, sein** and **werden** are given here:

Present Q-Subjunctive:

infinitive	haben	sein	werden
ich	*hätte*	sei	*würde*
du	habest	seiest	werdest
er, sie, es	habe	sei	werde
wir	*hätten*	seien	*würden*
ihr	habet	seiet	werdet
sie, Sie	*hätten*	seien	*würden*

In the table above you should recognize the words in italics as if-then subjunctive forms. Technically, there is a specific q-subjunctive form for all words, however some of these are identical to the present indicative. When this occurs, the if-then subjunctive is almost always used instead and this fact has been incorporated into the table. The q-subjunctive of all verbs is based on the *infinitive* stem; thus, there is no stem vowel change in the second- and third- person singular of **werden.**

Here is another example of a direct and indirect quote:

original statement: Ich habe einen besseren Vorschlag.
I have a better suggestion.

direct quote: Er sagte: ,,Ich habe einen besseren Vorschlag.''
He said, ''I have a better suggestion.''

indirect quote: Er sagte, er **habe** einen besseren Vorschlag.
He said he has a better suggestion.

The q-subjunctive is a formal grammatical construction in German. Many speakers simply use the indicative in indirect quotes. This is especially true in the spoken language. Nevertheless, the q-subjunctive often occurs in literature, and students in German-speaking countries are generally expected to use it in formal written assignments. When the q-subjunctive is intentionally replaced by the indicative in formal writing, this indicates that the speaker agrees with the statement being quoted. Conversely, the use of the if-then subjunctive when the q-subjunctive is expected suggests that the speaker questions the validity of the statement being quoted. However, in those grammatical cases where the q-subjunctive is identical to that of the if-then subjunctive, no doubt is implied.

Q-subjunctive is most common in the language of the press because it indicates a sense of neutrality towards the quoted material, i.e., it reinforces the idea of objective reporting. Often a series of sentences may be written in q-subjunctive thus indicating that the original quote is continuing. This technique avoids the necessity of having to repeat continually ''he further said etc.''

Approximately 90 percent of all sentences with the q-subjunctive are in the third person; most of the remaining cases are in the first person. In this book, the second person q-subjunctive forms are given only for reference; they are not covered in the exercises.

When the original statement is in the if-then subjunctive, the indirect quote retains the if-then subjunctive forms so that the original meaning is not lost:

original statement: Ich wäre zufrieden, wenn ich nur ein kleines Haus hätte.
I would be content if I only had a small house.

indirect quote: Er sagte, er wäre zufrieden, wenn er nur ein kleines Haus hätte.
He said he would be content if he only had a small house.

The verb **sagen** is normally followed directly by a dative object; however, when **sagen** introduces a *direct* quote, the dative object must be preceded by **zu:**

original statement: Ich bin krank.
I am sick.

direct quote: Er sagte **zu mir:** ,,Ich bin krank.''
He said to me, "I am sick."

indirect quote: Er sagte **mir,** er sei krank.
He told me he was sick.

It can be very monotonous to always introduce an indirect quote with **sagen.** The following is a list of verbs similar to **sagen** but more expressive:

antworten	*to answer*	berichten	*to report*	erwidern	*to retort*
äußern	*to utter*	bestätigen	*to confirm*	erzählen	*to tell*
behaupten	*to maintain*	beteuern	*to assert*	melden	*to report*
bekannt.geben	*to announce*	betonen	*to emphasize*	mit.teilen	*to inform*
bemerken	*to remark*	erwähnen	*to mention*	versichern	*to assure*

COMPREHENSION CHECK: *Insert the statement given into the incomplete sentence. Only the verb must be changed. Be careful to note whether the sentence is a direct or indirect quote.*

EXAMPLE: Klein ist der beste Kandidat.
Er sagte, _____
ANSWER: Er sagte, Klein sei der beste Kandidat.

1. Die Kosten sind zu hoch.
Der Chef äußerte die Meinung, _____
2. Der Strom ist ausgefallen.
Er sagte zu mir: _____
3. Er hat keine Geduld mehr mit uns.
Herr Kropp sagte, daß _____
4. Es wäre nett, wenn wir mehr Geld hätten.
Meine Frau bemerkte, _____
5. Beide haben die Grippe.
Der Arzt teilte uns mit, _____

B. Present Q-Subjunctive: Modal Verbs and *Wissen*

The following table lists the q-subjunctive forms for the modals and **wissen** (words in italics are identical to if-then subjunctive forms):

PRESENT TENSE Q-SUBJUNCTIVE: MODAL VERBS AND *WISSEN*

infinitive	dürfen	können	mögen	müssen	sollen	wollen	wissen
ich	dürfe	könne	möge	müsse	solle	wolle	wisse
du	dürfest	könnest	mögest	müssest	sollest	wollest	wissest
er, sie, es	dürfe	könne	möge	müsse	solle	wolle	wisse
wir	*dürften*	*könnten*	*möchten*	*müßten*	*sollten*	*wollten*	*wüßten*
ihr	dürfet	könnet	möget	müsset	sollet	wollet	wisset
sie, Sie	*dürften*	*könnten*	*möchten*	*müßten*	*sollten*	*wollten*	*wüßten*

Here is an example of a modal verb in a direct and indirect quote:

original statement:	Ich kann meine Brille nicht finden.
	I can't find my glasses.
direct quote:	Er antwortete: ,,Ich kann meine Brille nicht finden.''
	He answered, "I can't find my glasses."
indirect quote:	Er antwortete, er **könne** seine Brille nicht finden.
	He answered he couldn't find his glasses.

In the example that follows, the q-subjunctive of the modal is identical to the if-then subjunctive:

original statement:	Wir dürfen das Zimmer nicht betreten.
	We are not allowed to enter the room.
indirect quote:	Der Museumsführer betonte, wir **dürften** das Zimmer nicht betreten.
	The museum guide emphasized we were not allowed to enter the room.

COMPREHENSION CHECK: *Fill in the blank with the appropriate present q-subjunctive form of the modal given in parentheses.*

1. Die Zeitung berichtet, dieser Film _____ sehr gut sein. (sollen)
2. Mein Freund sagte mir, wir _____ ins Konzert gehen. (sollen)
3. Sie sagte mir, ich _____ nicht gut singen. (können)

4. Die Regierung hat heute bekanntgegeben, daß die Steuern nächstes Jahr erhöht werden _____. (müssen)

ANSWERS: 1. solle 2. sollten 3. könne 4. müßten

C. Present Q-Subjunctive: Strong and Weak Verbs

The q-subjunctive forms for strong and weak verbs are illustrated in the table below with **kommen** and **machen** as examples of a strong and weak verb respectively. Italicized forms are derived from the if-then subjunctive. Strong and weak verbs also take q-subjunctive endings shown in boldface:

PRESENT Q-SUBJUNCTIVE	STRONG VERBS	WEAK VERBS
infinitive	*kommen*	*machen*
ich	*käme*	*machte*
du	komm**est**	mach**est**
er, sie, es	komm**e**	mach**e**
wir	*kämen*	*machten*
ihr	komm**et**	mach**et**
sie, Sie	*kämen*	*machten*

Here are examples of a strong and a weak verb in the present q-subjunctive:

Strong verb

original statement:	Ich fahre gern mit dem Auto.
	I like to drive.
indirect quote:	Max sagte immer, er **fahre** gern mit dem Auto.
	Max always said he liked to drive.

Note: As always, the q-subjunctive is based on the infinitive stem, therefore strong verbs do not undergo a stem vowel change (i.e., not ***fähre**).

Weak verb

original statement:	Ich brauche keine Hilfe.
	I don't need any help.
indirect quote:	Sie versicherte mir, sie **brauche** keine Hilfe.
	She assured me she didn't need any help.

In the next two examples, the verb forms are identical to the if-then subjunctive:

Strong verb

original statement: Ich fahre lieber mit dem Zug.
I prefer to go by train.

indirect quote: Ich antwortete, ich **führe** lieber mit dem Zug.
I answered, I preferred to go by train.

Weak verb

original statement: Wir brauchen keine Hilfe.
We don't need any help.

indirect quote: Die zwei Touristen behaupteten, sie **brauchten** keine Hilfe.
The two tourists maintained they didn't need any help.

COMPREHENSION CHECK: *Fill in the blank with the appropriate present q-subjunctive form of the verb given in parentheses.*

1. Ich mußte nochmal sagen, daß meine Freundin kein Wort Deutsch _____. (verstehen)
2. Der Präsident sagte, er _____ auf eine politische Lösung des Problems. (hoffen)
3. Mein Vater erwiderte bloß, die anderen Autofahrer _____ zu schnell. (fahren)
4. Der Gewerkschaftssprecher beteuerte, daß wir alle einen Hungerlohn _____. (verdienen)
5. Der Beamte antwortete, die Formulare _____ auf dem Tisch. (liegen)

ANSWERS: 1. verstehe 2. hoffe 3. führen 4. verdienten 5. lägen

D. Past and Future Q-Subjunctive

The past tense of the q-subjunctive is formed by putting the auxiliary of the present perfect into the present q-subjunctive (see section A for the present q-subjunctive of **haben** and **sein**):

original statement: Er spielte die Rolle hervorragend.
He played the role magnificently.

indirect quote: Die Kritiker schrieben einstimmig, er **habe** die Rolle hervorragend **gespielt.**
The critics wrote unanimously that he had played the role magnificently.

The past q-subjunctive must be used when the *original* statement is in *any* past tense. In other words, all past tense verbs, whether they are present perfect, simple past or even past perfect, are replaced in indirect quotes by a single past q-subjunctive form, as shown above. The next example shows a past q-subjunctive for a verb with the auxiliary **sein:**

original statement:	Ich bin niemals in Rom gewesen.
	I have never been in Rome.
indirect quote:	Sie sagte, sie **sei** niemals in Rom **gewesen.**
	She said she had never been in Rome.

The future q-subjunctive is formed by putting the future auxiliary **werden** into the present q-subjunctive (the present q-subjunctive forms for **werden** are listed in section A):

original statement:	Ich werde diesen Entschluß ewig bereuen.
	I will always regret this decision.
indirect quote:	Der ehemalige Bundeskanzler schrieb in seinen Memoiren, er **werde** diesen Entschluß ewig **bereuen.**
	The former chancellor wrote in his memoirs, he would always regret this decision.

Here is an example of the future q-subjunctive where the auxiliary is equivalent to the if-then subjunctive:

original statement:	Sie werden nach Hamburg ziehen.
	They will move to Hamburg.
indirect statement:	Er schrieb mir, sie **würden** nach Hamburg ziehen.
	He wrote me they would move to Hamburg.

To review, the tense of a German q-subjunctive verb is determined by the tense of the verb in the *original* statement. In English, however, the tense of the verb in an indirect quote may be different from that of the original statement. As a result, the tense of an English indirect quote may not match the tense of the corresponding German indirect quote. Consider the examples below:

indirect quote:	Er sagte, er **sei** krank.
	He said he was sick.

The verb in the German indirect quote is *present* q-subjunctive. The verb in the English indirect quote, however, is *simple past* tense. To determine the proper tense of a German verb in an indirect quote, you must go back to the original statement:

original statement:	Ich **bin** krank.
	I am sick.

The verb in the original statement is *present* tense in both English and German, therefore the German indirect quote requires *present* q-subjunctive.

COMPREHENSION CHECK: *Insert the statement given into the sentence that follows. Change only the verb form.*

1. Sie hat ihren Aufsatz zu Hause gelassen.
    Die Studentin sagte, _____.
2. Er wird es nicht vergessen.
    Er antwortete, _____.
3. Die zwei Politiker machten einen Kompromiß miteinander.
    Unser Reporter berichtet, _____.
4. Petra und Elke sind für das Wochenende weggefahren.
    Uschi sagte mir, daß _____.
5. Sie *(they)* werden wohl nächsten Dienstag ankommen.
    Seine Freunde schrieben ihm, _____.

ANSWERS: 1. Die Studentin sagte, sie habe ihren Aufsatz zu Hause gelassen. 2. Er antwortete, er werde es nicht vergessen. 3. Unser Reporter berichtet, die zwei Politiker hätten einen Kompromiß miteinander gemacht. 4. Uschi sagte mir, daß Petra und Elke für das Wochenende weggefahren seien. 5. Seine Freunde schrieben ihm, sie würden wohl nächsten Dienstag ankommen.

E. Q-Subjunctive in Nonquote Sentences

In addition to indirect quotes, the present q-subjunctive can be used to express a wish:

Es **lebe** die Revolution!
Long live the revolution!

Es **lebe** der König!
Long live the King!

Möge das neue Jahr Ihnen viel Freude bringen!
May the new year bring you much joy!

Obviously, these are formal constructions. The q-subjunctive also occurs in a few common phrases and proverbs:

Gott **sei** Dank!
Thank God!

Ein jeder **kehre** vor seiner Tür!
Mind your own business. (literally: *Let each person sweep in front of his own door.*)

Es **sei** darauf hingewiesen, daß die Menge der Energie in einem geschlossenen System konstant bleibt.
It should be pointed out that the quantity of energy in a closed system remains constant.

The q-subjunctive can also serve as a formal substitute for the imperative:

So **sei** es!
Let it be!

Man **nehme** 100 Gramm Zucker.
Take 100 grams of sugar.
(in recipes)

X **sei** 20.
Let x be 20.
(in scientific German)

Der Leser **beachte** folgende Anmerkungen!
Let the reader note the following annotations.

Ein paar Widersprüche zu dieser Theorie **seien** unten besprochen.
Let us discuss below a few contradictions to this theory.

You do not need to write these forms, but you should be able to recognize and understand them when they occur.

COMPREHENSION CHECK: *Translate these sentences into English.*

1. Es lebe die Freiheit!
2. Möge auf Erden Frieden herrschen!
3. Man schlage drei Eier.
4. C sei die Lichtgeschwindigkeit.
5. Es sei erwähnt, daß der Bau dieses Gebäudes zwei Jahre dauern würde.

ANSWERS: 1. Long live freedom! 2. May peace reign on earth! 3. Beat three eggs. 4. Let c be the speed of light. 5. It should be mentioned that the construction of this building would last two years.

German-English Vocabulary

Learn the verbs on page 211 and the following:

die Adresse, -n	*address*	das Benzin	*gas*
an. geben (gibt), gab, gegeben	*to list*	berauben	*to rob*
		der Bericht, -e	*report*
die Annonce, -n	*advertisement*	bestehen, bestand, bestanden	*to be*
der Artikel, -	*article*		
auf.suchen	*to visit*	betreten (betritt), betrat, betreten	*to set foot on, to walk on*
der Außenminister,	*foreign minister*		
		bewilligen	*to approve*
der Autofahrer, -	*driver*	die Beziehung, -en	*relationship*
der Bankpräsident, -en, -en	*bank president*		
		der Botschafter, -	*ambassador*
behandeln	*to discuss, to deal with*	BRD = Bundesrepublik Deutschland	*Federal Republic of Germany = West Germany*
das Beispiel, -e	*example*		

das Bundesland, ¨er	Federal state	die Nase, -n	nose
DDR = Deutsche Demokratische Republik	German Democratic Republic = East Germany	die Natur-zeitschrift, -en	nature journal
		das Ohr, -en	ear
		die Oppositions-partei, -en	opposition party
der Diplomat, -en, -en	diplomat	die Pflanze, -n	plant
		der Politiker, -	politician
diskutieren	to discuss	die Politik	policy, politics
die Ecke, -n	corner	politisch	political
der Einbrecher, -	burglar	der Polizeichef, -s	police chief
entrüstet	indignant	der Präsident, -en, -en	president
die Erde, -n	earth		
erhöhen	to raise	die Rakete, -n	rocket
das Formular, -e	form	der Rasen, -	lawn
die Freiheit	freedom	die Regierung, -en	government
der Frieden	peace	das Reich, -e	kingdom
frühzeitig	early	der Reporter, -	reporter
die Garage, -n	garage	ruhen	to rest, to cool, to set
gefährden	to endanger		
der Geschäftsschluß	closing time	die Schluß-folgerung, -en	conclusion
der Gesprächs-partner, -	discussion partner	schmutzig	dirty
		die Schweiz	Switzerland
der Gewerkschafts-sprecher, -	union spokesman	sehr	very
		die Sekretärin, -innen	(female) secretary
gleich weit entfernt von	equidistant from	das Semester, -	semester
herrschen	to reign	der Sonntag, -e	Sunday
der Himmel	Heaven	der Spielplatz, ¨e	playground
hören	to hear	spionieren	to spy
der Hungerlohn, ¨e	starvation wage	der Sport	sports
der Kandidat, -en, -en	candidate	der Sprecher, -	speaker
		die Steuer, -n	tax
Köln	Cologne (city in Germany)	der Stiefel, -	boot
		der Süden	the South
der Kompromiß, -sse	compromise	der Teig, -e	dough
		treiben, trieb, getrieben	to engage in
der Kongreß, -sse	congress		
die Kosten	costs	überraschen	to surprise
Kurs: einen Kurs belegen	course: to register for a course	unleserlich	illegible
		verbrauchen	to use
die Lage, -n	situation	die Verhandlung, -en	negotiation
das Leid	sorrow		
die Licht-geschwindigkeit	speed of light	der Vertrag, ¨e	treaty
		vertreten (vertritt), vertrat, vertreten	to stand for
das Licht, -er	light		
die Mehrheit, -en	majority	wachsen (wächst), wuchs, gewachsen	to grow
der Nachrichten-sprecher, -	newscaster		

| die Wahl, -en | *choice* | zu.spitzen | *to come to a* |
| der Zuschauer, - | *viewer* | *(reflexive)* | *critical point* |

EXERCISE 1 (prerequisite: section A, topic: present q-subjunctive of **haben** and **sein**)

Insert the statement given into the sentence that follows it. You must distinguish between direct and indirect quotes. In this exercise and in the ones that follow, leave the subject as, but change the verb to the proper q-subjunctive form.

1. Der Patient ist nicht mehr krank.
   Der Arzt berichtete, _____.
2. Sie hat keine Zeit.
   Sylvia sagt immer, _____.
3. Wir sind schlechte Studenten.
   Er behauptet, daß _____.
4. Seine Eltern haben kein Auto.
   Mein Freund aus Deutschland erklärte mir, _____.
5. Sie hat eine Wohnung in der Stadt.
   Sie antwortete: _____.
6. Ich habe ihn trotzdem gern.
   Ich erwiderte, daß _____.
7. Er wäre überrascht, wenn die Geschäfte am Sonntag geöffnet wären.
   Er sagte, _____.
8. Das Haus hat keine Garage.
   In der Annonce habe ich gelesen, _____.
9. Er ist falsch informiert.
   Sein Gesprächspartner betonte, daß _____.
10. Die Kinder sind beide immer noch gesund.
    Gabriele schrieb ihrem Mann, _____.

EXERCISE 2 (prerequisite: section B, topic: present q-subjunctive of modal verbs and **wissen**)

Fill in the blank with the present q-subjunctive of the verb in parentheses.

1. Er sagte mir, er _____ meine Gründe nicht verstehen. (können)
2. Die Universität schrieb mir, ich _____ nächstes Semester einen Kurs mehr belegen. (müssen)
3. Dann sagte ich dem Kellner, wir _____ den Tisch in der Ecke haben. (wollen)
4. Der Arzt sagte mir, ich _____ mehr Sport treiben. (sollen)
5. Der Polizist erklärte den amerikanischen Touristen, sie _____ den Rasen nicht betreten. (dürfen)
6. Er behauptete, er _____ die Antwort wirklich nicht. (wissen)

7. Klemenz sagte, seine Freundin _____ ihn nicht mehr. (mögen)
8. Ich sagte den Kindern, sie _____ einen anderen Spielplatz finden. (müssen)
9. Der Zeuge beteuerte, er _____ sich gut an das Gesicht des Mannes erinnern. (können)
10. Er äußerte die Meinung, wir _____ nächstes Mal besser aufpassen. (sollen)

EXERCISE 3 (prerequisite: section C, topic: present q-subjunctive of strong and weak verbs)

Fill in the blank with the present q-subjunctive of the verb in parentheses.

1. Der Außenminister der DDR beteuerte, die DDR _____ eine Politik des Friedens. (vertreten)
2. Im Buch steht, diese Pflanze _____ gut mit nur wenig Wasser. (wachsen)
3. Die Regierung behauptet, er _____ für die Sowjetunion. (spionieren)
4. Der Artikel sagte, viele Leute _____ ihren Kindern zu wenig Aufmerksamkeit. (geben)
5. Ein Nachbar teilte uns mit, Horst und Frieda _____ nicht mehr im Haus. (wohnen)
6. Stefan erwähnte, daß er Helga sehr nett _____. (finden)
7. Der Lehrer sagte mir, ich _____ unleserlich. (schreiben)
8. Mein Vater sagte mir, er würde mir das Geld geben, wenn er es _____. (haben)
9. Der Nachrichtensprecher versicherte den Zuschauern, es _____ keine Gefahr. (bestehen)
10. Er behauptete, daß ich immer zu laut _____. (reden)
11. Der Verkäufer betonte, daß dieses Auto wenig Benzin _____. (verbrauchen)
12. Die anderen Mitglieder sagten, sie _____ nichts von diesem Vorschlag. (halten)

EXERCISE 4 (prerequisite: section D, topic: past and future q-subjunctive)

Insert the statement given into the sentence that follows it.

1. Ihr Vertreter wird mich nächste Woche aufsuchen.
   Die Firma schrieb mir, _____.
2. Der Außenminister diskutierte das Problem mit dem amerikanischen Botschafter.
   Die Zeitungen meldeten, _____.
3. Manche Vögel sind dieses Jahr frühzeitig nach dem Süden geflogen.
   Diese Naturzeitschrift berichtet, _____.
4. Wir hatten keine andere Wahl.
   Georg beteuerte, _____.
5. Alle Klassen werden abgesagt werden.
   Diese Sekretärin sagt, _____.
6. Er war gegen dieses Gesetz.
   Der Abgeordnete erwiderte, _____.

7. Er wird sie nie verlassen.
   Helmut versicherte ihr, daß _____.
8. Die Einbrecher haben die Bank kurz nach Geschäftsschluß beraubt.
   Der Polizeichef äußerte die Meinung, _____.
9. Er hätte einen Brief geschrieben, wenn er meine Adresse gehabt hätte.
   Er sagte mir später, _____.
10. Wir werden das Spiel verlieren.
    Jeder glaubt, _____.
11. Der Zug aus Köln ist angekommen.
    Entschuldigung, hat man gemeldet, daß _____?
12. Sie hatte den Boden gewaschen, bevor er mit den schmutzigen Stiefeln herein-
    kam.
    Sie sagte ihm entrüstet, _____.

EXERCISE 5 (comprehensive excluding section E)

Insert the statement given into the sentence that follows it.

1. Er braucht ein neues Auto.
   Er schrieb mir, _____.
2. Die politische Lage hat sich zugespitzt.
   Ein Sprecher der Oppositionspartei behauptete, _____.
3. Viele Bürger der BRD werden dieses Jahr weniger verdienen.
   Der Bericht hatte als Schlußfolgerung, daß _____.
4. Er muß heute abend wieder bis acht Uhr arbeiten.
   Ihr Mann erklärte, _____.
5. Ich habe ihre Nase.
   Meine Großmutter sagte immer, _____.
6. Er wird nächsten Monat nach Österreich fahren.
   Der Bundeskanzler gab bekannt, _____.
7. Der Bankpräsident ist in die Schweiz geflohen.
   Ein Angestellter der Bank teilte der Presse mit, _____.
8. Von jetzt an darf ich nicht mehr rauchen.
   Der Arzt sagte, _____.
9. Er würde dieses Semester bessere Noten bekommen.
   Er beteuerte, _____.
10. Diese Raketen gefährden die guten Beziehungen zwischen der BRD und der
    DDR.
    Der Verteidigungsminister äußerte die Meinung, _____.
11. Einige unserer Verwandten kommen in einer Woche.
    Sie erwähnte, daß _____.
12. Er hat kein Glück.
    Joachim sagte, _____.
13. Nur zwei Bundesländer gaben diesem Kandidaten die Mehrheit der Stimmen.
    Diese Zeitung meldete, _____.

14. Die Verträge müssen noch vom Kongreß bewilligt werden.
    Dies sei noch nicht das Ende der Verhandlungen, betonte der Diplomat, _____.

EXERCISE 6 (comprehensive, excluding section E)

Insert the statement given into the sentence that follows it. Then translate into German.

1. The fish has already gone bad.
   The customer explained that _____.
2. Austria will remain a neutral country.
   The foreign minister emphasized, _____.
3. They sing well, but not magnificently.
   He said _____.
4. She has slept only four hours.
   She mentioned that _____.
5. Many people will not appreciate his art.
   The artist said _____.
6. He wants a raise.
   Felix told the boss yesterday that _____.
7. He would sell that dog if anyone would buy it.
   My father often said to us that _____.
8. "I was once a Nazi."
   Mr. Finkelheim said to me, _____. *(direct quote)*
9. We can't find the plates and glasses.
   I told her _____.
10. Many people believe in ghosts.
    The speaker remarked that _____.
11. She is expecting a child.
    Walpurga Waldstrudel, the famous actress, announced today _____.
12. We had invented the entire story.
    He retorted that _____.

EXERCISE 7 (prerequisite: section E, topic: q-subjunctive in non-quote sentences)

Translate these sentences into English.

1. Man lasse den Teig fünfzehn Minuten ruhen.
2. Es lebe die Republik!
3. Wer Ohren hat, der höre!
4. Er ruhe in Frieden!

5. Der Verfasser behandelte diese Idee oft in seinen Werken; man denke an seinen ersten Roman.
6. Möge sie ihr Leid vergessen!
7. Dein Reich komme. Dein Wille geschehe auf Erden wie im Himmel.
8. X sei ein Punkt gleich weit entfernt von Punkt Y und Punkt Z.
9. Es werde Licht!
10. Ein letztes Beispiel sei hier angegeben.

Review Exercises Chapters 13–15

EXERCISE 1

Fill in the blank provided with the German word(s) corresponding to the English word(s) in parentheses or with the appropriate present tense form of the German verb given in parentheses.

1. Er konnte Deutsch sprechen, als ob er ein Deutscher _____. (sein)
2. _____ es schon spät ist, müssen wir jetzt nach Hause fahren. *(since)* *(= because)*
3. Gerhard antwortete, daß er keine andere Möglichkeit _____. (sehen)
4. Sie wird den Kaffee servieren, _____ sie abgewaschen hat. *(after)*
5. Viele Eltern äußerten die Meinung, ihre Kinder _____ zu wenig. (lesen)
6. Ludwig sagte, der Aufsatz _____ heute fertig sein. (müssen)
7. Ich werde in der Bibliothek sein, _____ jemand nach mir fragt. *(in case)*
8. Jeder will wissen, _____ du die Arbeit schon gemacht hast. *(if)*
9. Wir würden dir helfen, wenn wir Zeit _____. (haben)
10. Maria sagte, sie _____ es nicht. (glauben)
11. Weißt du, _____ Mantel das ist? *(whose)*
12. Die Regierung gab heute bekannt, der Außenminister _____ nächste Woche nach Washington fliegen. (werden)
13. Wenn er kommen _____, würde er mich besuchen. (können)
14. _____ du gekommen bist, sind viele Sachen in diesem Haus verschwunden. *(since)* *(that time)*
15. Diese Zeitung berichtet, ein Wissenschaftler in Berlin _____ dieses Problem gelöst. (haben)
16. Können Sie mir sagen, _____ dieser Mann in der Ecke ist? *(who)*
17. _____ ich Sie um Ihre Hilfe bitten? *(might)*
18. Katrine und Silke sagten mir, sie _____ auch kommen. (werden)
19. Kannst du mir helfen, _____ du das für mich hältst? *(by)*
20. Wenn ich all das _____, wäre ich ein Genie. (wissen)
21. Sie werden die Fahrkarten bekommen, _____ Sie bezahlen. *(when)*
22. _____ ich in diesem Haus wohne, wird es hier keinen Hund geben! *(as long as)*

EXERCISE 2

Translate into German.

1. Franz said Julia had already gone home. *(use past q-subjunctive)*
2. I would not have believed it if I had not seen it.
3. While I vacuum the rug, you can clean the bathroom.
4. He must have once been a famous scientist.

5. Oswald retorted he would not have done that if he had been there.
6. Can you tell me when the train from Heidelberg arrives?
7. Bismarck is said to have slept in this house.
8. Hartmut and Eva explained to me that they had bought a souvenir in every city. *(use past q-subjunctive)*
9. It would have been nice if you had been able to come.
10. Johann asked Luise, ''Do you want to go out with me tonight?''
11. When we were children, we would always steal the sugar.
12. He would be the best candidate unless we could get Heinrich.
13. You shouldn't have said that.
14. We were glad that after we had compared our notes we could eliminate many mistakes.
15. I would like a single room.

What's wrong with these?

1. Falls Sie sind damit nicht zufrieden, Sie können es zurückbringen.
2. Wenn ich nur mehr Geld hatte!
3. Der Diplomat sagte unserem Reporter, ''Die Verhandlungen waren sehr erfolgreich.''
4. Ich wußte das ich eine Dummheit gemacht hatte.
5. Was hättest du getan, wenn du den Koffer nicht finden können hättest?
6. Was sollen wir tun, nach wir gegessen haben?
7. Wissen Sie, wenn die Vorlesung fängt an?
8. Wir müssen bevor zehn Uhr zu Hause sein.
9. Ich würde haben dich gehört, wenn du lauter geredet hättest!
10. Es regnet, seit wir gekommen sind.

Relative Clauses and Related Topics

16

A. Relative Clauses: Introduction

The relative pronouns in German are listed below for your reference. Forms shown in italics differ from the corresponding definite article:

case	gender MASCULINE	NEUTER	FEMININE	PLURAL
nominative	der	das	die	die
accusative	den	das	die	die
dative	dem	dem	der	*denen*
genitive	*dessen*	*dessen*	*deren*	*deren*

The usage of a relative pronoun is illustrated by the following example:

Der Mann, **den** ich gestern getroffen **habe,** heißt Helmut.
The man whom I met yesterday is called Helmut.

To determine which German relative pronoun to use in a given relative clause, follow this rule:

> *The gender and number of a German relative pronoun is determined by the word it refers back to. The case is determined by its usage in the relative clause.*

In the example above, the English relative pronoun *whom* refers back to *the man;* the equivalent German relative pronoun refers back to **der Mann.** Therefore, the gender and number of the relative pronoun is masculine singular. But in the relative clause itself, the relative pronoun functions as the direct object and as a result takes the accusative case. The noun referred back to, namely, **der Mann,** is nominative; this, however, has no effect on the case of the relative pronoun.

As with subordinate clauses, the conjugated verb in a relative clause must go to the end of the clause, and the entire relative clause must be marked off by commas:

Der Kunde, dem Sie einen Regenschirm verkauft **haben,** hat sich über Sie beschwert.
The customer to whom you sold an umbrella complained about you.

Here are some additional examples of relative pronouns:

Ist das der Mann, **der** auf mich wartet?
Is that the man who is waiting for me?
(relative pronoun refers back to **Mann,** masculine singular, and is the subject, nominative, in the relative clause)

Das ist nicht der Brief, **den** ich geschrieben habe.
That is not the letter that I wrote.
(relative pronoun refers back to **Brief,** masculine singular, and is the direct object, accusative in the relative clause)

Wo ist die verletzte Frau, **der** ich helfen soll?
Where is the injured woman that I am supposed to help?
(relative pronoun refers to **Frau,** feminine singular, and is the dative object of the dative verb **helfen**)

Die Handschuhe, **die** ich gefunden hatte, gehörten einem Freund von mir.
The gloves that I found belonged to a friend of mine.
(relative pronoun refers to **Handschuhe,** plural noun, case in relative clause is accusative)

German relative pronouns are usually identical to the corresponding definite article, but as can be seen in the table in section A, the dative plural and the genitive relative pronouns are slightly different. A common mistake is to use the definite article in all cases instead of the relative pronoun:

*Die Waisenkinder, **den** wir die Weihnachtsgeschenke gaben, waren sehr glücklich darüber.
The orphans to whom we gave the Christmas presents were very happy with them.
correct: Die Waisenkinder, **denen** wir die Weihnachtsgeschenke gaben, waren sehr glücklich darüber.

The genitive relative pronouns in German correspond to the English *whose:*

> Die Frau, **deren** Mann verschwand, heiratete einen anderen.
> *The woman whose husband disappeared married someone else.*

Note that the relative pronoun in this sentence is **deren,** the feminine form, because the relative pronoun refers back to **Frau,** *not* to the word that follows it, i.e., **Mann.** In other words, do not make the mistake shown in the next example:

> *Der Student, **deren** Großmutter gestorben war, mußte sofort nach Hause fahren.
> *The student whose grandmother had died had to go home immediately.*
> correct: Der Student, **dessen** Großmutter gestorben war, mußte sofort nach Hause fahren. (relative pronoun refers back to **Student,** masculine noun)

Similarly, you must make sure that the genitive relative pronoun agrees in *number* with the noun referred back to and not to the noun following:

> *Wir gratulierten den stolzen Eltern, **dessen** Sohn die Aufnahmeprüfung zur Universität bestanden hatte.
> *We congratulated the proud parents, whose son had passed the entrance exam to the university.*
> correct: Wir gratulierten den stolzen Eltern, **deren** Sohn die Aufnahmeprüfung zur Universität bestanden hatte.
> (relative pronoun refers back to **Eltern,** plural)

COMPREHENSION CHECK: *Part A: Fill in the blank with the appropriate relative pronoun.*

1. Der Wagen, _____ wir kaufen wollten, war leider zu teuer.
2. Der Mann, _____ ich das Geld schulde, will es schon zurückhaben.
3. Die Aufsätze, _____ Sie diese Woche geschrieben haben, waren wirklich ausgezeichnet.
4. Der Mann in der nächsten Wohnung, _____ Katze vorige Woche Kätzchen bekam, will mir jetzt eines davon geben.
5. Viele Leute, _____ wir diesen Rat gegeben haben, sind dadurch reich geworden.

Part B: Rearrange these groups of words into meaningful sentences. The break between the relative clause and the main clause is shown by two slashes.

6. Die Antwort//die/Sie/haben/gegeben//leider/ist/falsch.
7. Gib mir die 20 DM//die/du/hast/in deiner Brieftasche.
8. Diese Mutter//deren Sohn/war/so eine Enttäuschung/geworden//ihn trotzdem/ verteidigte.

ANSWERS: 1. den 2. dem 3. die 4. dessen 5. denen 6. Die Antwort, die Sie gegeben haben, ist leider falsch. 7. Gib mir die 20 DM, die du in deiner Brieftasche hast. 8. Diese Mutter, deren Sohn so eine Enttäuschung geworden war, verteidigte ihn trotzdem.

B. *Was* as a Relative Pronoun

Was is used as a relative pronoun in certain circumstances:

1. When the relative pronoun refers back to an *indefinite noun,* namely:

alles	*everything*	manches	*much*
einiges	*several things*	nichts	*nothing*
etwas	*something*	vieles	*(very) much*

    Er gab mir **alles, was** er hatte.
    He gave me everything that he had.

    Manches, was er gesagt hat, glaube ich nicht.
    Much that he said I don't believe.

    Er hat uns **nichts** gebracht, **was** wirklich nützlich war.
    He brought us nothing, that was really useful.

2. When the relative pronoun refers back to **das, dasselbe,** or a *neuter superlative:*

    Du hast **dasselbe** getan, **was** ich getan hätte.
    You did the same thing that I would have done.

    Das Interessanteste, was sie sagte, war ihre Bemerkung über die moderne Kunst.
    The most interesting thing that she said was her comment about modern art.

3. When the relative pronoun refers back to an entire clause rather than to a specific word:

    Er sagte, daß er reich wäre, **was** ich persönlich nicht glaube.
    He said that he was rich, which I personally do not believe.

    Finally, you should be aware of the fact that in older texts, **welch-** may be used as a relative pronoun:

    Der Mann, **welcher** mich betrog, war mein eigener Bruder.
    The man who deceived me was my own brother.

In modern German, **welch-** is only rarely used as a relative pronoun, and it is never required.

COMPREHENSION CHECK: *Fill in the blank with the correct relative pronoun.* **Was** *is the appropriate relative pronoun in some but not all of the sentences.*

1. Das, _____ Sie wollen, kann ich Ihnen nicht geben.
2. Wer hat den Kuchen gebacken, _____ wir eben gegessen haben?
3. Das ist etwas, _____ ich nie vorher gesehen habe.

4. Unsere Nachbarn schreien ständig, _____ mich stört.
5. Das Licht, _____ die Tür beleuchten soll, ist ausgebrannt.
6. Das Schönste, _____ ich mir jetzt vorstellen kann, ist ein Bad und nachher ein bequemes Bett.

ANSWERS: 1. was 2. den 3. was 4. was 5. das 6. was

C. Relative Pronoun Deletions

In English, relative pronouns can be *optionally* deleted with no change in meaning. First consider a sentence with the relative pronoun *not* deleted:

The house that *you wanted to buy is no longer available.*

Here is the same sentence with the relative pronoun deleted:

The house you wanted to buy is no longer available.

In German, a relative pronoun can *never* be deleted; thus, the above sentence would be expressed in German as follows:

Das Haus, **das** Sie kaufen wollten, ist nicht mehr erhältlich.

Here is another example:

It was the most ridiculous thing I have ever done.

You should recognize that the relative pronoun in this sentence has been omitted. To determine the correct German equivalent, reinsert the relative pronoun in the English sentence:

It was the most ridiculous thing that *I have ever done.*

The German equivalent is therefore the following:

Es war das Lächerlichste, **was** ich jemals getan habe.

In English, when the verb after the relative pronoun is a form of *to be,* both the relative pronoun and the verb can be deleted:

The girl (who is) standing in the corner is your waitress.

German does not allow this deletion either; instead, the entire relative clause must be written out:

Das Mädchen, **das** in der Ecke steht, ist Ihre Kellnerin.

COMPREHENSION CHECK: *Reinsert the deleted relative pronouns in these English sentences. Then translate into German.*

1. The film I saw last night was very sentimental.
2. The people singing in the next apartment are too loud.

3. Everything you have said is a lie.

> ANSWERS: 1. The film *that* I saw last night was very sentimental. Der Film, den ich gestern abend gesehen habe, war sehr sentimental.   2. The people *who are* singing in the next apartment are too loud. Die Leute, die in der nächsten Wohnung singen, sind zu laut.   3. Everything *that* you have said is a lie. Alles, was Sie gesagt haben, ist eine Lüge.

D. Relative Clauses with Prepositions

In English, a relative clause sometimes ends with a preposition:

> *He is a man that you can depend* on.

This preposition can *optionally* be put in front of the relative pronoun, though the resulting sentence may sound somewhat formal:

> *He is a man* on *whom you can depend.*

The relative pronoun may change when the preposition is shifted to the front of the relative clause, e.g., *that → whom* in the example above, but this fact is not important for German. What is important is that in German the preposition must *always* precede the relative pronoun. Thus, a correct translation of the English example would be this:

> Er ist ein Mann, **auf den** man sich verlassen kann.

Notice that the case of the relative pronoun is determined by the preceding preposition, the gender and number are determined as usual by the word referred back to.

An English sentence may have the preposition at the end of the sentence *and* the relative pronoun deleted:

> *He is a man you can depend on.*

This sentence is equivalent to the previous example and has the same German translation. Here are two more examples:

> Ist das Grundstück, **über das** wir gesprochen haben, immer noch auf dem Markt?
> *Is the property (that) we talked about still on the market?*
> (i.e., *Is the property about which we talked still on the market?*)

> Wer kann den Philosophen nennen, **auf dessen** Schriften der Existenzialismus beruht?
> *Who can name the philosopher whose writings existentialism is based on?*
> (i.e., *Who can name the philosopher on whose writings existentialism is based?*)

In the previous German examples, the preposition was followed by a relative pronoun. This is always the case when the relative pronoun refers to a person. If, however, the relative pronoun refers to a thing, then the preposition + relative pronoun is often replaced by a so-called **wo-***compound:*

Ist dies der Aufsatz, **an dem** Sie arbeiten?

or

Ist dies der Aufsatz, **woran** Sie arbeiten?
Is this the essay you are working on?
(i.e., *Is this the essay on which you are working?*)

The **wo**-compound is actually a combination of **was** plus the preposition. As with **da**-compounds, an **r** is inserted before a preposition beginning with a vowel. Other typical **wo**-compounds would be, for example, **womit, worin, wozu, worauf,** etc.

The **wo**-compound *must* be used when the relative pronoun refers back to a word that requires **was** as the relative pronoun:

Er hat **einiges** überprüft, **woran** ich nicht gedacht hatte.
He checked some things that I had not thought of.
(**was** would be the relative pronoun referring back to **einiges,** this combines with the preposition **an** to give **woran**)

In English, a question may begin with a interrogative word and end in a preposition:

A. *Who were you talking with?*   B. *What should we drink to?*

As with relative clauses, these prepositions can also precede the interrogative word:

A. *With whom were you talking?*   B. *To what should we drink?*

In German, the preposition *must* precede the interrogative word. In addition, a **wo**-compound is formed if the interrogative word **was:**

A. **Mit wem** has du geredet?   B. **Worauf** sollen wir trinken?

COMPREHENSION CHECK: *Rewrite the English sentences below so that the preposition has been shifted to the front of the relative clause or question (even though the resulting sentence may sound awkward). Then translate into German.*

1. When does the train arrive that you are waiting for?
2. What do you believe in?
3. That is the teacher I am angry at.
4. Tell me something I can laugh about.

ANSWERS: 1. *When does the train arrive for which you are waiting?* Wann kommt der Zug an, auf den (*or* worauf) Sie warten? 2. *In what do you believe?* Woran glaubst du? 3. *That is the teacher at whom I am angry.* Das ist der Lehrer, auf den ich zornig bin. 4. *Tell me something about which I can laugh.* Sag mir etwas, worüber ich lachen kann.

E. Extended Modifiers

Consider the following sentence containing a relative clause:

> Dieses Gerät, das von einem unserer Wissenschaftler entwickelt wurde, wird die Produktionskosten senken.
> *This device, which was developed by one of our scientists, will reduce the production costs.*

In German, the relative clause can be replaced by an *extended modifier* (shown in parentheses):

> (Dieses von einem unserer Wissenschaftler entwickelte Gerät) wird die Produktionskosten senken.

The extended modifier turns the entire relative clause into a complex adjective modifying the noun **Gerät.** Note also that the verb in the relative clause has become a past participle and is being used as an adjective. Extended modifiers are commonly employed in scientific German and may also occur in other varieties of formal writing and literature. The example below will be used to show how to understand sentences containing extended modifiers:

> Diese im Jahre 1866 gefundene mittelalterliche Handschrift vermittelt uns eine neue Version der alten Legende.

1. The first step is to recognize the extended adjective modifier by observing these characteristic features:

> *An extended modifier usually consists of a **der**-word or **kein**-word followed by a series of words which are not adjectives, plus a present or past participle, ending in a noun.*

Applying this definition, the extended modifier in the example above can be identified and is shown in parentheses in the sentence that follows:

> (Diese im Jahre 1866 gefundene mittelalterliche Handschrift) vermittelt uns eine neue Version der alten Legende.

2. Next, underline the verb being used as a past or present participle:

> (Diese im Jahre 1866 <u>gefundene</u> Handschrift) vermittelt uns eine neue Version der alten Legende.

3. Put a bracket at the *first word* in the extended modifier that is *not* an *adjective* and put a closing bracket immediately after the underlined present or past participle. The parentheses can now be discarded:

> Diese [im Jahre 1866 <u>gefundene</u>] mittelalterliche Handschrift vermittelt uns eine neue Version der alten Legende.

4. Translate the sentence into English by putting everything outside of the brackets in a main clause and everything within the brackets in a relative clause, having the underlined present or past participle as the conjugated verb:

This medieval manuscript, (which was) found in the year 1866, conveys to us a new version of the old legend.

Here is an example in which a present participle is used. To save space, the example is followed immediately by the sentence corresponding to step 3 above:

Beobachten Sie genau das in der Flamme brennende Salz.
Beobachten Sie genau das [in der Flamme <u>brennende</u>] Salz.
Observe closely the salt (which is) burning in the flame.

A given German sentence may contain a series of extended modifiers before the noun. The process of analyzing these is essentially the same as before:

Dieser von den Griechen übernommene, in der westlichen Welt als selbstverständlich empfundene Gedanke gilt in manchen anderen Teilen der Welt als absurd.

Dieser [von den Griechen <u>übernommene</u>], [in der westlichen Welt als selbstverständlich <u>empfundene</u>] Gedanke gilt in manchen anderen Teilen der Welt als absurd.

This idea, which has been taken from the Greeks and which in the western world is perceived as being self–evident, is considered to be absurd in some other parts of the world.

A common type of extended modifier consists of **zu** plus a present participle. The English equivalent to this German construction is generally a past participle preceded by *to be, must be,* or *should be.* Here are two examples:

Das heute abend **zu** besprechende Thema beschäftigt sich mit der Zukunft der deutschen Wirtschaft.

Das [heute abend zu <u>besprechende</u>] Thema beschäftigt sich mit der Zukunft der deutschen Wirtschaft.

The topic to be discussed tonight deals with the future of the German economy.

Sie haben diese zwei voneinander **zu** unterscheidenden Begriffe nicht genügend erklärt.

Sie haben diese zwei [voneinander zu <u>unterscheidenden</u>] Begriffe nicht genügend erklärt.

You have not sufficiently explained these two concepts which must (should) be differentiated from each other.

COMPREHENSION CHECK: *Analyze the sentences below as shown in this section. Then translate into English.*

1. Diese vor kurzem in Wien eingeführten Straßenbahnen sind äußerst energiesparend.

2. Diese Droge ist nur gegen die im Anfangsstadium auftretenden Symptome wirksam.

3. Der Leser kann alle zu benutzenden Werkzeuge für weniger als 100 DM kaufen.

4. Eberhard wollte nicht in die Nähe des mit Schweiß bedeckten, nach Benzin stinkenden Arbeiters kommen.

ANSWERS: 1. Diese [vor kurzem in Wien eingeführten] Straßenbahnen sind äußerst energiesparend. *These streetcars, which were recently introduced in Vienna, are very energy-efficient.* 2. Diese Droge ist nur gegen die [im Anfangsstadium auftretenden] Symptome wirksam. *This drug is only effective against the symptoms which appear in the initial phase.* 3. Der Leser kann alle [zu benutzenden] Werkzeuge für weniger als 100 DM kaufen. *The reader can buy all tools which are to be used for less than 100 DM.* 4. Eberhard wollte nicht in die Nähe des [mit Schweiß bedeckten], [nach Benzin stinkenden] Arbeiters kommen. *Eberhard did not want to come near the worker who was covered with sweat and who stank of gasoline.*

German-English Vocabulary

Learn the words listed on page 229 and the following:

absolut	*absolute(ly)*	ein.führen	*to introduce*
der Agent, -en, -en	*agent*	das Einzelzimmer,	*single bedroom*
das Anfangs-	*initial phase*		
stadium, *plural*		der Elementarstoff,	*(chemical) element*
-stadien		-e	
auf.treten (tritt),	*to appear*	energiesparend	*energy-efficient*
trat, getreten		entwerfen	*to devise*
aus.brennen *(mixed*	*to burn out*	(entwirft),	
verb)		entwarf,	
ausgezeichnet	*excellent*	entworfen	
äußerst	*very, extremely*	erinnern einen an	*to remind one of*
backen	*to bake*	+ *acc.*	
das Bad, ̈er	*bath*	die Freude, -n	*joy*
bedecken	*to cover*	freuen auf + *acc.*	*to look forward to*
der Begriff, -e	*concept*	(*reflexive*)	
bei.bringen *(mixed*	*to teach*	gehören + *dat.*	*to belong to*
verb)		die Gesellschaft,	*organization,*
benützen	*to use*	-en	*society*
der Bleistift, -e	*pencil*	gründen	*to found*
borgen	*to loan*	die Hand, ̈e	*hand*
der Brauch, ̈e	*custom*	hängen, hing,	*to hang*
die Briefmarke, -n	*stamp*	gehangen	*(somewhere)*
chemikalisch	*chemical*	das Haustier, -e	*pet*
der Edelstein, -e	*jewel, precious*	die Heizung	*heating*
	stone	herrschen	*to prevail, to reign*

innen	inside, on the inside	die Schulbehörde, -n	schoolboard
das Jahres-einkommen, -	yearly income	der Schulunterricht	classroom instruction
das Jahrhundert, -e	century	der Schwager, ⸚	brother-in-law
die Jahrhundert-wende, -n	turn of the century	der Schweiß	sweat
		schwierig	difficult
das Jugendwerk, -e	early work (in one's youth)	sicher	certain(ly), for sure
das Kätzchen, -	kitten	die Sprache, -n	language
die Kirsche, -n	cherry	ständig	constant(ly)
der Kritiker, -	critic	stiften	to donate
die Krone, -n	crown	stinken, stank, gestunken	to stink
der Kuchen, -	cake		
kurzlebig	short-lived	stören	to bother, disturb
das Labor, -e	laboratory	das Symptom, -e	symptom
legen	to lay, put	das Thema, plural Themen	topic
leiden	to stand (someone), to suffer	ungesetzlich	illegal
der Leser, -	reader	ungesund	unhealthy
loben	to praise	ungewöhnlich	unusual
mieten	to rent	unpraktisch	impractical
nach.gehen, ging, gegangen	to run slow (clock)	verbieten, verbot, verboten	to forbid
namens	by the name of	verständlich	understandable
das Naturgesetz, -e	law of nature	verzieren	to decorate
oben	up there	vor.kommen, kam, gekommen	to occur
die Ohrfeige, -n	slap in the face		
ostdeutsch	East German	vor kurzem	a short time ago, recently
passen zu	to go with, be appropriate with	vor.schlagen (schlägt), schlug, geschlagen	to suggest
der Pfadfinder, -	boy scout		
die Pflanzenart, -en	plant type		
protestieren	to protest	weit	far
pünktlich	promptly	wiederauf.bauen	to rebuild
der Rat, plural Ratschläge	advice	wirksam gegen	effective against
		die Wüste, -n	desert
schief.gehen	to fail, go wrong	ziemlich	rather
schmecken	to taste		

EXERCISE 1 (prerequisite: section A, topic: basic relative pronouns)

Fill in the blank with the appropriate relative pronoun.

1. Die Geschichte, _____ sie erzählte, war äußerst interessant.
2. Der Mann, _____ er die Information gab, war ein ostdeutscher Agent.
3. Ist das der Kerl, _____ Hund dich gebissen hat?
4. Die meisten Pflanzenarten, _____ in der Wüste wachsen, brauchen nur wenig Wasser.

5. Die meisten Leute, _____ die Bank Geld borgt, bezahlen es auch pünktlich zurück.
6. Ich kann Nachbarn, _____ Auto besser ausschaut als meines, absolut nicht leiden.
7. Das Messer, _____ Sie in der Hand haben, ist schmutzig.
8. Viele der Soldaten, _____ wir dieses Denkmal widmen, sind nicht vom Krieg zurückgekommen.
9. Können Sie die Kirschen erreichen, _____ ganz weit oben hängen?
10. Die Gesellschaft, _____ er 1.000.000 DM stiftete, nannte ein neues Gebäude nach ihm.
11. Ich habe gestern einen alten Freund getroffen, _____ ich seit zehn Jahren nicht gesehen habe.
12. Diese Uhren, _____ wir von ihnen bestellt haben, gehen nach.
13. Der nächste Mensch, _____ etwas Schlechtes über meinen Hut sagt, kriegt von mir eine Ohrfeige.
14. Elisabeth, _____ Mann immer säuft, will zu ihrer Mutter gehen.
15. Die Armen, _____ wir geholfen haben, waren auch sehr dankbar dafür.

EXERCISE 2 (prerequisite: section A, topic: word order in relative clauses)

Rearrange the groups of words so as to form correct sentences. Double slashes indicate the break between the relative clause and the main clause.

1. Ich habe eine Briefmarke gefunden//die/lag/auf dem Boden.
2. Die meisten Leute//die/wohnen/in dieser Stadt//in der Fabrik/arbeiten.
3. Der Film//den/wir/haben/gestern abend/gesehen//war/ziemlich langweilig.
4. Viele Gebäude//die/während des Krieges/waren/zerstört/worden//wurden/ wiederaufgebaut.
5. Der Plan//den/Sie/vorlegen/hier//wird/schiefgehen/sicher.
6. Per//dessen Eltern/kommen/aus Schweden//einen Vortrag am Montag über dieses Land/wird/halten.

EXERCISE 3 (prerequisite: sections A–B, topic: deciding when to use **was** as the relative pronoun)

Fill in the blanks with the appropriate form of the relative pronoun.

1. Vieles, _____ ich in Deutschland gegessen habe, hat mir gut geschmeckt.
2. Das ist genau dasselbe, _____ ich gesagt habe!
3. Die Äpfel, _____ ich gestern hier gekauft habe, waren innen schlecht.
4. Glaub nicht alles, _____ du hörst.
5. Hast du den Bleistift gesehen, _____ ich auf diesen Tisch gelegt habe?
6. Dieses Jahr war der Sommer sehr naß, _____ für diese Gegend ungewöhnlich ist.

7. Wir untersuchten die Meinungen von Leuten, _____ Jahreseinkommen unter 40.000 DM lag.
8. Ich habe nichts getan, _____ ich jetzt bereue.
9. Die Wohnung, _____ er gemietet hatte, hatte keine Heizung.
10. Dort ist der Mann, _____ Sie wirklich danken sollten.
11. Das, _____ Sie vorschlagen, ist unpraktisch.
12. Wo sind diese Leute, _____ wir gehorchen müssen?
13. Das Merkwürdigste, _____ ich jemals gesehen habe, war ein Hund mit Schuhen.
14. Sind Sie die Person, _____ mit mir sprechen will?
15. Ich muß gegen einiges protestieren, _____ Sie über mich geschrieben haben.
16. Ich will ein Haustier für meine Kinder kaufen, _____ nicht zu teuer ist.
17. Hätten Sie vielleicht etwas, _____ zu diesem Anzug passen würde?
18. Manches, _____ er sagt, ist nicht wahr.

EXERCISE 4 (prerequisite: sections A–B, topic: review of previous exercises)

Translate into German.

1. We can't give the children everything that they want.
2. Is this the man who stole your purse?
3. The price which she had to pay was too high.
4. The tourists that I helped were from Greece.
5. That is something that you don't see every day.
6. What is the stupidest thing that you have ever done?
7. The lawyers whose office is in this building want to move out.
8. a. I wrote two essays which were very difficult.
   b. I wrote two essays, which was very difficult.
9. She always wears the same thing that her older sister wore.
10. What is the address of the woman to whom you want to send these flowers?

EXERCISE 5 (prerequisite: sections A–C, topic relative pronoun deletions)

Reinsert the deleted words in the English sentences. Then translate into German.

1. I couldn't eat the fish I had ordered.
2. The coat lying on the bed belongs to me.
3. Nothing you can do now will help.
4. The people you saw were workers in the factory.
5. Is that the same thing you did?
6. The meat cooking in the oven is burning.

EXERCISE 6 (comprehensive, excluding section E)

*Fill in the blank with the correct relative pronoun after the preposition. Where possible, state what the alternative **wo**-compound would be. In some sentences, the **wo**-compound may be mandatory.*

1. Es gibt doch niemand, auf _____ du eifersüchtig sein mußt!
2. Dies ist das Buch, nach _____ Sie gefragt haben.
3. Meine Eltern haben mir das Fahrrad gekauft, auf _____ ich mich gefreut hatte.
4. Es gibt vieles, vor _____ ich dich warnen muß.
5. Die Frau, auf _____ ich gewartet habe, kam nicht.
6. Das Gebäude, in _____ Sie jetzt sind, wurde im 15. Jahrhundert gebaut.
7. Was ist das Wichtigste, auf _____ wir achten müssen?
8. Das ist der Mann, mit _____ Tochter ich zur Partie gegangen bin.

EXERCISE 7 (comprehensive, excluding section E)

Translate into German.

1. The man I bought the rug from was a Turk.
2. What are you working on?
3. That is something I am not proud of.
4. The disease he died of was never identified.
5. The senator I wrote a letter to didn't write back.
6. What was the name of the movie he was enthusiastic about?
7. What must we do without?
8. I can't give you everything you ask for (use **bitten**).

EXERCISE 8 (prerequisite: section E, topic: extended modifiers)

Analyze these sentences as shown in section E, then translate into English.

1. Die moderne Physik fing mit den von Newton entworfenen Naturgesetzen an.
2. Die meisten im Leben zu genießenden Freuden sind entweder ungesetzlich, ungesund, oder zu teuer.
3. Diese nur im Labor vorkommenden Elementarstoffe sind sehr kurzlebig.
4. Wir wohnen in einem schönen um die Jahrhundertwende gebauten Haus.
5. Dieses von allen Kritikern gelobte, von einem unbekannten Verfasser geschriebene Buch erinnert einen an die Jungendwerke Hermann Hesses.
6. Die mit Edelsteinen verzierte Krone gehörte den Habsburgern.
7. Dieser Kandidat vertritt die für seine Partei herrschende Meinung.
8. Die Universität wollte diesen seit vielen Jahren bestehenden, von einem Studenten namens Smoot gegründeten Brauch verbieten.

9. Er konnte sogar die schwierig zu begreifenden Begriffe verständlich machen.
10. Die Schulbehörde hat die in diesem Buch beschriebenen chemikalischen Experimente für den Schulunterricht bewilligt.

GEDANKENPROBLEM: **Translate the sentence below into German.**

HINT: If you are acquainted with computer programming, you might think of this sentence in terms of nested loops.

I couldn't go to Russia because the visa I needed arrived too late.

What's wrong with these?

1. Wo ist der Wagen der Sie gekauft haben?
2. Der Pfadfinder, wer ein kleines Kind gerettet hatte, bekam eine Auszeichnung.
3. Der große Hund liegend vor der Tür ist ein Bernhardiner.
4. Der Kerl, den du hast eben gesehen, ist mein Schwager.
5. Sie sind der letzte Mensch ich werde verzeihen.
6. Er hat mir alles beigebracht, daß ich von der deutschen Sprache weiß.
7. Das Kind, deren Mutter krank war, wollte nicht mitspielen.
8. Das Beste ich kann Ihnen bieten ist ein Einzelzimmer ohne Bad.
9. Einige Leute, den du Geld schuldest, warten draußen vor der Tür auf dich.
10. Kannst du mir sagen, an was du hast gedacht?

Infinitive Clauses

17

A. Infinitive Clauses: Introduction

Infinitive clauses in English start with *to* plus the verb infinitive; in German they *end* with **zu** plus the infinitive:

> Wir fingen an, das Problem **zu** verstehen.
> *We began to understand the problem.*

An infinitive clause in German is usually preceded by a comma unless the clause consists only of **zu** + infinitive:

> Es fing an zu regnen.
> *It began to rain.*

If the verb in the infinitive clause has a separable prefix, then the **zu** is inserted between the prefix and the verb stem (just like the **ge-** of the past participle):

> Ich verspreche, sobald wie möglich zurück**zu**kommen.
> *I promise to come back as soon as possible.*

As in English, a German sentence may contain a series of infinitive clauses:

> Es wäre nett, die Chance zu haben, mit Ihnen zu sprechen.
> *It would be nice to have the chance to speak with you.*

The previous examples have shown the so-called *present infinitive*. The formation of the *past* infinitive can be seen in the example that follows:

> Es war mir eine hohe Ehre, ihn **gekannt zu haben.**
> *It was a great honor for me to have known him.*

In the past infinitive, the auxiliary verb appears in the infinitive form and goes at the end of the infinitive clause. Here is an example in which the auxiliary is **sein:**

> Er behauptet, ein Schachmeister **gewesen zu sein.**
> *He claims to have been a chess master.*

One problem students often have with infinitive clauses is deciding which elements in English belong in the main clause and which in the infinitive clause. The rule is this:

> *Everything before the "to" is in the main clause, everything after the "to" and up to the next clause is a part of the infinitive clause.*

For example, notice the position of **mir** in the German sentences below. Then compare this with the position of *me* in the English sentences:

Aber du hast versprochen, **mir** jeden Tag zu schreiben!
But you promised to write me every day!

Aber du hast **mir** versprochen, jeden Tag zu schreiben!
But you promised me to write every day!

The next example shows a common mistake involving an infinitive clause that follows a subordinate clause:

*Ich hoffe, daß es leicht dieses Problem zu lösen **ist**.
I hope that it is easy to solve this problem.
correct: Ich hoffe, daß es leicht **ist**, dieses Problem zu lösen.

The subordinate clause stops where the infinitive clause begins, and the verb must therefore go immediately before the infinitive clause, not at the end of the sentence.

COMPREHENSION CHECK: *Rewrite the second part of these sentences so as to form an infinitive clause. You will have to supply **zu** and a comma where necessary. The two slashes indicate the beginning of the infinitive clause.*

1. Ich war nicht geneigt//bezahlen/diesen Preis.
2. Hast du vergessen//deinen Ausweis/mitnehmen?
3. Wir waren froh//diese schwierige Arbeit/haben/beendet.
4. Endlich hörte es auf//schneien.

ANSWERS: 1. Ich war nicht geneigt, diesen Preis zu bezahlen. 2. Hast du vergessen, deinen Ausweis mitzunehmen? 3. Wir waren froh, diese schwierige Arbeit beendet zu haben. 4. Endlich hörte es auf zu schneien.

B. Infinitive Clauses and Some Irregular Verbs

Certain verbs in German are irregular in that they can be used with an additional verb preceded by **zu.** However, the second part of the sentence is not considered to be an infinitive clause. In practical terms, this means that no comma appears in such sentences. These verbs are:

brauchen	*to need*	scheinen	*to appear, to seem*
haben	*to have*	sein	*to be*
pflegen	*to usually do something*		

The following sentences illustrate this particular usage of these verbs:

Ich brauche das nicht zu tun.
I don't need to do that.

Hast du etwas zu tun?
Do you have something to do?

Er pflegt sein Frühstück im Bett zu essen. *(formal construction)*
He usually eats his breakfast in bed.

Das scheint richtig zu sein.
That appears to be correct.

Dieses Buch ist leicht zu verstehen.
This book is easy to understand.

The construction **sein + zu +** the infinitive shown in the last example often corresponds to English *can be, must be* or *should be +* past participle. Thus, the previous example could also be expressed in English as follows:

This book can be easily understood.

Here is another example of this construction:

Das Zerkratzen der Glasfläche ist zu vermeiden.
The scratching of the glass surface must be (should be) avoided.

A few verbs in German do not use **zu** at all where English may have an infinitive clause (this assumes that the German sentence is short). These verbs are:

heißen	*to command*
helfen	*to help*
lehren	*to teach*
lernen	*to learn*

Here are some practical examples of these verbs:

Der König hieß ihn kommen. *(formal construction)*
The king commanded him to come.

Hilf mir aufstehen!
Help me (to) get up.

Ich lehre ihn schwimmen.
I am teaching him to swim.

Er lernt schwimmen.
He is learning to swim.

Infinitive Clauses and Some Irregular Verbs 243

However, when additional elements are added to the middle field of a sentence with one of these verbs, then the sentence is usually broken up into a main clause and an infinitive clause, as in English:

> Ich lehrte sie, ausländische Filme mit oder ohne Untertiteln zu genießen.
> *I taught her to enjoy foreign films with or without subtitles.*

There is no clear-cut limit as to when a sentence with one of these verbs becomes too long to be used without **zu.** In general, however, **zu** is used with such verbs when the sentence contains more than just the direct and/or indirect object.

COMPREHENSION CHECK: *Rearrange these groups of words to form meaningful sentences. Insert **zu** and comma where necessary.*

1. Er/scheint/krank/sein.
2. Mein jüngstes Kind/lernt/radfahren/jetzt.
3. Das ist/leicht/sagen.
4. Er hat mir geholfen/diese Gruppe von wilden Kindern/überwachen.

> ANSWERS: 1. Er scheint krank zu sein. 2. Mein jüngstes Kind lernt jetzt radfahren. 3. Das ist leicht zu sagen. 4. Er hat mir geholfen, diese Gruppe von wilden Kindern zu überwachen.

C. English Infinitive Clauses That Correspond to German Subordinate Clauses

A common construction in English is to have the verb of the main clause followed by a noun object, which in turn is followed by an infinitive clause. In general, German deals with such sentences in a similar fashion:

> Ich bat **ihn,** die Arbeit sofort zu erledigen.
> *I asked him to take care of the job immediately.*
> (accusative noun object **ihn** followed by infinitive clause)

However, a small group of German verbs will not tolerate a noun object followed by an infinitive clause, even though their English counterparts do. Such verbs require a subordinate clause in German:

erwarten	*to expect*
möchten	*would like*
sagen	*to tell*
wollen	*to want*

> Die Firma erwartet, daß Sie mehr verkaufen.
> *The company expects you to sell more.*

> Ich will (möchte) nicht, daß Sie mich anlügen!
> *I don't want you to lie to me!*

Ich habe ihr gesagt, daß sie den Schlüssel in der Garage verstecken sollte.
I told her to hide the key in the garage.

In the last example, the German subordinate clause contains the verb **sollte.** The necessity for this can be seen by converting the equivalent English sentence into one with a subordinate clause:

I told her that she should hide the key in the garage.

In German do not write an infinitive clause after these verbs:

*Erwartest du mich, das zu tun?
Do you expect me to do that?
correct: Erwartest du, daß ich das tue?

A number of verbs in English can be followed by an interrogative word plus an infinitive clause. German does not allow this with any verb; instead, once again, a subordinate clause is used:

Wissen Sie, wie man (ich) das Meldeamt anrufen kann?
Do you know how to call the bureau of registry?

Note that the English sentence could also be rewritten with a subordinate clause:

Do you know how one (I) can call the bureau of registry?

In other words, whereas English allows an infinitive clause or a subordinate clause with such sentences, German permits only the subordinate clause.

COMPREHENSION CHECK: *Translate into German.*

1. He expects me to fulfill all his wishes.
2. He showed her how to fill out the form.
3. Our teacher wants us to write an essay.

ANSWERS: 1. Er erwartet, daß ich all seine Wünsche erfülle. 2. Er zeigte ihr, wie man (sie) das Formular ausfüllen kann. 3. Unser Lehrer will (möchte), daß wir einen Aufsatz schreiben.

German-English Vocabulary

der Abfall	*garbage*	erwarten	*to expect*
der Alligator, -en	*alligator*	faul	*lazy*
an.greifen, griff,	*to attack*	die Ferien (*plural*)	*vacation*
gegriffen		gar nicht	*not at all*
die Armee, -n	*army*	geneigt sein	*to be in the mood*
aus.packen	*to unpack*	der General, ̈-e	*general*
der Ausweis, -e	*identification card*	heißen, hieß,	*to command*
da	*there*	geheißen	

hinaus.tragen (trägt), trug, getragen	*to carry out*	in Ruhe lassen	*to leave alone, to not disturb*
das Krokodil, -e	*crocodile*	segeln	*to sail*
mit.nehmen (nimmt), nahm, genommen	*to take along*	überwachen	*to supervise*
		der Unterschied, -e	*difference*
		verbringen (*mixed verb*)	*to spend (time)*
natürlich	*naturally*	versuchen	*to try*
nützlich	*useful*	vor.rücken	*to advance*
pflegen	*to usually do something*	weiter	*additional, further*
		wild	*wild*
rad.fahren (fährt), fuhr, gefahren	*to ride a bicycle*	das Winter- semester, -	*winter semester*
die Ruhe	*peace, quiet*	das Ziel, -e	*goal*

EXERCISE 1 (prerequisite: section A, topic: word order in infinitive clauses)

Rearrange the groups of words in the second part of the sentence to make an infinitive clause. Supply zu and comma where necessary. The two slashes indicate where the infinitive clause begins.

1. Du versuchst gar nicht//tun/etwas Nützliches.
2. Empfiehlst du mir//diesen Kurs/belegen/im Wintersemester?
3. Ich war natürlich erstaunt//ihn/sehen/da.
4. Hitler hatte den Engländern versprochen//keine weiteren Länder/angreifen.
5. Wir waren froh//ein gutes Hotel/haben/gefunden.
6. Es war mein Ziel//der beste Schüler in der Klasse/werden.
7. Ich war zu faul//mit der Arbeit/anfangen.
8. Er bat uns//lassen/die Papiere auf seinem Tisch/in Ruhe.

EXERCISE 2 (prerequisite: section A, topic: formation of infinitive clauses)

Translate into German.

1. Suddenly it began to rain.
2. Will we have the opportunity to visit the old church in Zwentendorf?
3. My mother forced me to take along my winter coat.
4. It would be nice to have seen the famous cathedral in Mainz.
5. I promised her to find time to write her.
6. It's my task to feed the rabbits.

EXERCISE 3 (prerequisite: section B, topic: irregular verbs with infinitive clauses)

Rearrange these groups of words into meaningful sentences. Add **zu** *and comma where necessary.*

1. Was haben wir/trinken?
2. Der General hieß/die Armee/vorrücken.
3. Franz pflegte/seine Ferien zu Hause/verbringen.
4. Viele junge Leute in Österreich/lernen/tanzen.
5. Er lehrte uns/den Unterschied zwischen einem Alligator und einem Krokodil/erkennen.
6. Was/ist/machen?
7. Du/brauchst/die Handschuhe nicht/mitnehmen.
8. Hilfst du/mir/auspacken?

EXERCISE 4 (prerequisite: section B, topic: irregular verbs with infinitive clauses)

Translate into German.

1. The children are learning to read.
2. Our hotel was easy to find.
3. Give me something to eat.
4. Help her to carry the dishes into the kitchen.
5. Do I need to call him? (use **brauchen**)
6. Julia called her mother every weekend. (use **pflegen**)

EXERCISE 5 (prerequisite: section C, topic: English infinitive clauses that correspond to German subordinate clauses)

Translate into German.

1. I don't want you to buy it.
2. Can you tell me what to do?
3. We expect you to be home before eleven o'clock.
4. Who told you to wait here?
5. I expect him to arrive soon.
6. Do you know how to cook lobster?

EXERCISE 6 (comprehensive)

Translate into German.

1. He advised me to sell my stocks.
2. I told them to take along their cameras.
3. He taught me to paint.
4. It's beginning to snow.
5. I have a lot to do today.
6. My parents want me to work this summer.
7. These pills help me to sleep.
8. The doctor ordered me to breathe in deeply. (use **befehlen**)
9. Can you explain to me how to order a taxi in Germany? (use **bestellen**)
10. I would like you to be happy.
11. My teacher expects us to know everything.
12. He claimed to have been born in Russia.
13. Renate was nowhere to be found.
14. Do you believe that a woman has the duty to obey her husband?

GEDANKENPROBLEM: How would you say this in German?

It would be nice to be able to speak with you.

HINT: Use the structure of the past infinitive as a guide.

What's wrong with these?

1. Ich begann zu verstehen den Artikel.
2. Wir haben keine Zeit, auf alle Themen zu eingehen.
3. Wir erwarten dich da zu sein.
4. Er hat uns den Film erlaubt zu sehen.
5. Vorigen Sommer lernte ich zu segeln.
6. Ich war so überrascht, daß ich nicht wußte, was zu sagen.

The English Construction: Verb + Verb + -ing: German Equivalents and Related Topics

18

A. *Fühlen, Hören, Sehen,* and *Lassen*

In English, the verbs *to feel, to hear* and *to see* are often followed by a verb + *-ing*; in German, the equivalent verbs **fühlen, hören** and **sehen** are followed by an infinitive:

> **Fühlst** du das Fieber schlimmer **werden?**
> *Do you feel the fever getting worse?*

> Ich **höre** jemanden **kommen.**
> *I hear someone coming.*

> Er **sieht** mich **weinen.**
> *He sees me crying.*

The simple past of these German verbs is formed in a straightforward fashion:

> **Fühltest** du das Fieber schlimmer werden?
> *Did you feel the fever getting worse?*

> Ich **hörte** jemanden kommen.
> *I heard someone coming.*

Er **sah** mich weinen.
He saw me crying.

The present perfect, however, is formed with the *infinitive* of the verbs **fühlen, hören,** or **sehen:**

Hast du das Fieber schlimmer werden **fühlen?**

Ich habe jemand kommen **hören.**

Er hat mich weinen **sehen.**

(These sentences have the same meanings as the previous examples in the simple past tense.)

Sometimes the English verb + *-ing* is contracted to the verb stem alone; the German translation is the same:

Hast du den Baum fallen hören?
Did you hear the tree fall(ing)?

These verbs can also take two accusative objects. The meaning of such sentences can be seen in the examples below:

Wir hörten **ihn ein Lied** singen.
We heard him singing a song.

Ich habe **dich meinen Mantel** stehlen sehen.
I saw you stealing my coat.

The German verb **lassen** (*to let, allow*) functions in the same manner as **fühlen, hören** and **sehen:**

Er **läßt** mich nicht ins Kino gehen.
He doesn't let me go to movies.
(present tense)

Er **ließ** mich nicht ins Kino gehen.

or

Er **hat** mich nicht ins Kino gehen **lassen.**
He didn't let me go to movies.
(simple past or present perfect)

Another common meaning of **lassen,** when used with another verb, is *to have* (something) *done:*

Ich **lasse** den Rasen mähen.
I am having the lawn mowed.
(present tense)

Ich **ließ** den Rasen mähen.

or

Ich **habe** den Rasen mähen **lassen.**
I had the lawn mowed.
(simple past or present perfect)

In sentences such as the above containing a form of **lassen,** the person actually doing the activity is indicated by an accusative object. The resulting sentence has a double accusative object:

> Ich ließ **meinen Sohn den Rasen** mähen.
> *I had my son mow the lawn.*

The person for whom the activity is being done is indicated by a dative pronoun:

> Ich lasse **mir** eine Garage bauen.
> *I am having a garage built (for myself).*

Finally, the following examples show how these verbs can be used in the future tense:

> Willst du ihn singen hören?
> *Do you want to hear him sing?*

> Wirst du dir eine Garage bauen lassen?
> *Will you have a garage built for you?*

COMPREHENSION CHECK: *Part A: Translate the sentences into English.*

1.   Ich höre ihn lachen.
2.   Dieser Lärm läßt mich nicht schlafen!
3.   Siehst du jemand auf mich warten?
4.   a. Ich ließ mein Auto reparieren.
         b. Ich ließ ihn mein Auto reparieren.
5.   Wir wollen den Teppich reinigen lassen.

Part B: Rewrite sentences 1–3 above in the present perfect tense.

ANSWERS: Part A 1. I hear him laughing.   2. This noise won't let me sleep.   3. Do you see someone waiting for me?   4.a. I had my car repaired.   4.b. I had him repair my car.   5. We want to have the carpet cleaned.   Part B: 1. Ich habe ihn lachen hören. 2. Dieser Lärm hat mich nicht schlafen lassen.   3. Hast du jemand auf mich warten sehen?

B. *Ohne... Zu, (An)statt... Zu,* and *Um... Zu* in Infinitive Clauses

English often uses verb + *-ing* after the prepositions *without* and *instead of.* The German equivalent of these verb forms is usually an infinitive clause based on **ohne... zu** and **(an)statt... zu,** respectively:

> Tue es nicht, **ohne** mich vorher **zu** fragen.
> *Don't do it without asking me beforehand.*

Du solltest mehr essen, **(an)statt** so viel Bier **zu** trinken.
You should eat more instead of drinking so much beer.

Note: **Anstatt** is more formal than **statt.**

The infinitive clause can also begin the sentence:

Statt so viel Bier **zu** trinken, solltest du mehr essen.
Instead of drinking so much beer, you should eat more.

Here is an example in which the infinitive has a separable prefix:

Kannst du dieses Seil halten, ohne diesmal **los**zulassen?
Can you hold onto this rope without letting go this time?

The German **um... zu** construction, which corresponds to English *in order to,* functions in the same manner as **ohne... zu** and **(an)statt... zu:**

Ich gehe heute zur Apotheke, **um** Hustentropfen **zu** kaufen.
I'm going to the pharmacy today in order to buy cough syrup.

The English construction *in order to* is often shortened to simply *to.* This may mislead you to write an **um... zu** construction in German as an infinitive clause with **zu** alone:

*Normalerweise sind zwei Wochen notwendig, den Wagen **zu** richten.
Normally two weeks are necessary (in order) to fix the car.
correct: Normalerweise sind zwei Wochen notwendig, **um** den Wagen **zu** richten.

In other words, if you could say *in order to* in English, you must say **um... zu** in German.

The **ohne, (an)statt,** and **zu** in these infinitive constructions do not function as prepositions, therefore they do not determine the case of any nouns following them. Instead, the case of nouns in the infinitive clause is determined solely by the verb infinitive:

Der gerettete Mann ging weg, ohne **seinen Rettern** zu danken.
The rescued man walked away without thanking his rescuers.
(**Seinen Rettern** is dative because of **danken,** the accusative preposition **ohne** has no effect on the noun.)

Any of these infinitive constructions can be used with a past infinitive:

Ich habe sie angerufen, ohne vorher an die Kosten **gedacht zu haben.**
I called her without having thought of the cost beforehand.

The English example above could also be stated as follows:

I called her without *my* having thought of the cost beforehand.

The possessive pronoun *my* has been added to the sentence, but the meaning is the same. The *my* shows that the subject of the sentence applies to the first verb as well as to the second. In some sentences with two verbs, however, each verb has, in effect, its own subject. This can be seen in the example below:

We want to buy him a present without his knowing it.

The possessive adjective *his* cannot be deleted without changing the meaning of the sentence. In effect, the sentence is saying: *"We want to buy him a present. He must not know it."* However, the **ohne... zu, (an)statt... zu** and **um... zu** constructions can only be used if the subject of the first verb is *identical* to the understood subject of the second verb. When the subjects are *not* identical, **ohne... zu** must be replaced by **ohne daß**, **(an)statt... zu** by **(an)statt daß**, and **um... zu** by **so daß** or **damit**. All of these latter forms are subordinate conjunctions and must therefore be followed by a subordinate clause. Therefore, the last English example must be expressed in German as follows:

> Wir wollen ihm ein Geschenk kaufen, **ohne daß** er es weiß.

Here is an example to illustrate **(an)statt daß**:

> *Instead of his cooking the meal for me, I had to do it for him.*

The possessive adjective *his* does not agree with the subject *I;* therefore the usual **(an) statt... zu** construction must be replaced by **(an)statt daß**:

> **Statt daß** er das Essen für mich gekocht hat, mußte ich es für ihn tun.

The next example shows the use of **so daß (damit)**:

> *The resistance leader died in order that (so that) we can live in freedom.*

The subject, *resistance leader*, does not agree with the second subject *we*, therefore **um... zu** is replaced by **so daß** or **damit**:

> Der Widerstandskämpfer starb, **so daß (damit)** wir in Freiheit leben können.

The table below summarizes the preceding information:

SAME SUBJECT, INFINITIVE CLAUSE	DIFFERENT SUBJECT, SUBORDINATE CLAUSE
ohne... zu	ohne daß
(an)statt... zu	(an)statt daß
um... zu	so daß (damit)

COMPREHENSION CHECK: *Fill in the blank with the appropriate German words corresponding to the English words in parentheses.*

1. Er ging nach Hause, _____. *(instead of staying here)*
2. Wir feuern Sie, _____. *(in order to save money)*
3. Er redete zwei Stunden, _____. *(without stopping a single time)*
4. Die Krankenschwester kam, _____. *(in order to help him)*
5. Ich kann nicht zum Kühlschrank gehen, _____. *(without my dog coming)*

ANSWERS: 1. statt hier zu bleiben 2. um Geld zu sparen 3. ohne ein einziges Mal aufzuhören 4. um ihm zu helfen 5. ohne daß mein Hund kommt

C. Possessive + Verb + *-ing:* German Equivalents

This section deals with the general problem of English sentences in which a verb is followed by a possessive + verb + *-ing:*

> *How can you justify his sleeping during work?*

In effect, sentences of this type are a contracted form of an *underlying* main clause and a subordinate clause, namely:

> ~*How can you justify it   that he sleeps during work?*
> (The symbol ~ is used to indicate that these are underlying forms that do not necessarily correspond to an actual sentence in the English language.)

Note: The pronoun *it* is supplied in the underlying main clause to give the verb *justify* an object.

The German equivalent of such sentences is very similar in form to the underlying main clause and subordinate clause shown above:

> Wie können Sie es rechtfertigen, daß er während der Arbeit schläft?

Note: The pronoun **es** is usually inserted in the main clause of such German sentences to "anticipate" the subordinate clause that follows the main clause. This so-called *anticipatory* **es** corresponds to the *it* of the English underlying main clause.

Now consider this example:

> *He prefers sleeping in a bed.*

The possessive adjective does not appear because it is unnecessary; in this example, the person who prefers and who sleeps is the same. Such sentences should be thought of in terms of an underlying main clause and an *infinitive* clause:

> ~*He prefers it   to sleep in a bed.*

The German equivalent will again be similar in form to the underlying clauses:

> Er zieht es vor, in einem Bett zu schlafen.

Here is another example:

> *The university does not allow us to smoke in the classroom.*

The two verbs have different subjects (i.e., it is not the university that is smoking in the classroom), therefore the sentence should be broken up into a main clause and a subordinate clause:

> ~*The university does not allow it   that we smoke in the classroom.*

The German equivalent will be:

> Die Universität erlaubt es uns nicht, daß wir im Klassenzimmer rauchen.

Here is another example in which an infinitive clause is needed:

I haven't finished (my) talking with you.

This is reduced to:

≈*I haven't finished it   to talk with you.*

The German equivalent is:

Ich habe nicht aufgehört, mit dir zu reden.
(No anticipatory **es** is used in this sentence because the verb **aufhören** does not take a direct object in German.)

Finally, if the verb + *-ing* in the English sentence is the past auxiliary, i.e., *having*, then the German equivalent will have a past tense verb or a past infinitive according to whether a subordinate clause or an infinitive clause is used:

He denies your having killed the victim.

The underlying form is:

≈*He denies it   that you killed the victim.*

In German:

Er leugnet es ab, daß Sie das Opfer ermordeten.

Here is the same example slightly modified:

He denies (his) having killed the victim.

The underlying form is:

≈*He denies it   to have killed the victim.*

The German equivalent will be:

Er leugnet es ab, das Opfer ermordet zu haben.

Most infinitive clauses in German can be converted into subordinate clauses, though the reverse is not necessarily true. In colloquial language, past infinitives are usually avoided in favor of subordinate clauses; therefore, in everyday speech the previous example would most likely be stated as follows:

Er leugnet ab, daß er das Opfer ermordet hat.
He denies that he killed the victim.

COMPREHENSION CHECK: *First reduce these sentences to their underlying form, i.e., main clause plus subordinate or infinitive clause. Then translate into German. Do not forget the anticipatory* **es**.

1.   I appreciate your coming.
2.   He always avoided drinking the water.
3.   a. She denies your having given her the money.
      b. She denies having given you the money.

ANSWERS: 1. ~*I appreciate it   that you come:* Ich schätze es, daß du kommst. 2. ~*He always avoided it   to drink the water:* Er hat es immer vermieden, das Wasser zu trinken. 3.a. ~*She denies it   that you gave her the money:* Sie leugnet es ab, daß Sie ihr das Geld gegeben haben. 3.b. ~*She denies it   to have given you the money:* Sie leugnet es ab, Ihnen das Geld gegeben zu haben. *or* Sie leugnet es ab, daß sie Ihnen das Geld gegeben hat.

D. Preposition + Possessive + Verb + -ing: German Equivalents

The German sentences discussed in this section are identical to those dealt with in the previous section, except that the possessive is preceded by a preposition:

We talked earlier about your wanting more money.

Again, this example can be thought of as being derived from an underlying main clause followed by a subordinate clause:

~*We talked earlier about it   that you want more money.*

The German equivalent is similar to the underlying forms shown above:

Wir haben früher darüber geredet, daß du mehr Geld willst.

Note that the English preposition is expressed as a **da**-compound in the German sentence. The preposition itself is always determined by the first verb, i.e., the preposition is specific; the first verb is the dominant word. Here is an example in which an infinitive clause can be used:

Do you still insist on (your) becoming our leader?

The underlying form is:

~*Do you still insist on it   to become our leader?*

The German equivalent is:

Bestehen Sie immer noch darauf, unser Leiter zu werden?

All of the previous examples have involved possessive adjectives, but the possessive can be a noun too:

Can we depend on Helmut's being there?

The underlying form is:

~*Can we depend on it   that Helmut will be there?*

The German equivalent is:

Können wir uns darauf verlassen, daß Helmut da sein wird?

In colloquial English, the possessive **s** is often dropped in such sentences:

Can we depend on Helmut being there?

The German equivalent is the same, regardless. The next example shows a past infinitive:

> *I was happy about having received a raise.*

This sentence is based on:

> *˜I was happy about it   to have received a raise.*

The German equivalent would therefore be:

> Ich war froh darüber, eine Gehaltserhöhung bekommen zu haben.

or more simply:

> Ich war froh darüber, daß ich eine Gehaltserhöhung bekommen hatte.

Finally, go back and look at the sentences in section B. You should notice that the **ohne... zu, (an)statt... zu** and **um... zu** constructions are a special subtype of the sentences discussed in this section.

COMPREHENSION CHECK: *Rewrite each sentence in terms of the underlying main clause and subordinate or infinitive clause. Then translate into German.*

1. We are used to the squirrels' stealing our bread.
2. Are you interested in buying my car?
3. He is proud of having been an officer in the army.

> ANSWERS: 1. *˜We are used to it   that the squirrels steal our bread:* Wir sind daran gewöhnt, daß die Eichhörnchen unser Brot stehlen. 2. *˜Are you interested in it   to buy my car:* Sind Sie daran interessiert, mein Auto zu kaufen? 3. *˜He is proud of it   to have been an officer in the army:* Er ist stolz darauf, ein Offizier in der Armee gewesen zu sein. *or* Er ist stolz darauf, daß er ein Offizier in der Armee war.

German-English Vocabulary

an.spucken	*to spit at*	der Pantoffel, -n	*slipper*
auf.heben, hob, gehoben	*to pick up*	der Schwarzmarkt, ¨-e	*black market*
fühlen	*to feel*	servieren	*to serve*
der Gehorsam	*obedience*	das Spielzeug, -e	*toy*
das Gratisgetränk, -e	*free drink*	steigen, stieg, gestiegen	*to rise*
handeln	*to act*	tragen (trägt), trug, getragen	*to wear*
die Kneipe, -n	*bar*		
der Kühlschrank, ¨-e	*refrigerator*	vorbei.fahren (fährt), fuhr, gefahren	*to drive by*
lassen (läßt), ließ, gelassen	*to have something done*		
malen	*to paint*	weiterhin: etwas weiterhin tun	*to continue to do something*

EXERCISE 1 (prerequisite: section A, topic: **fühlen, hören, sehen** and **lassen**)

Rewrite these sentences in the simple past and the present perfect tenses. Then translate the original sentence and the rewritten sentences into English.

1. Ich sehe meinen Nachbarn vorbeifahren.
2. Die Eltern lassen ihre Tochter nicht ausgehen.
3. Wir hören jemand singen.
4. a. Ich lasse mein Haus malen.
   b. Ich lasse ihn mein Haus malen.
5. Fühlst du die Temperatur in diesem Zimmer steigen?

EXERCISE 2 (prerequisite: section A, topic: **fühlen, hören, sehen** and **lassen**)

Translate into German.

1. Do you hear the telephone ring?
2. Let him speak.
3. Rosa saw the sun go down in the West. *(simple past)*
4. You should have this garbage taken away.
5. I saw him hitting the child.
6. I had the suitcases brought to me. *(simple past)*
7. No one really wants to see you cry.
8. I am having my neighbor's son mow the lawn.

EXERCISE 3 (prerequisite: section B, topic: **ohne... zu, statt... zu, um... zu**)

Fill in the blank with the German words corresponding to the English words in parentheses.

1. Ich esse Äpfel, _____. *(in order to stay healthy)*
2. Er handelt immer, _____. *(without thinking beforehand)*
3. Manfred blieb in der Kneipe, _____. *(instead of going home)*
4. Leonora hob einen Stein auf, _____. *(in order to chase away the dog)*
5. _____, spuckte er ihn an. *(instead of forgiving his brother)*
6. Moritz bekam eine gute Note, _____. *(without having cheated)*
7. _____, servieren wir lhnen Gratisgetränke. *(in order to make your flight more pleasant)*
8. Das Kind spielte im Bett mit seinen Spielzeugen, _____. *(instead of falling asleep)*
9. Wir haben unserem Sohn etwas Geld geschickt, _____. *(in order that he can pay his tuition)*
10. Sie ging weiterhin in die Kirche, _____. *(without believing in it)*

11. Arnold trug Pantoffeln zu Hause, _____. *(in order to please his wife)*
12. Er erwartet Gehorsam, _____. *(without our understanding the reasons for it)*

EXERCISE 4 [prerequisite: section C, topic: (possessive) + verb + -*ing:* German equivalents]

Translate into German.

1. We anticipated your refusing our offer.
2. I appreciate your helping me.
3. He enjoyed tormenting me.
4. I can't stand his constantly bragging about his car.
5. We postponed our buying a new house.
6. Someone in the audience began shouting obscenities. *(Do not use an anticipatory es in this sentence.)*
7. He admitted his having been surprised. *(Do not use an anticipatory es in this sentence.)*
8. I wanted to avoid his seeing me.

EXERCISE 5 (prerequisite: section D, topic: preposition + (possessive) + verb + -*ing:* German equivalents)

Translate into German.

1. We insist on your being there.
2. I have been thinking of opening my own restaurant.
3. Are you accustomed to getting up early?
4. You are responsible for his being so lazy.
5. That is the end result of your having eaten so much.
6. He is interested in finding old manuscripts.
7. I am astonished at his believing in this nonsense.
8. She is working on developing a better computer.

EXERCISE 6 (comprehensive)

Translate into German.

1. Do you hear all the people laughing?
2. We enjoyed watching the film.
3. I paid 100 DM to get these tickets.
4. They were not used to eating so little meat.
5. Instead of turning on the light, she preferred to sit in the twilight.
6. Have him come to me.

7. Do you anticipate her saying no?
8. Without having understood the question, I could not give the correct answer.
9. We are against your leaving the university.
10. I heard Frieda laughing.
11. Wolf fell asleep during the lecture without anyone noticing it.
12. Do you want to have this suit cleaned?
13. She admitted having eaten the cookies. *(Do not use an anticipatory* es *in this sentence.)*
14. Instead of flattering the boss, you should try to work harder.

GEDANKENPROBLEM: **Look again at sentence 6 in exercise 3; then translate this sentence into German:**

Moritz received a good grade without having to cheat.

What's wrong with these?

1. Der Arzt hörte auf gebend Großmutter diese Tabletten.
2. Nach dem Krieg mußten wir zum Schwarzmarkt gehen, Obst zu kaufen.
3. Wir haben ein Haus gebaut für uns. *(intended meaning: We are having a house built for ourselves.)*
4. Ich habe es wirklich nur getan, um dich zu helfen!

Review Exercises Chapters 16–18

EXERCISE 1

Fill in the blanks with the German words corresponding to the English words in parentheses.

1. Viele Leute, _____, glauben nicht daran. *(to whom I tell this story)*
2. Es war mein Ziel, _____. *(to bring these two people together)*
3. Ich kann sie nicht ansehen, _____. *(without laughing)*
4. Meine Nachbarin, _____ ältester Sohn Arzt wurde, ist sehr stolz auf ihn. *(whose)*
5. Er ging nach Wien, _____. *(to become a great painter)*
6. Der Hund, _____, hat mich heute gebissen. *(I bought yesterday)*
7. Er hat etwas gesagt, _____. *(that was incredibly stupid)*
8. Es war sehr schwierig, _____. *(to find the cabin in this snowstorm)*
9. Ich habe aufgehört, _____. *(writing her letters)*
10. Ist dieses Problem _____? *(easy to solve)*
11. Der junge Mann bestellte dasselbe, _____. *(that his girlfriend wanted)*
12. Ihr Ausweis _____. *(appears to be in order)*
13. Ist dies das Buch, _____? *(you were thinking of)*
14. _____, solltest du mehr Sport treiben. *(instead of taking vitamins)*
15. Ich lerne _____. *(to swim)*
16. Manches, _____, will ich sowieso nicht. *(that I have to do without)*
17. Können Sie ihm die schlechte Nachricht mitteilen, _____? *(without his getting angry)*
18. Ich weiß nicht, _____. *(what to do)*

EXERCISE 2

Translate into German.

1. Do you really want me to do this?
2. This cathedral has a tower that is 50 meters high.
3. I am interested in studying German.
4. Do you have anything to sell?
5. The man I am pointing at is our director.
6. I ate 20 eggs, which was too much for me.
7. Why do you avoid visiting her?
8. My brother told me to buy this car.
9. Do you insist on eating in a Chinese restaurant?
10. We saw him stumble.
11. They drove to Berlin because they wanted to have the opportunity to see the Wall.
12. Because the advice you gave me was bad, I now have to sell this house.

What's wrong with these?

1. Der Mann, wer besuchte uns vorige Woche, war ein alter Freund meines Vaters.
2. Ich hatte kein Interesse daran, an dem Projekt zu teilnehmen.
3. Er starb, ohne mich zu verzeihen.
4. Sie lehrte ihn zu lesen.
5. Das Schönste, das wir gesehen haben, war das Schloß.
6. Man braucht viel Geld, an der Universität zu studieren.
7. Wenn ich nur wüßte wo anzufangen!
8. Damals wohnten wir in einer kleinen Wohnung, daß nur ein Fenster hatte.
9. Ich habe die Platte gefunden du wolltest kaufen.
10. Du willst mich nicht zu sein glücklich!
11. Wir fuhren mit einer Straßenbahn, weil wir waren zu faul zu gehen zu Fuß.
12. Die Leute, bei den ich wohne, sind alle ganz nett.

Capitalization

19

A. Capitalization: Introduction

You already know that nouns are capitalized in German, but that basic rule will be modified in this chapter as follows:

> *Words that function as nouns are capitalized.*

The emphasis in this modified rule is on *function*, because many words that are not normally nouns in German can be used as such and are then capitalized:

Das ist das große **Aber.**
That's the catch.

Jedem das **Seine.**
To each his own.

Wollen Sie mir doch nicht das traute **Du** sagen?
Don't you really want to say "du" to me? (literally: *Don't you really want to say the intimate "du" to me?*)

Conversely, a word that in other circumstances would be a noun is not capitalized when it functions as some other part of speech. For example, the sentence below shows the German noun **Schuld** *(guilt, fault),* which is capitalized:

Es ist deine **Schuld!**
It's your fault!

But in the next example, **Schuld** is used as a predicate adjective and is therefore not capitalized:

> Du bist **schuld** daran!
> *It's your fault!*

Here are some more examples to show how the same word can function as a noun or some other part of speech:

> Sollte nicht **jemand** etwas sagen?
> *Shouldn't someone say something?*
> (pronoun, not capitalized)

> Ein gewisser **Jemand** hat Sie gestern gesehen.
> *A certain someone saw you yesterday.*
> (noun, capitalized)

> Du solltest nicht so **schnell fahren!**
> *You shouldn't drive so fast!*
> (adverb **schnell**, verb **fahren**)

> Ich habe Angst vor dem **Schnellfahren.**
> *I am afraid of fast driving.*
> (noun formed from adverb + verb)

Note the distinction in meaning of the word **paar** depending on whether or not it is capitalized:

> ein **paar** Leute: *a few people*
> ein **Paar** Schuhe: *a pair of shoes*

In contrast to English, proper names in German are capitalized only when they actually function as nouns:

> Sagen Sie das auf **deutsch!**
> *Say that in German.*
> (adverbial phrase, tells how you should say it)

> Sprechen Sie **Deutsch?**
> *Do you speak German?*
> (noun, i.e., the language itself)

> Wollen Sie **amerikanische** Dollar kaufen?
> *Do you want to buy American dollars?*
> (just another adjective in German)

> Ich bin **Amerikaner.**
> *I am an American.*
> (noun)

However, proper names ending in **-er** are considered nouns and are therefore always capitalized:

> Gibt es wirklich so etwas wie den **Wiener** Charme?
> *Is there really such a thing as Viennese charm?*

Proper names are also capitalized when they occur in geographical names and in titles:

> Wie groß ist der **Atlantische Ozean?**
> *How large is the Atlantic Ocean?*
> (**Atlantisch** is part of the name for this ocean.)

> Er ist der Direktor des **Deutschen Instituts für Wirtschaftsforschung.**
> *He is the director of the German Institute for Economic Research.*
> (everything after **des** is a title)

The second person polite pronoun **Sie** *(you)* is always capitalized, as is **Ihnen,** the dative form of this, and the corresponding possessive adjective **Ihr** *(your).* However, *in letters, all* second person pronouns and their corresponding possessive adjectives are capitalized:

> Liebste Ingeborg!
> Ich vermisse **Dich** schrecklich! Ich habe **Dein** Bild immer bei mir!
> *Dearest Ingeborg!*
> *I miss you terribly! I have your picture with me at all times!*

The reflexive pronoun **sich** is not capitalized, even when it refers to the second person polite pronoun:

> Warum haben Sie **sich** heute nicht rasiert?
> *Why didn't you shave today?*

However, **sich** is capitalized when combined with a reflexive verb to form a noun:

> Das **Sichselbstverstehen** ist eben das Schwierige im Leben.
> *Understanding yourself is after all the hard part in life.*

Finally, here is some useful terminology with respect to capitalization in German:

> Die Großschreibung   *capitalization*
> Die Kleinschreibung   *noncapitalization*

> Schreibt man das **groß** oder **klein?**
> *Is that capitalized or not?*

COMPREHENSION CHECK: *Only the first word in each sentence below has been capitalized. Rewrite the sentence and capitalize where necessary.*

1. Wo hast du russisch gelernt?
2. Ich habe genug von deinem nichtstun!
3. Sein vater war ein dänischer einwanderer.
4. Ich möchte gern zur leipziger messe fahren.
5. Wir haben nur ein paar sachen gekauft.

ANSWERS: 1. Wo hast du Russisch gelernt? 2. Ich habe genug von deinem Nichts-tun! 3. Sein Vater war ein dänischer Einwanderer. 4. Ich möchte gern zur Leipziger Messe fahren. 5. Wir haben nur ein paar Sachen gekauft.

B. Problematic Cases of Capitalization in German

Certain common words and expressions in German may appear to be nouns but are nevertheless not capitalized. Consider the examples below:

Im Prinzip stimme ich mit dir überein.
In principle I agree with you.

Im allgemeinen stimme ich mit dir überein.
In general I agree with you.

The two expressions **im Prinzip** and **im allgemeinen** both appear to involve nouns, but only **Prinzip** is capitalized. The reason for this is that **Prinzip** is a noun in its own right, i.e., **das Prinzip**, whereas **allgemein** is actually an adjective. The number of *nouns* that can be used after **im** is virtually endless, but only a few expressions exist in which **im** is followed by a word that is not a noun. The most common of these are listed here:

im allgemeinen	*in general*	im großen und ganzen	*in general*
im folgenden	*in the following*	im übrigen	*in addition*
nicht im geringsten	*not at all*	im voraus	*in advance*

You will recall from Chapter 9 that adjectival nouns are capitalized but adjective fragments are not. Certain adjectives, however, when used with the definite article, are *not* capitalized even though they may appear to be adjectival nouns. The most common of these are:

ander	*other*	gleich	*same*	selb	*same*
beid	*both*	meist	*most*	übrig	*remaining*
einzeln	*individual*	mindest	*least*	wenigst	*least, few*
einzig	*single, only*				

Here are a few examples:

Sogar der **einzelne** darf nicht vernachlässigt werden.
Even the individual must not be neglected.

Ich habe den **beiden** meine Antwort gesagt.
I told the two my answer.

Die **wenigsten** verstehen diese Theorie vollkommen.
Few understand this theory completely.

Sie hatte das **gleiche (dasselbe)** an.
She wore the same thing.
(Note: The definite article is written separately from **gleich-** but together with **selb-**.)

The expression **ein bißchen** (*a little*) is not capitalized because it functions as an adjective or adverb. Literally it means *a little bite*:

Ich will mich **ein bißchen** ausruhen.
I want to rest a little.

A small group of nouns can function as separable prefixes to certain verbs. Some of these nouns are written as one word with the verb, others are always separate from the verb. In either case, the noun may or may not be capitalized. The list below gives the most common of these:

INFINITIVE	AS SEPARABLE PREFIX	MEANING
Auto fahren	Ich fahre Auto.	*I am driving.*
eis.laufen	Ich laufe eis.	*I am skating.*
ernst nehmen	Ich nehme ihn nicht ernst.	*I don't take him seriously.*
leid tun	Es tut mir leid.	*I am sorry.*
rad.fahren	Ich fahre Rad.	*I am riding a bicycle.*
Schi laufen	Ich laufe Schi.	*I am skiing.*
weh tun	Das tut mir weh.	*That hurts me.*

COMPREHENSION CHECK: *Only the first word in each sentence has been capitalized. Rewrite the sentence and capitalize where necessary.*

1. Das ist das wenigste, was wir für die arme witwe tun können.
2. Im übrigen ist das haus zu teuer.
3. Udo ist im vergleich zu ihr gescheiter.
4. Wir wollen dieses wochenende schi laufen.
5. Wo sind die anderen?

ANSWERS: 1. Das ist das wenigste, was wir für die arme Witwe tun können. 2. Im übrigen ist das Haus zu teuer. 3. Udo ist im Vergleich zu ihr gescheiter. 4. Wir wollen dieses Wochenende Schi laufen. 5. Wo sind die anderen?

German-English Vocabulary

Learn the words listed on pages 266 and 267, and the following:

der Achtund-fünfziger	*Number fifty-eight (streetcar)*	die Geschichte	*history*
		die Großschreibung	*capitalization*
der Akzent, -e	*accent*	Grund: im Grunde genommen	*basically*
der Anhänger, -	*supporter*		
begrüßen	*to greet*	der Gruß, ⸚e	*greeting*
die Beschwerde, -n	*complaint*	herzlich	*hearty*
da drüben	*over there*	Holländisch	*Dutch (language)*
dänisch	*Danish (adjective)*	hüten vor + *dat.* (*reflexive*)	*to watch out for*
der Einwanderer, -	*immigrant*		
erdulden	*to tolerate*	das Ich	*the self*
etwas	*somewhat*	die Klein-schreibung	*noncapitalization*
das Fleisch	*meat*		
französich	*French (adjective)*	Latein	*Latin (language)*

leidenschaftlich	*passionate*	das Selbst	*the self*
die Leipziger Messe	*Leipzig trade fair*	das Sichgehenlassen	*letting yourself go*
die Leistung, -en	*achievement*	die Sozialdemo- kratische Partei Deutschlands (SPD)	*Social Democratic Party of Germany*
das Nichtstun	*doing nothing*		
die Öffentlichkeit	*public*		
die Oma, -s	*grandma*	die Spritze, -n	*(needle) shot*
polnisch	*Polish (adjective)*	die Stadtbehörde, -n	*city authorities*
richtig	*real*		
die Ringstraße	*Ring Street (in Vienna)*	der Stolz	*pride*
		der Südbahnhof, ⸚e	*south train station*
das Rote Meer	*Red Sea*	die Untergrund- bahn, -en	*subway*
Russisch	*Russian (language)*		
das Schwarzfahren	*using public transportation without paying*	der Vergleich, -e	*comparison*
		die Weimarer Republik	*Weimar Republic*
das Schwein, -e	*pig, despicable person*	die Witwe, -n	*widow*

EXERCISE 1 (prerequisite: section A, topic: basic problems of capitalization in German)

*In the sentences below, only the first word and the second person polite pronoun **Sie** have been capitalized. Rewrite the sentences and capitalize where necessary.*

1. Er hat einen französischen akzent.
2. Herzliche grüße! Dein dich liebender sohn! *(an ending in a letter)*
3. Nur ein paar *(a few)* städte in deutschland haben eine untergrundbahn.
4. Die Stadtbehörde wird kein schwarzfahren mehr erdulden!
5. Die Studenten im mittelalter mußten latein sprechen.
6. Sie können mit dem achtundfünfziger vom südbahnhof zur ringstraße fahren.
7. Hüten Sie sich vor dem sichgehenlassen!
8. In der öffentlichkeit bin ich etwas scheu, aber unter freunden zeige ich mein wahres ich.
9. Ich habe ein paar *(a pair)* socken gekauft.
10. Wer a sagt, muß auch b sagen.
11. Wir sind ans rote meer gefahren.
12. a. Er wird niemals seinen stolz verlieren.
    b. Wir sind stolz auf deine leistung.

EXERCISE 2 (prerequisite: section B, topic: problematic cases of capitalization in German)

Translate into German. Each sentence must contain an expression discussed in section B.

1. I want the same thing.
2. The trip was in general a success.
3. She likes to skate.
4. The political situation is discussed in the following.
5. I take my duty very seriously.
6. That is the least thing that you can do!
7. You have to pay in advance.
8. He isn't sorry.
9. It costs a little too much.
10. We drove for nine hours. *(present perfect tense)*
11. Most don't believe him. *(use the definite article before the German word for most)*
12. Does it hurt you?
13. He is the only one who can do it.
14. Do you often ride a bicycle?

EXERCISE 3 (comprehensive)

Only the first word of each sentence and the second person polite pronoun **Sie** *have been capitalized. Rewrite the sentences and capitalize where necessary. As a review from Chapter 9, a few adjectival nouns have been included.*

1. Wie sagt man das auf deutsch?
2. Alles gute!
3. Im allgemeinen bin ich mit diesem kurs zufrieden.
4. Diese kleine spritze wird dir nicht weh tun.
5. Mein besseres selbst erlaubte es mir nicht.
6. Die beiden da drüben sind schwestern.
7. Der außenminister begrüßte den polnischen botschafter.
8. Können Sie schi laufen?
9. Laß den alten in ruhe!
10. Ein paar *(pair)* handschuhe lagen auf dem tisch.
11. Wir nehmen seine beschwerden nicht mehr ernst.
12. Ich kann holländisch verstehen, aber nicht sprechen.
13. Der film war ein bißchen langweilig.
14. Im grunde genommen ist er ein richtiges schwein.
15. Liebe oma! Danke für dein geschenk! *(letter)*
16. Ja, ich habe einmal jemanden geliebt.
17. Er war ein leidenschaftlicher anhänger der sozialdemokratischen partei deutschlands.
18. Ich will etwas besseres als das haben!
19. Die nachricht hat mich eigentlich nicht im geringsten überrascht.
20. Du bist ein nichts!
21. Mein bruder aß das weiße fleisch und ich das dunkle.
22. Das ist das meiste, was ich dafür bezahlen werde.

23. Das buch behandelt die geschichte der weimarer republik.

24. Wollen Sie auch etwas anderes bestellen?

EXERCISE 4 (optional exercise, topic: using a dictionary to determine capitalization in German)

A good German dictionary should give not only the meaning of a given word but also its exact spelling. Check the expression **ernst nehmen** *in your dictionary to see if it indicates that* **ernst** *should not be capitalized. Look it up under both the noun* **Ernst** *and the verb* **nehmen.** *Also, go to your library and get the authoritative source for spelling in German, namely,* Der Große Duden, Rechtschreibung, Band 1. *Look up* **Ernst** *in this book. How does the* Duden *indicate when to capitalize and when not to?*

EXERCISE 5 (optional exercise, topic: using a dictionary to solve difficult problems of capitalization in German)

Each of the sentences below contains a word in italics. By using a good reference dictionary, decide whether the word in italics should be capitalized or not.

1. a. Mein Onkel wohnt in der *deutschen* Schweiz.
   b. Meine Schwester arbeitet bei der *deutschen* Bundesbahn.
2. a. Ich schreibe Ihnen mit *bezug* auf Ihren vorigen Brief.
   b. Ihr Vorschlag in *bezug* auf unser Problem klingt vielversprechend.
3. a. Ich war natürlich der *letzte* in der Reihe.
   b. Er gab sein *letztes* für die Revolution.
   c. Das Thema wurde bis ins *letzte* untersucht.
4. a. Die Miete ist am *ersten* des Monats fällig.
   b. Wir nannten ihn den Wunderknaben, weil er der *erste* in unserer Klasse war.
   c. Ich war der *erste,* der den Fehler bemerkte.
5. a. Nur das *beste* ist für mich gut genug.
   b. Ich halte es für das *beste,* ein billiges Zimmer in einer Pension zu nehmen.
6. a. Wir haben alles *mögliche* getan. *(all kinds of things)*
   b. Wir haben alles *mögliche* getan. *(everything possible)*

Noun Suffixes, Compound Nouns

20

A. Noun Suffixes: Gender and Plural Recognition

A constant problem in German is knowing what gender and plural form a given noun has. Fortunately, many German nouns end in a certain suffix, and this suffix determines the gender and plural form of the noun, as can be seen in the list on next page. Some of these suffixes are not always consistent with regard to gender:

-e

Almost all nouns ending in **-e** are feminine; the exceptions are a few masculine weak nouns which are listed in chapter 9, section D and **das Auge** *(eye)* and **das Ende** *(end)*.

-er

Nouns ending in **-er** are consistently masculine *only* when they refer to a person who does something, e.g., **der Jäger** *(hunter)*, i.e., the person who hunts. Other types of nouns ending in **-er** may or may not be masculine, e.g., **der Vater** *(father)*, **die Mutter** *(mother)*.

-nis

Words with this suffix can be either neuter or feminine, though neuter is more com-

SUFFIX	GENDER(S)	PLURAL FORM	GERMAN EXAMPLE	ENGLISH EQUIVALENT
-chen	neuter	(same)	das Heftchen, pl. Heftchen	small notebook
-e	feminine	-en	die Bluse, pl. Blusen	blouse
-ei	feminine	-eien	die Bäckerei, pl. Bäckereien	bakery
-er	masculine	(same)	der Jäger, pl. Jäger	hunter
-heit	feminine	-heiten	die Mehrheit, pl. Mehrheiten	majority
-ie	feminine	-ien	die Familie, pl. Familien	family
-in	feminine	-innen	die Freundin, pl. Freundinnen	girlfriend
-ismus	masculine	-ismen	der Organismus, pl. Organismen	organism
-ität	feminine	-itäten	die Universität, pl. Universitäten	university
-keit	feminine	-keiten	die Möglichkeit, pl. Möglichkeiten	possibility
-lein	neuter	(same)	das Bächlein, pl. Bächlein	little brook
-nis	neut./fem.	-nisse	das Ergebnis, pl. Ergebnisse	result
-schaft	feminine	-schaften	die Gesellschaft, pl. Gesellschaften	organization
-(t)ion	feminine	-(t)ionen	die Diskussion, pl. Diskussionen	discussion
-tum	neut./masc.	-tümer	das Eigentum, pl. Eigentümer	possession
-ung	feminine	-ungen	die Leistung, pl. Leistungen	achievement

mon, e.g., **das Ergebnis** (result), **die Erlaubnis** (permission). However, the plural form is the same regardless of the gender of the noun.

-tum

Words with this suffix are neuter except for two nouns: **der Irrtum** (mistake) and **der Reichtum** (wealth).

The meanings and usage of the suffixes listed here will be discussed in the next section. For this section, it is sufficient that you memorize the list of suffixes and know what gender and plural form to use with them.

COMPREHENSION CHECK: *On the basis of the suffix, determine the gender and plural form of the nouns shown. For your convenience, the English equivalent is given for each word.*

1. Erkältung *a cold*
2. Konditorei *pastry shop*
3. Euphemismus *euphemism*
4. Brötchen *bread roll*

5. Krankheit *sickness*
6. Fürstentum *principality*
7. Pfadfinder *boy scout*
8. Komödie *comedy*

ANSWERS: 1. *feminine; plural:* Erkältungen 2. *feminine; plural:* Konditoreien 3. *masculine; plural:* Euphemismen 4. *neuter; plural:* Brötchen 5. *feminine; plural:* Krankheiten 6. *neuter; plural:* Fürstentümer 7. *masculine; plural:* Pfadfinder 8. *feminine; plural:* Komödien

B. Noun Suffixes: Meanings and Usage

The function of a suffix is to create a noun out of an adjective, verb, or another noun. In many cases, the suffix imparts a specific meaning to the new noun. A suffix may also produce an umlaut in the *base word,* i.e., the word without the suffix. The information that follows outlines the pertinent facts in this matter:

-chen = -lein

These two suffixes both function as diminutives, i.e., they impart to the base word the idea of *little* or *dear.* They also produce an umlaut in the base word if the vowel is "umlautable," e.g., **der Bach** *(brook),* **Bächlein** *(little brook),* **die Tochter** *(daughter),* **Töchterlein** *(dear daughter).* The nouns **Fräulein** *(miss)* and **Mädchen** *(girl)* have lost any diminutive sense and now have the meanings shown. If the stem noun is a feminine noun ending in **-e,** then this **e** is dropped before **-chen** or **-lein,** e.g., **Blume** *(flower),* **Blümchen** *(little flower),* **Rose** *(rose),* **Röslein** *(little rose).* The suffix **-chen** is more common in Northern German, **-lein** is favored in Southern German.

-ei

This suffix often indicates a place of business, e.g., **Bäckerei** *(bakery),* **Brauerei** *(brewery),* **Molkerei** *(dairy).* In other cases, this suffix may indicate a pejorative (bad) activity, e.g., **Pinselei** *(painting badly),* **Schweinerei** *(disgraceful act),* **Wichtigtuerei** *(pomposity).*

-er

This suffix converts verbs into nouns meaning "the person who does what the verb does," e.g., **jagen** *(to hunt)*, **Jäger** *(hunter)*. Often the *base word* may take an umlaut when the **-er** suffix is added, as in the previous example, but not always: e.g., **malen** *(to paint)*, **Maler** *(painter)*.

-heit = -keit

These two suffixes both convert adjectives into nouns, but the choice of which to use is determined by the last syllable of the adjective. Follow this rule:

> Use **-keit** when the adjective ends in **-bar, -er, -ig, -lich,** or **-sam;**
> use **-heit** for adjectives that do not have these endings.

Examples: Frucht**barkeit** *(fertility)*, Tapf**erkeit** *(bravery)*, Eif**rigkeit** *(eagerness)*, Feier**lichkeit** *(ceremony)*, Bieg**samkeit** *(pliability)*, Trocken**heit** *(dryness)*, Faul**heit** *(laziness)*, Gesamt**heit** *(totality)*, Mensch**heit** *(human race)*.

-ie

This suffix can have two different pronunciations:

1. The **ie** can be pronounced as the *ia* at the end of *encyclopedia*, e.g., **die Familie** *(family)*.

2. The **ie** can be pronounced as the *y* in the English word *geography*, e.g., **die Geographie** *(geography)*.

The names of academic subjects in German, such as **Geographie, Philosophie, Anatomie** etc., are always pronounced with the second pronunciation given above. However, with other German words ending in **-ie,** you will have to consult a dictionary to determine the correct pronunciation.

-in

This suffix indicates that the person named is a female, e.g., **Arbeiter** *(male worker)*, **Arbeiterin** *(female worker)*. The suffix **-in** usually gives the noun stem an umlaut, assuming that the vowel is "umlautable": **der Arzt** *(male doctor)*, **die Ärztin** *(female doctor)*, **Storch** *(stork)*, **Störchin** *(female stork)*. Sometimes the umlaut does not occur: **der Gatte** *(husband)*, **die Gattin** *(wife)*.

-nis

This suffix makes nouns out of verbs or adjectives, e.g., **gleich** *(like)*, **Gleichnis** *(likeness)*. The addition of this suffix to a given word may produce an umlaut as well as other changes to the base word, e.g., **verstehen** *(to understand)*, **Verständnis** *(understanding)*.

You may have learned elsewhere or deduced yourself that some of the suffixes discussed in this chapter correspond to certain English suffixes, e.g., **-heit** = *-hood*, **-nis** = *-ness*, **-schaft** = *-ship*, **-tum** = *-dom*. To a certain extent these correspondences hold true:

Kindheit	*childhood*	**Freundschaft**	*friendship*
Finsternis	*darkness*	**Märtyrertum**	*martyrdom*

However, in many cases, the German suffixes may correspond to the "wrong" English suffix or to no suffix at all:

Freiheit	*freedom*	**Brüderschaft**	*brotherhood*
Zeugnis	*certificate*	**Sklaventum**	*slavery*

As a further example, note that **finster** *(dark)* + **-nis** does yield **Finsternis** *(darkness)*, but **dunkel** *(dark)* + **-nis** yields ***Dunkelnis,** a word that doesn't exist. Correct would be **Dunkelheit,** using again the "wrong" suffix.

Certain English and German suffixes do correspond very well to each other, namely, **-ismus** = *-ism*, **-ität** = *-ity*, **-(t)ion** = *-(t)ion:*

Pessim**ismus**	*pessimism*	Diskuss**ion**	*discussion*
Univers**ität**	*university*	Inform**ation**	inform*ation*

These suffixes almost always correspond because the base words to which they are attached are essentially the same in English and in German. But even here exceptions exist:

das Christen**tum**	*Christianity*	*not* *die Christian**ität**

In short, be careful of creating German words on the basis of the corresponding suffix; check your German dictionary to see if the word you want to create really exists.

COMPREHENSION CHECK: *Part A: Using a dictionary for reference, not the glossary, add the suffix given to the word shown. Translate the original word and the new word into English.*

1. Koch + -in	**3.** entwickeln + -ung	**5.** geschehen + -nis
2. rauben + -er	**4.** Flasche + -chen	**6.** obszön + -ität

*Part B: Decide whether to add **-heit** or **-keit** to these two words using the rule given* *in this section. Do not use the glossary. Translate the original word and the new word into English.*

7. kahl   **8.** ähnlich

Part C: Using a German dictionary, determine the pronunciation of these words.

9. Astronomie *(astronomy)*   **10.** Serie *(series)*

ANSWERS: 1. Koch *(male cook)*, Köchin *(female cook)* 2. rauben *(to rob)*, Räuber *(robber)* 3. entwickeln *(to develop)*, Entwicklung *(development)* 4. Flasche *(bottle)*, Fläschchen *(small bottle)* 5. geschehen *(to occur)*, Geschehnis *(occurrence)* 6. obszön *(obscene)*, Obszönität *(obscenity)* 7. kahl *(bald)*, Kahlheit *(baldness)* 8. ähnlich *(similar)*, Ähnlichkeit *(similarity)* 9. Astronomie: like *y* in *geography* 10. Serie: like *ia* in *encyclopedia*

C. Compound Words: Formation

Where English has two nouns next to each other, German usually combines these two words into one compound noun:

> Ich mache dieses Jahr einen **Sommerkurs.** (*not* *Sommer Kurs)
> *I'm going to take a summer course this year.*

The gender and plural of a compound noun in German is determined by the last noun of the compound (exceptions are discussed in chapter 21, section A):

> **die** Jahres**zeit**   die Jahres**zeiten**
> *the season*   *the seasons*
> (gender of **Zeit**, not **Jahr**)   (plural of **Zeit**, not **Jahr**)

A word can also be combined with an adjective to form a compound adjective:

> Liebe + bedürftig = liebesbedürftig
> *love + needy = in need of love*

When two words are combined into one in German, a *connecting sound* is sometimes added between the two words, e.g., the **s** in the previous example of **liebesbedürftig**. For words ending in certain suffixes, the connecting sound is predictable:

---
*The connecting sound is **s** for nouns ending in **-heit, -keit, -schaft, -tät, -(t)ion, -tum,** or **-ung**.*

Note: All of these are feminine suffixes except **-tum.** Here are a few examples:

die Schönheit + die Königin	= die Schönheitskönigin
beauty + the queen	= *the beauty queen*
die Arbeitslosigkeit + das Problem	= das Arbeitslosigkeitsproblem
the unemployment + the problem	= *the unemployment problem*
die Freundschaft + das Abkommen	= das Freundschaftsabkommen
friendship + the agreement	= *the friendship agreement*
die Scheidung + der Grund	= der Scheidungsgrund
the divorce + the reason	= *the reason for the divorce*

The **s** is added to such words even if the second noun begins with an **s**:

die Krankheit + die Symptome	= die Krankheitssymptome
the disease + the symptoms	= *the disease symptoms*

For words with other endings, you will have to consult the glossary or a dictionary to determine which connecting sound, if any, to use. Certain types of words, however, have a *tendency* to take specific connecting sounds. These tendencies are listed here:

1. Words that already end in an **s**-sound (**s, ß, sch, z**) usually add no connecting sound:

Gas + Heizung	= Gasheizung
gas + heating	= *gas heating*
Holz + Ware	= Holzware
wood + article	= *wooden article*

2. Feminine nouns of one syllable usually add no connecting sound:

Bahn + Hof	= Bahnhof
train + courtyard	= *train station*

3. Feminine nouns ending in **e** generally add **n** as the connecting sound (most likely) or drop the **e** and add no connecting sound (less likely):

Pflanze + Garten	= Pflanzengarten
plant + garden	= *botanical garden*
Grenze + Gegend	= Grenzgegend
border + region	= *border region*

For other types of nouns, and for compound adjectives, no reliable rules can be stated. Some of the possibilities are shown here:

Geist + Stadt	= Geisterstadt
ghost + city	= *ghost town*

Bauer + Hof	= Bauernhof
farmer + courtyard	= *farm*
Sieg + Armee	= Siegesarmee
victory + army	= *victorious army*
Sieg + reich	= siegreich
victory + rich	= *victorious*
Mensch + Fresser	= Menschenfresser
person + eater	= *cannibal*

If you want to combine two words into a compound and the dictionary does not list that particular compound, you must determine the necessary connecting sounds, if any, by *extrapolation*. See how the first word combines with other words that *are* listed in the dictionary and then assume that your particular compound combines in the same fashion. For example, let us assume that you want to create the compound *side street* out of the words **Seite + Straße,** but this particular compound is not listed in your dictionary. Instead, you find **Seitenausgang** (*side exit*) and **Seitenweg** (*side road*). You could then reasonably assume that *side street* would be **Seiten-straße.** This method is, however, not always reliable, for example:

Geburtstag	Geburtenregelung
birthday	*birth control*

Note that the word **Geburt** uses a different connecting sound depending on the noun that follows. However, such idiosyncrasies generally occur only with common compounds given in the dictionary anyway.

COMPREHENSION CHECK: *Using a dictionary for reference, combine the two words shown into a compound word. If the compound is a noun, give its gender. List also the meaning of each newly formed compound word. Try to predict the connecting sound where possible.*

1. Rose + farbig
2. Fakultät + Mitglied
3. Fleisch + Messer
4. Pflicht + Lehre
5. Eigentum + Wohnung
6. Geburt + Ort

ANSWERS: 1. rosenfarbig (*rose-colored*)   2. Fakultätsmitglied (*faculty member*)
3. Fleischmesser (*meat knife*)   4. Pflichtenlehre (*study of ethics*)   5. Eigentumswohnung (*condominium, literally: property apartment*)   6. Geburtsort (*birthplace*)

D. Compound Nouns: Deciphering

An endless number of German compound nouns can be constructed. In fact, in German, a writer or speaker is permitted to create a compound on the spot, assuming that the compound is plausibly constructed. As a result, even a good German dictionary can list only the shorter, more common compound nouns. When you encounter a compound that is not listed in the dictionary, you must break it down into its component words in order to understand it:

> Telefongespräch = Telefon + Gespräch, *meaning: telephone conversation*

However, with some compounds in German, the individual words that make up the compound may not be so obvious, particularly when the compound consists of three words or more. With these compounds, you may be able to decipher the individual words by doing the following:

1. Look for the connecting sounds. If present, they will show where one word stops and the next begins.

2. Look for any suffixes. They mark the end of a word. (Of course, some compounds will contain a suffix *and* a connecting sound.)

Here are two examples to illustrate this process:

Gefängniswärter	(original compound)
Gefäng**nis**wärter	(suffix found)
Gefängnis + Wärter	(broken up into two words)
prison guard	(meaning)
Gewissensqual	(original compound)
Gewissen**s**qual	(connecting sound found)
Gewissen + Qual	(broken up into two words)
pangs of conscience	(meaning) (literally: *conscience torment*)

Both of the compounds shown above could be looked up directly in any good German dictionary. But the process of deciphering a compound becomes essential with long compounds such as this:

Bezirksversammlungsgebäude	(original compound)
Bezirksversamml**ungs**gebäude	(connecting sounds and suffix found)
Bezirk + Versammlung + Gebäude	(broken up into three words)
district council building	(meaning)

An alternative method for deciphering compound nouns is to look up the first syllable and try to match it with a word in the dictionary. Add the next syllable(s) if necessary. Once you have found the first word, try to match up the next syllable and continue until you reach the end of the compound:

Kernkettenreaktion	(original compound)
Kern + kettenreaktion	(first word match up)
Kern + ket + tenreaktion	(no match up)
Kern + Ketten + reaktion	(second word match up)
Kern + Ketten + reak + tion	(no match up)
Kern + Ketten + Reaktion	(third word match up)
nuclear chain reaction	(meaning)

You could probably recognize **Reaktion** immediately without needing to match up each syllable, but the point is that this method can be used to decipher any compound no matter how long or complicated, even when there are no suffixes or connecting sounds.

The meaning of a compound may not be immediately obvious even if broken down into its individual parts. For example, the word **Kern,** given in the example above, can take on many meanings, but the correct meaning *nuclear* becomes clear in the context of the other words of the compound. In the context of an entire sentence, the appropriate meaning would be even clearer.

COMPREHENSION CHECK: *Using a German dictionary, not the glossary in this book, break these words down into their individual parts. Translate the individual words into English. Then give a translation of the original compound.*

1. Heiratsantrag
2. Feindschaftsäußerung
3. Erbschaftsstreitprobleme
4. Scheinangriffstaktik

ANSWERS: 1. Heirat *(marriage)* + Antrag *(proposal), marriage proposal* 2. Feind-schaft *(hostility)* + Äußerung *(remark), hostile remark* 3. Erbschaft *(inheritance)* + Streit *(dispute)* + Probleme *(problems), problems of an inheritance dispute* 4. Schein *(false appearance)* + Angriff *(attack)* + Taktik *(tactic), tactic of a feigned attack*

Important! Use a dictionary for reference in these exercises, not the glossary.

EXERCISE 1 (prerequisite: section A, topic: gender and plural assignment with suffixes)

Identify the gender and plural form that these nouns must have.

1. Tragödie	11. Kleinigkeit	21. Gitarre
2. Besitztum	12. Million	22. Verkäufer
3. Sekretärin	13. Mädchen	23. Wirtschaft
4. Metzgerei	14. Anglizismus	24. Fräulein
5. Verwaltung	15. Dummheit	25. Operation
6. Fähigkeit	16. Bärchen	26. Abrüstung
7. Rätin	17. Quacksalberei	27. Bürgermeisterin
8. Nationalismus *(no plural)*	18. Trivialität	28. Fußgänger
9. Heiligtum	19. Burschenschaft	29. Rivalität
10. Küste	20. Rehlein	30. Theologie

EXERCISE 2 (prerequisite: sections A–B, topic: formation and meaning of nouns with some common suffixes)

Convert each row of words into nouns using the suffix shown. Give the translation of the original word and the resulting noun.

-ität

1. brutal   2. moral   3. kriminal   4. objektiv

-schaft

5. Herr   6. bekannt   7. Wissen   8. schwanger

-ung

9. ausbeuten   10. beleuchten   11. unterstützen   12. warnen

EXERCISE 3 (prerequisite: sections A–B, topic: suffixes that may have concomitant umlaut)

Convert the words in each row into nouns using the suffix shown. Add an umlaut where necessary. Give a translation of the original word and the new word created.

EXAMPLE: **jagen + -er**
ANSWER: **Jäger,** original word: *to hunt,* new word: *hunter*

-er

1. laufen   3. wandern   5. fahren
2. malen   4. backen   6. morden

-in

7. ein Gott   9. Franzose   11. Wolf
8. Bauer   10. Pole   12. Graf

-chen

13. Lamm   14. Lied   15. Katze   16. Apfel

-lein

17. Rad   18. Frau   19. Bub   20. Bauch

EXERCISE 4   (prerequisite: sections A–B, topic: **-heit** vs. **-keit**)

*Form nouns from these adjectives by adding either **-heit** or **-keit** as appropriate, using the rule given in section B. As usual, give the English translation for the original word and the resulting noun.*

1. frech
2. lesbar
3. gesund
4. nackt
5. sauber
6. beweglich
7. scheu
8. einfach
9. tätig
10. reinlich
11. seltsam
12. wahr
13. bissig
14. erreichbar
15. unbestimmt
16. folgsam
17. klug
18. bitter

EXERCISE 5   (prerequisite: sections A–B, topic: **-nis**)

*Find the nouns ending in **-nis** derived from these verbs. Indicate whether the resulting noun is neuter or feminine. Also give a translation of the verb and the noun.*

EXAMPLE: **ärgern**
ANSWER: **das Ärgernis**, verb: *to irritate*, noun: *irritation*

1. erleben
2. bedürfen
3. erlauben
4. wagen
5. besorgen
6. gestehen
7. kennen
8. erzeugen
9. ersparen
10. hindern

EXERCISE 6   (prerequisite: sections A–B, topic: pronunciation of the *-ie* suffix)

*Using a dictionary that gives the pronunciation of German words, determine the pronunication of the final *-ie* suffix in these words. State also the meaning of each word.*

1. Kastanie
2. Melodie
3. Technologie
4. Lappalie
5. Biologie
6. Linie
7. Lilie
8. Chemie

EXERCISE 7 (prerequisite: section C, topic: formation of compound nouns)

Combine the two words shown into a compound word. If the compound is a noun, give its gender. Also list the meaning of each compound word. Where possible, predict the connecting sound; otherwise, try to make an educated guess.

1. Universität + Ball
2. Fahrt + Verbot
3. Maus + Loch
4. Klasse + Kampf
5. Kindheit + Erinnerungen
6. Prozeß + Kosten
7. Zins + Berechnung
8. Diskussion + Runde
9. Existenz + Berechtigung
10. Rasen + Mäher
11. Liebe + Geschichte
12. Altertum + Kunde
13. Bild + Buch
14. Hilfe + reich
15. Börse + Geschäft
16. Wirtschaft + Krise
17. Nacht + Wache
18. Anständigkeit + Bestrebung
19. Krieg + fähig
20. Überzeugung + Kraft

EXERCISE 8 (prerequisite: section D, topic: deciphering compound words)

Split each compound into its individual words. Give the meaning of each individual word and of the compound word.

1. Koalitionsregierung
2. Reinlichkeitsfanatiker
3. Versuchskaninchen
4. Befreiungskrieg
5. Wachstumsprognosen
6. Spesenvergütung
7. Produktivitätsaufstieg
8. Glaubenszwang
9. gesellschaftswidrig
10. Beamtendeutsch
11. Lebensversicherungsgesellschaft
12. militärdienstpflichtig
13. Empfängnisverhütungsmittel
14. Luftdruckabnahme
15. Pfefferkuchengeschmack

EXERCISE 9 (comprehensive)

To the teacher: Choose a German reading passage from current readings.
To the student: Underline all nouns in the given reading passage for which the gender is determined by a suffix. Without looking the word up, state what the gender and plural form must be. Then draw a circle around each compound word in the reading passage and determine the meaning of the compound.

GEDANKENPROBLEM: **Here is a famous example of an actual compound in German. Decipher it:**

Donaudampfschiffahrtsgesellschaftskapitän

What's wrong with these?

1. Das ist das neue Universitätgebäude.
2. Er war immer mein Bruderchen.
3. Ich zweifle nicht an seiner Fähigheit, das zu tun.
4. Wo ist der Film Fest?
5. Er hat ein Irrtum gemacht.
6. Ich will bloß ein bißchen Zärtlichnis von dir.

Problems with the Gender, Plural, Number, and Definite Article of Some Nouns

21

A. Problems with the Gender or Plural of Certain Nouns

Some nouns have two different genders, each gender corresponding to a different meaning:

> **der** See *(the lake)*   **die** See *(the sea)*
> (plural of both of these is: **die Seen**)

Other nouns have two different plurals corresponding to two meanings. For example, **das Wort** *(the word)* has the plural **die Worte** meaning words in connected discourse:

> Was waren seine letzten **Worte?**
> *What were his last words?*

However, **Wort** has another plural, **die Wörter,** which refers to isolated, unrelated words, e.g., **das Wörterbuch** *(dictionary)*.

In other cases, the difference in meaning corresponds to a difference in gender *and* plural:

> **der** Schild *(shield),* plural: die Schilde
> **das** Schild *(street sign),* plural: die Schilder

Other examples of such nouns will be given in the exercises. Some German nouns do not have plural forms even though the equivalent English words do. With such words, the plural is formed by using the plural of another, similar noun:

> der **Tod** *(death),* plural: die Tod**esfälle** *(deaths)*
> (The plural is derived from **der Todesfall,** meaning: *a case of death*)

Common nouns that function like **Tod** are given here:

SINGULAR	PLURAL	MEANING
der Atem	Atemzüge	*breath(s)*
der Betrug	Betrügereien	*deception(s)*
der Kohl	Kohlköpfe	*cabbage(s)*
der Raub	Raubfälle	*robbery(s)*
der Tod	die Todesfälle	*death(s)*
das Unglück	Unglücksfälle	*accident(s)*

As stated in the previous chapter, the gender and plural of a compound noun is normally determined by the last element. In a few cases, this rule does not hold, e.g., the plural of **das Mal** *(point in time)* is **die Male,** as shown in the sentence below:

> Wie viele **Male** waren Sie in Paris?
> *How many times were you in Paris?*

However, the plural of **das Denkmal** *(monument)* is **die Denkmäler.** A similar problem exists with the gender of compound nouns ending in **-teil.** The noun **Teil** *(part)* is masculine, but as a part of a compound noun the gender can be masculine or neuter. The plural of such compounds ends in **-teile** regardless of gender. The list below gives the most common compounds with **-teil:**

MASCULINE		NEUTER	
Bestandteil	*component*	Erbteil	*inheritance*
Elternteil	*parent*	Gegenteil	*opposite*
Erdteil	*continent*	Hinterteil	*back part*
Nachteil	*disadvantage*	Urteil	*judgement*
Vorteil	*advantage*	Vorderteil	*front part*

The word **Mut** *(courage)* is masculine but compounds ending in **-mut** can be masculine or feminine. These compounds refer to abstract concepts and therefore have no plural forms:

MASCULINE		FEMININE	
Edelmut	*noble-mindedness*	Großmut	*magnanimity*
Frohmut	*cheerfulness*	Sanftmut	*gentle temper*

MASCULINE		FEMININE	
Gleichmut	*equanimity*	Schwermut	*melancholy*
Hochmut	*arrogance*	Wehmut	*wistfulness*
Kleinmut	*pettiness*		
Wagemut	*daring*		
Wankelmut	*fickleness*		

COMPREHENSION CHECK: *Fill in the blanks with the missing information.*

	noun	gender	plural	meaning
1. a.	See	_____	Seen	*lake*
b.	See	_____	Seen	*sea*
2. a.	Schild	_____	_____	*street sign*
b.	Schild	_____	_____	*shield*
3. a.	Erbteil	_____	Erbteile	_____
b.	Erdteil	_____	Erdteile	_____
4.	Raub	masculine	_____	*robbery*

ANSWERS: 1. a. *masculine* b. *feminine* 2. a. *neuter*, Schilder b. *masculine*, Schilde 3. a. *neuter, inheritance* b. *masculine, continent* 4. Raubfälle

B. Problems with the Number of Some German Nouns

Some nouns are used in the *plural* in English but are *singular* in German:

> Wo **ist** meine **Brille?**
> *Where are my glasses?*

When the plural form of these words is used, it refers to a plural number of that item:

> Zwei **Brillen** liegen auf dem Tisch.
> *Two pairs of glasses are lying on the table.*

Common nouns that function like **Brille** are the following:

die Brille	*eyeglasses*	die Polizei	*police*
das Gemüse	*vegetables*	die Schere	*scissors*
die Hose	*pants*	die Statistik	*statistics*
der Inhalt	*contents*	die Treppe	*stairs*

Here are some additional examples:

> Iß **dein** Gemüse!
> *Eat your vegetables!*

> Diese Hose **paßt** mir nicht.
> *These pants don't fit me.*

Wo **ist** die Polizei, wenn man sie braucht?
Where are the police when you need them?

Gib mir **eine** Schere!
Give me a pair of scissors.

Note that the German equivalent of **a pair** in the last example is the indefinite article; you do not use the German expression **ein Paar** (*a pair*) because the German nouns discussed in this section are singular. The correct usage of **ein Paar** is shown here for contrast:

Hast du **ein Paar** Handschuhe?
Do you have a pair of gloves?

The list that follows shows the plural form of these nouns, where it exists:

die Brillen	*pairs of eyeglasses*	die Scheren	*pairs of scissors*
die Gemüsearten	*types of vegetables*	die Treppen	*sets of stairs*
die Hosen	*pairs of pants*		

Here is another example of one of these nouns used as a plural:

Ich esse viele **Gemüsearten.**
I eat many types of vegetables.

The German word **die Möbel** (*furniture*) is usually plural in German but singular in English:

Unsere neuen **Möbel sind** sehr schön.
Our new furniture is very beautiful.

A single piece of furniture in German is **das Möbelstück:**

Dieses **Möbelstück ist** mir zu teuer.
This piece of furniture is too expensive for me.

Die Ferien (*the vacation*) is a plural noun in German, singular in English:

Wie **waren** deine **Ferien?**
How was your vacation?

COMPREHENSION CHECK: *Translate into German.*

1. What are the contents of this book?
2. Your furniture has arrived.
3. I bought a shirt and (a pair of) pants.
4. Do you have two pairs of scissors?

ANSWERS: 1. Was ist der Inhalt dieses Buches? 2. Ihre Möbel sind angekommen. 3. Ich habe ein Hemd und eine Hose gekauft. 4. Haben Sie zwei Scheren?

C. German Words That Require the Definite Article

A number of German nouns are used with the definite article where this would not be possible with the English equivalent:

So ist **das** Leben!
That's life!

Common nouns that function in this manner are:

das Christentum	*Christianity*	die Natur	*nature*
die Jugend	*youth*	das Schicksal	*fate*
das Leben	*life*	der Tod	*death*
die Liebe	*love*		

plus all seasons and the names of daily meals:

der Winter	*winter*	das Frühstück	*breakfast*
der Frühling	*spring*	das Mittagessen	*lunch*
der Sommer	*summer*	das Abendessen	*dinner*
der Herbst	*autumn*		

Here are a few examples of these words:

Ist **die** Liebe nicht schön!
Isn't love beautiful!

Der Winter war dieses Jahr lang.
Winter was long this year.

Wann wird **das** Abendessen serviert?
When is dinner served?

Was willst du **zum** Frühstück haben?
What do you want for breakfast?

With another group of German nouns, the definite article is used in prepositional phrases, but the English equivalent has no definite article:

Sie liegt seit drei Wochen **im** Bett.
She has been lying in bed for three weeks.

Er sprang aus **dem** Bett.
He jumped out of bed.

Here is a list of such nouns in German:

in der Arbeit	*at work*	in der Kirche	*in church*
im Bett	*in bed*	in der Öffentlichkeit	*in public*
im Gefängnis	*in prison*	in der Schule	*in school*

plus the biblical regions:

im Fegefeuer	*in purgatory*	in der Hölle	*in hell*
im Himmel	*in heaven*	im Paradies	*in paradise*

plus the days of the week and the months:

am Montag	*on Monday*	im Januar	*in January*
am Dienstag	*on Tuesday*	im Februar	*in February*
usw.	*etc.*	usw.	*etc.*

Here are a few examples:

Heinz ist in **der** Schule.
Heinz is in school.

Heinz ging in **die** Schule.
Heinz went to school.
(accusative to indicate motion toward something)

Wo wirst du **am** Mittwoch sein?
Where will you be on Wednesday?

Ich habe **im** April Geburtstag.
My birthday is in April.

COMPREHENSION CHECK: *Fill in the blank with the German words corresponding to the English words in parentheses.*

1. Was hast du heute _____ gelernt? *(in school)*
2. _____ ist in Österreich oft regnerisch. *(summer)*
3. Man sollte _____ nicht zerstören. *(nature)*
4. Ich fahre jedes Jahr _____ an die Küste. *(in July)*
5. Wann mußt du heute _____ gehen? *(to work)*

ANSWERS: 1. in der Schule 2. der Sommer 3. die Natur 4. im Juli 5. in die Arbeit

German-English Vocabulary

Learn the nouns listed on pages 285–290 and the following:

aus sein	*to be over*	die Jahreszeit, -en	*season*
bekannt	*renowned*	die Küste, -n	*coast*
das Dach, ⸚er	*roof*	die Leiter, -n	*ladder*
fürchten vor +	*to be afraid of*	mittelalterlich	*medieval*
dat. *(reflexive)*		regnerisch	*rainy*
das Paar, -e	*pair*	der Schnee	*snow*
der Pfarrer, -	*pastor*	die Schokolade	*chocolate*

EXERCISE 1 (prerequisite: section A, topic: words with more than one gender and/or plural)

For the German word given, indicate the gender and plural form that corresponds to the meaning listed. These words are not necessarily listed in the glossary; you should use a German dictionary for reference.

      EXAMPLE: See *lake* _____ (answer: der, *pl.* Seen)
                            sea _____ (answer: die, *pl.* Seen)

1. Leiter   *ladder* _____
               director _____
2. Bank   *bench* _____
               bank (where money is kept) _____
3. Gehalt   *capacity* _____
               salary _____
4. Rat   *advice, suggestion* _____
               advisor, councilor _____
5. Tor   *fool* _____
               door, or goal in a game _____
6. Tau   *rope* _____
               dew _____
7. Strauß   *flower bouquet* _____
               ostrich _____
8. Mann   *man (a male person)* _____
               man (in a crew or military unit) _____
               vassal (poetic) _____
9. Steuer   *rudder* _____
               tax _____
10. Band   *volume (of a book)* _____
               ribbon _____
               bond (for holding captive) _____

EXERCISE 2 (prerequisite: section A, topic: words with unpredictable genders or irregular plural forms)

Fill in the blanks with the necessary information. You will derive the most benefit from this exercise if you first memorize the meanings, genders, and plural forms of the words discussed in section A. Then test yourself by doing this exercise.

	Noun	Gender	Plural	Meaning
1.	Nachteil	_____	Nachteile	_____
2.	Atem	*masculine*	_____	_____
3.	_____	_____	*(no plural)*	*gentle temper*
4.	_____	*neuter*	_____	*point in time*
5.	Gegenteil	_____	_____	*opposite*

Noun	Gender	Plural	Meaning
6. Frohmut	_____	*(no plural)*	_____
7. Kohl	_____	_____	*cabbage*
8. Denkmal	neuter	_____	_____
9. _____	das	_____	*back part*
10. Unglück	_____	_____	*accident*
11. Kleinmut	_____	*(no plural)*	_____
12. Bestandteil	_____	Bestandteile	_____
13. Großmut	_____	*(no plural)*	_____
14. _____	der	_____	*deception*
15. Urteil	_____	Urteile	_____

EXERCISE 3 (prerequisite: section B, topic: problems with the number of certain nouns)

Translate into German.

1. The police could not catch him.
2. She is standing on the stairs.
3. The statistics show that the average income has risen.
4. I eat many types of vegetables.
5. The contents were flammable.
6. I need a pair of scissors.
7. He only owns two pairs of pants.
8. My vacation was too short.
9. I have new sunglasses.
10. These vegetables taste good.

EXERCISE 4 (prerequisite: section C, topic: German words that require the definite article)

Fill in the blanks with the German words corresponding to the English words in parentheses.

1. Er saß drei Jahre _____. *(in prison)*
2. _____ ist immer schwer. *(life)*
3. Wo sollen wir _____ kaufen? *(lunch)*
4. Dieser Schnee wird erst _____ schmelzen. *(in spring)*
5. Die Prüfung ist _____. *(on Friday)*
6. Jeder fürchtet sich vor _____. *(death)*
7. Unser Semester ist _____ aus. *(in June)*
8. _____ erlaubte es mir nicht. *(fate)*
9. Gibt es Schokolade _____? *(in heaven)*

10.   _____ ist die schönste Jahreszeit. *(autumn)*
11.   Sag das nicht _____! *(in public)*
12.   Sie ging jeden Sonntag _____. *(to church)*

EXERCISE 5 (comprehensive)

Translate into German.

1.   He always wore green pants.
2.   How many times have you seen these monuments?
3.   When will we eat dinner?
4.   Can I have the large scissors?
5.   The advantage and the disadvantage are the opposite of each other.
6.   When did the police come?
7.   This year it snowed in May.
8.   Where are my glasses?
9.   Why are you lying in bed?
10.   I criticized my teacher's arrogance.
11.   Christianity teaches that there is life in heaven after death.
12.   Both banks didn't have any benches.
13.   I'm going home on Thursday.
14.   You must overcome this melancholy.
15.   He is at work.

What's wrong with these?

1.   Schicksal ist gegen mich.
2.   Die mittelalterlichen Könige waren wegen ihres Großmuts bekannt.
3.   Herr Kellner! Ich kann diese Gemüse nicht essen!
4.   Der Pfarrer fragte mich, wann ich zum letzten Mal in Kirche war.
5.   Ich muß ein Paar Hosen waschen lassen.
6.   Um das Dach zu reparieren, mußte ich zuerst einen Leiter holen.

Review Exercises Chapters 19–21

EXERCISE 1

Fill in the blank with the German words corresponding to the English words in parentheses.

1. Sagen Sie das nicht _____! *(in English)*
2. Bist du ein Anhänger _____? *(of this football team)*
3. _____ keine Erklärung für das Verbrechen. *(the police have)*
4. Nur _____ Leute haben ihn gern. *(a few)*
5. Das ist _____, was ich nicht verstehe. *(the only thing)*
6. Er war mein _____. *(Physics teacher)*
7. Niemand nimmt mich _____. *(seriously)*
8. Zeigen Sie mir _____ dieses Koffers. *(the contents)*
9. Er versteht _____. *(Swedish)*
10. Es war ein gutes Beispiel von _____. *(mass production)*
11. Sie heiratete _____. *(in spring)*
12. Warum hast _____ mir nicht geschrieben? *(you)* (in a letter)
13. Dieses Geschäft verkauft nur _____. *(men's clothing)* (write as one word)
14. Ich liebe _____! *(nature)*
15. Hast du die meisten _____ gern? *(types of vegetables)*
16. Unsere Wohnung ist _____ dazu kleiner. *(in comparison)*
17. Ich will nicht _____ gehen. *(to school)*
18. Mein Arzt verlangt, daß ich _____ bezahle. *(in advance)*
19. Ich habe leider nichts _____ zu berichten. *(good)*
20. Das Buch behandelt das Problem _____. *(of capital punishment)*

EXERCISE 2

Give the gender, plural, and meaning of the words listed. These words are not necessarily listed in the glossary. If you do not know the answer already, you will have to use a German dictionary.

1. Technologie
2. Atem
3. Tätigkeit
4. Entchen
5. Edelmut
6. Panzerdivision
7. Pause
8. Kohl
9. Einwanderer
13. Zuweisung
14. Staatseigentum
15. Wehmut
16. a. Steuer *(tax)*
    b. Steuer *(rudder)*
17. Wirtin
18. Idealismus
19. Vorderteil
20. Arbeitserlaubnis

10.	Buchbinderei	21.	Demokratie
11.	Bestandteil	22.	a. Tor *(fool)*
12.	Angelegenheit		b. Tor *(goal)*
		23.	Botschaft
		24.	Strahlungsintensität

What's wrong with these?

1. Wir sind in August in die Schweiz gefahren.
2. Der Verkaufer hat mir sehr geholfen.
3. Er war ein Polnischer Prinz.
4. Jeder Einzelne muß sein eigenes Essen mitnehmen.
5. Ich habe eine Beschwerde Brief geschrieben.
6. Wollen Sie Sich die Hände waschen?
7. Ich habe mich mit einem Paar von Schere geschnitten.
8. Im Allgemeinen trinke ich jeden Tag eine Tasse Tee.
9. Das tut mir Leid.
10. Ich habe seine Wörter nicht verstanden.
11. Wo hast du den Wohnungschlüssel?
12. Ich werde dich im frankfurter Bahnhof treffen.

Verb Types

22

A. Reflexive Verbs

As you know from Chapter 4, section E, many verbs in German and English can be used reflexively:

> Er hat **sich** erschossen.
> *He shot himself.*

The use of the reflexive pronoun in this example is necessitated by the fact that the subject and the object of the sentence are identical. If this were not the case, a non-reflexive pronoun would be used:

> Er hat **sie** erschossen.
> *He shot her.*

But with many verbs in German, the reflexive pronoun must be used regardless of whether the subject is identical to the object. Furthermore, the equivalent English verb is generally not reflexive:

> Er fürchtet **sich** vor dem Hund.
> *He is afraid of the dog.*

The reflexive pronoun is "illogical" in this sentence because the subject does not fear *himself;* instead he fears *the dog*. Verbs such as **sich fürchten** will be called *reflexive verbs*. Here is another example of a reflexive verb:

> Du mußt **dich** um dieses Problem **kümmern.**
> *You have to take care of this problem.*
> (reflexive verb: **sich kümmern**)

The reflexive pronoun usually appears at the beginning of the middle field and thus may be separated from the verb on which it depends, e.g., the **dich** and **kümmern** in the previous example.

Here is a list of some common reflexive verbs. Note the specific prepositions that accompany many of these:

sich amüsieren	to have a good time
sich aus.ruhen	to take a rest
sich beeilen	to hurry
sich benehmen	to behave
sich bewegen	to move
sich bewerben um	to apply for
sich entschließen	to decide
sich erinnern an + *accusative*	to remember
sich erkälten	to catch a cold
sich freuen auf + *accusative*	to look forward to
sich freuen über + *accusative*	to be happy about
sich fürchten vor + *dative*	to be afraid of
sich genieren	to be embarrassed
sich gewöhnen an + *accusative*	to get used to
sich interessieren für	to be interested in
sich irren	to be wrong, mistaken
sich kümmern um	to take care of, concern oneself with
sich schämen wegen	to be ashamed of
sich verlassen auf + *accusative*	to depend on
sich wundern über + *accusative*	to be astonished at

The verbs shown in the examples below are used with a *dative* reflexive pronoun:

Ich kann es **mir** nicht leisten.　　(sich etwas leisten)
I can't afford it.　　*(to afford something)*

Ich mache **mir** Sorgen um dich.　　(sich Sorgen um etwas machen)
I'm worried about you.　　*(to be worried about something)*

Stell **dir** das vor!　　(sich etwas vorstellen)
Just imagine that!　　*(to imagine something)*

Sentences dealing with parts of the body often contain a dative reflexive pronoun:

Ich putze **mir** die Zähne jeden Abend.
I brush my teeth every evening.

Willst du **dir** zuerst die Haare kämmen?
Do you want to comb your hair first?

Note that English uses a possessive adjective before the body part; however, German uses the definite article (and plural for *hair*). The verb **lassen** is frequently used in conjunction with sentences such as the above:

Ich muß mir bald die Haare schneiden **lassen.**
I have to have my hair cut soon.

1. You should hurry. *(use the **Sie**-form)*
2. He is not having a good time.
3. I can't afford this house.
4. Wash your hands. *(use the **du**-form)*
5. She wants to have her hair dyed.

ANSWERS: 1. Sie sollten sich beeilen. 2. Er amüsiert sich nicht. 3. Ich kann mir dieses Haus nicht leisten. 4. Wasch dir die Hände! 5. Sie will sich die Haare färben lassen.

B. Dative Verbs

You have already dealt with dative verbs starting with Chapter 4, section D. Here is a more complete list of dative verbs that includes those given previously:

antworten	*to answer*	gratulieren	*to congratulate*
begegnen (sein)	*to meet*	helfen	*to help*
danken	*to thank*	mißfallen	*to displease*
dienen	*to serve*	schaden	*to hurt*
drohen	*to threaten*	schmeicheln	*to flatter*
entfliehen (sein)	*to flee (from)*	trauen	*to trust*
folgen (sein/haben)	*to follow, obey*	verzeihen	*to forgive*
gefallen	*to please*	widersprechen	*to contradict*
gehorchen	*to obey*	widerstehen	*to resist*
glauben	*to believe*	zu.stimmen	*to agree with*
gleichen	*to be like*	zuvor.kommen (sein)	*to forestall*

Note: **Folgen** uses **sein** in the past tense in the meaning of *follow,* but **haben** in the meaning of *obey:*

Warum **bist** du mir gefolgt?
Why did you follow me?

Warum **hast** du mir nicht gefolgt?
Why didn't you obey me (follow my advice)?

Note: **Antworten** and **glauben** require the dative only when the object is a person, not a thing:

Antworten Sie **mir!**
Answer me.

Antworten Sie **auf meine Frage!**

or alternatively:

Beantworten Sie meine Frage!
Answer my question.

Ich glaube **dir** nicht.
I don't believe you.

Ich glaube **das** nicht.
I don't believe that.

Dative verbs, by definition, are intransitive and therefore use **sein** as the auxiliary in the present and past perfect tenses if the verb also indicates motion or change of condition. Moreover, dative verbs sometimes use **sein** as the auxiliary even when the idea of motion or change of condition is not altogether clear. Consider, for example, **begegnen** and **zuvorkommen:**

Wo **bist** du ihm begegnet?
Where did you meet him?

Damals **ist** die Armee dem Putschversuch zuvorgekommen.
At that time the army forestalled the coup attempt.

In short, when you look up a German word in the dictionary and discover that the word is listed as a dative verb, also check to see what auxiliary it takes.

COMPREHENSION CHECK: *Translate these sentences into German using a dative verb.*

1. May I congratulate you? *(use **Sie-** form)*
2. We don't trust him.
3. I met her in the library. *(present perfect tense)*
4. Will you answer him? *(use **du-** form)*

ANSWERS: 1. Darf ich Ihnen gratulieren? 2. Wir trauen ihm nicht. 3. Ich bin ihr in der Bibliothek begegnet. 4. Wirst du ihm antworten?

C. Genitive Verbs

A few verbs in German require a *genitive* object:

Gedenke deines Versprechens!
Remember your promise.

Such verbs have an archaic or poetic ring to them and are therefore usually avoided in everyday speech. The previous example could be expressed more conventionally as follows:

Erinnere dich an dein Versprechen!

The list below gives the most common genitive verbs:

Bedürfen *(to need):*

Er bedarf des Trostes.
He is in need of comfort.
more commonly: Er braucht Trost. (accusative object)

Sich Bemächtigen *(to seize):*

Der jüngste Sohn bemächtigte sich des Thrones.
The youngest son seized the throne.
more commonly: Der jüngste Sohn übernahm den Thron mit Gewalt.

Sich Erinnern *(to remember):*

Lotte erinnerte sich noch des alten Familienhauses.
Lotte still remembered the old family home.
more commonly: Lotte erinnerte sich noch an das alte Familienhaus.

Sich Schämen *(to be ashamed of):*

Er schämte sich seines Aussehens.
He was ashamed of his appearance.
more commonly: Er schämte sich wegen seines Aussehens.

Sich Vergewissern *(to make sure of):*

Wir haben uns zuerst seiner Verläßlichkeit vergewissert.
We first made sure of his dependability.
more commonly: Wir haben uns zuerst über seine Verläßlichkeit vergewissert.

Note: As can be seen with the examples above, most genitive verbs are also reflexive.

COMPREHENSION CHECK: *Translate each German sentence into English. Then rewrite the German sentence using a more conventional, nongenitive verb.*

1. Ich bedarf einer Erklärung.
2. Sie schämte sich ihrer niedrigen Herkunft.

ANSWERS: 1. *I am in need of an explanation.* Ich brauche eine Erklärung. 2. *She was ashamed of her low origin.* Sie schämte sich wegen ihrer niedrigen Herkunft.

D. Impersonal Verbs

An *impersonal* verb is one which always or nearly always has **es** as the subject. This **es** does not refer to any particular object but simply provides a subject for the sentence. Most verbs indicating weather activities fall into this category:

Es blitzt.	Es donnert.	Es hagelt.
It's lightening.	*It's thundering.*	*It's hailing.*
Es nieselt.	Es regnet.	Es schneit.
It's drizzling.	*It's raining.*	*It's snowing.*

Not every impersonal verb deals with the weather:

Es lohnt sich, diesen Film anzuschauen.
It's worthwhile (pays) to see this film.

German has a number of impersonal verbs for which the equivalent English verb is not impersonal:

Es geht mir gut.   Es ist ihr kalt.   Es ist ihm warm.

or

Mir geht's gut.	Ihr ist kalt.	Ihm ist warm.
I am fine.	*She is cold.*	*He is warm.*

Note that the **es** disappears in the last two examples when the indirect object is put in first position. If the English sentences are translated literally into German, the meaning becomes quite different:

Ich bin gut in der Mathematik.
I am good at mathematics.

Sie ist kalt.
She is cold. (i.e. impersonal, or sexually frigid)

Er ist warm. (slang expression)
He is gay. (i.e. a homosexual)

Here are three more impersonal verbs in German:

Es **ist** mir nicht **gelungen,** das Problem zu lösen.
I was unsuccessful at solving the problem.
(from **gelingen,** strong verb, auxiliary **sein**)

Es graut mir vor ihm.

or

Mir graut vor ihm.
I am horrified by him.

Mir schwindelt.
I am dizzy.
(more conventionally: Mir ist schwindlig.)

In the previous examples, the English subject corresponds to the dative object of the German impersonal verb. Sometimes the German impersonal verb has an accusative object:

Mich schaudert bei diesem Gedanken.
I shudder at this thought.

Mich friert.
I am cold.
(more conventionally: Mir ist kalt.)

Mich dürstet.
I am thirsty.
(more conventionally: Ich habe Durst. *or* Ich bin durstig.)

Mich hungert.
I am hungry.
(more conventionally: Ich habe Hunger (bin hungrig).)

The impersonal verb **es gibt** corresponds to the English *there is/there are* and indicates the general *existence* of the object:

Es gibt keine bessere Alternative.
There is no better alternative. (i.e., no better alternative exists)

The same sentence in the plural would be:

Es gibt keine besseren Alternativen.
There are no better alternatives.

The next example shows this construction used in a past tense:

Es gab keine besseren Alternativen.
There were no better alternatives.

Here is another example of **es gibt:**

Es gibt nur einen Arzt, der diese Operation durchführen kann.
There is only one doctor who can perform this operation. (i.e., only one exists)

Compare the previous example with this one:

Da ist der Arzt, der diese Operation durchführen wird.
There is the doctor who will perform this operation. (i.e., you are pointing at him)

or in the plural:

Da sind die Ärzte, die die Operation durchführen werden.
There are the doctors who will perform the operation.

German uses **da ist/sind** to indicate that the object is being pointed out.

COMPREHENSION CHECK: *Translate into German.*

1. It's been drizzling for three days.
2. We succeeded in helping him. *(use present perfect tense)*
3. I was dizzy. *(use the more conventional form)*
4. Are you warm?
5. Is there a God?
6. Look. There is the train station.

ANSWERS: 1. Es nieselt seit drei Tagen. 2. Es ist uns gelungen, ihm zu helfen. 3. Mir war schwindlig. 4. Ist es dir warm? 5. Gibt es einen Gott? 6. Schau! Da ist der Bahnhof.

E. Transitive and Intransitive Verbs

The distinction between transitive and intransitive verbs was discussed in chapter 3, section C. To summarize, a transitive verb in German takes an accusative object, an intransitive verb does not. A good German dictionary will tell you if a given verb is transitive or intransitive. This information is important because the German verb may be transitive whereas the equivalent English verb is not, or vice versa. The examples below illustrate this problem:

> Ich wache jeden Tag um acht Uhr auf.
> *I wake up every day at eight o'clock.*
> (intransitive verb **aufwachen**)

> Weck mich um acht Uhr!
> *Wake me up at eight o'clock.*
> (transitive verb **wecken**)

The two German verbs cannot be interchanged in the sentences shown because the one is transitive, the other intransitive. However, both mean *to wake up*.

In some cases, a transitive and an intransitive verb can be used to express the same idea, but not in the same way:

> Wir bekämpften den Feind.
> *We fought the enemy.*
> (**bekämpfen:** transitive verb only)

> Wir kämpften gegen den Feind.
> *We fought against the enemy.*
> (**kämpfen:** intransitive verb only)

Your dictionary would probably list both **bekämpfen** and **kämpfen** under the English verb *to fight,* but to use either verb correctly you would also have to check whether the verb is transitive or intransitive (many verbs are both) and write the intended German sentence accordingly. Remember: An intransitive verb in German is one that does not allow an *accusative* object. However, it may still allow a dative, genitive, or prepositional object, e.g., **kämpfen gegen etwas,** or it may allow no object at all, e.g., **aufwachen.**

Note: Verbs with the **be-** prefix are usually transitive; the same verb without this prefix may not be transitive.

COMPREHENSION CHECK: *Consult a German dictionary, instead of the glossary, to do this exercise.*

Part A: Translate the English sentence into German using the appropriate verb from the two given in parentheses.

1. He rang the bell every day. (klingeln, läuten)
2. We delayed the trip. (verzögern, zögern)

Part B: Translate the English sentence into German using both of the verbs shown.

3. I continued the work. (fortfahren, fortsetzen) *(use simple past tense)*

Part C: Translate the English sentence into German using the German verb shown.

4. She pressed the button. (drücken)

> ANSWERS: 1. Er läutete die Glocke jeden Tag.   2. Wir verzögerten die Reise.
> 3. Ich fuhr mit der Arbeit fort. Ich setzte die Arbeit fort.   4. Sie drückte auf den Knopf.

German-English Vocabulary

Learn the reflexive verbs listed on page 297, the dative verbs on page 298, the genitive verbs on page 300, the impersonal constructions in section D, and the following:

antworten auf +	*to answer*	niedrig	*low*
acc.	*(something)*	die Richtigkeit	*correctness*
die Aussage, -n	*statement*	der Staat, -en	*state (country)*
das Eigentum	*property*	der Urlaub, -e	*vacation*
die Herkunft, ⁔e	*origin*		

EXERCISE 1   (prerequisite: section A, topic: reflexive verbs)

Translate the English sentences into German using a reflexive verb.

1. I am afraid of the consequences.
2. You are mistaken. *(use **du**-form)*

3. He burnt his finger. *(present perfect tense)*
4. I remember him well.
5. The children should brush their teeth.
6. Are you interested in this topic? *(use **Sie**-form)*
7. She was worried about her husband.
8. I can't get used to this weather.
9. Why did you have your hair cut? *(use **du**-form) (present perfect tense)*
10. She is applying for a scholarship.
11. Can we really depend on him?
12. Why are you embarrassed?
13. Can't you behave? *(use **du**-form)*
14. I have to take a rest.
15. a. We are looking forward to your visit.
    b. We are happy about your visit.

EXERCISE 2 (prerequisite: section B, topic: dative verbs)

Translate into German using a dative verb in each sentence.

1. That displeases me very much.
2. We aren't supposed to contradict him.
3. He is like his brother.
4. We forestalled the danger. *(present perfect tense)*
5. I serve my country.
6. Are you threatening me?
7. I agree with you.
8. He fled from prison. *(present perfect tense)*
9. I couldn't resist the temptation.
10. a. How long did you follow him? *(use **folgen** and present perfect tense for 10a and 10b)*
    b. Your son didn't obey me again.

EXERCISE 3 (prerequisite: section C, topic: genitive verbs)

Translate into English. Then rewrite the original German sentence in the more conventional form.

1. Gedenke des Todes!
2. Nachher schämte er sich seiner Worte.
3. Erinnern Sie sich dieses Mannes?
4. Ich bedarf eines langen Urlaubs.
5. Der Staat bemächtigte sich des Eigentums vieler Leute.
6. Er hat sich der Richtigkeit meiner Aussage vergewissert.

EXERCISE 4 (prerequisite: section D, topic: impersonal verbs)

Translate into German. Use an impersonal verb construction where possible.

1. She was horrified.
2. How is he today?
3. Suddenly I was dizzy.
4. It doesn't pay to talk to him.
5. It's thundering and lightening outside.
6. Are you cold?
7. I shudder when I think of it.
8. There were many possibilities.
9. Were you successful in finding her house? *(present perfect tense)*
10. There is your pen.

EXERCISE 5 (prerequisite: section E, topic: transitive and intransitive verbs)

The verbs used in this exercise are not necessarily listed in the glossary. You should consult a German dictionary for help.

Part A: Translate the sentences into German using the words in parentheses. Each word is correct in only one sentence.

1. a. The ship sank.
    b. The rocket sank the ship.
    (versenken, versinken)
2. a. He is probably lying.
    b. Don't lie to me!
    (anlügen, lügen)
3. a. I want to grow spinach in my garden.
    b. Rice grows well in this country.
    (anbauen, wachsen)
4. a. The murderer drowned his victim.
    b. Her husband drowned.
    (ertränken, ertrinken)

Part B: Translate the sentences into German using both verbs listed.

5. Let's discuss the problem. (besprechen, sprechen)
6. I want to marry her. (heiraten, verheiraten)

Part C: Translate the sentence into German using the German verb given.

7. We are waiting for the rain to be over. (abwarten)
8. May I ask you for a favor? (erbitten)

306 VERB TYPES

EXERCISE 6 (comprehensive)

Translate these sentences into German using the verb given in parentheses. Use the present perfect tense for all verbs written in the past tense. Most of these verbs are not given in the glossary. You must use a German dictionary to determine whether the verb is reflexive, dative, genitive, impersonal, transitive or intransitive, or a combination of these.

1. I overslept. (verschlafen)
2. That doesn't impress me. (imponieren)
3. Do you like it? (gefallen)
4. I set him right. (belehren)
5. He stems from a royal family. (entstammen)
6. You should listen to me. (anhören)
7. I longed for a soft bed. (sehnen)
8. He craves only money. (gelüsten)
9. We encountered some difficulties. (stoßen)
10. The audience applauded the actors. (applaudieren)
11. Did you inquire about it? (erkundigen)
12. The judge withheld his judgement. (enthalten)
13. She came toward me slowly. (entgegenkommen)
14. We got lost. (verfahren)

What's wrong with these?

1. Mit unserer neuen Heizung sind wir immer warm im Haus.
2. Warum wollen Sie meine Frage nicht antworten?
3. Ich kann nicht entschließen, was ich tun sollte.
4. Wo hast du ihn begegnet?
5. Sie bedürfen meine Hilfe wirklich.
6. Wie geht es Ihnen? Ich bin gut.

Proverbs, Common Sayings, Figurative Expressions, and Multiple Meanings

23

A. Proverbs

Proverbs are sentences that stand for a certain idea in a poetic or figurative way. Here are two examples of proverbs in English and German:

> Liebe macht blind.
> *Love is blind.*

> Not bricht Eisen.
> *Necessity is the mother of invention.*
> (The German sentence means literally: *Necessity breaks iron.*)

The proverbs that exist in any language are largely a result of cultural tradition. English and German are based on related cultures, therefore they often have similar proverbs, as can be seen in the first example above. *However, only rarely can an English proverb be literally translated into German or vice versa.* In practical terms, this means that you should always check your dictionary before attempting to render an English proverb into German. Proverbs are, however, easy to recognize and a good dictionary should list the German equivalent of an English proverb or vice versa (though you may have to look up several key words in the proverb before you find the proverb itself listed).

Here are a few more examples of German and English proverbs:

> Ende gut, alles gut.
> *All's well that ends well.*

Übung macht den Meister.
Practice makes perfect.

Ein Unglück kommt selten allein.
When it rains, it pours.

Morgenstund' hat Gold im Mund.
The early bird catches the worm. (literally: *Morning hour has gold in the mouth.*)

Sometimes English does not have an equivalent proverb to translate a German proverb. In these cases you simply have to state what the proverb in effect means:

German proverb:	Es wird niemals so heiß gegessen, wie es gekocht wird.
literal meaning:	*It's never eaten as hot as it is cooked.*
best English equivalent:	*Things never turn out as bad as we fear.*

Conversely, German may not have an equivalent proverb for an English proverb:

English proverb:	*Curiosity killed the cat.*
best German equivalent:	Sei nicht so neugierig!
meaning:	*Don't be so curious!*

Note this terminology: **Das Sprichwort** *(proverb)*, plural: **die Sprichwörter.**

COMPREHENSION CHECK: *Part A: Translate into English using a dictionary instead of the glossary for reference.*

1. Der Spatz in der Hand ist besser als die Taube auf dem Dach.
2. Was ich nicht weiß, macht mich nicht heiß.

Part B: Translate into German using a dictionary for reference.

3. Hunger is the best sauce.
4. Birds of a feather flock together.

ANSWERS: 1. A bird in the hand is worth two in the bush. 2. What I don't know can't hurt me. 3. Hunger ist der beste Koch. 4. Gleich und gleich gesellt sich gern.

B. Common Sayings

Common sayings are similar to proverbs in that they are poetic and figurative. But in contrast to proverbs they are not separate sentences; instead, they are inserted, as needed, into a sentence. For example, note how the common saying *to kill two birds with one stone* is made a part of the sentence below:

I killed two birds with one stone. (i.e., *I was able to do two things at the same time.*)

The sentence could easily be literally translated into German:

??Ich habe zwei Vögel mit einem Stein getötet.

The German sentence makes perfectly good sense; but it means that you literally killed two innocent birds with a single rock. The *proper* German equivalent of the English example would be as follows:

> Ich habe zwei Fliegen mit einer Klappe geschlagen.
> (literally: *I struck two flies with one swat.*)

As with proverbs, *an English saying is likely to be wrong if translated literally into German or vice versa.* Again, consult your dictionary for the correct equivalent.

Here are a few more examples of common sayings in English and German:

> Warum hast du die Katze im Sack gekauft?
> *Why did you buy a pig in a poke?*

> Er ist auf den Hund gekommen.
> *He has gone to the dogs.*

> Ich werde dir den Daumen halten.
> *I will cross my fingers for you.* (literally: *I will hold the thumb for you.*)

> Sie wollte nicht ins Fettnäpfchen treten.
> *She didn't want to put her foot in her mouth.* (literally: *She didn't want to step into the bowl of fat.*)

Note this terminology: **die Redensart** (*common saying*), plural: **die Redensarten.**

COMPREHENSION CHECK: *Part A: Translate into English using a dictionary instead of the glossary for reference.*

1. Er war ein Arzt von echtem Schrot und Korn.
2. Die ganze Arbeit war für die Katz'.

Part B: Translate into German using a dictionary for reference.

3. You are making a mountain out of a molehill.
4. I have a bone to pick with you.

> ANSWERS: 1. He was a doctor of the old school. 2. The whole work was in vain. 3. Du machst aus einer Mücke einen Elefanten. 4. Ich habe ein Hühnchen mit dir zu rupfen.

C. Figurative Meanings

In speaking or writing German, you must distinguish between *literal* and *figurative* meanings. For example, the English verb *to pick up* has the literal German equivalent **aufheben:**

> Er hat den Sessel aufgehoben.
> *He picked up the chair.*

But in the next example, the verb *to pick up* clearly has a figurative meaning:

He always tries to pick up girls.

If you translate this sentence into German using **aufheben,** you will produce a peculiar sentence:

??Er versucht immer, Mädchen aufzuheben.

The German sentence sounds as if he is constantly trying to hoist girls over his head. The point is this:

A word in English may have numerous literal and figurative meanings; however, there is no guarantee that the German word equivalent to the literal meaning can also be used for any of the figurative meanings.

In other words, you will probably make a mistake if you use the literal translation for a figurative meaning. Fortunately, a good English-German dictionary will list not only the literal meanings for a given word but also the figurative meanings (usually the literal meanings come first). For example, you should find under the general heading *to pick up* the figurative meaning *to pick up (a girl):* **jemanden aufgabeln** (literally: *to fork someone up*). Therefore, the correct translation of the English example would be:

Er versucht immer, Mädchen aufzugabeln.

Sometimes the figurative nature of an expression may be very subtle. Consider, for example, the English sentence below:

I had a good time.

This expression is so common that you might not realize that it is figurative, but in fact, you cannot really ''have'' (possess) a good time. An acceptable German translation would be as follows:

Ich habe mich amüsiert.
(not: *Ich hatte eine gute Zeit.)

Check the word in your dictionary if there is any doubt that you might be dealing with a figurative meaning.

As with proverbs and common sayings, the German equivalent of an English sentence containing a figurative meaning may bear little resemblance to the English sentence:

Ich erwarte, daß du dich so brav wie möglich benimmst.
I expect you to be on your best behavior.

If you are speaking German and using a dictionary would be impractical, then try to avoid figurative meanings when you are unsure of the correct German equivalent.

Nearly any sentence containing a figurative meaning can be restated in simpler, more literal terms. For example, consider the sentence below:

He will always be in love with me.

You should recognize the figurative expression *to be in love with someone*. If you translate literally you will get a nonsense sentence:

*Er wird immer in Liebe mit mir sein.

The correct translation would be:

Er wird immer in mich verliebt sein.

Obviously, the correct translation differs significantly and unpredictably from the literal, incorrect, translation. However, if the original English sentence is made more literal as shown below:

He will always love me.

then the translation becomes straightforward:

Er wird mich immer lieben.

COMPREHENSION CHECK: *Each sentence contains a figurative meaning. Translate into German using a dictionary for reference.*

1. Some people are never on time.
2. This machine doesn't work any more. (i.e., is broken)
3. Can you make room for me?

ANSWERS: 1. Manche Leute sind niemals pünktlich. 2. Diese Maschine funktioniert nicht mehr. 3. Können Sie mir Platz machen?

D. Multiple Meanings

A word can have several meanings without any of them being figurative. Consider, for example, the word *memory* as shown in the sentences below:

1. That is a good *memory*. (i.e., That is a good remembrance.)
2. He has a good *memory*. (i.e., He has the ability to remember things well.)

The above sentences describe different types of memory, but neither is any more figurative than the other. Such *multiple meanings* for words are quite common in any language. Consider now the German equivalents of the examples above:

1. Das ist eine gute **Erinnerung.**
2. Er hat ein gutes **Gedächtnis.**

German uses a different word for each of the two meanings expressed by the single word *memory* in English. Graphically, the problem can be illustrated as follows:

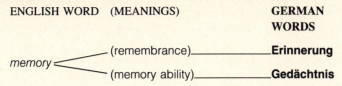

ENGLISH WORD (MEANINGS)   **GERMAN WORDS**

memory
- (remembrance)——————**Erinnerung**
- (memory ability)——————**Gedächtnis**

Here is another example of multiple meanings. Observe the German equivalents for the English word *suspicious:*

Ich bin sehr **mißtrauisch** gegen ihn.
I am very suspicious of him. (i.e., I don't trust him.)

Er sieht sehr **verdächtig** aus.
He looks very suspicious. (i.e., He looks strange in a bad way.)

There is a subtle distinction in meaning between the words *suspicious* in the two English sentences. But an English speaking person would probably be unaware of that fact precisely because both meanings are expressed by the same word. In German, however, the distinction is quite obvious because each meaning is expressed by a different word. The problem can be summarized as follows:

> *A given word in English may have a number of literal meanings, and there is no way of knowing in advance whether the German word that corresponds to one of those meanings will also share the others. In fact, you will probably not even realize that the multiple meanings exist.*

This problem is not limited to a few specific examples, rather it affects a large proportion of English and German vocabulary. You can, at best, improve your chances of finding the right word by checking all words in the dictionary except those with which you are very familiar.

When you do look up an English word in an English-German dictionary, you will probably be presented with a string of German words. You should not assume that all of these words are acceptable in your sentence. Some of them will probably correspond to different meanings of the English word. Look at the explanations after each word and especially the sample sentences, if they exist. When you think you have found the German word that corresponds *exactly* to your intended meaning, look that word up in the German-English part of the dictionary and see if it translates back to your original English word. Of course, carefully check all the information given on the German word, such as gender, plural, transitive verb, reflexive, etc.

After completing this process, your chances of finding the correct word are good but still not certain. If you simply choose the first German word listed, or the shortest one, or the one that looks most like English, then your chances of finding the correct word are poor.

COMPREHENSION CHECK: *Fill in the blank with the appropriate form of the German word corresponding to the English word in parentheses. You are given two German words to choose from; however, each word is correct in only one of the sentences. You should be able to do the first set of sentences immediately, but you will probably have to use a dictionary to do the other sentences.*

1. a. Sie war sehr _____, als sie ihn mit einer anderen Frau sah.
   b. Seine Ausreden klingen _____.
      (*suspicious:* mißtrauisch, verdächtig)
2. a. Ich _____ den Platz mit der Frau neben mir.
   b. Ich _____ meinen Plan ein bißchen.
      (*changed:* ändern, wechseln)
3. a. Er ist ein _____ Mensch. Er tut immer merkwürdige Sachen.
   b. Eine _____ Katze sitzt in unserer Garage. Weißt du vielleicht, wem sie gehört?
      (*strange:* fremd, komisch)

ANSWERS: 1. a. mißtrauisch b. verdächtig 2. a. wechselte b. änderte
3. a. komischer b. fremde.

Important! For all of the exercises in this chapter you must use a dictionary instead of the glossary for reference.

EXERCISE 1   (prerequisite: section A, topic: understanding German proverbs)

Translate into English. Be prepared to state the literal meaning of the German translation.

1. Ehrlich währt am längsten.
2. Man muß das Eisen schmieden, solange es heiß ist.
3. Aller Anfang ist schwer.
4. Man soll den Tag nicht vor dem Abend loben.
5. Geiz ist die Wurzel allen Übels.

EXERCISE 2   (prerequisite: section A, topic: translating English proverbs into German)

Translate into German. Be prepared to state the literal meaning of the German translation.

1. The proof of the pudding is in the eating.
2. No news is good news.
3. Out of sight, out of mind.
4. A stitch in time saves nine.
5. Every cloud has a silver lining.

EXERCISE 3 (prerequisite: section B, topic: understanding common sayings in German)

Translate into English. Be prepared to state the literal meaning of the German translation.

1. Er jagt mich immer ins Bockshorn.
2. Diesem Kind muß man auf die Finger schauen.
3. Wie kannst du das auf die leichte Schulter nehmen?
4. Er gerät immer außer Rand und Band, wenn er von seinem Auto spricht.
5. Ich wette, ich kann ihn in den April schicken.

EXERCISE 4 (prerequisite: section B, topic: translating common English sayings into German)

Translate into German. Be prepared to state the literal meaning of the German translation.

1. They sent me on a wild goose chase.
2. These radios are selling like hot cakes.
3. I hate it when she beats around the bush.
4. He finally kicked the bucket.
5. My sister wanted to poke her nose into my business.

EXERCISE 5 (optional exercise)

Just for fun, ask friends who know another foreign language to translate the sentences in exercises 2 and 4 into that language and then give you a literal translation of the result. Compile a listing of each sentence in as many languages as possible and compare the results. Try to get some of your examples from a non-European language such as Chinese, Japanese or Hebrew.

EXERCISE 6 (prerequisite: section C, topic: figurative meanings)

Translate into German. If you cannot find a suitable translation in the dictionary, rewrite the sentence more literally so that it expresses the same idea but is easier to translate.

1. The line is busy.
2. Your essay reads well.

3. Can't you bend the rules a little?
4. My car looks its age.
5. Who will run the office while you are away?
6. I lost my temper.
7. You can't beat this offer.
8. This room holds forty people.
9. You can always turn to me if you need help.
10. These plastic sweaters don't sell.

EXERCISE 7 (prerequisite: section D, topic: finding the German word with the correct meaning)

Fill in the blank with the German word which corresponds to the meaning of the English word(s) in parentheses.

1. Mexikanisches Essen ist mir zu _____. *(hot)*
2. Es gibt keine _____ mehr zwischen uns. *(communication)*
3. Was _____ dieses Wort? *(mean)*
4. Sie dürfen _____ dann nach Hause gehen, wenn die Arbeit fertig ist. *(only)*
5. Jemand hat den Präsidenten _____! *(shot and killed) (Use only one word in German.)*

EXERCISE 8 (prerequisite: section D, topic: finding the verb with the right meaning)

Translate each pair of sentences using the two verbs shown in parentheses. Each verb is correct in only one of the sentences.

1. a. We want to rent a house.
   b. A friend rented a house to us.
      (mieten, vermieten)
2. a. The scientist invented a better solar cell.
   b. How can you invent such a ridiculous story?
      (erdichten, erfinden)
3. a. I missed you while you were away.
   b. I must have missed you in the crowd.
      (vermissen, verpassen)
4. a. He refused me his help.
   b. He refused my offer.
      (ablehnen, verweigern)
5. a. We had to swear an oath.
   b. We were not allowed to swear.
      (fluchen, schwören)

EXERCISE 9 (comprehensive)

Translate into German.

1. Can you give me a light? *(for a cigarette)*
2. I became extremely frustrated.
3. The baby makes great demands on my time.
4. You were lucky.
5. I know which way the wind blows.
6. She is very bright.
7. I can't stand this heat any longer.
8. Where there is smoke, there is fire.
9. We were bored stiff.
10. What will we do if the theory proves to be wrong?

GEDANKENPROBLEM: **Explain why a German might say this when speaking English.**

a. *Would you please borrow me a pen.*
b. *Let the book on the table.*
c. *How much clock is it?*
d. *I never eat flesh on Friday.*

What's wrong with these?

1. Ich muß zugeben, daß du richtig bist.
2. Dieses Brot ist aus Weizen und Hühnerauge.
3. Ich war grün mit Neid.
4. Für ein Genie wäre es sehr einfältig, das Problem zu lösen.
5. Ein neuer Besen kehrt rein.
6. Wir haben eine Party geworfen.

Flavoring Words and False Cognates

24

A. Flavoring Words

Consider the German sentence below:

> Ich bin **eben** ein sehr heikler Mensch.
> *I'm just a very particular person.*

The German word **eben** is a so-called *flavoring word:* it gives the sentence a certain extra meaning, though the sentence would mean basically the same thing without it. In this example, the meaning imparted by the word **eben** is fairly obvious and a straightforward English equivalent, namely *just,* can be found. In other cases, however, the effect of a flavoring word on a German sentence is more subtle and may be untranslatable by a single word. The examples that follow illustrate the most common flavoring words in German (only the major meanings are listed):

Aber:

> Das ist **aber** nett von dir.
> *That's really nice of you.*
> (meaning: *really*)

Do not confuse the flavoring word **aber** with its normal meaning of *but, however:*

> Orangensaft trinke ich selten. Ich habe **aber** Apfelsaft gern.
> *I seldom drink orange juice. However, I like apple juice.*

Denn:

1. Wo bist du **denn?**
   Where are you anyway?
   (indicates impatience in questions)

2. Ich habe schon gegessen. Wann **denn**?
   I've already eaten. When?
   (emphasizes the speaker's interest in finding out the answer to the question)

Doch:

1. Du bist **doch** gekommen.
   So, you did come after all.
   (meaning: *after all*, stress on **doch**)

2. Das ist **doch** ein Unsinn.
   That's really a stupidity.
   (meaning: *really*)

3. Du wirst mich **doch** anrufen?
   You will call me, (won't you)?
   (asks for a confirmation of the statement)

Eben/Halt:

Wenn du dich nicht brav benehmen kannst, kriegst du **eben (halt)** keine Schokolade.
If you can't behave, you just won't get any chocolate.
(meaning: *just*)

Note: **Eben** and **halt** are used synonymously, but **halt** is more common in Southern German.

Ja:

1. Heute ist es **ja** kalt.
   Today it's cold (of course).
   (meaning: *of course* or *as we know*, level tone of voice)

2. Das ist **ja** unglaublich.
   That's really unbelievable.
   (meaning: *really*, emotional tone of voice, stress on **unglaublich** in this example)

Langsam:

Es ist schon spät. Wir sollten **langsam** nach Hause fahren.
It's already late. We should start going home soon.

or

It's already late. It's about time that we should be going home.

Note: Do not confuse **langsam** as a flavoring word with its normal meaning of *slow* as shown in the example below:

Die Straßen sind eisig. Du solltest **langsam** fahren.
The streets are icy. You should drive slowly.

Mal:

Schau **mal,** was er gefunden hat.
Take a look at what he found.
(used with commands, English equivalent, if any, depends on context)

Nur:

1. Wie kommst du **nur** auf diese Idee?
   How in the world did you come up with that idea?

or

   How could you possibly think that?
   (indicates astonishment)

2. Heirate ihn **nur!**
   Go ahead and marry him for all I care!
   (said scornfully)

3. Spiel nicht mit deinem Essen, iß es **nur!**
   Don't play with your food, just eat it!
   (meaning: *just,* said angrily)

Note: As a nonflavoring word, **nur** means *only:*

Ich will **nur** das essen.
I only want to eat that.

Ruhig:

1. Du kannst **ruhig** sagen, was du von meiner neuen Frisur hältst.
   Feel free to say what you think of my new hair style.
   (meaning: *feel free to*)

2. Diese Portion Fleisch könnte **ruhig** ein bißchen größer sein.
   It wouldn't hurt if this meat portion were a little bigger.
   (adds sarcasm)

Note: As a nonflavoring word, **ruhig** means *quiet* or *peaceful:*

Sei **ruhig!**
Be quiet.

Schon:

1. Das ist **schon** wahr, aber ich will trotzdem keinen BMW kaufen.
   Yes, that's true, but I still don't want to buy a BMW.
   (meaning: *yes, but*)

2. Das ist **schon** wahr!
   That is (indeed) true!
   (meaning: *indeed,* stress on *is* in English, on **schon** in German)

3. Wir werden Ihre Koffer **schon** finden.
   (Don't worry) we'll find your luggage.
   (conveys the idea that everything will turn out all right)

Note: As a nonflavoring word, **schon** means *already:*

Wir haben Ihre Koffer **schon** gefunden.
We have already found your luggage.

Flavoring words are most common in the spoken language. By their very nature, they are not essential to the meaning of a given sentence, but their presence makes the sentence more interesting and expressive. If used correctly and not overdone, flavoring words will make your German more natural and authentic.

COMPREHENSION CHECK: *Translate into English.*

1. Du solltest langsam daran denken, was du auf der Uni studieren willst.
2. Ich liebe dich schon, aber...
3. Geh nur weg! *(said angrily)*
4. Irgendwer muß es ja tun. *(said unemotionally)*
5. Das ist ja fantastisch! *(said emotionally)*

ANSWERS: 1. It's time you started thinking about what you want to study at the university. 2. Yes I do love you, but . . . 3. Just go away! 4. Of course, someone has to do it. 5. That's really fantastic!

B. False Cognates

Cognates are words in two languages which have the same or similar sound and meaning. For example, the German word **Pfeffer** is a cognate of English *pepper,* **Salz** of *salt,* **Glas** of *glass,* etc. In a few cases, however, a German word may only appear to be a cognate of an English word when in fact the meaning is quite different. For example, the German word **Jalousie** would seem to mean *jealousy* but actually means *venetian blind.* Of course, if you heard a sentence with **Jalousie** in it, you might not know what the correct meaning is, but you would probably realize immediately that it cannot mean *jealousy.* Some false cognates, however, are not so obvious:

Wir werden **eventuell** nach Amerika gehen.

The sentence appears to mean:

??*We will eventually go to America.*

But **eventuell** actually means *possibly*. The correct translation is:

We will possibly go to America.

Fortunately the number of false cognates in German is small. The list that follows gives the most common of these:

false cognate	actual meaning	*apparent meaning
aktuell	*topical*	*actually
effektiv	*in effect*	*effective
eventuell	*possibly*	*eventually
die Fabrik	*factory*	*fabric
die Jalousie	*venetian blind*	*jealousy
die Kaution	*deposit*	*caution
komisch	*strange*	*comical
die Konfession	*religious denomination*	*confession
der Lump (*weak noun*)	*scoundrel*	*lump
ordinär	*vulgar*	*ordinary
der Rock	*skirt, coat*	*rock
sensibel	*sensitive*	*sensible
spenden	*to donate*	*to spend
sympathisch	*likable*	*sympathetic

The next two examples illustrate two verbs which do not mean what you might think:

sich blamieren (*to make a fool of oneself*):
Er hat **sich** durch sein Benehmen **blamiert.**
He made a fool of himself by his behavior.
(not: *to blame oneself)

überhören (*to not hear*):
Ich habe leider **überhört,** was Sie eben gesagt haben.
Unfortunately I didn't hear (didn't catch), what you just said.
(not: *to overhear)

COMPREHENSIVE CHECK: *Translate into English.*

1. Wieviel Kaution muß ich bezahlen?
2. Er war immer ein komischer Mensch.
3. Ich fürchte, ich bin mit einem Lumpen verheiratet.
4. Sei nicht so sensibel!
5. Ich muß es überhört haben.

ANSWERS: 1. How much deposit do I have to pay? 2. He was always a strange person. 3. I'm afraid I am married to a scoundrel. 4. Don't be so sensitive! 5. I must not have heard it.

German-English Vocabulary

Learn the flavoring particles listed in section A, the false cognates given on page 322, and the following:

(die) Angst haben	*to be afraid*	irgendwer	*someone*
bekennen	*to profess*	der Onkel, -	*uncle*
(*reflexive, mixed*		der Protest, -e	*protest*
verb)		die Reise, -n	*trip*
die Bemerkung,	*remark*	die Sahne	*whipped cream*
-en		der Schilling, -e	*shilling (Austrian*
besprechen	*to discuss*		*coin)*
(bespricht),		So was!	*What do you know!*
besprach,		üben	*to exercise*
besprochen			*(caution)*
betragen (beträgt),	*to amount to*	der Übermensch,	*superman*
betrug, betragen		-en, -en	
es ist mir (ihm)	*it's all the same to*	verabschieden	*to say good-bye*
egal	*me (him)*	(*reflexive*)	
fantastisch	*fantastic*	verheiratet sein	*to be married*
das Ferienhaus, ̈er	*vacation home*	verschwenden	*to squander*
fürchten	*to fear*	die Wirklichkeit	*reality*
der Geburtstag, -e	*birthday*		

EXERCISE 1 (prerequisite: section A, topic: flavoring words)

Translate into English. Be prepared to state the effect of the flavoring word on the sentence if it is not clear in the translation.

1. Heute ist doch Dienstag, oder?
2. Wann bist du denn endlich fertig?
3. Was kann er nur gegen uns haben?
4. Ich bin ja so froh, daß ihr da seid!
5. Unser Lehrer könnte uns ruhig mehr Zeit für diesen Aufsatz geben!
6. Ich kann dir schon sagen, wo er ist, weil er mich eben angerufen hat.
7. Sie ist aber schön!
8. Wann haben Sie denn Geburtstag?
9. Wir müssen langsam ein Hotel finden, es ist schon elf Uhr.
10. Tu' es nur, ob du willst oder nicht!
11. Wir müssen eben auf ein neues Auto verzichten.
12. Sie dürfen mich ruhig zu jeder Zeit anrufen.
13. Sag mal, kannst du mir ein bißchen Geld borgen?
14. Ich habe doch eine gute Note bei der letzten Prüfung bekommen!
15. Hab keine Angst! Er wird schon kommen.
16. Verschwende dein Geld nur!

EXERCISE 2 (prerequisite: section A, topic: flavoring words)

This exercise has two sections. Within each section, fill in the blank with the appropriate flavoring word chosen from those listed at the beginning of the section. Use each word only once and only in its meaning as a flavoring word.

aber, denn, ja, langsam, ruhig

1. Wir müssen uns _____ verabschieden, es ist schon spät.
2. Haben Sie _____ ein Ferienhaus?
3. Sie können _____ etwas mehr Sahne mit Ihrem Kaffee haben.
4. Unsere Reise war _____ schön!
5. Ruf mich morgen an, du kennst _____ meine Telefonnummer.

doch, eben, mal, nur, schon

6. Entschuldigung, wann fährt der Zug nach Freiburg ab? Sie haben Pech, er ist _____ vor einer Minute weggefahren.
7. Bleib _____ zu Hause, es ist mir egal, ob du mitfährst.
8. Warte _____, ich kann es für dich holen.
9. Aber Onkel Gerhard, wir sind _____ froh, daß du uns besuchen willst, bloß ist es jetzt eine schlechte Zeit für uns.
10. So was! Es schneit _____, ich habe gedacht, es wäre zu warm dafür.

EXERCISE 3 (prerequisite: section B, topic: false cognates)

Translate into English.

1. Können Sie mir eventuell helfen?
2. Die Kaution beträgt 3000 Schilling.
3. Hast du diesen komischen Mann gesehen?
4. Er war sensibler als seine Brüder.
5. Du Lump!
6. Zu welcher Konfession bekennen Sie sich?
7. Wo kann ich meinen Rock aufhängen?
8. Du hast dich durch deinen Protest nur blamiert.
9. Sie ist ein äußerst unsympathischer Mensch.
10. Ich wollte nicht in der Fabrik arbeiten.
11. Sei nicht so ordinär!
12. Er hat effektiv dasselbe gesagt.
13. Ich habe seine Bemerkung überhört.
14. Dieses Buch bespricht viele aktuelle Probleme.

EXERCISE 4 (comprehensive)

Choose five words from section A and write a sentence for each illustrating the usage of the word as a flavoring word. Then choose five false cognates from the list in section B and write a sentence for each showing the correct meaning of the word.

GEDANKENPROBLEM: **Explain why a German might say this in English.**

---

a. May I give you a rat?
b. The room costs 20 marks and in the morning you become breakfast.

What's wrong with these?

1. Die Droge scheint nicht besonders effektiv zu sein.
2. Er ist kein aktuelles Mitglied der Regierung.
3. Sie ist niedergefallen und hat jetzt einen Lumpen auf dem Kopf.
4. Ich muß eine Konfession machen.
5. Üben Sie Kaution bei dem Hund, und falls er versucht zu beißen, werfen Sie einen Rock auf ihn.
6. Die Fabrik in diesem Kleid ist nicht schlecht.
7. Ich bin wirklich sympathisch, aber ich kann Ihnen nicht helfen.
8. Manche Leute behaupten, Bismarck sei ein Übermensch gewesen, aber in Wirklichkeit war er nur ein ordinärer Mensch so wie du und ich.

Review Exercises Chapters 22–24

Important! Use a dictionary instead of the glossary for reference.

EXERCISE 1

Translate into German.

1. We had a good time in Vienna.
2. Feel free to tell me what's on your mind.
3. He doesn't look very likable.
4. I am cold.
5. You can't teach an old dog new tricks.
6. I want to tell you what I overheard.
7. Have you reached a conclusion?
8. I couldn't afford to buy the car.
9. Familiarity breeds contempt.
10. Were you successful at getting a job?
11. I got the tickets after all.
12. She fled from the Nazis.
13. I am interested in German. That is why I am taking this course.
14. The hunters didn't make a single sound.
15. This film is no longer topical.
16. You should brush your teeth after every meal.
17. Can you see who is at the wheel of the car?
18. Do you want to be woken up in the morning?
19. We will just have to start from scratch.
20. I can't remember her name.
21. How can you possibly say that!
22. Please hurry.
23. A new architect continued the design of the church.
24. Why are you always contradicting me?

What's wrong with these?

1. Das Streichholz zwischen den zwei Ringern war sehr spannend.
2. Wir haben eine Stunde lang ausgeruht.
3. Deine Jalousie ist völlig unberechtigt, sie ist nur eine alte Bekannte meiner Familie.
4. Das Gras ist immer grüner auf der anderen Seite des Zauns.
5. Es ist wichtig, daß Sie ihn nachgehen.
6. Du wirst nicht gelingen.

7. Mit einer klugen Antwort drehte ich die Tische auf ihm.
8. Voriges Jahr haben wir Tomaten gewachsen.
9. Ruhen Sie versichert, Frau Lenz, wir werden Ihren Mann finden.
10. Sei ruhig! Ich muß konzentrieren.

List of Strong Verbs in German

Note: Verbs which regularly use **sein** as the auxiliary in the present and past perfect tense are preceded by **ist** in the past participle. With some verb forms, two possibilities exist; these are indicated by a slash between the forms:

INFINITIVE	MEANING	3RD PERSON SG.	SIMPLE PAST	PAST PARTICIPLE
backen	to bake	bäckt	buk/backte	gebacken
befehlen	to command	befiehlt	befahl	befohlen
beginnen	to begin	beginnt	begann	begonnen
beißen	to bite	beißt	biß	gebissen
bergen	to save	birgt	barg	geborgen
bersten	to burst	birst	barst	ist geborsten
betrügen	to deceive	betrügt	betrog	betrogen
biegen	to bend	biegt	bog	gebogen
bieten	to offer	bietet	bot	geboten
binden	to tie	bindet	band	gebunden
bitten	to ask	bittet	bat	gebeten
blasen	to blow	bläst	blies	geblasen
bleiben	to stay	bleibt	blieb	ist geblieben
braten	to fry	brät	briet	gebraten
brechen	to break	bricht	brach	gebrochen
dringen	to penetrate	dringt	drang	ist gedrungen
empfehlen	to recommend	empfiehlt	empfahl	empfohlen
erschrecken	to be frightened	erschrickt	erschrak	ist erschrocken
essen	to eat	ißt	aß	gegessen
fahren	to drive	fährt	fuhr	ist gefahren
fallen	to fall	fällt	fiel	ist gefallen
fangen	to catch	fängt	fing	gefangen
finden	to find	findet	fand	gefunden
fliegen	to fly	fliegt	flog	ist geflogen
fliehen	to flee	flieht	floh	ist geflohen
fließen	to flow	fließt	floß	ist geflossen
fressen	to eat (with animals)	frißt	fraß	gefressen
frieren	to freeze	friert	fror	gefroren
geben	to give	gibt	gab	gegeben
gedeihen	to thrive	gedeiht	gedieh	ist gediehen
gehen	to go	geht	ging	ist gegangen
gelingen	to succeed	gelingt	gelang	ist gelungen
gelten	to be worth	gilt	galt	gegolten
genießen	to enjoy	genießt	genoß	genossen
geschehen	to happen	geschieht	geschah	ist geschehen
gewinnen	to win	gewinnt	gewann	gewonnen
gießen	to pour	gießt	goß	gegossen
gleichen	to be like	gleicht	glich	geglichen
gleiten	to glide	gleitet	glitt	ist geglitten
graben	to dig	gräbt	grub	gegraben

INFINITIVE	MEANING	3RD PERSON SG.	SIMPLE PAST	PAST PARTICIPLE
greifen	*to grasp*	greift	griff	gegriffen
haben	*to have*	hat	hatte	gehabt
halten	*to hold*	hält	hielt	gehalten
hängen	*to hang*	hängt	hing	gehangen
heben	*to raise*	hebt	hob	gehoben
heißen	*to be called*	heißt	hieß	geheißen
helfen	*to help*	hilft	half	geholfen
klingen	*to sound*	klingt	klang	geklungen
kneifen	*to pinch*	kneift	kniff	gekniffen
kommen	*to come*	kommt	kam	ist gekommen
kriechen	*to crawl*	kriecht	kroch	ist gekrochen
laden	*to load*	lädt	lud	geladen
lassen	*to let*	läßt	ließ	gelassen
laufen	*to run*	läuft	lief	ist gelaufen
leiden	*to suffer*	leidet	litt	gelitten
leihen	*to lend*	leiht	lieh	geliehen
lesen	*to read*	liest	las	gelesen
liegen	*to lie*	liegt	lag	hat/ist gelegen
lügen	*to (tell a) lie*	lügt	log	gelogen
meiden	*to avoid*	meidet	mied	gemieden
messen	*to measure*	mißt	maß	gemessen
nehmen	*to take*	nimmt	nahm	genommen
pfeifen	*to whistle*	pfeift	pfiff	gepfiffen
preisen	*to praise*	preist	pries	gepriesen
raten	*to advise*	rät	riet	geraten
reiben	*to rub*	reibt	rieb	gerieben
reißen	*to tear*	reißt	riß	gerissen
reiten	*to ride*	reitet	ritt	ist geritten
riechen	*to smell*	riecht	roch	gerochen
ringen	*to wrestle*	ringt	rang	gerungen
rinnen	*to run (flow)*	rinnt	rann	ist geronnen
rufen	*to call*	ruft	rief	gerufen
saufen	*to drink (with animals)*	säuft	soff	gesoffen
scheinen	*to seem*	scheint	schien	geschienen
schelten	*to scold*	schilt	schalt	gescholten
schieben	*to shove*	schiebt	schob	geschoben
schießen	*to shoot*	schießt	schoß	geschossen
scheiden	*to separate*	scheidet	schied	geschieden
schlafen	*to sleep*	schläft	schlief	geschlafen
schlagen	*to strike*	schlägt	schlug	geschlagen
schleichen	*to sneak about*	schleicht	schlich	ist geschlichen
schließen	*to close*	schließt	schloß	geschlossen
schmeißen	*to fling*	schmeißt	schmiß	geschmissen
schmelzen	*to melt*	schmilzt	schmolz	ist geschmolzen
schneiden	*to cut*	schneidet	schnitt	geschnitten
schreiben	*to write*	schreibt	schrieb	geschrieben
schreien	*to scream*	schreit	schrie	geschrien

INFINITIVE	MEANING	3RD PERSON SG.	SIMPLE PAST	PAST PARTICIPLE
schreiten	to stride	schreitet	schritt	ist geschritten
schweigen	to be quiet	schweigt	schwieg	geschwiegen
schwellen	to swell	schwillt	schwoll	ist geschwollen
schwimmen	to swim	schwimmt	schwamm	ist geschwommen
schwingen	to swing	schwingt	schwang	geschwungen
schwören	to pledge	schwört	schwur	geschworen
sehen	to see	sieht	sah	gesehen
sein	to be	ist	war	ist gewesen
singen	to sing	singt	sang	gesungen
sinken	to sink	sinkt	sank	ist gesunken
sitzen	to sit	sitzt	saß	hat/ist gesessen
spinnen	to weave	spinnt	spann	gesponnen
sprechen	to speak	spricht	sprach	gesprochen
sprießen	to sprout	sprießt	sproß	ist gesprossen
springen	to jump	springt	sprang	ist gesprungen
stechen	to sting	sticht	stach	gestochen
stehen	to stand	steht	stand	hat/ist gestanden
stehlen	to steal	stiehlt	stahl	gestohlen
steigen	to climb	steigt	stieg	ist gestiegen
sterben	to die	stirbt	starb	ist gestorben
stinken	to stink	stinkt	stank	gestunken
stoßen	to push	stößt	stieß	gestoßen
streichen	to stroke	streicht	strich	gestrichen
streiten	to argue	streitet	stritt	gestritten
tragen	to carry	trägt	trug	getragen
treffen	to meet	trifft	traf	getroffen
treiben	to set in motion	treibt	trieb	getrieben
treten	to step	tritt	trat	ist getreten
trinken	to drink	trinkt	trank	getrunken
tun	to do	tut	tat	getan
verderben	to ruin	verdirbt	verdarb	verdorben
verdrießen	to irritate	verdrießt	verdroß	verdrossen
vergessen	to forget	vergißt	vergaß	vergessen
verlieren	to lose	verliert	verlor	verloren
verschlingen	to devour	verschlingt	verschlang	verschlungen
verschwinden	to disappear	verschwindet	verschwand	ist verschwunden
verzeihen	to forgive	verzeiht	verzieh	verziehen
wachsen	to grow	wächst	wuchs	ist gewachsen
waschen	to wash	wäscht	wusch	gewaschen
weichen	to retreat	weicht	wich	ist gewichen
weisen	to show	weist	wies	gewiesen
werben	to advertise	wirbt	warb	geworben
werden	to become	wird	wurde	ist geworden
werfen	to throw	wirft	warf	geworfen
wiegen	to weigh	wiegt	wog	gewogen
ziehen	to pull	zieht	zog	gezogen
zwingen	to force	zwingt	zwang	gezwungen

German-English Glossary

List of abbreviations for the glossaries:

acc.	*accusative*	**dat.**	*dative*	**pl.**	*plural*
adj.	*adjective*	**gen.**	*genitive*	**prep.**	*preposition*
adv.	*adverb*	**imp.**	*impersonal verb*	**refl.**	*reflexive verb*
aux.	*auxiliary verb*	**nom.**	*nominative*	**sg.**	*singular*

This list contains the total German-English vocabulary of the book. The number after the German entry indicates the chapter in which the German word is first used with that particular meaning. If no number follows, the German word is used at some point in chapters 1–9 but is not a part of the core vocabulary for those chapters. The auxiliary of the verb is indicated only when this is not obvious from the verb itself. Strong verbs are followed by the past tense forms. If the verb undergoes a stem vowel change, the third person singular form of the present tense is given in parentheses. The dot after a prefix indicates that the prefix is separable. For strong verbs with separable prefixes, only the past tense forms of the base verb are listed. For weak nouns, the genitive singular ending and the plural ending are given. Adjectival nouns are indicated by the ending **-e(r)**.

A

das **Abendessen**, *dinner*
ab.fahren (fährt), fuhr, gefahren 3 *to depart, to leave*
der **Abfall 17** *garbage*
der **Abfallkorb, ⁻e 5** *garbage can*
ab.führen 2 *to lead away*
Abgeordnet-e(r) 9 *elected representative*
ab.lehnen 3 *to refuse*
die **Abreise, -n 13** *departure*
ab.sagen 12 *to call off, to cancel*
ab.schicken 10 *to send off*
ab.schneiden, schnitt, geschnitten 2 *to cut off, to slice off*
die **Absicht, -en** *intention*
absolut 16 *absolutely*
abstoßend 8 *revolting*
ab.waschen (wäscht), wusch, gewaschen 11 *to wash dishes*
achten auf + *acc.* **6** *to pay attention to, heed, respect*
der **Achtundfünfziger 19** *number fifty-eight (streetcar)*
die **Adresse, -n 15** *address*
der **Affe, -n, -n 9** *ape, monkey*
der **Agent, -en, -en 16** *agent*
ähneln 1 *to resemble*
die **Ahnung, -en 13** *idea*
der **Akzent, -e 19** *accent*
der **Alkohol, -e** *alcohol*
all 4 *all*
alles 16 *everything*
allgemein: im allgemeinen 19 *in general*
der **Alligator, -en 17** *alligator*
allmählich *gradually*
als 13 *as, while*
als ob 14 *as if*
alt, älter, ältest 4 *old, older, oldest*
am liebsten 8 *most preferred, best of all*
amerikanisch 4 *American*

an (*2-way prep.*) **5** *on, at, to*
das **Andenken,** *souvenir*
ander 4 *other*
ändern 10 *to change*
anders 14 *differently*
anderswo *elsewhere*
der **Anfang, ⁻e 4** *beginning,* **am Anfang** *in the beginning*
an.fangen (fängt), fing, gefangen 2 *to begin*
das **Anfangsstadium,** *pl.* **-ien 16** *initial phase*
an.geben (gibt), gab, gegeben 15 *to list*
angeblich 10 *supposedly*
das **Angebot, -e 6** *offer*
Angestellt-e(r) 9 *employee*
angewiesen auf + *acc.* **12** *dependent on*
an.greifen, griff, gegriffen 17 *to attack*
die **Angst, ⁻e 12** *fear,* **Angst haben 24** *to be afraid*
an.haben (hat), hatte, gehabt 10 *to have on, wear*
der **Anhänger, 19** *supporter*
an.kommen, kam, gekommen 2 *to arrive*
an.lügen, log, gelogen 3 *to lie to (someone)*
an.machen 2 *to turn on*
an.malen 10 *to paint*
an.nehmen (nimmt), nahm, genommen 3 *to accept*
die **Annonce, -n 15** *advertisement*
an.reden *to address*
der **Anruf, -e** *(telephone) call*
an.rufen, rief, gerufen 3 *to call (on the telephone)*
an.schauen *to look at*
an.schreien, schrie, geschrien 14 *to scream at*
die **Anschuldigung, -en 14** *accusation*
an.sehen (sieht), sah, gesehen 14 *to look at*

an.spucken 18 *to spit at*
anständig 13 *respectable*
anstatt *(prep. + gen.)* **5** *instead of*
die **Antwort, -en auf + acc. 10** *answer to*
  antworten + dat. *(person)* **auf + acc.**
  (thing) **4** *to answer*
die **Anweisung, -en 13** *direction*
der **Anzug, ⁻e 7** *suit*
der **Apfel, 8** *apple*
die **Apotheke, -n 5** *pharmacy*
der **April** *April*
die **Arbeit, -en 4** *work*
  arbeiten an + dat. 1 *to work on*
der **Arbeiter, 8** *worker*
  arg, ärger, ärgst 8 *bad, worse, worst*
  arm, ärmer, ärmst an + dat. 5 *poor,*
  poorer, poorest in
die **Armee, -n 17** *army*
die **Art, -en** *manner*
der **Artikel, 15** *article*
der **Arzt, ⁻e 4** *doctor*
die **Ärztin, -innen** *female doctor*
der **Asphalt** *asphalt*
der **Astronaut, -en, -en 9** *astronaut*
der **Astronom, -en, -en 9** *astronomer*
  ästhetisch 9 *esthetic*
  atmen 1 *to breathe*
  auch 10 *also*
  auch wenn 14 *even if*
  auf *(2-way prep.)* **5** *on,* **auf alle Fälle 12**
  no matter what
  auf.blasen (bläst), blies, geblasen 2 *to*
  blow up (put air into)
der **Aufenthalt, -e 13** *stay*
  auf.führen 10 *to perform*
  auf.geben (gibt), gab, gegeben 11 *to give*
  up
  auf.heben, hob, gehoben 18 *to pick up*
  auf.hören 14 *to stop*
die **Auflage, -n** *edition*
  auf.lockern *to loosen up*
  auf.machen 2 *to open*
die **Aufmerksamkeit 6** *attentiveness, attention*
  auf.muntern 3 *to cheer up*
  auf.passen auf + acc. 10 *to watch out*
  for, pay attention to, **13** *take care of*
  aufregend 8 *exciting*
der **Aufsatz, ⁻e 9** *essay*
  auf.stehen, stand, gestanden 2 *to get up*
  auf.stellen *to put up*
  auf.suchen 15 *to visit*
  auf.treten (tritt), trat, getreten 16 *to*
  appear
der **Augenblick, -e 8** *moment*
der **August 21** *August,* **im August** *in August*
  aus *(prep. + dat.)* **5** *from, out of, made*
  out of
  aus sein (ist), war, gewesen 21 *to be over*
  aus.brechen (bricht), brach, gebrochen
  13 *to begin, break out, open*
  aus.brennen *(mixed verb)* **16** *to burn out*
der **Ausdruck, ⁻e** *expression*
  Ausflug: einen Ausflug machen 14 *to go*
  on an outing
  aus.fallen (fällt), fiel, gefallen 11 *to fail,*
  break down

der **Ausgang, ⁻e** *exit*
  aus.gehen, ging, gegangen 2 *to go out (on*
  a date)
  ausgerechnet mir 12 *to me of all persons*
  ausgezeichnet 16 *excellent*
  aus.halten, hielt, gehalten *to stand*
  (someone)
die **Auskunft, ⁻e** *information*
  aus.lachen 14 *to laugh at*
der **Ausländer,** *foreigner*
das **Ausmaß 4** *extent*
  aus.packen 17 *to unpack*
  aus.probieren *to try out*
die **Ausrede, -n 7** *excuse*
  aus.rufen, rief, gerufen 2 *to call out*
die **Aussage, -n 22** *statement*
  aus.schauen 3 *to look (like), appear (to be)*
  aus.sehen (sieht), sah, gesehen 2 *to look*
  (like), appear (to be)
  aus.spritzen 2 *to squirt out*
  ausverkauft *sold out*
der **Ausweis, -e 17** *identification card*
die **Auszeichnung, -en 12** *commendation,*
  award
das **Auto, -s 4** *car*
  Auto fahren (fährt), fuhr, gefahren 14 *to*
  drive a car
die **Autobahn, -en** *highway*
der **Autobus, -sse** *bus*
der **Autofahrer, 15** *driver*
der **Automat, -en, -en** *vending machine*
der **Autoschlüssel,** *car key*
der **Außenminister, 15** *foreign minister*
  außer *(prep. + dat.)* **5** *except for, in*
  addition to
  äußern 15 *to utter*
  äußerst 16 *very, extremely*

B

das **Baby, -s 13** *baby*
  backen 16 *to bake*
das **Bad, ⁻er 16** *bath*
  baden 3 *to bathe*
die **Badewanne, -n** *bathtub*
der **Bahnhof, ⁻e 5** *train station*
  bald 12 *soon*
der **Ball, ⁻e 10** *ball*
der **Ballon, -s** *balloon*
die **Banane, -n 12** *banana*
die **Bank, -en 4** *bank*
der **Bankpräsident, -en, -en 15** *bank president*
der **Bär, -en, -en 9** *bear*
der **Bau 6** *construction*
  bauen 10 *to build*
der **Baum, ⁻e 4** *tree*
die **Baustelle, -n** *construction site*
  Beamt-e(r) *public official*
  beantworten 1 *to answer*
  bedecken 16 *to cover*
  bedienen *to serve*
  bedürfen + gen. *(modal verb)* **22** *to need*
  beenden 1 *to end*
der **Befehl, -e 13** *command*
  befehlen (befiehlt), befahl, befohlen 1 *to*
  command, order
  begegnen + dat. 4 *to meet*

begeistert von 6 *enthusiastic about*
beginnen, begann, begonnen 1 *to begin*
begleiten 3 *to accompany*
begreifen, begriff, begriffen 2 *to understand*
der Begriff, -e 16 *concept*
begrüßen 19 *to greet*
behandeln 15 *to discuss, deal with*
behaupten 3 *to maintain*
beherrschen 10 *to control*
bei (*prep. + dat.*) 5 *at, with, near*
bei.bringen (*mixed verb*) 16 *to teach*
beichten 12 *to confess*
beid 5 *both*
das Beispiel, -e 15 *example*
beißen (beißt), biß, gebissen 10 *to bite*
bei.stehen, stand, gestanden 2 *to stand by (someone)*
bekannt 21 *renowned*
Bekannt-e(r) 9 *acquaintance*
bekannt.geben (gibt), gab, gegeben 15 *to announce*
bekennen (*refl., mixed verb*) 24 *to profess*
bekommen 12 *to get, receive*
belästigen 1 *to bother*
beleidigend 9 *insulting*
beleuchten 7 *to light up, illuminate*
bemerken 15 *to remark*
die Bemerkung, -en 24 *remark*
das Benehmen *behavior*
benehmen (*refl.*) *to behave*
benützen 16 *to use*
das Benzin 15 *gas*
bequem 8 *comfortable*
berauben 15 *to rob*
bereit 14 *ready*
bereuen 14 *to regret*
der Berg, -e 5 *mountain*
die Bergluft *mountain air*
der Bergsteiger, *mountain climber*
die Bergstraße, -n *mountain road*
der Bericht, -e 15 *report*
berichten 15 *to report*
beruhen auf + dat. 6 *to be based on*
beruhigt 14 *reassured*
berühmt 14 *famous*
beschädigen 10 *to damage*
beschäftigt 14 *busy*
beschlagnahmen 13 *to confiscate*
beschließen, beschloß, beschlossen 10 *to agree upon, decide*
beschreiben, beschrieb, beschrieben 13 *to describe*
die Beschreibung, -en 4 *description*
die Beschwerde, -n 19 *complaint*
der Beschwerdebrief, -e *letter of complaint*
besetzt 10 *busy*
besitzen *to own*
der Besitzer, 4 *owner*
besoffen *drunken*
besonder(s) 12 *especially, special*
besprechen (bespricht), besprach, besprochen 24 *to discuss*
best 4 *best*
bestätigen 15 *to confirm*

das Bestechungsgeld *bribe (money)*
bestehen, bestand, bestanden 15 *to be*
bestellen 14 *to order*
bestimmen 13 *to determine*
bestimmt 11 *for sure, certainly*
bestrafen 12 *to punish*
der Besuch, -e *visit,* zu Besuch kommen *to come for a visit*
besuchen 1 *to visit*
der Besucher, 4 *visitor*
betäuben 7 *to anesthetize*
beteuern 15 *to assert*
betonen 15 *to emphasize*
betragen (beträgt), betrug, betragen 24 *to amount to*
betreffen (betrifft), betraf, betroffen, *to concern,* was das betrifft *as far as that is concerned*
betreten (betritt), betrat, betreten 2 *to enter, set foot on*
der Betrieb, -e 6 *order, operation*
der Betrug, *pl.* Betrügereien 21 *deception*
betrügen, betrog, betrogen 7 *to deceive*
das Bett, -en 5 *bed*
das Bettuch, ̈er 7 *bed sheet*
beunruhigend 9 *upsetting, disturbing*
die Bevölkerung 13 *population*
bevor 13 *before*
der Beweis, -e 7 *proof*
beweisen, bewies, bewiesen 1 *to prove*
bewilligen 15 *to approve*
bezahlen 10 *to pay*
die Beziehung, -en 15 *relationship*
die Bibliothek, -en 5 *library*
das Bier, -e 9 *beer*
der Bierbauch, ̈e *beer belly*
bieten, bot, geboten 1 *to offer*
das Bild, -er *picture*
billig 4 *cheap*
die Biologie 13 *biology*
bis (*prep. + acc.*) 5 *as far as, until*
bissig 9 *mean, sarcastic*
bitte *please*
bitten, bat, gebeten um 1 *to ask for*
blasen (bläst), blies, geblasen 1 *to blow*
das Blatt, ̈er *leaf*
blau *blue*
blaß 8 *pale*
bleiben, blieb, ist geblieben 1 *to stay, remain*
der Bleistift, -e 16 *pencil*
der Blitz 10 *lightning*
blöd *stupid*
bloß 13 *merely*
die Blume, -n 14 *flower*
der Blumenkranz, ̈e *floral wreath*
die Bluse, -n 7 *blouse*
das Blut *blood*
der Boden, ̈ 5 *floor*
die Bohne, -n 14 *bean*
die Bombe, -n 12 *bomb*
borgen 16 *to loan*
die Börse, -n *stock market*
bösartig 4 *mean*
böse auf + acc. 6 *angry at*
der Botschafter, -15 *ambassador*

braten (brät), briet, gebraten 10 *to roast*
der Brauch, ⸚e 16 *custom*
brauchen 1 *to need*
braun 4 *brown*
brav *good (with respect to behavior)*
BRD = Bundesrepublik Deutschland 15 *Federal Republic of Germany, i.e., West Germany*
brechen (bricht), brach, gebrochen 2 *to break*
breit *wide*
brennen (mixed verb) 1 *to burn*
der Brief, -e an + acc. 4 *letter to*
die Briefmarke, -n 16 *stamp*
der Briefträger, *mailman*
die Brille, -n 13 *eyeglasses*
bringen, brachte, gebracht 1 *to bring*
das Brot, -e 7 *bread*
der Bruder, ⸚ *brother*
brummen 1 *to purr*
der Brunnen, *fountain*
der Bub, -en, -en 4 *boy*
das Buch, ⸚er 5 *book*
der Buchstabe, -ns, -n 9 *letter (of the alphabet)*
die Bundesbahn, -en 11 *Federal Railway*
der Bundeskanzler, 7 *Federal Chancellor*
das Bundesland, ⸚er 15 *Federal state*
der Bürgermeister, 13 *mayor*
das Büro, -s *office*
der Bürokrat, -en, -en 9 *bureaucrat*

C

die Chance, -n 7 *chance*
das Charterflugzeug, -e *charter plane*
der Chauffeur, -e *chauffeur*
der Chef, -s 12 *boss*
die Chefin, -innen *female boss*
die Chemie *chemistry*
chemikalisch 16 *chemical*
chemisch 13 *chemical*
der Chor, ⸚e *choir*

D

da 13 *since (for that reason),* **17** *there*
da drüben 19 *over there*
das Dach, ⸚er 21 *roof*
damals 7 *at that time*
die Dame, -n *lady*
dänisch 19 *Danish (adj.)*
dankbar 14 *grateful, thankful*
danken + dat. 4 *to thank*
der Dankzettel, 10 *thank-you note*
dann 14 *then*
das Darleihen, 12 *loan*
dauern 14 *to last*
daß 13 *that*
DDR = Deutsche Demokratische Republik 15 *German Democratic Republic, i.e., East Germany*
dein (du-form) 4 *your*
Delegiert-e(r) 9 *delegate*
dementieren 3 *to deny*
denken, dachte, gedacht an + acc. 1 *to think of*
das Denkmal, ⸚er 10 *monument*

deprimieren 7 *to depress*
deshalb 10 *therefore*
deutlich 8 *clear, distinct*
deutsch (adj.), Deutsch (language) 4 *German*
Deutsch-e(r) 9 *(a) German*
Deutschland 5 *Germany*
der Deutschlehrer, *German teacher*
der Dichter, 14 *poet*
dick 13 *thick*
der Dieb, -e 14 *thief*
der Dienstag, -e 5 *Tuesday*
dies 4 *this*
das Ding, -e *thing*
das Diplom, -e *diploma*
der Diplomat, -en, -en 15 *diplomat*
direkt *directly*
der Direktor, -en *director*
diskutieren 15 *to discuss*
die DM (=Deutsche Mark) 4 *German mark (monetary unit)*
dokumentieren 7 *to document*
der Dollar, - 7 *dollar*
der Dom, -e 4 *cathedral*
der Domturm, ⸚e *cathedral tower*
der Donner *thunder*
das Doppelzimmer, *double (bed) room*
das Dorf, ⸚er 12 *village*
dort 12 *there*
der Dramatiker, *dramatist*
draußen 14 *outside*
drei *three*
dreimal *three times*
drinnen 13 *inside*
dritt *third*
die Droge, -n 14 *drug*
der Druckkochtopf, ⸚e 14 *pressure cooker*
dumm, dümmer, dümmst 8 *stupid, stupider, stupidest*
die Dummheit, -en 14 *stupidity*
dunkel 8 *dark*
durch (prep. + acc.) 5 *through*
durch.fliegen, flog, geflogen 2 *to fly (straight through)*
durchfliegen, durchflog, durchflogen 2 *to skim*
dürfen (modal verb) 1 *to be allowed (permitted) to, may*
duschen 11 *to take a shower*

E

die Ecke, -n 15 *corner*
edel 7 *noble*
der Edelstahl 4 *high-grade steel*
der Edelstein, -e 16 *jewel, precious stone*
egal 24 *no matter (how, what, etc.),* **es ist mir (ihm) egal** *it's all the same to me (him)*
der Egoismus 4 *egotism*
ehe 13 *before*
ehemalig *former*
der Ehemann, ⸚er 7 *husband*
das Ehepaar, -e *married couple*
die Ehre, -n 7 *honor*
das Ei, -er 6 *egg*
das Eichhörnchen, *squirrel*

die **Eifersucht auf** + *acc.* **6** *jealousy of*
eifersüchtig auf + *acc.* **6** *jealous of*
eigen 13 *own*
eigentlich *really, actually*
das **Eigentum 22** *property*
ein.atmen 2 *to breathe in*
ein bißchen 14 *a little*
der **Einbrecher, 15** *burglar*
eindeutig *definite(ly), clear(ly)*
einfach 5 *simple, simply*
ein.führen 16 *to introduce*
einig 4 *several*
einiges 16 *several things*
die **Einkaufstasche, -n** *shopping bag*
ein.laden 10 *to invite*
die **Einladung, -en** *invitation*
einmal 14 *once*
ein paar 5 *a few*
ein.schenken 3 *to pour*
ein.streuen 2 *to slip in, insert*
der **Einwanderer, 19** *immigrant*
einzeln 19 *individual*
das **Einzelzimmer, 16** *single (bed) room*
einzig 5 *single, only*
das **Eis** *ice cream*
das **Eisen** *iron*
eis.laufen 19 *to skate*
eitel 7 *vain*
der **Elefant, -en, -en 9** *elephant*
der **Elementarstoff, -e 16** *(chemical) element*
die **Eltern** *(pl.)* **4** *parents*
der **Empfang, ¨e 13** *reception*
**empfangen (empfängt), empfing,
empfangen 2** *to receive*
**empfehlen (empfiehlt), empfahl,
empfohlen 1** *to recommend*
empor.arbeiten *(refl.)* **2** *to work oneself
up*
das **Ende, -n 10** *end*
endlich 13 *finally*
energiesparend 16 *energy-efficient*
Englisch *(language) English*
engstirnig 12 *narrow-minded*
entdecken 10 *to discover*
die **Ente, -n 10** *duck*
entfernt von *distanced from*
die **Entfernung, -en** *distance*
entgegen.wirken 2 *to work against, hinder*
entrüstet 15 *indignant*
entschließen, entschloß, entschlossen
(refl.) **22** *to decide*
der **Entschluß, ¨sse 12** *decision*
Entschuldigung! 13 *Excuse me.*
die **Enttäuschung, -en 6** *disappointment*
entweder... oder 12 *either . . . or*
**entwerfen (entwirft), entwarf, entworfen
16** *to devise*
entwerten 3 *to invalidate*
entwickeln 2 *to develop*
die **Erde, -n 15** *earth*
erdulden 19 *to tolerate*
erfahren (erfährt), erfuhr, erfahren 13 *to
find out, learn, discover*
erfassen 1 *to comprehend*
erfinden, erfand, erfunden 2 *to invent*
der **Erfolg, -e** *success*

erfolgreich 7 *successful*
das **Ergebnis, -nisse 9** *result*
erhalten (erhält), erhielt, erhalten 14 *to
receive*
erhöhen 15 *to raise*
erinnern an + *acc.* *(refl.)* **12** *to remember*
erinnern einen an + *acc.* **16** *to remind
one of*
die **Erkältung, -en 14** *cold*
erkennen *(mixed verb)* **3** *to recognize*
erklären 12 *to explain*
die **Erklärung, -en 7** *explanation*
erkranken an + *dat.* **12** *to become sick
with*
erlauben 14 *to allow*
erleben 14 *to experience*
**ernst nehmen (nimmt), nahm, genommen
19** *to take seriously*
erobern 10 *to conquer*
erraten (errät), erriet, erraten 13 *to guess*
erreichen 10 *to reach*
erröten 13 *to blush*
erscheinen, erschien, erschienen 3 *to
appear*
erschrecken 1 *to terrify*
erst 13 *first*
erstaunt über + *acc.* **6** *astonished at*
ersticken 14 *to suffocate,* **im Keim
ersticken** *to nip in the bud*
Erwachsen-e(r) 9 *adult*
erwähnen 3 *to mention*
erwarten 17 *to expect*
erwidern 1 *to return, reciprocate
(greeting),* **15** *to retort*
erwünschen 10 *to desire, wish for*
erzählen 15 *to tell*
erziehen, erzog, erzogen 10 *to raise*
die **Erziehung, -en 6** *upbringing*
es sei denn, daß 13 *unless*
essen (ißt), aß, gegessen 1 *to eat*
das **Essen 6** *meal*
etwas 12 *some,* **16** *something,* **19** *somewhat*
euer (ihr-*form)* **4** *your*
europäisch *European*
das **Experiment, -e 10** *experiment*
der **Experte, -n, -n 7** *expert*

F

das **Fach, ¨er** *field, area of expertise*
fahren (fährt), fuhr, gefahren 1 *to drive*
die **Fahrkarte, -n 13** *ticket*
das **Fahrrad, ¨er 13** *bicycle*
der **Fahrschein, -e** *ticket*
fallen (fällt), fiel, gefallen 1 *to fall*
falls 13 *in case*
falsch 9 *false*
die **Familie, -n 4** *family*
fantastisch 24 *fantastic*
die **Farbe, -n 4** *color*
färben 7 *to dye*
die **Fassung, -en 7** *version*
faul 6 *rotten,* **17** *lazy*
der **Februar** *February*
die **Fehde, -n 6** *feud*
der **Fehler, 5** *mistake*
feiern 10 *to celebrate*

der **Feiertag, -e** *holiday*
    feilschen um 6 *haggle over*
der **Feind, -e 7** *enemy*
das **Fenster, 5** *window*
die **Ferien** *(pl.)* **17** *vacation*
das **Ferienhaus, ¨er 24** *vacation home*
das **Fernrohr, ¨e** *telescope*
    fern.sehen (sieht), sah, gesehen 11 *to watch television*
der **Fernseher, 5** *television set*
    fertig 12 *finished*
    festigen 1 *to bolt, secure*
    fest.stellen *to determine*
das **Feuer, 10** *fire*
    feuern 10 *to fire*
das **Fieber, 7** *fever*
der **Film, -e 4** *film, movie*
    finden, fand, gefunden 1 *to find*
die **Firma,** *pl.* **Firmen 4** *firm, company*
der **Fisch, -e 4** *fish*
das **Fischen** *fishing*
das **Fleisch 19** *meat*
    fleißig 8 *industrious*
    flexibel 8 *flexible*
die **Fliege, -n** *fly*
    fliegen, flog, geflogen 1 *to fly*
    fliehen, floh, geflohen 3 *to flee*
der **Flug, ¨e 6** *flight*
der **Flughafen, ¨** *airport*
das **Flugzeug, -e 6** *airplane*
der **Fluß, ¨sse** *river*
die **Folge, -n** *consequence*
    folgen + *dat.* **4** *to follow*
    folgend: im folgenden 19 *in the following*
das **Formular, -e 15** *form*
    fort.setzen 2 *to continue*
das **Fotogeschäft, -e** *photography store*
die **Frage, -n 10** *question*
    fragen nach 6 *to ask about*
    Frankfurt 5 *Frankfurt (city in Germany)*
der **Franzose, -n, -n 9** *Frenchman*
    französisch *(adj.),* **Französisch** *(language)* **19** *French*
die **Frau, -en 4** *woman, wife*
das **Fräulein, - 4** *miss, young lady*
die **Frechheit, -en 7** *impudence*
die **Freiheit, -en 15** *freedom*
    frei.lassen (läßt), ließ, gelassen 11 *to free, release*
der **Freitag, -e 7** *Friday*
    freiwillig 12 *voluntarily*
    Fremd-e(r) 9 *stranger, foreigner*
der **Fremdenführer, - 4** *tour guide*
    fressen (frißt), fraß, gefressen 1 *to eat (of animals), to devour (of humans)*
die **Freude, -n 16** *joy*
    freuen auf + *acc.* *(refl.)* **16** *to look forward to*
der **Freund, -e 4** *friend*
die **Freundin, -innen 6** *girlfriend*
der **Frieden 15** *peace*
    friedlich 8 *peaceful*
    frisch 4 *fresh*
der **Friseur, -e 5** *hairdresser*
die **Frisur, -en** *hairstyle*
    froh über + *acc.* **6** *happy with*

die **Frucht, ¨e** *fruit*
das **Frühstück, -e** *breakfast*
    frühzeitig 15 *early*
    fühlen 18 *to feel*
    führen *to lead*
der **Funke, -ns, -n 9** *spark*
    funktionieren *to function*
    für *(prep.* + *acc.)* **5** *for*
    furchtbar 5 *terrible*
    fürchten 24 *to fear*
    fürchten vor + *dat.* *(refl.)* **21** *to be afraid of*
der **Fürst, -en, -en 9** *sovereign*
    füttern 10 *to feed*
der **Fuß, ¨e 6** *foot*
der **Fußball 11** *soccer*

G

    ganz 7 *whole, entire*
    gar nicht 17 *not at all*
die **Garage, -n 15** *garage*
die **Garderobe, -n** *cloakroom*
die **Gartentür, -en** *garden door*
der **Gast, ¨e 4** *guest*
    gastfreundlich *hospitable*
die **Gastgeberin, -innen** *hostess*
das **Gebäude, 4** *building*
    gebaut 4 *built*
    geben (gibt), gab, gegeben 1 *to give,* **es gibt 3** *there is/are*
    geboren *born*
der **Geburtstag, -e 24** *birthday*
das **Geburtstagskind, -er** *birthday child*
das **Gebüsch, -e 5** *bush*
der **Gedanke, -ns, -n 7** *thought*
das **Gedicht, -e** *poem*
die **Geduld 14** *patience*
    geehrt 4 *honored, dear (in letters)*
die **Gefahr, -en 6** *danger*
    gefährden 15 *to endanger*
    gefährlich 6 *dangerous*
    gefallen (gefällt), gefiel, gefallen + *dat.* **2** *to please*
der **Gefallen, - 14** *favor*
    Gefangen-e(r) 9 *prisoner*
    gefaßt auf + *acc.* **6** *prepared for*
das **Gefühl, -e 9** *emotion, feeling*
    gegen *(prep.* + *acc.)* **5** *against, approximately (but no more than)*
die **Gegend, -en 8** *region*
das **Gegenteil, -e 13** *opposite*
    gegenüber *(prep.* + *dat.)* **5** *opposite*
das **Geheimnis, -nisse 12** *secret*
    gehen, ging, gegangen 1 *to go*
    gehorchen + *dat.* **3** *to obey*
    gehören + *dat.* **16** *to belong to*
der **Gehorsam 18** *obedience*
die **Geige, -n 13** *fiddle*
der **Geist 6** *spirit, intellect*
das **Geld -er 5** *money*
die **Gelegenheit, -en 14** *opportunity*
    Geliebt-e(r) 9 *lover*
    genau *exactly*
    geneigt sein 17 *to be in the mood*
der **General, ¨e 17** *general*
das **Genie, -s 7** *genius*
    genießen, genoß, genossen 1 *to enjoy*

genug 10 *enough*
gerade 11 *just*
geraten (gerät), geriet, geraten in + *acc.* 14 *to get into*
gering: nicht im geringsten 19 *not at all*
gern (+ *verb*) 8 *like (to do something), gladly*
das **Gerücht, -e** *rumor*
das **Geschäft, -e** 5 *store*
die **Geschäftsreise, -n** 13 *business trip*
der **Geschäftsschluß** 15 *closing time*
geschehen (geschieht), geschah, ist geschehen 1 *to happen, occur*
gescheit 14 *clever*
das **Geschenk, -e** 7 *present*
die **Geschichte, -n** 12 *story,* 19 *history*
die **Geschwindigkeit, -en** 13 *speed*
die **Gesellschaft, -en** 16 *organization, society*
das **Gesetz, -e** 10 *law*
das **Gesicht, -er** 7 *face*
gespannt *strained*
der **Gesprächspartner, -** 15 *discussion partner*
gestern abend 12 *yesterday evening, last night*
gesund, gesünder, gesündest- 8 *healthy, healthier, healthiest*
die **Gesundheit** 10 *health*
die **Gewalt** 6 *force, violence*
der **Gewerkschaftssprecher, -** 15 *union spokesman*
gewinnen, gewann, gewonnen 3 *to win*
der **Gewinner, -** 6 *winner*
das **Gewitter, -** 7 *thunderstorm*
gewiß 5 *certain*
die **Gitarre, -n** *guitar*
das **Glas, ̈-er** 4 *glass*
der **Glaube, -ns (no pl.)** 9 *belief*
glauben + *dat. (person),* **an** + *acc. (thing)* 4 *to believe in*
gleich 14 *immediately,* 19 *same*
gleich weit entfernt von 15 *equidistant from*
die **Gleichung, -en** *equation*
die **Glocke, -n** *bell*
das **Glück** 7 *luck*
glücklich 12 *happy*
das **Gold** *gold*
der **Goldfisch, -e** *goldfish*
Gott *God,* **um Gottes willen** *for God's sake*
der **Grad, -e** *degree*
graduieren 13 *to graduate*
der **Graf, -en, -en** 9 *count*
das **Gras, ̈-er** 5 *grass*
das **Gratisgetränk, -e** 18 *free drink*
die **Grenze, -n** 5 *border*
Griechenland *Greece*
das **Grillhendl, -** *grilled chicken*
die **Grippe, -n** 12 *flu*
grob, gröber, gröbst- 8 *uncouth, more uncouth, most uncouth*
Grönland *Greenland*
der **Groschen, -** 7 *groschen (Austrian coin), penny*

groß, größer, größt- 4 *large, larger, largest,* **im großen und ganzen** 19 *in general*
großartig 7 *fantastic*
die **Großeltern** 13 *grandparents*
die **Großmutter, ̈-** 5 *grandmother*
die **Großschreibung** 19 *capitalization*
grün *green*
der **Grund, ̈-e** 6 *reason,* **im Grunde genommen** 19 *basically*
gründen 16 *to found*
die **Gruppe, -n** 12 *group*
der **Gruß, ̈-e** 19 *greeting*
grüßen 1 *to greet*
gültig 13 *valid*
der **Gummistiefel, -** *rubber boots*
die **Gurke, -n** 7 *pickle*
gut, besser, best- 4 *good, better, best*

H

das **Haar, -e** 7 *hair*
haben (hat), hatte, gehabt 3 *to have*
der **Hagel** 4 *hail*
der **Haken, -** *hook*
halb 7 *half*
die **Hälfte, -n** 8 *half*
der **Hals, ̈-e** 5 *neck*
halten (hält), hielt, gehalten 1 *to hold,* **halten von** *to think of, be of an opinion,* **jemand für etwas halten** 12 *to consider someone to be something*
die **Hand, ̈-e** 16 *hand*
handeln 18 *to act*
der **Handschuh, -e** 4 *glove*
hängen (*transitive, weak verb*) 2 *to hang (something)*
hängen, hing, gehangen (*intransitive, strong verb*) 16 *to hang (somewhere)*
hart, härter, härtest 8 *hard, harder, hardest*
der **Hase, -n, -n** 9 *rabbit*
hassen 1 *to hate*
hastig *hasty*
das **Haus, ̈-er** 4 *house*
die **Hausaufgabe, -n** 6 *homework assignment*
das **Haustier, -e** 16 *pet*
der **Haß** *hatred*
die **Häßlichkeit** 5 *ugliness*
heikel 7 *picky, fussy*
die **Heilfähigkeit, -en** 6 *healing ability*
die **Heimat, -en** 6 *homeland*
heim.fahren 2 *to go home*
heiraten 12 *to marry*
die **Heizung** 16 *heating (system)*
heiß 8 *hot*
heißen, hieß, geheißen 1 *to be called,* 17 *to command*
der **Held, -en, -en** 9 *hero*
helfen (hilft), half, geholfen + *dat.* 1 *to help*
hell *light, bright*
die **Herkunft, ̈-e** 22 *origin*
der **Herr, -n, -en** 9 *gentleman, mister*
herrschen 15 *to reign,* 16 *to prevail*
herum.liegen, lag, gelegen 7 *to lie around*

das **Herz, -ens, -en 9** *heart*
   herzlich 19 *hearty*
das **Heu** *hay*
   heute 12 *today*
   heute früh 11 *this morning*
   hier 10 *here*
die **Hilfe, -n 12** *help*
der **Himmel 15** *heaven, sky*
   hin sein *to be broken*
   hinab.führen 2 *to lead down*
   hinab/herab.lassen (läßt), ließ, gelassen 2
    to lower
   hinauf.blasen (bläst), blies, geblasen 2 *to*
    move upward by blowing
   hinaus.gehen, ging, gegangen 2 *to go out*
   hinaus.spritzen 2 *to squirt out*
   hinaus.tragen (trägt), trug, getragen 17
    to carry out
   hinter *(2-way prep.)* **5** *behind,* **14** *back*
   hinterlassen (hinterläßt), hinterließ,
    hinterlassen 2 *to leave behind*
   hinweg.schauen 2 *to look away*
die **Hitze 5** *heat*
   hoch, höher, höchst 7 *high, higher,*
    highest
   hoffen auf + *acc.* **6** *to hope for*
   hoffentlich 12 *it is to be hoped*
   holen 12 *to get, fetch*
   Holländisch 19 *Dutch (language)*
das **Holz** *wood*
   hören auf + *acc.* **14** *to listen to*
    (someone's advice), **15** *to hear*
das **Hotel, -s 5** *hotel*
   hübsch 7 *pretty*
   Hunger haben 14 *to be hungry*
der **Hungerlohn, ¨e 15** *starvation wage*
   hungrig 13 *hungry*
   husten 14 *to cough*
der **Hut, ¨e 7** *hat*
   hüten vor + *dat. (refl.)* **19** *to watch out*
    for

I

das **Ich 19** *the self*
die **Idee, -n 6** *idea*
   ihr 4 *hers, theirs*
   Ihr (Sie-form) 4 *your*
   immer 12 *always*
   immer noch 6 *still*
   impfen 10 *to immunize*
   in *(2-way prep.)* **5** *in*
   indem 13 *by (doing something)*
die **Information 13** *information*
   informieren über + *acc.* **10** *to inform*
    about
   innen 16 *inside, on the inside*
   interessant 9 *interesting*
das **Interesse an** + *dat.* **6** *interest in*
   interessieren für *(refl.)* **12** *to be interested in*
   irgendwann 14 *sometime*
   irgendwer 24 *someone*
   irgendwo 10 *somewhere*
   Italien *Italy*

J

die **Jacke, -n 5** *jacket*
der **Jäger** *hunter*

das **Jahr, -e 6** *year*
das **Jahreseinkommen 16** *yearly income*
die **Jahreszeit, -en 21** *season*
das **Jahrhundert, -e 16** *century*
die **Jahrhundertwende, -n 16** *turn of the*
    century
   jed 4 *each, every*
   jemals 21 *ever*
   jemand 10 *someone*
   jetzt 10 *now*
   je... desto 13 *the . . . the*
die **Jugend 4** *youth*
   Jugendlich-e(r) *youth*
das **Jugendwerk, -e 16** *early work (in one's*
    youth)
   jung, jünger, jüngst 4 *young, younger,*
    youngest
der **Junge, -n, -n 9** *boy*
das **Juwel, -en** *jewel*

K

der **Kaffee, -s 7** *coffee*
   kalt, kälter, kältest 8 *cold, colder, coldest*
die **Kälte** *cold*
der **Kamerad, -en, -en 9** *comrade*
   kämmen 1 *to comb*
der **Kandidat, -en, -en 15** *candidate*
   kapieren 3 *to understand, catch on*
die **Karte, -n 8** *ticket, seat*
die **Kartoffel, -n 8** *potato*
der **Kater, 14** *tomcat*
der **Katholik, -en, -en 9** *Catholic*
der **Katholizismus** *Catholicism*
das **Kätzchen, 16** *kitten*
die **Katze, -n 7** *cat*
   kaufen 7 *to buy*
das **Kaufhaus, ¨er 8** *department store*
   kein 4 *no, none*
der **Kellner, 4** *waiter*
   kennen *(mixed verb)* **1** *to know*
   kennen.lernen 7 *to become acquainted*
    with, get to know
der **Kerl, -e 9** *guy*
die **Kerze, -n** *candle*
die **Kette, -n** *chain*
das **Kind, -er 4** *child*
der **Kinderchor, ¨e 10** *children's choir*
das **Kino, -s 13** *movie house,* **ins Kino gehen**
    to go to a movie
die **Kirche, -n 10** *church*
die **Kirsche, -n 16** *cherry*
das **Kissen, - 5** *pillow*
die **Kiste, -n** *box*
   klar 8 *clear*
die **Klasse, -n 14** *class*
das **Klassenzimmer, - 13** *classroom*
   klatschen 10 *to clap*
das **Klavier, -e** *piano*
der **Klavierspieler, - 11** *piano player*
das **Kleid, -er 4** *dress,* **die Kleider** *(pl.)* **6**
    clothing
der **Kleiderschrank, ¨e 5** *clothes closet*
   klein 4 *small*
das **Kleingeld** *change*
die **Kleinschreibung 19** *noncapitalization*
   klingeln 3 *to ring*

klopfen *to knock*

klug, klüger, klügst 8 *clever, more clever, most clever*

die **Kneipe, -n 18** *bar*

der **Knoblauch 7** *garlic*

kochen 10 *to cook*

der **Koffer, - 10** *suitcase*

der **Kollege, -n, -n 9** *colleague*

Köln 15 *Cologne (city in Germany)*

der **Komet, -en, -en 9** *comet*

kommen, kam, gekommen 1 *to come*

der **Kommunist, -en, -en 10** *communist*

kompliziert 12 *complicated*

der **Kompromiß, -sse 15** *compromise*

der **Kongreß, -sse 15** *congress*

der **König, -e 9** *king*

können *(modal verb)* **1** *to be able, can*

das **Konzert, -e 5** *concert*

die **Konzertkarte, -n** *concert ticket*

der **Kopf, ⁻e 5** *head*

die **Kopfwehtablette, -n** *headache pill*

kopieren 3 *to copy*

die **Kosmetikfirma,** *pl.* **-firmen** *cosmetics company*

kosten 3 *to cost*

die **Kosten 15** *costs*

das **Kostüm, -e** *costume*

kräftig 8 *powerful*

krank, kränker, kränkst 4 *sick, sicker, sickest*

das **Krankenhaus, ⁻er** *hospital*

die **Krankenschwester, -n 13** *nurse*

die **Krankheit, -en 6** *disease*

kratzen *to scratch*

der **Kräutertee, -s** *herbal tea*

die **Krawatte, -n 4** *tie*

die **Kreditkarte, -n 10** *credit card*

der **Kreis, -e** *circle*

kreisen *to circle*

kriechen, kroch, gekrochen 3 *to crawl*

der **Krieg, -e 5** *war*

kriegen 13 *to get*

das **Kriegsopfer,** *war victim*

der **Kriminalroman, -e 7** *detective novel*

der **Kritiker, 16** *critic*

das **Krokodil, -e 17** *crocodile*

die **Krone, -n 16** *crown*

die **Küche, -n 11** *kitchen*

der **Kuchen, 16** *cake*

der **Kugelschreiber,** *pen*

der **Kühlschrank, ⁻e 18** *refrigerator*

der **Kunde, -n, -n 9** *customer*

die **Kunst, ⁻e 12** *art*

der **Kurs, -e 6** *course,* **einen Kurs machen 12** *to take a course,* **einen Kurs belegen 15** *to register for a course*

die **Kurve, -n** *curve*

kurz, kürzer, kürzest 8 *short, shorter, shortest*

kurzlebig 16 *short-lived*

küssen 1 *to kiss*

die **Küste, -n 21** *coast*

L

das **Labor, -e 16** *laboratory*

lachen über *+ acc.* **3** *to laugh about, at*

lächerlich *ridiculous*

laden (lädt), lud, geladen 1 *to load*

die **Lage, -n 15** *situation*

das **Lagerfeuer, -** *campfire*

das **Lamm, ⁻er** *lamb*

das **Land, ⁻er 7** *country, land*

lang, länger, längst 8 *long, longer, longest*

lange 12 *a long time*

langsam 8 *slow*

langweilig 10 *boring*

der **Lärm 7** *noise,* **viel Lärm um nichts** *much ado about nothing*

lassen (läßt), ließ, gelassen 1 *to leave, let,* **18** *to have something done*

Latein 19 *Latin (language)*

der **Lauf** *run,* **im Laufe** *+ gen. in the course of*

das **Laufen** *running*

laufen (läuft), lief, gelaufen 1 *to run*

der **Läufer, 4** *runner*

laut 8 *loud*

läuten 13 *to ring*

leben 13 *to live*

das **Leben, 4** *life*

die **Lebensmittel** *(pl.) groceries*

ledig 13 *single (unmarried)*

legen 16 *to lay, put*

lehren 10 *to teach*

der **Lehrer, 4** *teacher*

leicht 14 *easy*

das **Leid 15** *sorrow,* **leid tun 19** *to be sorry,* **es tut mir leid** *I am sorry*

leiden, litt, gelitten an *+ dat.* **1** *to suffer from,* **16** *to stand (someone)*

leidenschaftlich 19 *passionate*

leider 12 *unfortunately*

die **Leipziger Messe 19** *Leipzig trade fair*

leise 12 *softly*

die **Leistung, -en 19** *achievement*

die **Leiter, -n 21** *ladder*

lernen 1 *to learn*

lesen (liest), las, gelesen 1 *to read*

der **Leser, 16** *reader*

letzt *last*

die **Leute 4** *people*

das **Licht, -er 15** *light*

die **Lichtgeschwindigkeit 15** *speed of light*

lieb *dear*

lieben 10 *to love*

lieber *(+ verb)* **8** *prefer (to do something) to rather*

lieber sollen 6 *ought to, should rather*

die **Liebesszene, -n** *love scene*

das **Lied, -er 9** *song*

liefern 12 *to deliver*

liegen, lag, hat/ist gelegen 13 *to lie (somewhere), be (somewhere)*

der **Lippenstift, -e** *lipstick*

die **List, -en 10** *subterfuge*

loben 16 *to praise*

das **Loch, ⁻er 5** *hole*

der **Löffel, - 5** *spoon*

der **Lohn, ⁻e 8** *salary, wage*

lösen 10 *to solve*

los.lassen (läßt), ließ, gelassen 2 *to let go*

die **Lösung, -en 4** *solution*

der Löwe, -n, -n 9 *lion*
die Luft 4 *air*
die Luftpost *airmail*
lügen, log, gelogen 1 *to (tell a) lie*
der Lump, -en, -en 9 *scoundrel*
lustig 9 *funny*

M

machen 1 *to do, make*
die Macht, ⁼e 13 *power,* **an die Macht
    kommen** *to come to power*
das Mädchen, 4 *girl*
das Mal, -e 11 *time (period)*
malen 18 *to paint*
manch 4 *some, much*
manches 16 *much*
manchmal 12 *sometimes*
der Mann, ⁼er 4 *man, husband*
die Mannschaft, -en 8 *team*
der Mantel, ⁼7 *coat*
die Mark *mark (German coin)*
die Maschine, -n 4 *machine*
der Mathematiklehrer,- *mathematics teacher*
der Matrose, -n, -n 9 *sailor*
die Matte, -n 5 *mat*
die Mauer, -n *wall*
die Maus, ⁼e *mouse*
der Mechaniker, *mechanic*
die Medaille, -n *medal*
die Medizin *medicine*
mehrer 4 *several*
die Mehrheit, -en 15 *majority*
die Meile, -n 7 *mile*
mein 4 *my*
meinen 12 *to mean*
meinetwegen *for all I care*
die Meinung, -en 6 *opinion*
meist 4 *most*
meistens 12 *mostly, usually*
melden 15 *to report*
der Mensch, -en, -en 4 *person, human being*
merkwürdig 9 *peculiar, strange*
das Messer, 8 *knife*
der/das Meter, 7 *meter*
die Methode, -n 12 *method*
die Miete, -n 4 *rent*
mieten 16 *to rent*
die Mieterin, -innen 13 *female renter*
das Mikroskop, -e *microscope*
die Milch *milk*
der Milchmann, ⁼er 7 *milkman*
der Millionär, -e *millionaire*
mindest 19 *least*
mindestens 13 *at least*
mit *(prep. + dat.)* 5 *with*
miteinander 14 *with each other*
das Mitglied, -er 8 *member*
mit.kommen, kam, gekommen 2 *to come
    along*
der Mitmensch, -en, -en *fellow man*
mit.nehmen (nimmt), nahm, genommen
    17 *to take along*
mit.spielen 2 *to join in the game*
der Mittag, -e 12 *noon*
das Mittagessen 6 *lunch*
mit.teilen 15 *inform*

mittelalterlich 21 *medieval*
der Mittwoch, -e 5 *Wednesday*
mißverstehen, mißverstand,
    mißverstanden 2 *to misunderstand*
modern 4 *modern*
mögen *(modal verb)* 1 *to like*
möglich 12 *possible*
die Möglichkeit, -en 4 *possibility*
der Monat, -e 11 *month*
der Mörder,- *murderer*
morgen 10 *tomorrow*
der Morgen, - 7 *morning*
der Morgenschlaf 6 *morning sleep*
müde 6 *tired*
munter 13 *awake*
das Museum, *pl.* Museen 8 *museum*
müssen *(modal verb)* 1 *to must, have to*
die Mutter, ⁼ 5 *mother*
die Mutti, -s 11 *mom*

N

nach *(prep. + dat.)* 5 *after, to, according
    to*
der Nachbar, -n, -n 9 *neighbor*
nachdem 13 *after*
nach.gehen, ging, gegangen 16 *to run
    slow (clock)*
nachher 13 *afterwards*
der Nachmittag, -e *afternoon*
die Nachricht(en) 6 *news*
der Nachrichtensprecher, - 15 *newscaster*
nach.schlagen (schlägt), schlug,
    geschlagen 2 *to look up*
die Nachspeise, -n *dessert*
nächst 5 *next*
die Nacht, ⁼e 5 *night*
nachts *evenings*
nah, näher, nächst- 8 *near, nearer,
    nearest (next)*
Nähe: in der Nähe 13 *near, nearby*
der Name, -ns, -n 9 *name*
namens 16 *by the name of*
das Namensverzeichnis, -nisse 4 *directory of
    names*
der Narr, -en, -en 9 *fool*
die Nase, -n 15 *nose*
das Naturgesetz, -e 16 *law of nature*
natürlich 17 *naturally*
die Naturzeitschrift, -en 15 *nature journal*
naß 8 *wet*
neben *(2-way prep.)* 5 *next to, beside*
nebenan 14 *next door*
die Nebenstraße, -n *sidestreet*
nehmen (nimmt), nahm, genommen 1 *to
    take*
nennen *(mixed verb)* 1 *to name*
nett 4 *nice*
neu 4 *new*
neugeboren *newborn*
neugierig 13 *curious*
Neuschwanstein 13 *name of a famous
    castle in Bavaria*
nicht 7 *not*
nicht mehr 10 *no longer*
die Nichte, -n 5 *niece*
nichts 16 *nothing*

das Nichtstun **19** *doing nothing*
nie(mals) 10 *never*
nieder.brennen *(mixed verb)* **14** *to burn down*
nieder.fahren (fährt), fuhr, gefahren 2 *to run over*
die Niederlage, -n **7** *defeat*
nieder.reißen, riß, gerissen 12 *to tear down*
nieder.stellen 2 *to put down*
niedrig 22 *low*
niemand 13 *no one*
das Niveau, -s **8** *level*
noch nicht 7 *not yet*
noch nie *never, not yet*
nochmal 14 *again*
Norwegen *Norway*
die Note, -n **13** *grade*
das Notizbuch, ⁻er **4** *notebook*
notwendig *necessary*
die Nummer, -n **10** *number*
nur 10 *only*
nützlich 17 *useful*
nutzlos *uselessly*
die Nuß, ⁻sse **nut**

O

ob 13, *if, whether*
oben 16 *up there*
obgleich 13 *although*
das Obst **4** *fruit*
obwohl 13 *although*
öde 8 *desolate*
der Ofen, ⁻ **5** *oven*
offensichtlich *apparently*
die Öffentlichkeit **19** *public*
öffnen 1 *to open*
oft, öfter, am öftesten 8 *often, more often, most often*
ohne *(prep. + acc.)* **5** *without*
das Ohr, -en **15** *ear*
die Ohrfeige, -n **16** *slap in the face*
die Ökonomie, -n **12** *economy*
ölen 1 *to oil*
die Oma, -s **19** *grandma*
der Onkel, **24** *uncle*
die Oper, -n *opera*
die Operation, -en **12** *operation*
der Opernsänger, **14** *opera singer*
die Oppositionspartei, -en **15** *opposition party*
ostdeutsch 16 *East German*
Ostdeutsch-e(r) *(an) East German*
Ostern *(pl.)* **6** *Easter*
Österreich 13 *Austria*
österreichisch 5 *Austrian*

P

das Paar, -e **21** *pair*
das Paket, -e *package*
die Panne, -n **14** *breakdown*
der Pantoffel, -n **18** *slipper*
das Papier, -e **7** *paper*
der Park, -s **5** *park*
der Passant, -en, -en **9** *passer-by*
passen + dat. 1 *to fit,* **passen zu 16** *to go with, be appropriate with*

passieren *(aux. sein)* **13** *to happen*
der Patient, -en, -en **10** *patient*
das Pech **7** *bad luck,* **Pech haben** *to be unlucky, to be out of luck*
die Pension, -en *cheaper type of hotel*
die Perlenkette, -n *pearl chain*
die Person, -en **4** *person*
der Pessimismus **4** *pessimism*
der Pfadfinder, **16** *boy scout*
die Pfanne, -n *pan*
der Pfarrer, - **21** *minister (Reverend)*
das Pferd, -e **8** *horse*
die Pflanze, -n **15** *plant*
die Pflanzenart, -en **16** *plant type*
pflegen 17 *to usually do something*
die Pfütze, -n **5** *puddle*
der Philosoph, -en, -en **9** *philosopher*
die Philosophie, -n *philosophy*
photographieren 10 *to photograph*
die Physik **6** *physics*
der Physiklehrer, **7** *physics teacher*
der Pilot, -en, -en *pilot*
der Pilz, -e *mushroom*
der Pirat, -en, -en **9** *pirate*
die Pistole, -n *pistol*
die Pizza, -s *pizza*
der Plan, ⁻e **8** *plan*
Platz nehmen *to take a seat, sit down*
plausibel 7 *plausible*
plötzlich *suddenly*
die Politik **15** *policy, politics*
der Politiker, **15** *politician*
politisch 15 *political*
die Polizei *(sg.)* **4** *police*
der Polizeichef, -s **15** *police chief*
der Polizist,-en, -en **9** *policeman*
polnisch 19 *Polish (adj.)*
pompös 8 *pompous*
positiv *positive*
die Post *mail*
das Postamt, ⁻er *post office*
praktisch 4 *practical*
der Präsident, -en, -en **15** *president*
der Preis, -e **4** *price,* **um jeden Preis** *at any cost,* **14** *prize*
preiswert *a good value*
die Presse, -n **12** *press*
der Prinz, -en, -en **9** *prince*
die Prinzessin, -innen *princess*
das Prinzip, *pl.* **Prinzipien 12** *principle*
das Privathaus, ⁻er *private home*
das Problem, -e **5** *problem*
das Projekt, -e **11** *project*
der Protest, -e **24** *protest*
protestieren 16 *to protest*
die Prüfung, -en **5** *test*
pudelnaß *''poodle-wet'' i.e., drenched*
pünktlich 16 *promptly*
die Puppe, -n *doll*
pur 5 *pure*

Q

die Quelle, -n **8** *source*

R

rad.fahren (fährt), fuhr, gefahren 17 *to ride a bicycle*

der **Radfahrer,** *cyclist*
das **Radio, -s** *radio*
die **Rakete, -n 15** *rocket*
rasch 8 *quick*
der **Rasen, 15** *lawn*
die **Rasierklinge, -n 8** *razor blade*
der **Rat,** *pl.* **Ratschläge 16** *advice*
raten (rät), riet, geraten 1 *to advise*
das **Rathaus, ̈er 5** *city hall*
rauchen 11 *to smoke*
der **Raufbold, -e 6** *bully, tough guy*
raufen 14 *to fight*
reagieren auf + acc. 6 *to react to*
die **Reaktion auf + acc. 6** *reaction to*
rechnen mit 1 *to expect*
die **Rechnung, -en 10** *bill*
recht haben 14 *to be right*
der **Rechtsanwalt, ̈e 5** *lawyer*
rechtzeitig 14 *on time*
die **Rede, -n 6** *speech, talk*
reden 1 *to talk*
der **Redner,** *speaker*
Referat halten *to give a report*
regeln 13 *to control*
der **Regenmantel, ̈ 5** *rain coat*
der **Regenschirm, -e 9** *umbrella*
die **Regierung, -en 15** *government*
regnen 1 *to rain*
regnerisch 21 *rainy*
das **Reh, -e** *deer*
reich an + dat. 6 *rich in*
das **Reich, -e 15** *kingdom*
reichen 2 *to pass, hand over*
der **Reichstag 10** *(German) parliament*
die **Reihe, -n 14** *row*
reinigen 1 *to clean*
die **Reise, -n 24** *trip*
reisen 1 *to travel*
der **Reisepaß, ̈sse 4** *passport*
der **Reisescheck, -s 13** *traveler's check*
die **Religion, -en 6** *religion*
die **Renaissance** *Renaissance*
rennen *(mixed verb)* **1** *to run*
der **Rennwagen,** *racing car*
reparieren 10 *to repair*
der **Reporter, 15** *reporter*
die **Republik, -en 13** *republic*
respektieren 10 *to respect*
das **Restaurant, -s 4** *restaurant*
das **Resultat, -e 6** *result*
retten 1 *to save*
der **Rhythmus** *rhythm*
der **Richter, -** *judge*
richtig 19 *real, correct*
die **Richtigkeit 22** *correctness*
riechen, roch, gerochen nach 3 *to smell like*
das **Rindsgulasch** *beef goulash*
der **Ring, -e 7** *ring*
die **Ringstraße 19** *famous boulevard in Vienna*
der **Roman, -e 10** *novel*
die **Rose, -n 4** *rose*
rot *red,* **bei Rot 4** *on a red light*
das **Rote Meer 19** *the Red Sea*
rufen, rief, gerufen 1 *to call*

die **Ruhe 17** *peace, quiet,* **in Ruhe lassen** *to leave alone, not disturb*
ruhen 13 *to rest,* **15** *to cool, sit*
ruhig *quiet*
die **Ruine, -n** *ruin*
ruinieren 10 *to ruin*
der **Russe, -n, -n 9** *(a) Russian*
Russisch 19 *Russian (language)*
Rußland 5 *Russia*

S

die **Sache, -n 6** *matter, thing*
sagen 1 *to say, tell*
die **Sahne, -n 24** *whipped cream*
sammeln 1 *to collect*
sarkastisch *sarcastic*
sauber *clean*
saufen (säuft), soff, gesoffen 1 *to drink (of animals), to consume alcohol (of humans)*
schaden + dat. 4 *to hurt*
der **Schaden, ̈ 13** *damage*
der **Schäferhund, -e** *German shephard*
scharf, schärfer, schärfst 8 *sharp, sharper, sharpest*
schätzen *to appreciate*
das **Schauspiel, -e** *play*
scheiden lassen *(refl.) to get a divorce*
scheinen, schien, geschienen 14 *to seem*
schenken *to give (for a present), present*
die **Schere** *(sg.)* **21** *scissors*
scheu bei 12 *shy with*
Schi laufen (läuft), lief, gelaufen 19 *to ski*
schicken 12 *to send*
schieben, schob, geschoben *to shove*
schief.gehen, ging, gegangen 16 *to fail, go wrong*
das **Schiff, -e 7** *ship*
der **Schiläufer,** *skier*
der **Schilling, -e 24** *shilling (Austrian coin)*
der **Schlaf** *sleep*
schlafen (schläft), schlief, geschlafen 1 *to sleep*
schlagen (schlägt), schlug, geschlagen 1 *to hit, beat*
schlau 8 *clever*
schlecht 4 *bad*
schließen, schloß, geschlossen 1 *to close*
schließlich *finally, eventually*
schlimm 8 *bad*
das **Schloß, ̈sser 4** *castle, palace*
schluchzen 1 *to sob*
der **Schlüssel, 13** *key*
die **Schlußfolgerung, -en 15** *conclusion*
schmal 8 *narrow*
schmecken 16 *to taste*
schmeicheln + dat. 4 *to flatter*
schmeißen, schmiß, geschmissen 1 *to fling*
schmelzen (schmilzt), schmolz, geschmolzen 1 *to melt*
schmerzstillend *painkilling*
schmutzig 15 *dirty*
die **Schmutzwäsche** *dirty wash*
der **Schnee 21** *snow*
schneiden, schnitt, geschnitten 1 *to cut,* **7** *mince*

schneien 14 *to snow*
schnell 8 *fast*
schockieren 3 *to shock*
die Schokolade 21 *chocolate*
schön 7 *beautiful*
schon 10 *already*
die Schönheitskonkurrenz, -en *beauty pageant*
schrecklich *terrible*
schreiben, schrieb, geschrieben 3 *to write*
schreien, schrie, geschrien 10 *to scream*
die Schrift, -en *writing*
der Schriftsteller, 5 *writer*
der Schritt, -e *step*
der Schuh, -e 9 *shoe*
die Schulbehörde, -n 16 *schoolboard*
schulden 12 *to owe*
die Schulden (pl.) *debts*
    schuldig an + dat. 6 *guilty of*
der Schuldirektor, -en *school director,*
    principal
die Schule, -n 10 *school*
der Schüler 4 *student, pupil*
die Schulgruppe, -n *school group*
der Schulunterricht 16 *classroom instruction*
    schwach, schwächer, schwächst 8 *weak,*
    weaker, weakest
der Schwager, - 16 *brother-in-law*
    schwänzen *to skip class*
    schwarz, schwärzer, schwärzest 8 *black,*
    blacker, blackest
das Schwarzfahren 19 *using public*
    transportation without paying
der Schwarzmarkt, -e 18 *black market*
    schweigen, schwieg, geschwiegen 1 *to be*
    silent
das Schwein, -e 19 *pig, despicable person*
die Schweinerei *outrageous act*
die Schweiz 15 *Switzerland*
der Schweiß 16 *sweat*
    schwer 7 *severe, difficult, with difficulty*
die Schwester, -n 4 *sister*
    schwierig 16 *difficult*
die Schwierigkeit, -en 10 *difficulty*
das Schwimmbecken, *swimming pool*
    schwimmen, schwamm, geschwommen 1
    to swim
    schwindeln *to cheat*
    segeln 17 *to sail*
    sehen (sieht), sah, gesehen 1 *to see*
die Sehenswürdigkeit, -en 10 *tourist sight*
die Sehnsucht nach 6 *longing for*
    sehr 15 *very much*
die Seife, -n *soap*
das Seil, -e *rope*
    sein 4 *his, its*
    sein (ist), war, ist gewesen 1 *to be*
    seit (prep. + dat.) 5 *since, for*
    seitdem 13 *since (that time), since then*
die Seite, -n *side*
die Sekretärin, -innen 15 *female secretary*
    selb 19 *same*
    selber 13 *yourself, himself, myself, etc.*
    selbst 12 *even; yourself, myself, etc.*
das Selbst 19 *the self*
    selten 12 *seldom*
das Semester, 15 *semester*

der Senator, -en *senator*
    senden (mixed verb) 1 *to send*
    sensibel 8 *sensitive*
    servieren 18 *to serve*
der Sessel 5 *chair*
    setzen (refl.) *to sit down*
    siamesisch *Siamese*
    sicher 16 *certain(ly), for sure*
das Sichgehenlassen 19 *letting yourself go*
das Silber 5 *silver*
das Silberbesteck *silverware*
die Sinfonie, -n 10 *symphony*
    singen, sang, gesungen 1 *to sing*
die Sitte, -n *custom*
    sitzen, saß, hat/ist gesessen 1 *to sit*
    so (et)was 14 *such a thing,* So was! 24
    What do you know!
    sobald 13 *as long as*
die Socke, -n 4 *sock*
    soeben *just*
    sofort 7 *immediately*
der Sohn, -e 6 *son*
    solange 13 *as long as*
    solch 4 *such*
der Soldat, -en, -en 4 *soldier*
    sollen (modal verb) 1 *to be supposed to,*
    should
der Sommer, 12 *summer*
die Sonne, -n *sun*
der Sonntag, -e 15 *Sunday*
    sowieso 14 *anyway*
der Sozialdemokrat, -en, -en 12 *social*
    democrat
der Sozialist, -en, -en *socialist*
    Spanien *Spain*
    sparen *to save*
    spät 8 *late*
    spazieren.gehen, ging, gegangen 12 *to*
    take a walk
    spenden 1 *to donate*
    spezialisieren 3 *to specialize*
das Spiel, -e 14 *game*
    spielen 1 *to play*
der Spielplatz, -e 15 *playground*
die Spielsache, -n *toy*
das Spielzeug, -e 18 *toy*
    spionieren 15 *to spy*
der Sport 15 *sports*
der Sportler, 14 *athlete*
der Sportverein, -e *sports club*
die Sprache, -n 16 *language*
    sprechen (spricht), sprach, gesprochen 1
    to speak
der Sprecher, 15 *speaker*
    springen, sprang, gesprungen *to jump*
die Spritze, -n 19 *(needle) shot*
    spüren *to feel*
der Staat, -en 22 *state (country)*
die Stadt, -e 5 *city*
die Stadtbehörde, -n 19 *city authorities*
das Stadtlicht, -er *city light*
    stammen aus *to stem from, come from*
    ständig 16 *constantly*
    stark, stärker, stärkst 8 *strong, stronger,*
    strongest
die Stärke, -n *strength*

statt *(prep. + gen.)* **5** *instead of*
stattdessen *instead*
statt.finden, fand, gefunden 2 *to take place*
staunen 14 *to be astonished*
stecken 10 *to put,* **in Brand stecken** *to set on fire*
stehen, stand, ist/hat gestanden 10 *to stand, be (somewhere)*
stehen.bleiben, blieb, ist stehengeblieben 10 *to stop*
stehlen (stiehlt), stahl, gestohlen 1 *to steal*
steigen, stieg, gestiegen 18 *to rise*
der **Stein, -e 14** *rock*
die **Stellage, -n 12** *shelf*
Stelle: an seiner (deiner) Stelle sein 14 *to be in his (your) place*
stellen 1 *to put*
sterben (stirbt), starb, gestorben 3 *to die*
die **Steuer, -n 15** *tax*
der **Stiefel, 15** *boot*
stiften 16 *to donate*
die **Stimme, -n 12** *vote, voice*
stimmen 14 *to be correct*
die **Stimmung** *atmosphere, mood*
stinken, stank, gestunken 16 *to stink*
das **Stipendium,** *pl.* **-ien 13** *scholarship*
der **Stolz 19** *pride*
stolz auf + acc. 6 *proud of*
stören 16 *to bother, disturb*
stoßen (stößt), stieß, gestoßen 1 *to knock, shove*
der **Strafzettel,** *police ticket*
die **Straße, -n 9** *street*
die **Straßenbahn, -en 9** *streetcar*
der **Streit, -e** *argument*
streng 7 *strict*
der **Strom 11** *electricity*
das **Stück, -e** *piece*
der **Student, -en, -en 4** *student*
die **Studentenermäßigung, -en** *student discount*
das **Studentenheim, -e 6** *dormitory*
die **Studentin, -innen 5** *female student*
studieren 1 *to study*
das **Studium** *course of studies*
der **Stuhl, -̈e 11** *chair*
die **Stunde, -n 5** *hour, classroom hour*
stur 13 *stubborn*
der **Sturm, -̈e** *storm*
stürzen 14 *to stumble*
Stuttgart 5 *Stuttgart (city in Germany)*
suchen nach *to look for*
der **Südbahnhof 19** *South train station*
der **Süden 15** *(the) South*
die **Sünde, -n 12** *sin*
die **Suppe, -n 7** *soup*
süß 8 *sweet*
die **Süßigkeit, -en** *candy*
das **Symptom, -e 16** *symptom*
die **Szene, -n 5** *scene*

T

die **Tablette, -n 13** *pill*
der **Tag, -e 5** *day*
das **Talent, -e 6** *talent*

die **Tante, -n 5** *aunt*
tanzen 3 *to dance*
die **Tapferkeit** *bravery*
die **Tasche, -n 5** *bag, pocket*
die **Tasse, -n 14** *cup*
die **Tat, -en** *deed*
die **Tatsache, -n** *fact*
der **Tee, -s 5** *tea*
der **Teig, -e 15** *dough*
der **Teil, -e 4** *portion, part*
teil.nehmen (nimmt), nahm, genommen an + dat. 3 *to participate in*
das **Telefon, -e 11** *telephone*
die **Telefonnummer, -n 13** *telephone number*
der **Teller, 14** *plate*
die **Temperatur, -en 7** *temperature*
der **Teppich, -e 5** *rug, carpet*
teuer 7 *expensive*
das **Thema,** *pl.* **Themen 16** *topic*
die **Theorie, -n 13** *theory*
tief 8 *deep*
der **Tisch, -e 14** *table*
die **Tochter, -̈ 12** *daughter*
der **Tod,** *pl.* **Todesfälle 21** *death*
die **Toilette, -n 8** *toilet*
die **Tomate, -n** *tomato*
der **Ton, -̈e 7** *tone, sound*
tot 9 *dead*
der **Tourist, -en, -en 9** *tourist*
tragen (trägt), trug, getragen 1 *to carry,* **18** *to wear*
die **Tragödie, -n 7** *tragedy*
die **Traube, -n 8** *grape*
trauen + dat. 4 *to trust*
trauern um 6 *to mourn for*
traurig 12 *sad*
treffen (trifft), traf, getroffen 12 *to meet*
treiben, trieb, getrieben 15 *to engage in*
treten (tritt), trat, getreten 1 *to step*
treu *faithful*
trinken, trank, getrunken 10 *to drink*
das **Trinkgeld, -er 4** *tip*
der **Trost 7** *comfort*
der **Trottel, 9** *fool*
trotz *(prep. + gen.)* **5** *in spite of*
trotzdem 14 *just the same, in spite of that*
die **Truppe, -n 7** *army, troops*
das **Tuch, -̈er** *cloth*
tüchtig 8 *competent, industrious*
die **Tulpe, -n** *tulip*
tun, tat, getan 12 *to do*
die **Tür, -en 5** *door*
der **Türhüter, 9** *doorman*
der **Turm, -̈e 7** *tower*

U

üben 11 *to practice,* **24** *to exercise (caution)*
über *(2-way prep.)* **5** *over*
überhaupt nicht 12 *not at all*
über.laufen (läuft), lief, gelaufen 2 *to run over*
überlaufen (überläuft), überlief, überlaufen 2 *to bombard*
der **Übermensch, -en, -en 24** *superman*
übermorgen 12 *day after tomorrow*

übernachten 11 *to spend the night*
überraschen 15 *to surprise*
die **Überraschung, -en 7** *surprise*
der **Überstundenlohn, -e 13** *overtime pay*
überwachen 17 *to supervise*
überzeugt von 14 *convinced of*
übrig: im übrigen 19 *remaining, in addition*
die **Übung, -en 7** *exercise*
die **Uhr, -en 5** *watch, clock, o'clock*
um *(prep. + acc.)* **5** *around, at*
umarmen 2 *to embrace*
um.bringen *(mixed verb)* **12** *to kill, murder*
umgekehrt 14 *reversed*
um.rechnen 3 *to convert*
um.werfen (wirft), warf, geworfen 10 *to knock over*
unabhängig 13 *independent*
unbekannt 13 *unknown*
unerwartet 13 *unexpectedly*
unfreundlich *unfriendly*
ungeheuer 7 *enormous*
ungesetzlich 16 *illegal*
ungesund 16 *unhealthy*
ungewöhnlich 16 *unusual*
unglaublich *unbelievable*
die **Uni, -s** *(colloquial)* **13** *university*
die **Universität, -en 11** *university*
unleserlich 15 *illegible*
unpraktisch 16 *impractical*
unrasiert *unshaved*
unregelmäßig *irregular*
unser 4 *our*
unter *(2-way prep.)* **5** *under, among*
unterbrechen (unterbricht), unterbrach, unterbrochen 11 *to interrupt*
die **Untergrundbahn, -en 19** *subway*
der **Unterschied, -e 17** *difference*
untersuchen 10 *to examine, study, investigate*
die **Untertasse, -n 7** *saucer*
der **Urlaub, -e 22** *vacation*
der **Ursprung, -̈e** *origin*

V

der **Vater, -̈ 4** *father*
das **Vaterland** *fatherland*
der **Vati, -s** *daddy*
verabschieden *(refl.)* **24** *to say good-bye*
verachten 1 *to despise*
verbannen von 11 *to expel from, exile from*
verbieten, verbot, verboten 16 *to forbid*
verblühen 3 *to fade*
verbrauchen 15 *to use*
das **Verbrechen, 6** *crime*
der **Verbrecher,** *criminal*
verbrennen *(mixed verb)* **2** *to burn*
verbringen *(mixed verb)* **17** *to spend (time)*
verdienen 14 *to earn*
der **Verfasser, 5** *author*
die **Vergangenheit, -en 6** *past*
vergessen (vergißt), vergaß, vergessen 1 *to forget*
vergeuden 1 *to squander*
der **Vergleich, -e 19** *comparison*

verhaften 13 *to arrest*
verhandeln 13 *to deal*
die **Verhandlung, -en 15** *negotiation*
verheiratet sein 24 *to be married*
verkaufen 1 *to sell*
der **Verkäufer, 6** *seller, salesperson*
die **Verkäuferin, -innen** *female salesperson*
der **Verkehrspolizist, -en, -en** *traffic policeman*
verkennen *(mixed verb)* **7** *to not recognize*
verlangen 14 *to demand*
verlassen (verläßt), verließ, verlassen 3 *to leave*
verletzen 10 *to injure*
verliebt 9 *in love*
verlieren, verlor, verloren 3 *to lose*
verlockend 8 *tempting*
vermeiden 1 *to avoid*
die **Vermieterin, -innen** *person who rents out (female)*
vermissen 1 *to miss*
das **Vermögen,** *fortune*
verschwenden 24 *to squander*
verschwinden, verschwand, verschwunden 3 *to disappear*
versichern 15 *to assure; insure*
das **Versicherungsgeld 14** *insurance money*
die **Verspätung 7** *lateness*
verspielen 13 *to lose at playing*
versprechen (verspricht), versprach, versprochen 12 *to promise*
das **Versprechen,** *promise*
der **Verstand 7** *common sense*
verständlich 16 *understandable*
das **Verständnis 4** *understanding*
verstärkt 4 *strengthened*
verstehen, verstand, verstanden 13 *to understand*
versteigern 10 *to auction off*
versuchen 17 *to try*
verteidigen 1 *to defend*
der **Verteidigungsminister, 11** *defense minister*
der **Vertrag, -̈e 15** *treaty*
vertreten (vertritt), vertrat, vertreten 15 *to stand for, represent*
der **Vertreter, 12** *representative*
Verwandt-e(r) 9 *relative*
verwenden 14 *to use*
die **Verwendung, -en 4** *use*
Verwundet-e(r) 9 *wounded person*
verzeihen + dat. 4 *to forgive*
verzichten auf + acc. 6 *to do without, renounce*
verzieren 16 *to decorate*
der **Vetter, -n** *cousin*
viel, mehr, meist 4 *much, more, most*
vieles 12 *(very) much*
vielleicht 12 *perhaps*
das **Vitamin, -e 6** *vitamin*
der **Vogel, -̈ 9** *bird*
die **Vogelart, -en** *bird type*
von *(prep. + dat.)* **5** *from, by*
vor *(2-way prep.)* **5** *in front of, before, ago*
vor allem 12 *above all*
voraus: im voraus 19 *in advance*
vorbei 13 *over*

vorbei.fahren (fährt), fuhr, gefahren 18 *to drive by*
vorbereiten 10 *to prepare*
der **Vorgänger,** *predecessor*
Vorgesetzt-e(r) 9 *superior (at work)*
vorgestern 11 *day before yesterday*
vorher 13 *before*
vorig 7 *last*
vor.kommen, kam, gekommen 14 *to seem,* **16** *to occur*
vor kurzem 16 *a short time ago*
vor.legen, lag, gelegen 2 *to submit, to present*
die **Vorlesung, -en 11** *lecture, course*
der **Vormittag, -e 7** *morning*
der **Vorname, -ns, -n** *first name*
vorne *up ahead*
vor.rücken 17 *to advance*
der **Vorschlag, ̈e 5** *suggestion*
vor.schlagen (schlägt), schlug, geschlagen 16 *to suggest*
vorsichtig 12 *carefully*
Vorsitzend-e(r) 9 *chairman*
vor.stellen *(refl.)* **12** *to imagine*
die **Vorstellung, -en** *presentation*
der **Vortrag, ̈e 13** *talk, lecture*
Vortrag halten *to hold a talk*

W

wach *awake*
wachen 14 *to be awake*
wachsen (wächst), wuchs, gewachsen 15 *to grow*
wagen 14 *to dare*
der **Wagen, 4** *car*
die **Wahl, -en 15** *choice, election*
der **Wahlkampf, ̈e 13** *political campaign*
wahr 14 *true*
während *(prep. + gen.)* **5** *during,* **10** *(subordinate conjunction) while*
die **Wahrheit 14** *truth*
die **Wahrscheinlichkeit 12** *probability*
die **Wand, ̈e 5** *wall*
wann 10 *when*
die **Ware, -n 8** *merchandise*
warm, wärmer, wärmst 8 *warm, warmer, warmest*
warnen vor + *dat.* **1** *to warn about, against*
warten 1 *to wait*
warten auf + *acc.* **6** *to wait for*
warum 10 *why*
was 13 *what*
waschen (wäscht), wusch, gewaschen 3 *to wash*
das **Wasser 10** *water*
wecken 10 *to wake (someone) up*
der **Wecker, 13** *alarm*
weg 10 *away*
der **Weg, -e 8** *way*
wegen *(prep. + gen.)* **5** *because of*
weg.fahren (fährt), fuhr, gefahren 14 *to drive away, go away*
weg.fliegen, flog, geflogen 3 *to fly away*
weg.jagen 2 *to chase away*

weg.laufen (läuft), lief, gelaufen 3 *to run away*
weg.schauen 2 *to look away*
weg.stellen 14 *to put away*
weg.werfen (wirft), warf, geworfen 10 *to throw away*
weg.ziehen, zog, gezogen 13 *to move away*
weh tun *to hurt,* **das tut mir weh 19** *that hurts me*
Weihnachten 12 *Christmas*
der **Weihnachtsmann, ̈er 6** *Santa Claus*
weil 13 *because*
die **Weimarer Republik 19** *Weimar Republic*
der **Wein, -e 7** *wine*
weinen 10 *to cry*
die **Weinstube, -n 5** *wine tavern*
weise 8 *wise*
weit 16 *far*
weiter 17 *additional, further*
weiter.fahren (fährt), fur, gefahren 10 *to continue on*
weiter.gehen, ging, gegangen 2 *to go on, continue*
weiterhin: etwas weiterhin tun 18 *to continue to do something*
weiß 4 *white*
welch 4 *which*
die **Welt, -en 13** *world*
die **Weltreise, -n** *trip around the world*
wem *(dat.)* **12** *whom*
wen *(acc.)* **13** *whom*
wenden *(mixed verb)* **1** *to turn*
wenig 4 *few, little*
wenigst 19 *least, few*
wenn 13 *if, when*
wer *(nom.)* **10** *who*
werden (wird), wurde, geworden 3 *to become*
werfen (wirft), warf, geworfen 1 *to throw*
das **Werk, -e 7** *work*
das **Werkzeug, -e 5** *tool*
der **Wert, -e 14** *value*
wesentlich *essential*
wessen *(gen.)* **13** *whose*
der **Wettbewerb** *competition*
wetten *to bet*
das **Wetter 5** *weather*
wichtig 7 *important*
widmen 1 *to dedicate*
wie 10 *how*
wiederauf.bauen 16 *to rebuild*
wiederholen 10 *to repeat*
Wien 12 *Vienna*
das **Wiener Schnitzel** *breaded veal cutlet*
wieso 13 *why*
wieviel 13 *how much*
wild 17 *wild*
der **Wille, -ns, -n 9** *will*
der **Wind, -e 5** *wind*
der **Winter** *winter*
das **Wintersemester, 17** *winter semester*
wirklich 13 *really*
die **Wirklichkeit 24** *reality*
wirksam gegen 16 *effective against*
der **Wirt, -e** *host*
wissen *(modal verb)* **1** *to know*

der Wissenschaftler, 7 *scientist*
die Witwe, -n 19 *widow*
der Witz, -e 13 *joke*
    wo 13 *where*
die Woche, -n 12 *week*
    wohl 11 *probably*
das Wohl *welfare, well-being*
das Wohlfahrtsgeld *welfare money*
    wohnen 1 *to live*
die Wohnung, -en 4 *apartment*
der Wohnungsschlüssel, *apartment key*
das Wohnzimmer, *living room*
    wollen *(modal verb)* 1 *to want*
das Wort, -e *or* ⸚er *(see chap. 21, sec. A)* 14
    word
das Wörterbuch, ⸚er *dictionary*
der Wunsch, ⸚e 5 *wish*
die Wüste, -n 16 *desert*

Z

    zählen 10 *to count*
der Zahn, ⸚e 7 *tooth*
der Zahnarzt, ⸚e *dentist*
der Zaun, ⸚e *fence*
    zehn *ten*
    zeichnen 3 *to draw*
    zeigen 9 *to show*
die Zeit, -en 4 *time*
die Zeitung, -en 5 *newspaper*
der/das Zentimeter, 7 *centimeter*
die Zentralbank, -en 12 *central bank*
    zerbrechen (zerbricht), zerbrach,
        zerbrochen 10 *to shatter*
    zerfließen, zerfloß, zerflossen 2 *to melt*
        away
    zerplatzen 3 *to burst*
    zerreißen, zerriß, zerrissen 2 *to tear*
    zerstören 10 *to destroy*

der Zeuge, -n, -n 9 *witness*
das Ziel, -e 17 *goal*
    zielen auf + *acc.* 6 *to point at*
    ziemlich 16 *rather*
die Zigarette, -n *cigarette*
das Zimmer, - 5 *room*
der Zoo, -s *zoo*
der Zorn 5 *anger*
    zornig auf + *acc* 6 *angry at*
    zu *(prep. + dat.)* 5 *to*
der Zucker *sugar*
    zuerst 13 *first*
der Zufall, ⸚e 6 *coincidence, chance*
    zufällig *by coincidence*
    zufrieden 13 *content*
der Zug, ⸚e 8 *train*
die Zugspitze *name of highest mountain in*
    Bavaria
    zu.nehmen (nimmt), nahm, genommen
        14 *to gain weight*
    zurück.halten (hält), hielt, gehalten 2 *to*
        hold back, keep to oneself
    zurück.kommen, kam, gekommen 3 *to*
        come back
    zusammen *together*
    zusammen.brechen (bricht), brach,
        gebrochen *to break down*
der Zusammenbruch 4 *collapse*
    zusammen.mischen 10 *to mix together*
    zusammen.stellen 2 *to put together*
der Zuschauer, 15 *viewer*
    zu.sperren 2 *to lock*
    zu.spitzen *(refl.)* 15 *to come to a critical*
        point
die Zutat, -en *added ingredient*
    zwanzig *twenty*
    zwei *two*
    zweit 12 *second*
    zwischen *(2-way prep.)* 5 *between*

English-German Glossary

This list contains the total English-German vocabulary of the book. A summary of the abbreviations used can be found at the beginning of the German-English glossary.

A

above all *vor allem*
accomplishment *die Leistung, -en*
accustomed to *gewöhnt an + acc.*
acquaintance *Bekannt-e(r)*
actress *die Schauspielerin, -innen*
address *die Adresse, -n*
admit *zu.geben (gibt), gab, gegeben*
adult *Erwachsen-e(r)*
advance: in advance *im voraus*
advantage *der Vorteil, -e*
advice *der Rat, pl. Ratschläge*
advise *raten (rät), riet, geraten*

afford something *etwas leisten (dat. refl.)*
afraid: be afraid of *fürchten vor + dat. (refl.)*
after *nach + dat.*
again *wieder*
against *gegen + acc.*
agree with *zu.stimmen + dat.*
all *all*
allusion to *die Anspielung, -en auf + acc.*
already *schon*
always *immer*
American *amerikanisch*
angry *zornig*
annihilate *vernichten*

answer (the) *die Antwort, -en*
answer (verb) *antworten + dat.*
anticipate *voraus.ahnen*
anyone *irgendjemand*
anything *irgendetwas*
apartment *die Wohnung, -en*
apparently *offensichtlich*
apply for *bewerben (bewirbt), bewarb,*
  beworben um (refl.)
appreciate *schätzen*
army *die Armee, -n*
arrive *an.kommen, kam, gekommen*
arrogance *der Hochmut*
art *die Kunst*
artist *der Künstler,*
as if *als ob*
ask about *fragen nach*
ask for *bitten um*
astonished at *erstaunt über + acc.*
as . . . as *so... wie*
attack *an.greifen, griff, gegriffen*
audience *das Publikum*
aunt *die Tante, -n*
Austria *Österreich*
autumn *der Herbst*
average income *das Durchschnittseinkommen*
avoid *vermeiden, vermied, vermieden*

B

baby *das Baby, -s*
bad *schlecht*
bank *die Bank, -en*
basement *der Keller,*
bathroom *das Badezimmer,*
be *sein (ist), war, ist gewesen*
bear *der Bär, -en, -en*
beautiful *schön*
become *werden (wird), wurde, ist geworden*
bed *das Bett, -en*
before *bevor*
beforehand *vorher*
begin *an.fangen (fängt), fing, gefangen*
beginning *der Anfang, ¨e*
behave *benehmen (benimmt), benahm,*
  benommen (refl.)
believe *glauben + dat. (someone)*
believe in *glauben an + acc.*
belong to *gehören + dat.*
better *besser*
bicycle *das Fahrrad, ¨er*
big *groß*
bill *die Rechnung, -en*
black *schwarz*
blind *blind*
blitzkrieg *der Blitzkrieg, -e*
blond *blond*
body (dead) *die Leiche, -n*
book *das Buch, ¨er*
born: be born *geboren sein*
boss *der Chef, -s*
both *beid*
brag about *prahlen mit*
bread *das Brot, -e*
break *brechen (bricht), brach, gebrochen*
breath *der Atem*
breathe in *ein.atmen*

bridge *die Brücke, -n*
bring *bringen (mixed verb)*
bring out *heraus.bringen (mixed verb)*
brother *der Bruder, ¨*
brown *braun*
brush (teeth) *putzen*
building *das Gebäude,*
burn *brennen (mixed verb)*
bus *der Autobus, -sse*
buy *kaufen*

C

calcium *der Kalk*
call (on the telephone) *an.rufen*
called: be called *heißen, hieß, geheißen*
camera *der Fotoapparat, -e*
can *können (modal verb)*
candidate *der Kandidat, -en, -en*
capital punishment *die Todesstrafe*
capture *fangen (fängt), fing, gefangen*
car *das Auto, -s*
careful *vorsichtig*
carry *tragen (trägt), trug, getragen*
cat *die Katze, -n*
catch *fangen (fängt), fing, gefangen*
cathedral *der Dom, -e*
Catholic *der Katholik, -en, -en*
certain *sicher*
chair *der Sessel,*
chairman *Vorsitzend-e(r)*
change *ändern*
chase away *weg.jagen*
cheap *billig*
cheat *schwindeln*
child *das Kind, -er*
Chinese *chinesisch (adj.)*
choose *wählen*
Christianity *das Christentum*
Christmas *die Weihnachten (pl.)*
church *die Kirche, -n*
circle *der Kreis, -e*
city *die Stadt, ¨e*
city hall *das Rathaus, ¨er*
claim *behaupten*
class *die Klasse, -n*
clean *reinigen*
clear *klar*
clever, cleverer, cleverest *klug, klüger,*
  klügst
close *schließen, schloß, geschlossen*
clothes *die Kleider*
clothing *die Bekleidung,* **men's clothing** *die*
  Herrenbekleidung
club *der Verein, -e*
coat *der Mantel, ¨*
coffee *der Kaffee, -s*
coincidence *der Zufall, ¨e*
cold (weather) *die Kälte*
cold, colder, coldest *kalt, kälter, kältest*
comb *der Kamm, ¨e*
come *kommen, kam, gekommen*
company (business) *die Firma, pl. Firmen*
compare *vergleichen, verglich, verglichen*
comparison *der Vergleich, -e,* **in comparison**
  im Vergleich
computer *der Computer,*

confidentiality: in all confidentiality *unter vier Augen*
confiscate *beschlagnahmen*
congratulate *gratulieren + dat.*
consequence *die Folge, -n*
consequence: as a consequence *infolgedessen*
consist of *bestehen, bestand, bestanden aus*
constant(ly) *ständig*
contents *der Inhalt (sg.)*
contradict *widersprechen (widerspricht), widersprach, widersprochen + dat.*
cook *kochen*
cookie *der Keks, -e*
copy *die Kopie, -n*
correct *richtig*
cost *kosten*
costume *das Kostüm, -e*
cough *husten*
country *das Land, ⁻er*
crazy *verrückt*
criticize *kritisieren*
cry *weinen*
curious about *neugierig auf + acc.*
customer *der Kunde, -n, -n*
cut *schneiden, schnitt, geschnitten*
Czechoslovakia *die Tschechoslowakei*

D

damage *beschädigen*
dance *tanzen*
danger *die Gefahr, -en*
dangerous *gefährlich*
dark *dunkel*
day *der Tag, -e*
day before yesterday *vorgestern*
death *der Tod, pl. Todesfälle*
dedicate *widmen*
deed *die Tat, -en*
deeply *tief*
delegate *Delegiert-e(r)*
deny (refuse) *verweigern*
deny (something) *ab.leugnen*
depend on *verlassen auf + acc. (refl.)*
dependent on *abhängig von*
dessert *die Nachspeise, -n*
destroy *zerstören*
develop *entwickeln*
diameter *der Durchmesser,*
die of *sterben (stirbt), starb, gestorben an + dat.*
difficult *schwierig*
dinner *das Abendessen*
director *der Direktor, -en*
dirty *schmutzig*
disadvantage *der Nachteil, -e*
disappointment *die Enttäuschung, -en*
discuss *diskutieren*
disease *die Krankheit, -en*
dishes *das Geschirr (sg.)*
displease *mißfallen (mißfällt), mißfiel, mißfallen + dat.*
divided by *durch*
dizzy *schwindlig*
do *tun, tat, getan*
do without *verzichten auf + acc.*
doctor *der Arzt, ⁻e*

dog *der Hund, -e*
drink (a lot of alcohol) *saufen (säuft), soff, gesoffen*
drink to *trinken, trank, getrunken auf + acc.*
drive *fahren (fährt), fuhr, gefahren*
drive away *weg.fahren (fährt), fuhr, gefahren*
drizzle *nieseln*
drug *die Droge, -n*
during *während + gen.*
duty *die Pflicht, -en*
dye *färben*

E

each other *einander,* **of each other** *voneinander*
early *früh*
earthquake *das Erdbeben, -*
easily, easy *leicht*
eat *essen (ißt), aß, gegessen*
economic *ökonomisch*
effect on *die Wirkung auf + acc.*
egg *das Ei, -er*
eliminate *eliminieren*
else *ander*
embarrassed: be embarrassed about *genieren (refl.)*
empty *leer*
end result *das Endresultat, -e*
energetic *energisch*
English *Englisch (language),* **in English** *auf englisch*
enjoy *genießen, genoß, genossen*
enthusiastic about *begeistert von*
entire *ganz*
essay *der Aufsatz, ⁻e*
European *europäisch*
even *selbst*
even (before a comparative) *(sogar) noch*
even if *auch wenn, sogar wenn*
everyone *jeder*
everything *alles*
example *das Beispiel, -e*
exciting *aufregend*
expect *erwarten*
expensive *teuer*

F

factory *die Fabrik, -en*
fall asleep *ein.schlafen (schläft), schlief, geschlafen*
family *die Familie, -n*
famous *berühmt*
fast *schnell*
fate *das Schicksal, -e*
father *der Vater, ⁻*
feed *füttern*
few (a) *ein paar*
fill out *aus.füllen*
film *der Film, -e*
finally *endlich*
find *finden*
finger *der Finger*
first *erst*
fish *der Fisch, -e*
flammable *leicht entzündbar*
flatter *schmeicheln + dat.*

flee from *entfliehen, entfloh, entflohen + dat.*
flight *der Flug, -̈e*
floor *der Boden, -̈*
flower *die Blume, -n*
follow *folgen + dat. (aux. sein)*
following: in the following *im folgenden*
foot *der Fuβ, -̈e*
football team *die Fuβballmannschaft, -en*
for *für (prep. + acc.)*
forbid *verbieten, verbot, verboten*
force *(the) die Gewalt, -en*
force *(verb) zwingen, zwang, gezwungen*
foreign language *die Fremdsprache, -n*
foreign minister *der Auβenminister*
forestall *zuvor.kommen, kam, gekommen + dat. (aux. sein)*
forgive *verzeihen, verzieh, verziehen + dat.*
fork *die Gabel, -n*
form *das Formular, -e*
former *ehemalig*
fraternity *die Burschenschaft, -en*
Frenchman *der Franzose, -n, -n*
Friday *der Freitag, -e*
fulfill *erfüllen*
full *voll*
funny *lustig*
furniture *die Möbel (pl.)*

G

garbage *der Abfall, -ë*
gas *das Benzin*
general: in general *im allgemeinen*
German *Deutsch (language)*
Germany *Deutschland*
get *kriegen*
get up *auf.stehen, stand, gestanden*
get used to *gewöhnen an + acc. (refl.)*
ghost *das Gespenst, -er*
girl friend *die Freundin, -innen*
give *geben (gibt), gab, gegeben*
glad *froh*
glass *das Glas, -̈er*
glasses *die Brille (sg.)*
go *gehen, ging, gegangen*
go down *unter.gehen, ging, gegangen*
go home *nach Hause gehen*
go out *aus.gehen, ging, gegangen*
God *der Gott*
gold *das Gold*
good *gut*
grade *die Note, -n*
Greece *Griechenland*
green *grün*
grow *wachsen (wächst), wuchs, gewachsen*
growl at *an.knurren*

H

hair *das Haar, -e*
hand *die Hand, -̈e*
happy *glücklich, froh*
happy: be happy about *freuen über + acc. (refl.)*
hard *schwer*
have *haben (hat), hatte, gehabt*
have a good time *amüsieren (refl.)*
have to *(must) müssen*

head *der Kopf, -̈e,* **from head to toe** *von Kopf bis Fuβ*
health *die Gesundheit*
healthy *gesund*
hear *hören*
heaven *der Himmel*
help *(the) die Hilfe*
help *(verb) helfen (hilft), half, geholfen + dat.*
her *ihr*
here *hier*
high *hoch*
his *sein*
hit *schlagen (schlägt), schlug, geschlagen*
home: be home *zu Hause sein*
homeowner *der Hausbesitzer*
horrified: be horrified *grauen (dat. imp.)*
hotel *das Hotel, -s*
hour *die Stunde, -n*
house *das Haus, -̈er*
how *wie*
how long *wie lange*
hungry *hungrig*
hurry *beeilen (refl.)*
hurt: that hurts me *das tut mir weh*
husband *der Mann, -̈er*

I

identify *identifizieren*
impractical *unpraktisch*
insist on *bestehen, bestand, bestanden auf + dat.*
instead of *(an)statt*
intelligent *intelligent*
interested: be interested in *interessiert sein an + dat., interessieren für (refl.)*
interesting *interessant*
introduce *vor.stellen*
invent *erfinden, erfand, erfunden*
invention *die Erfindung, -en*

J

job *die Arbeit, -en*
July *der Juli, -s*
June *der Juni, -s*
just as . . . as *genauso (ebenso)... wie*

K

kill *töten*
kitchen *die Küche, -n*
know *wissen, wuβte, gewuβt*
know *(someone) kennen (mixed verb)*

L

large, larger, largest *groβ, gröβer, gröβt*
last *vorig*
last night *gestern abend*
late *spät*
laugh about *lachen über + acc.*
lawn *der Rasen,*
lawn mower *der Rasenmäher, -*
lawyer *der Rechtsanwalt, -̈e*
lazy *faul*
lead *führen*
leader *der Leiter,*
learn *lernen*
least thing *(the) das wenigste*

leave *verlassen (verläβt), verlieβ, verlassen*
lecture *der Vortrag, ¨e*
let *lassen (läβt), lieβ, gelassen*
letter *der Brief, -e*
library *die Bibliothek, -en*
lie *lügen, log, gelogen*
lie *(somewhere) liegen, lag, hat/ist gelegen*
life *das Leben,*
light *das Licht, -er*
like: be like *gleichen + dat.*
like: would like *möchte*
little *klein (= small), wenig (= not much)*
little *(a) ein biβchen*
live *(somewhere) wohnen*
loan *leihen, lieh, geliehen*
lobster *der Hummer*
long, longer, longest *(time) (adv.) lange,*
    länger, am längsten
long, longer, longest *(adj.) lang, länger, längst*
look *schauen*
look forward to *freuen auf + acc. (refl.)*
lose *verlieren, verlor, verloren*
lot *(a) viel*
loud *laut*
lunch *das Mittagessen*

M

magnificent *hervorragend*
main building *das Hauptgebäude*
main dish *das Hauptgericht, -e*
main street *die Hauptstraβe, -n*
make *machen*
man *der Mann, ¨er*
manuscript *die Handschrift, -en*
mass production *die Massenproduktion*
May *der Mai, -e*
may *dürfen (modal verb)*
mayor *der Bürgermeister,*
meal *das Essen*
measure *ab.messen (miβt), maβ, gemessen*
meat *das Fleisch*
meet *begegnen + dat. (aux. sein)*
melancholy *die Schwermut*
men's clothing *die Herrenbekleidung*
messenger *der Bote, -n, -n*
meter *der/das Meter,*
method *die Methode, -n*
million *die Million, -en*
minute *die Minute, -n*
missing: be missing *fehlen*
mistake *der Fehler,*
mistaken: be mistaken *irren (refl.)*
mister *der Herr, -n, -en*
money *das Geld*
month *der Monat, -e*
monument *das Denkmal, ¨er*
most *die meisten*
mother *die Mutter, ¨*
mountain cabin *die Berghütte, -n*
mouse trap *die Mausefalle, -n*
move out *aus.ziehen, zog, gezogen*
movie *der Film, -e*
mow *mähen*
much *(adv.) viel*
much *(pronoun) vieles*
murder *ermorden*

N

name *der Name, -ns, -n*
nature *die Natur*
need *brauchen*
neighbor *der Nachbar, -n, -n*
nephew *der Neffe, -n, -n*
neutral *neutral*
never *nie(mals)*
nevertheless *nichtsdestoweniger*
new *neu*
news *die Nachricht, -en*
next *nächst*
nice *nett*
night *die Nacht, ¨e*
no longer *nicht mehr*
no one *niemand*
noble *edel*
nonsense *der Unsinn*
noon *der Mittag, -e*
not *nicht*
note *die Notiz, -en*
notebook *das Notizbuch, ¨er*
nothing *nichts*
notice *bemerken*
novel *der Roman, -e*
now *jetzt*
nowhere *nirgendwo*

O

o'clock *Uhr*
obey *gehorchen + dat, folgen + dat.*
obscenity *die Obszönität, -en*
office *das Büro, -s*
officer *der Offizier, -e*
often, more often, most often *oft, öfter, am*
    öftesten
old, older, oldest *alt, älter, ältest*
once *einmal*
one *ein (as adj.), eins (in counting)*
only *nur, einzig (= only one)*
only thing *(the) das einzige*
open *auf.machen*
opinion *die Meinung, -en*
opportunity *die Gelegenheit, -en*
opposite *das Gegenteil, -e*
or *oder*
order *(give a command) befehlen (befiehlt),*
    befahl, befohlen
order *(something) bestellen*
organization *die Gesellschaft, -en*
other *ander*
outrageous *ungeheuer*
outside *drauβen*
oven *der Ofen, ¨*
overcome *überwinden, überwand, überwunden*
owe *schulden*
own *(adj.) eigen*
own *(verb) besitzen, besaβ, besessen*

P

package *das Paket, -e*
paint *malen*
painting *das Bild, -er*
pants *die Hose (sg.),* **pair of pants** *die Hosen*
    (pl.)
parents *die Eltern*

parents-in-law *die Schwiegereltern*
patience *die Geduld*
pay, *(spend money) bezahlen*
pay, *(be worthwhile) lohnen (refl.)*
pen *der Kugelschreiber*
pencil *der Bleistift, -e*
people *die Leute*
philosopher *der Philosoph, -en, -en*
Physics teacher *der Physiklehrer,*
pickle *die Gurke, -n*
pill *die Tablette, -n*
pity *das Mitleid*
plan *der Plan, ¨-e*
plate *der Teller,*
pleasant *angenehm*
please *(adv.) bitte*
please *(verb) gefallen (gefällt), gefiel, gefallen + dat.*
poem *das Gedicht, -e*
point at *deuten auf + acc.*
Poland *Polen*
police *die Polizei (sg.)*
political *politisch*
poor, poorer, poorest *arm, ärmer, ärmst*
possibility *die Möglichkeit, -en*
postpone *hinaus.schieben, schob, geschoben*
pragmatic *pragmatisch*
prefer *(verb) vor.ziehen, zog, gezogen,* **I prefer to do that** *ich ziehe es vor, das zu tun*
prefer *lieber (adv.),* **I prefer to do that** *ich tue das lieber*
pregnant *schwanger*
president *der Präsident, -en, -en*
pretty *hübsch*
price *der Preis, -e*
primarily *hauptsächlich*
prison *das Gefängnis, -nisse*
problem *das Problem, -e*
program *das Programm, -e*
promise *versprechen (verspricht), versprach, versprochen*
protection from *der Schutz vor + dat.*
proud of *stolz auf + acc.*
prove *beweisen, bewies, bewiesen*
public *die Öffentlichkeit*
purse *die Geldbörse, -n*
put *stellen*

Q

question *die Frage, -n*
quick *schnell*

R

rabbit *der Hase, -n, -n*
rain *(verb) regnen*
raise *die Gehaltserhöhung, -en*
read *lesen (liest), las, gelesen*
really *wirklich*
reason *der Grund, ¨-e*
reasonable *vernünftig*
receive *bekommen, bekam, bekommen*
refuse *ab.lehnen*
reject *ab.lehnen*
reliable *zuverlässig*
remark *die Bemerkung, -en*

remember *erinnern an + acc. (refl.)*
rent *mieten*
repair *reparieren*
report *der Bericht, -e*
representative *Abgeordnet-e(r)*
resist *widerstehen, widerstand, widerstanden + dat.*
responsible for *verantwortlich für*
rest *(the) die Ruhe, -n*
rest: take a rest *aus.ruhen (refl.)*
restaurant *das Restaurant, -s*
return *die Rückkehr*
revise *revidieren*
reward *belohnen*
rich *reich*
ride a bicycle *rad.fahren (fährt), fuhr, gefahren*
ridiculous *lächerlich*
right: the right *das Recht, -e*
ring *(the) der Ring, -e*
ring *(verb) läuten*
rise *steigen, stieg, gestiegen*
rock *der Stein, -e*
room *das Zimmer,*
rug *der Teppich, -e*
run *laufen (läuft), lief, gelaufen*
Russia *Rußland*

S

sad *traurig*
same thing *(the) dasselbe*
save *sparen*
say *sagen*
scholarship *das Stipendium, pl. -ien*
school *die Schule, -n*
shudder *schaudern (acc. imp.)*
scientist *der Wissenschaftler, -*
scissors *die Schere (sg.),* **pair of scissors** *die Scheren (pl.)*
scream *schreien, schrie, geschrien*
seasick *seekrank*
see *sehen (sieht), sah, gesehen*
sell *verkaufen*
semester *das Semester,*
senator *der Senator, -en*
send *schicken*
sentimental *sentimental*
serve *dienen + dat., bedienen*
several *einig*
sharp, sharper, sharpest *scharf, schärfer, schärfst*
shirt *das Hemd, -en*
shock *schockieren*
short, shorter, shortest *kurz, kürzer, kürzest*
should *sollte*
shout *aus.rufen, rief, gerufen*
show *zeigen*
sick, sicker, sickest *krank, kränker, kränkst*
simple, simply *einfach*
since *(that time) seit (prep. + dat.),* **since** *(for that reason) da*
sing *singen*
single *einzig*
sister *die Schwester, -n*
sit *sitzen, saß, hat/ist gesessen*
situation *die Situation, -en*
skate *eis.laufen (läuft), lief, gelaufen*

slave *der Sklave, -n, -n*
sleep *schlafen (schläft), schlief, geschlafen*
small *klein*
smile *das Lächeln*
smoke *rauchen*
snow *schneien*
so *so*
Social Democratic Party *die Sozialdemokratische Partei*
sock *die Socke, -n*
sofa *das Sofa, -s*
soft *leise*
solve *lösen*
someone *jemand*
something *etwas*
sometimes *manchmal*
son *der Sohn, ⸚e*
soon *bald*
sorry: I am sorry *es tut mir leid*
sour *sauer*
souvenir *das Andenken,*
speak *sprechen (spricht), sprach, gesprochen*
speaker *der Sprecher*
special *besonder*
spring *der Frühling*
squirrel *das Eichhörnchen,*
stairs *die Treppe (sg.)*
stand *stehen, stand, hat/ist gestanden*
stand *(something) aus.halten (hält), hielt, gehalten*
statistics *die Statistik (sg.)*
stay *bleiben, blieb, ist geblieben*
steal *stehlen (stiehlt), stahl, gestohlen*
stem *stammen*
stock *die Aktie, -n*
stop *auf.hören*
store *das Geschäft, -e*
storm *der Sturm, ⸚e*
story *die Geschichte, -n*
stranger *Fremd-e(r)*
streetcar *die Straßenbahn, -en*
strong, stronger, strongest *stark, stärker, stärkst*
student *der Student, -en, -en*
study *studieren*
stumble *stolpern*
stupid, stupider, stupidest *dumm, dümmer, dümmst-*
succeed *gelingen, gelang, ist gelungen (dat. imp.)*
success *der Erfolg*
successful: be successful *gelingen, gelang, ist gelungen (dat. imp.)*
suddenly *plötzlich*
sugar *der Zucker*
suggestion *der Vorschlag, ⸚e*
suit *der Anzug, ⸚e*
suitcase *der Koffer,*
summer *der Sommer, -*
sun *die Sonne, -n*
sunglasses *die Sonnenbrille (sg.)*
supposed: be supposed to *sollen*
surprise *überraschen*
suspenseful *spannend*
swear by *schwören auf + acc.*
sweater *der Pullover,*

Swedish *Schwedisch (language)*
sweet *süß*
Switzerland *die Schweiz*

T

table *der Tisch, -e*
take a rest *aus.ruhen (refl.)*
take along *mit.nehmen (nimmt), nahm, genommen*
take away *weg.nehmen (nimmt), nahm, genommen*
take seriously *ernst nehmen (nimmt), nahm, genommen*
talk *reden,* **talk to** *reden mit*
task *die Aufgabe, -n*
taste *schmecken*
taxi *das Taxi, -s*
teach *lehren*
teacher *der Lehrer,*
team *die Mannschaft, -en*
teddy bear *der Teddybär, -en, -en*
telephone *das Telefon, -e*
tell *(a story) erzählen*
tell *(say) sagen*
temptation *die Versuchung, -en*
test *die Prüfung, -en*
than *(in the comparative) als*
their *ihr*
theory *die Theorie, -n*
there *da*
there is/are *es gibt*
thin *dünn*
think of *denken an + acc. (mixed verb)*
third *dritt*
this morning *heute früh*
threaten *drohen + dat.*
thrive *gedeihen, gedieh, ist gediehen*
throw away *weg.werfen (wirft), warf, geworfen*
thunder *donnern*
Thursday *der Donnerstag, -e*
ticket *die Karte, -n*
time *die Zeit, -en*
time *(period) das Mal, -e*
time: have a good time *amüsieren (refl.)*
tired *müde*
today *heute*
tomcat *der Kater,*
tonight *heute abend*
too *zu*
tooth *der Zahn, ⸚e*
topic *das Thema, pl. Themen*
torment *quälen*
tourist *der Tourist, -en, -en*
tower *der Turm, ⸚e*
train *der Zug, ⸚e*
tree *der Baum, ⸚e*
trip *die Reise, -n*
trust *trauen + dat.*
try *versuchen*
tuition *der Studienbeitrag, ⸚e*
Turk *der Türke, -n, -n*
Turkey *die Türkei*
Turkish *türkisch*
turn on *an.machen*
twilight *die Abenddämmerung, -en*
two *zwei*

U

unbelievable *unglaublich*
uncouth, more uncouth, most uncouth *grob, gröber, gröbst*
under *unter (2-way prep.)*
understand *verstehen, verstand, verstanden*
understanding *das Verständnis*
unfortunately *leider*
university *die Universität, -en*
used to *gewöhnt an + acc.*
unusual *ungewöhnlich*

V

vacation *die Ferien (pl.)*
vacuum *staubsaugen*
vegetables *das Gemüse (sg.),* **types of vegetables** *Gemüsearten (pl.)*
very (much) *sehr*
visa *das Visum, pl. Visa*
visit (the) *der Besuch, -e*
visit (verb) *besuchen*
voice *die Stimme, -n*

W

wait for *warten auf + acc.*
wall *(i.e., the Berlin Wall) die Mauer*
want *wollen (modal verb)*
war *der Krieg, -e*
warm, warmer, warmest *warm, wärmer, wärmst*
wash *waschen (wäscht), wusch, gewaschen*
watch (the) *die Uhr, -en*
watch (verb) *an.schauen*
watch television *fern.sehen (sieht), sah, gesehen*
water *das Wasser*

weak, weaker, weakest *schwach, schwächer, schwächst*
wear *tragen (trägt), trug, getragen*
weather *das Wetter*
week *die Woche, -n*
weekend *das Wochenende, -n*
West (the) *der Westen*
what *was*
when *(in a question) wann*
where *wo*
who(m) *wer (nom.), wen (acc.), wem (dat.)*
why *warum*
wide *breit*
wife *die Frau, -en*
win *gewinnen, gewann, gewonnen*
window *das Fenster,*
wintercoat *der Wintermantel, ¨*
wish *der Wunsch, ¨e*
without *ohne*
wolf *der Wolf, ¨e*
woman *die Frau, -en*
word *das Wort, -e*
work *die Arbeit, -en*
work on *arbeiten an + dat.*
worker *der Arbeiter,*
worried: be worried about *Sorgen machen um (refl.)*
worthwhile: be worthwhile *lohnen (refl.)*
write to *schreiben, schrieb, geschrieben an + acc.*

Y

year *das Jahr, -e*
yellow *gelb*
yesterday *gestern*
young, younger, youngest *jung, jünger, jüngst*
your *dein (du-form), euer (ihr-form), lhr (Sie-form)*

Index

Extended modifiers, 233–234

False cognates, 321–322
False vs. true passive, 149
Figurative meanings,
    translation problems,
    310–312
Flavoring words, 318–321
for in time expressions,
    German equivalents,
    159–161
fühlen + another verb, 249–
    250
für in time expressions, 160–
    161
Future tense
    English progressive,
    German equivalents,
    157–158
    formation and usage in
    German, 34, 41–42
    future perfect tense, 47
    (Gedankenproblem)
    in the passive, 143
    q-subjunctive, 215
    with modals, 42

genauso...wie, 120
Gender
    compound nouns with
    multiple genders, 286–287
    nouns with multiple
    genders, 285, 291
    (exercise 1)
General/specific prepositions,
    distinguishing between
    the two, 89–90
Genitive case,
    comparison with English
    possessive 's, 59–60
    in time expressions, 102
    noun endings, 55–56
Genitive verbs, 299–300
gerade, progressive tense
    meaning, 158

haben
    conjugation
    indicative, 35
    if-then subjunctive, 195
    q-subjunctive, 210
    past participle, 36
    + **zu** + verb, 243
    usage as auxiliary, 39–41
halt (flavoring word), 319
halten, 4
heißen + another verb, 243–
    244
helfen + another verb, 243–
    244

her-prefix, 25
her-/hier-, distinguishing
    between the two, 25
Herrn, preceding genitive
    noun, 60
hin- prefix, 25
hoch, 107
hören + another verb, 249–
    251

-ieren, verbs with this ending,
    41
if, German equivalents, 184–
    185
if-then subjunctive
    alternative uses, 200–201
    conjugation and usage
    haben, sein, werden,
    195
    modals and **wissen,** 195
    weak, strong, mixed
    verbs, 197–198
    incorrectly used, 196
    past tense, 199–200
    würde + infinitive vs.
    single-word form, 198–
    199
immer + comparative
    adjective, 121
Imperative
    formation and usage, 6–7
    expressed by q-subjunctive,
    216–217
Impersonal passive, 147–148
Impersonal verbs, 301–302
in order to, German
    equivalent, 252–253
Indefinite pronoun, 102–103
indem, 181
Indirect quotes. *See* chapter
    on q-subjunctive
Indirect/direct object, word
    order, 170–171
Infinitive clauses
    English
    corresponding to German
    subordinate clauses, 244–
    245
    German
    corresponding to English
    possessive + verb +
    -ing, 254–255
    corresponding to English
    preposition + possessive
    + verb + *-ing,* 256–
    257
**ohne...zu, anstatt...zu,
    um...zu** constructions,
    251–253

Infinitive clauses (*cont'd*)
    with irregular verbs, 242–
    244
    with modals, 248
    (Gedankenproblem),
    260 **(Gedankenproblem)**
    word order in, 241–242
Infinitive verbs
    past infinitive, examples,
    241, 252, 255, 257
    present infinitive, definition,
    241
Inseparable prefixes
    meanings, 32
    (Gedankenproblem)
    present perfect and past
    perfect, 40–41
    present tense and simple
    past, 21–23
    stress with, 22–23
    table summarizing, 24
instead of + verb + *-ing,*
    German equivalent, 251–
    253
Interjections, word order after,
    168
Interrogative words
    list, 180
    usage, 183–185
Intransitive/transitive verbs
    definition, 39
    translation problems, 303–
    304
Inverted sentences, 99–100
Irregular
    comparative/superlative
    adjectives, 117–118
Irregular verbs in the present
    tense, **halten, laden,
    raten,** 4
Isolated pronouns, 100–101

ja (flavoring word), 319
je...desto, 181–182
just as: **genauso(ebenso),** 120

kein-words
    as adjective fragments,
    130–131
    list, 54

laden, 4
langsam (flavoring word),
    319–320
lassen
    + another verb, 250–251
    + dative reflexive verbs,
    297
lehren + another verb, 243–
    244

lernen + another verb, 243–244

mal (flavoring word), 320
Mal = time period, 161
man (indefinite pronoun), 102–103
Mann vs. **man,** 103
mehr, usage in the comparative, 121
Middle field, word order, 169–171
Mixed verbs
  if-then subjunctive, 197–198
  present and simple past indicative, 7–8
  present perfect and past perfect, 37
Modal verbs
  future tense, 42
  in infinitive clauses, 248 **(Gedankenproblem),** 260 **(Gedankenproblem)**
  present if-then subjunctive, 195
  present indicative, 10
  present q-subjunctive, 212
  subjective usage, 202–203
  with the passive, 143–144
more, in the comparative, German equivalents, 120–121
most, in the superlative, German equivalents, 121
Multiple meanings, translation problems, 312–313
-mut, genders with this ending, 286–287

nicht, 173
nichts + adjectival nouns, 129
noch + comparative adjective, 121
Nouns
  adjectival, 127–130
  capitalization, 263–265
  dative plural ending, 55
  genitive endings, 55–56
  plural in English/singular in German or vice-versa, 287–288
  suffixes, 271–275
  that require the definite article in German, 289–290
  weak, 132–134

Nouns (*cont'd*)
  with irregular plurals, 286
  with multiple genders and/or plurals, 285–286
Number, English/German nouns differing in number, 287–288
nur (flavoring word), 320

ob, 184–185
ohne...zu, 251–253

Paar (das)
  correct and incorrect usage, 288
  das Paar vs. **ein paar,** 264
pair (a) of, 264, 288
Participles. *See* present participle, past participle
Passive
  derived from active sentences, 144–147
  distinguishing between true/false passive, 149
  impersonal, 147–148
  modal verbs, 143–144
  subjunctive, 208 **(Gedankenproblem)**
  tenses, 142–143
  use of **von** or **durch** before agent, 145
Past infinitive verb, 241, 252, 255, 257
Past participle
  as adjectival noun, 129
  as adjective, 107–108
  formation
    of basic forms, 36–37
    with mixed verbs, 37
    with verbs ending in **-ieren,** 41
    with verbs having separable and inseparable prefixes, 40–41
  position in clause, 36
Past perfect tense
  basic formation and usage, 35, 38
  in the passive, 142
Past tense if-then subjunctive, 199–200
Past tense q-subjunctive, 214–215
pflegen + **zu** + verb, 243
Plural nouns
  in English, singular in German, or vice-versa, 287–288

Plural nouns (*cont'd*)
  with irregular or multiple plurals, 285–286
Possessive + verb + *-ing,* German equivalents, 254–255
Predicate
  adjective/nominative, word order with, 170
Prefixes. *See* inseparable, separable, uncertain
Prepositional phrases, word order, 170
Prepositions
  case determined by, 72
  common contractions, 72–73
  da-compounds
    formation and basic usage, 77
    with subordinate and infinitive clauses, 256–257
  distinguishing between general/specific type
  general meanings, 67–71
  less common meanings, 84–86
  + possessive + verb + *-ing,* German equivalents, 256–257
  specific type, 87–88
  2-way, 73–76
  with relative pronouns, 231–232
Present infinitive verb type, 241
Present participles
  as adjectival noun, 129
  as adjective, 107
Present perfect tense
  English progressive, German equivalent, 159–160
  formation in German, 35–37
  in the passive, 142
  vs. simple past, 38
Present tense
  conjugation, 1–5
  English progressive: German equivalents, 157–158
  if-then subjunctive **haben, sein, werden,** 195
  modals and **wissen,** 195
  weak, strong, mixed verbs, 197–198